The Graphics of
Communication

The Graphics of Communication

TYPOGRAPHY · LAYOUT · DESIGN
THIRD EDITION

Arthur T. Turnbull · Russell N. Baird
Ohio University

Holt, Rinehart and Winston

New York Chicago San Francisco Atlanta Dallas Montreal Toronto London Sydney

This book was set, both text and display, in Palatino, a face designed in 1948 by Hermann Zapf, a noted German designer and calligrapher. (Among other faces Zapf has designed are Melior and Optima.) Palatino is a Modern Roman face that has some properties of Renaissance Old Style faces; it was therefore named for a famous sixteenth-century calligrapher, Giambattista Palatino. This face is both beautiful and versatile: it is suitable for books and for commercial graphics.

Linofilm composition and camera work by
Ruttle, Shaw & Wetherill, Inc., Philadelphia, Pennsylvania

Printing and binding by
The Maple Press Company, York, Pennsylvania

Book and cover design by Arthur Ritter

Library of Congress Cataloging in Publication Data

Turnbull, Arthur T
The graphics of communication.

Bibliography: p.
Includes index.
1. Printing, Practical. I. Baird, Russell N.,
joint author. II. Title.

Z244.T86   1975   686.2'2   74-26949

ISBN 0-03-089580-4

Preface

THIS THIRD EDITION of *The Graphics of Communication* stems from two strong and basic convictions that we both hold.

The first conviction is that it is now impossible for good schools of journalism and communication to ignore the new electronic technology involved in text processing and mass communication. With the computer at its center, an explosion of technological innovations has burst upon us more quickly and with far greater force than anyone at first imagined. When the second edition was being prepared, some of the important innvoations had begun to appear, but they were viewed as isolated examples of changes that would probably have a widespread effect only in the far-off future. In just a few short years, however, what was blue-sky dreaming has become day-to-day routine.

As a result, staff members working in all kinds of print media have been undergoing rush "retreading" in order to become proficient with new technical systems. For future college graduates this retraining on the job will not be available. Therefore it is essential that their professional education provide them with a good foundation of technical knowledge that is absolutely up-to-date. We hope that the detailed explanations of the latest technological innovations presented in this edition will provide such a foundation.

The second conviction is that this foundation of technical knowledge can no longer be separate and distinct from the understanding of theoretical aspects of communication which is also a must for professional communicators. Exploration in the area of human information processing has been closely paralleling the startling innovations in technology; as technology has opened new vistas for graphic communication, theoretical explorations have served to provide a better, more solid basis for decision-making in the preparation of pieces of graphic communication. The theoretical and the practical have become so intertwined that the old tradesmen's approach to a course dealing with printing technology is no longer feasible. The processing of information in the human mind cannot be separated from the processing of information in the computer; the methodologies of both are so similar that what we can learn from one can be helpful in working with the other.

We hope that the theoretical bases of the first two chapters will provide for a much better understanding of many of the "whys" associated with the preparation of visual communication. It seems to us that rules learned in a framework that fully explores their reasons will usually be better rules and will be more easily learned and understood.

Some reorganization seemed to be necessary for this edition so that we could include complete coverage of the theoretical concepts and the new technology. Therefore we decided to expand the theoretical material and place it first as Section 1. The verbal (words) aspects of graphic communication are explored in Section 2, followed by the visual (illustrations) aspects in Section 3. Design, the arrangement of the verbal and visual elements into a functional piece of graphic communication, is discussed in Section 4. This is followed by production, the use of technology for accomplishing communication, in Section 5.

We have moved the discussion of the evolution of man's ability to communicate graphically to the final section for a number of reasons. Although it seemed logical in the last edition to place the history first, the realities of teaching have revealed some shortcomings to this approach; the most important of these shortcomings is that students find it very difficult to understand the significance of earlier technical advances without first understanding contemporary technology. We believe that this new order of presentation will provide a more logical step-by-step approach to the subject.

. . .

We owe a special debt of gratitude to scores of individuals and business firms who graciously provided material for this edition and the previous editions. More than 250 illustrations have been used in this edition, and most of these were contributed by newspapers, magazines, printers, and others associated with graphics-related industries. Although credit is given wherever such material appears in the text, we wish to add here our special thanks for these valuable contributions.

Our gratitude goes also to John E. Leard, executive editor of the Richmond, Virginia, newspapers; Dennis Shere and Al Abbott, city editor and communications editor, respectively, of the *Detroit News;* Ralph Squire, special projects director of the Gannett Newspaper

Foundation, Inc.; Dick Paynter, assistant to the publisher of the *Athens Messenger;* Forrest Kilmer, editor of the *Davenport* (Iowa) *Times Democrat;* and the personnel of the American Newspaper Publishers Association Research Institute for their valuable assistance in our search for understanding of the new technological marvels associated with newspaper production.

A.T.T.
R.N.B.

Contents

Preface   v

SECTION 1
THEORETICAL ASPECTS OF GRAPHIC
COMMUNICATION   1

1 Graphics and Communication Theory   3

Graphic Communication 4 | The Communication
Process 7 | Information Theory 11

2 Human Information Processing   15

Human Perception 16 | Concept Formation 22 |
Memory Systems 24 | Decision Making 28 | Emotion
and Motivation 30

SECTION 2
VERBAL ELEMENTS OF COMMUNICATION   33

3 Type and Type Faces   35

Type Materials 37 | Measurement of Type 38 |
The Type Body 40 | Type Classification 41 | How to
Identify Type 52 | The Point System 52 | Hand
Composition 57 | Spacing of Type 57

4 Elements of Good Typography 60

Legibility 62 | Appropriateness of Type 70 |
Check List 72

5 Using Type Creatively 74

Visual Syntax 75 | Display Legibility 76 | The New
Typography 76 | Symmetrical Design 82 | Asymmetrical
Design 86 | Headline Size 89 | Initial Letters 93 |
Conclusion 93

SECTION 3
VISUAL ELEMENTS OF COMMUNICATION 95

6 Illustrations in Graphic Communication 97

The Many Functions and Forms of Illustrations 98 |
The Production Aspects of Illustrations 102 | Adding
Color to Illustrations 120 | Process Plates for
Full-Color Reproduction 121

7 Color in Graphic Communication 125

The Nature of Color 126 | Color Dimensions in
Pigment 127 | Psychological Aspects of Color 128 |
Functions of Color 130 | Types of Color Printing 133 |
The Cost Factor in Color Printing 135 | Fidelity
in Process Color 136 | Practical Pointers in the Use
of Color 138

SECTION 4
DESIGN: COMBINING THE VERBAL
AND VISUAL ELEMENTS 141

8 Design Principles and Advertising Layout 143

Meaning in Design 143 | Design Vocabulary 145 |
Putting It All Together 151 | Design Principles 154 |
Making Design Articulate 167

9 Principles of Magazine Layout 176

The First Step: Break-of-the-Book 179 | Dimensions of the Stage: Format 181 | Some Theoretical Bases for Magazine Design 181 | Achieving Meaning Through Orderly Presentation 183 | Balance and Simplicity Help Create Order 184 | Controlling Direction 191 | Controlling Contrast to Achieve Harmony and Unity 195 | A Word About Special Pages and Problem Pages 198

10 Newspaper Typography and Makeup 202

Influence of Heritage and News Policy on Makeup 204 | Kinds of Headlines and Their Importance 205 | Other Makeup Components 213 | Makeup: Putting the Parts Together in an Attractive Package 222 | Modern Trends in Newspaper Design 231

11 Planning and Designing Other Printed Literature 241

Kinds of Direct Literature 241 | What Kind of Printed Piece? 248 | Standard Unit Sizes 248 | Special Paper Considerations 250 | Other Design Considerations 252 | Checking Press Sheets 255

SECTION 5
PRODUCTION OF GRAPHIC COMMUNICATION 257

12 Graphic Reproduction Processes 259

Basic Principles of Common Graphic Reproduction Processes 260 | Relief, or Letterpress, System of Printing 261 | Uses and Capabilities of Letterpress Printing 267 | Photo-Offset Lithography 267 | Advantages of Offset Printing 273 | The Big Switch to Photo-Offset Lithography 279 | Gravure Printing 281 | Silk-Screen Printing 286 | Photogelatin

Printing 290 | Electrostatic Printing 292 | Jet Printing 294 | Selection of the Process 295

13 Preparing Verbal Copy for Production   296

Copy Correction 298 | Marking Printer's Instructions 302 | Copyfitting 315 | Fitting Display Type to Space 322

14 Preparing Visual Copy for Production   325

Cropping Photographs 325 | Scaling Instructions 327 | Finding the Percentage of Reductions or Enlargements 332 | Other Methods of Altering Photo Content 332 | Specifying Screen and Metal for Halftones 334 | Line Drawings 335 | Color in Illustrations 336 | Reading Proofs of Illustrations 336

15 Machine Composition and Presses   339

Type Composition 339 | Presses 367

16 Paper: Selection, Folding, Binding, Finishing   377

Paper Selection 377 | Basic Kinds of Paper 379 | Paper Surfaces 380 | Paper Weight and Sheet Sizes 381 | Imposition, Binding, and Folding 382

SECTION 6
HISTORICAL BACKGROUND   397

17 Evolution of Graphic Communication   399

At the Beginning: Prehistoric Efforts 400 | Contributions of Early Civilizations 400 | The Renaissance and Printing from Movable Type 403 | Effects of the Industrial Revolution 405 | Improvements in Composition Methods 409 | Machine Papermaking 412 | Reproduction of Photographs 412 | Discovery of Offset Printing 412 | The Era of the Computer and Video Tube 414

Glossary   417

Bibliography   432

APPENDIX A
Characters Per Pica: Selected Type Faces   438

APPENDIX B
Some Commonly Used Type Faces   440

Index   449

The Graphics of
Communication

SECTION 1   # THEORETICAL ASPECTS OF GRAPHIC COMMUNICATION

CHAPTER 1
Graphics and Communication Theory

CHAPTER 2
Human Information Processing

CHAPTER 1 # Graphics and Communication Theory

Where would we be—you and I—if it weren't for communication? The answer is simple: Nowhere.

All living organisms, even the microscopic, have ancestors. According to Oparin's theory, the most widely accepted, life sprang into being through a series of chemical reactions among large quantities of organic materials (Oparin, 1962). This was perhaps two billion years ago. The recipe for life, or genetic information, was coded in deoxyribonucleic acid (DNA) and has been communicated through the countless generations to the present. Through evolution various life forms emerged, the result of slow changes in these genetic codes, culminating in the appearance of man.

Thus the genetic codes—recipes for life—dictate that here we are, kindred to other forms of life, all springing from a common origin in the dim past. Our evolution has been determined by communication.

That we continue to live day to day we owe to our *internal* communication systems. These involve hormones and the nervous system. Hormones are information messengers released into the bloodstream. As they are carried to various parts of the body, they affect the metabolic processes leading to maintenance, growth, development, and reproduction. We will consider the nervous system in some detail later.

Graphic Communication

Usually when we talk about communication we mean external communication that keeps us in touch with other people. In this text we are concerned with a specific form of external communication— graphic communication.

Despite competition from radio and television, the written word is still the major means of communication. The written word is, of course, an extension of the spoken word. Transforming speech into writing unfortunately bypasses facial expression, tonal inflection, and gestures, which are vital in conveying meanings in face-to-face communication. Thus it becomes necessary in presenting a written message to make up for this loss by putting words in as effective a *visual* form as possible. This accounts for the fact that before the widespread use of the typewriter, penmanship was prominent in the school curriculum and "social writing" was an art.

Printing is the means of reproducing the written message for mass communication. It is the presentation or form of the printed message that concerns us in this book. However, a word of caution. Form is inextricably involved with message content, or meaning. As Henry James put it, form and content are inseparable in a work of art. The writer works with vocabulary and syntax. The graphic designer also works with a vocabulary—lines, shapes, colors, textures, and so on. And according to how he (or she) uses these elements of his vocabulary, he too can affect meanings. Thus the effectiveness of a printed message is the result of writer and designer expressing a common meaning.

The importance of form (graphics) may be primary or secondary, depending on the circumstances. In general, the importance of form is reduced as the reader interest in word content increases. Readers will overcome formidable graphic obstacles to get information they strongly desire. For example, the want ads are dull in appearance, yet they are among the best-read parts of a newspaper. Students scan monotonous lists of scores in small type to find the result of the hometown school's football game. The interest in content is so great that graphics are cast in a secondary role.

On the other side of the coin is the wastebasket fate of much printed material. Tests have shown the importance of form: material of the same content has been received, read, and acted on in one form, but discarded in another. Also, a newspaper story may gain readership from one edition to another simply by a change in headline size or placement on a page. And the addition of a second color may dramatically increase response to a direct-mail piece.

These examples, along with the general fact that any reader is offered much more than he can ever assimilate, indicate that graphic techniques are too important to be ignored.

WHY NOT CALL IT GRAPHIC ART?

The designer must combine communication and creativity. To the extent that his task is to present an esthetically pleasing message, there may be some justification for calling his work *graphic art.* We prefer the term *graphic communication* because the designer of printed literature must be primarily concerned with communication, not art. What he or she creates must not produce the exclamation, "how attractive!" Rather, printed literature must be a vehicle that successfully transmits the substance of communications.

Three objectives confront the designer: (1) to attract attention to the message; (2) to present it so that it can be easily read and understood; (3) to make an impression. The desired impression depends on circumstances. He may want to transmit knowledge that the reader will retain or win the reader to a point of view or get acceptance of a product or create an emotional response. Whichever it is, the first two objectives must work toward its achievement.

THE EXTENT OF GRAPHIC COMMUNICATION

Since our immediate concern is graphic communication, we might ask: How extensive is it? Printing and publishing revenues were estimated in 1970 as $25.7 billion, representing some 2.6 percent of the Gross National Product of $989 billion.[1]

Graphic communication is a major, sustaining force of our economic, political, and cultural existence. We play watchdog to our government via the printed newspaper. We pay our printed bills with printed money, checks, or credit cards. We learn about goods through printed advertising and take them home in printed cartons after we have bought them. It has been estimated — but not verified — that a typical metropolitan family is exposed to 1,518 ads per day (Bauer and Greyser, 1968). Deducting 53 radio commercials, this leaves 1,465 visual ads that even so do not include all forms of printed advertising.

Our day is brightened by magazines, books, and greeting cards. We broaden our knowledge through textbooks and technical or professional journals. Great works of art, past and present, come to us from far-off museums as accurate reproductions. We travel about guided by printed maps. Libraries, drugstore display racks, home bookshelves and attics and basements everywhere are crammed with

---

[1] *Inland Printer/American Lithographer,* January, 1970, p. 47.

printed materials. So are millions of wastebaskets that are emptied each night into trash cans. But the unending deluge can be expected to continue tomorrow — and the day after.

Naturally, the public can be expected to be selective in what it reads. It's a matter of self-defense! It follows also that designers of printed materials need every skill and technique to prevent their handiwork from going to the wastebasket unread. Competition for the reader's time is keen. Messages in newspapers, for example, must vie for attention not only with television, magazines, other newspapers, and scores of one-shot printed pieces, but with internal competition, too. Few of us read everything in a newspaper. Consequently, each page, story, illustration, and headline must battle for readership with all the other pages.

Only the publications and individuals offering the best in content and form can win out in such a competitive struggle.

WHY BOTHER WITH MECHANICS?

A considerable portion of this text discusses the machines and techniques involved in getting the message into print.

The mechanics of printing place certain constraints on the efforts of the designer. Just as the actor is limited to the dimensions of the stage, the graphics designer is limited to the dimensions of the page. An actor must recognize the limitations of his voice and his gestures, but he does not consider them to be unduly restrictive. He also is very unlikely to wish he could fly or change his costume magically while on stage. He accepts all the limitations on him and uses his skills to bring his performance to the highest level in spite of them.

The graphic communicator must operate in similar fashion. Before he can use his creative talent effectively he must know both the mechanics and the limitations of his medium. The mechanics are complicated, but they can be learned. In fact, one can only marvel at the intricacies of even the most elementary graphic communication. A simple note to a friend represents a marvelous achievement of man — the ability to combine letter symbols to transfer meaning from one mind to another. Johann Gutenberg's invention of printing from movable type in the fifteenth century extended man's ability to communicate visually and to reach mass audiences. Later advancements made possible mass distribution of pictures, as well as words.

If Gutenberg's were the only printing method, the mechanics would be complicated enough. But today many printing systems are available. Some are mechanical, others electronic. To communicate effectively in print, the communicator must have a basic understanding of these systems and the technology involved.

The Communication Process

A knowledge of the basic concepts of communication theory can be of inestimable help to the designer of printed literature. With this thought in mind we will consider in the rest of this chapter certain significant concepts in the communication process, including information theory. In the next chapter we will take a look at human information processing.

Then, in succeeding chapters, we will refer again to these concepts and the principles involved. Thus the designer, when planning his presentation, can be made aware of its rationale.

Particularly since the end of World War II authorities in many fields have shown keen interest in the area of external communication, which we will henceforth refer to simply as communication. Among the fields these experts represent are mathematics, psychology, sociology, linguistics, philosophy, computer science, education, biology, and journalism.

Two books published in 1948 and 1949 gave particular impetus to the study of communication: *The Mathematical Theory of Communication* by Claude Shannon and Warren Weaver (1949) and *Cybernetics: Control and Communication in the Animal and the Machine* by Norbert Wiener (1948).

Shannon's book, which was done within the context of communication engineering, offered a model of communication that is as applicable to human communication as it is to engineering—see Figure 1-1. The channel is the medium for carrying a signal from

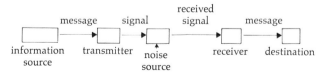

Figure 1-1. *Shannon's Communication Model.*

the source to the message destination: it can be wire, cable, radio frequency, light, and so on. In graphic communication it might be the paper or any other printing surface.

Perhaps you noticed that the Shannon model is linear, moving directly, step-by-step from source to destination. To get a better understanding of the communication process we need to introduce the concept of *feedback*. Wiener, like Shannon a mathematician, developed this concept within the context of communication. He brought the subject of cybernetics to public attention and defined it as the study of control mechanisms and communication in animals and machines.

An application can be seen in an artillery gunfire control system, which receives information from a moving target through radar. The system calculates what should be done to hit the target. By control, the gun is brought into position and fired at what should be the proper time. If it is off-target, the feedback of information from the target allows the system to make further adjustment.

Feedback is an integral part of our own information processing systems as we shall see later.

Let us now examine the individual components of the communication process. It should be pointed out, however, that communication is a continuing and complex process and to look at the component parts one after the other is to take them out of the process context. Therefore it is necessary to discuss them with a degree of overlap.

THE SOURCE

The source or sender of a message is the individual or organization *perceived by the receiver to be the sender.* In an ad where the sender clearly identifies himself he is known at once. In five ads in a national magazine five products made by five different manufacturers are advertised. Five sources are identifiable. But if the five products comprise a retail ad for a large department store, the store is perceived to be the sender.

Publicity stories appearing in magazines or newspapers present a different situation. The stories appear as a part of the format of the publication and so the implication to the reader is that the publication must be the source, although the real source may be a publicity agent or advertising agency.

The task of the sender when he prepares a printed message is to inform, to alter the attitudes of the receiver toward the object of the message, or to reinforce the attitudes already held. Attitudes may be defined as *willingness to make value judgments.* It is possible, of course, for them to remain unchanged, despite the sender's intentions.

The message may result in changed attitudes toward either the object of the message, the perceived sender, or both. Attitudes toward the medium—for example, the magazine or the newspaper —may even be changed. These changes may occur even in cases where the task of the sender is to inform, as is the purpose of the editorial content of a newspaper. Change may be pro or con in varying degrees.

People develop attitudes as a result of reacting to their total socioeconomic environment; the media are a small part of this environment. Attitudes reflect the meanings people have assigned to their various experiences.

To fashion successful printed communication the sender should learn all he can about people, their environment, and how it affects their status, role, and attitudes.

THE MESSAGE

The graphic communication message involves the use of symbols— verbal (words) and graphic (illustrations)—to convey meanings. Symbols serve as *cues* to meaning. Thus meaning is not in the symbol but in the mind of the receiver. The success of a message depends in large part on a common interpretation of the meanings between source and receiver.

The content of messages—the ideas being presented—is less under the graphic designer's control than is the presentation of the message. But the method of presentation carries meanings in its own right as we shall see later.

What we perceive in our environment comes through the several senses. Stimuli to the senses give us cues. We categorize the events and things we experience and react to them, thereby establishing meanings. For example, many people consider that the category of soft drinks includes primarily the leading cola drinks, followed by various other types of soft drinks. Thus, when they think of soft drinks, they think first of a cola. The makers of Seven Up, through many advertisements, have attempted to set their product apart as the "Uncola," so that people will categorize soft drinks as colas, the Uncola, and others. In a separate subcategory, Seven Up may thus take on a new meaning.

Categories that prove rewarding or need-reducing—an analog to the goal-seeking action of the gunfire control system—are said to be learned and stored in memory.

In print, cues to meaning are given through the sense of sight. A cue in print can, by association, recall feelings developed through senses other than visual. Thus, reproduction of a photograph in full color may suggest taste, smell, touch, and so on to a greater degree than in black and white, or better than the single word "cake."

Before turning our attention to the channels of communication let us look briefly at two other terms common to communication theory: *encoding and decoding*. Encoding refers to the selection of symbols or cues to be used in communicating a message. Decoding refers to extracting meaning from these cues.

THE CHANNEL

The channel can be considered to be the vehicle for carrying the message. A more common term for the channel, for our purposes, is the *medium.* Newspapers, magazines, folders, leaflets, posters can all be termed media. Don't forget, these media can themselves be sources. Messages can affect attitudes toward the object of the message and toward the sender, as well as toward the medium, as was mentioned previously. Moreover, the attitudes of receivers toward the media can affect the attitudes toward the message and toward the sender, or both.

NOISE

The concept of noise in the electronic theory of communication relates to disturbances which impair efficiency of delivery of symbols. This concept is carried over to sociopsychological adaptations of the theory.

Interference can occur through (1) selection of symbols the meanings of which are not clear to receivers, (2) channel noise, and (3) other messages or outside activities competing for receiver attention.

Interference of the first instance can be verbal or graphic. Verbal noise involves semantic difficulties and is therefore beyond the scope of this text. We shall consider "graphic noise" here, however. This involves such considerations as selection and arrangement of graphic elements.

Channel noise refers to the relative quality of printing when reproducing a message. This we shall also consider.

There are graphic techniques for combating the third type of noise. These are an essential element of later chapters of this book.

THE RECEIVER

We have already indicated the position of the receiver in the communication process. The receiver can often, of course, be a source, just as the sender is a receiver of many messages from other sources. And naturally, in an exchange of information face-to-face, one may alternately be source and sender.

FEEDBACK

The purpose of feedback is to effect some degree of control over the communication process. Through feedback the source is able to obtain information concerning the receiver's reactions to a message. This allows the source to alter his message to make it more effective.

Feedback is direct in face-to-face communication. It is indirect and delayed in printed communication. In the latter case it must be gathered after the message is delivered. It may be secured through survey, formal or informal, by either the sender or the medium or both.

A productive use of this sort of feedback is in the development of principles to be applied in subsequent communication. Many principles have also been developed by students of the communication process working in laboratory situations.

Be prepared to find feedback in other contexts. It is, after all, an integral part of any communication system. Human information processing involves communication systems functioning internally. More will be said about this in the next chapter.

Various theorists have developed communication models. We offer the one in Figure 1-2 not as an improvement but as a means to bring into focus the particular elements we have discussed and the points we made concerning them.

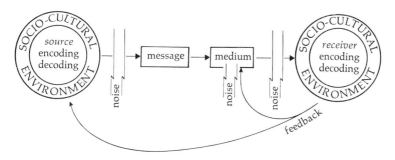

Figure 1-2. *A suggested communication model.*

Information Theory

Information Theory is a product largely of the efforts of the mathematicians Shannon and Weaver. It is sometimes also referred to as Communication Theory, since it relates closely to Shannon's model. We prefer to consider Information Theory separately, since it defines *amounts of information* and *channel capacity,* two important concepts in our view of man as an information processing system, to be considered later.

The communication process cannot be understood adequately unless we can quantify the amounts of information. Only then can we measure the efficiency of the process. That is, we must know *how much information is communicated* and *how much is acquired.*

Thus it becomes necessary first to define information. When somebody or a machine (computer) tells us something we didn't know, we have received information.

If you are told it's Tuesday and you already know it's Tuesday, you receive no information. If you don't know the date, ask a friend, and he says, "It's the ninth," you receive information.

Communication provides information to the extent that it reduces uncertainty. The amount we get is in no way related to whether it is correct or incorrect. Measured scientifically, amount of information involves quantities sent and received but not values.

Suppose you toss a coin. Will it fall heads or tails? There is *a priori* uncertainty. How it falls will reduce the uncertainty. Amount of information and uncertainty are closely related concepts.

If we can measure amount of uncertainty we can measure amount of information. Suppose you roll a die. It can stop with any of six sides up. You receive more information after it stops than you received when the coin fell.

What if you toss two coins together? There are four possible outcomes: HH, TT, TH, and HT. But if you toss three there are eight possible outcomes. Can you list them—HHH, TTT, and so on?

By now you should sense that the relationship between amount of information received and amount of uncertainty is not direct. Do you? Here's why:

one coin toss resolves two units of uncertainty (two alternatives)
two coin tosses resolve four units
three coin tosses resolve eight units

There is a measure that covers the situation. It is logarithmic and is stated: $\log_2 N$, where N = the number of alternatives. When the uncertainty is eight alternatives, $\log_2 8 = 3$. The 3 represents three "bits" of information.[2] The term *bit* is a contraction of "binary digit." The two binary digits are 0 and 1.

Can you answer this: How many bits are needed to resolve uncertainty in the case of 64 alternatives? Read no further until you have thought about it.

Suppose 64 cards are spread before you. Pick the one I have in mind; they're numbered 1 through 64. A bit is a "Yes" or "No" answer to any questions you ask. Your most efficient approach is to start with "Is it between 33 and 64, inclusive?" If you get a "No," next ask, "Is it between 1 and 16, inclusive?" And so on. You need to ask a total of six questions ($\log_2 64$).[3]

If you should start off with a "wild guess" and ask, "Is it 11?" and get a "Yes," you have asked a 6-bit question and got a 6-bit answer.

[2] Ordinary or common log tables are for base ten N ($\log_{10} N$). $\log_2 N$ is the same as $3.32 \times \log_{10} N$.
[3] This is a fine point but worth mentioning: The formula is better stated $\log_2(\frac{1}{p})$. If a biased coin turns up heads six out of ten tosses, then $\log_2(1.66) = .73$, which means a fall of heads contains .73 bits of information.

To indicate further how the communication process works let us establish an alphabet of eight symbols: *A, B, C, D, E, F, G, H*. We will be the source, you the receiver, and, using the alphabet, we will send you an intelligible message.

Since each symbol will require three bits of information ($\log_2 8$) for discrimination, we need to structure a means of allowing you to select each symbol.

DECISIONS

Symbol	In first half of 8?	In first half of its group of 4?	In first half of its group of 2?
A	1	1	1
B	1	1	0
C	1	0	1
D	1	0	0
E	0	1	1
F	0	1	0
G	0	0	1
H	0	0	0

In our alphabet 1 = Yes and 0 = No. But why, for example, does 111 code the symbol *A?* In the first decision column you are signaled that the *A* is in the first four letters of our alphabet. In the second column you are told it is in the first two of *A, B, C, D*. In the third column you are told it is the first half of the pair *A* and *B*.

Here's our message: 110,011 − 111 − 101, 111, 100. Commas represent space between letters and dashes space between words.

At this point you may be wondering, "But why the binary coding and its logarithms to base 2?" Computers operate on a binary system. They use switches or other components that are on ("Yes" or 1) or off ("No" or 0) to code information.

In both animals and man, the signals that move along the nervous systems from the sense organs to the brain and from the brain to effectors are coded into electrical pulses that are either on or off; nerve cell synapses function like on-off switches (Travers, 1970). Analogies between man's information processing and that of the computer are frequently drawn. We shall refer to some of them in the next chapter. But first let us summarize several important points made in this section.

A bit of information is that necessary for making a decision between two alternatives. Each time the number of alternatives doubles, the amount of information increases by one bit.

For our purposes the math aspects of information theory are less important than these considerations:

1. The amount of information can be measured or quantified.
2. Information in and of itself contains no meaning. Meaning arises in the mind of the receiver and only after decision-making. The purpose of information is to reduce doubt. When we receive information we use it to select from alternatives. Most of our time is spent in making such selections or discriminations unconsciously.
3. Communication is an ordered system of sending and receiving information. Both sender and receiver must have a memory in which is stored a common alphabet of symbol coding that allows the receiver to find meanings the sender hopes to arouse.

CHAPTER 2

Human Information Processing

ใเレ ่ึเ ็ง

What you see above may look like madness. It isn't meant to be. Can you tell what it says? If not, don't worry about it. You'll learn later. Its purpose is to dramatize an important aspect of this section.

Three basic subsystems characterize any information processing system (IPS) — for example, the computer. They are: (1) input, (2) information processing, (3) output.

So it is with man, also an IPS. Our nervous system, divisible into three parts, comprises an IPS. Through our senses we receive information from the environment. Information received and utilized is for the most part processed within the brain. An integral part of the processing subsystem is memory, as is also the case with the computer. And continuing the metaphor, output is in the form of behavior.

At this point, "Why does man take in information?" becomes a fundamental question. An analogy offers a good answer. On the physiological-biochemical level, raw materials (food and so on) are received, broken down, then synthesized to sustain life. Waste materials are rejected or eliminated. The processes involved are self-regulatory and integrating, functioning on an unconscious level. Information systems controlling the processes involve the autonomic nervous system and the information-bearing hormones.

On the psychological level, information from the environment is received, broken down, and somehow synthesized to sustain life. Inasmuch as we can move about in our environment we must some-how determine its constancies and structuring that offer information necessary for survival. Unneeded information is rejected, as we shall see.

Consciousness — being aware of existence — is common to animal and to man. Both are capable of sensing information, selecting that which they need, and interpreting the input to form perceptions — intelligible "pictures of reality."

But man's consciousness functions not only on a perceptual but on a conceptual level as well. Animals seem to be limited to the perceptual level of consciousness (Adler, 1967).

Human Perception

What turns man on? What starts him moving toward adaptive be-havior? The same question might be asked about animals. Tradi-tionally, psychology has usually referred us to motivations, primary or innate, and secondary or learned motives. In terms of information processing, however, we are "programmed" to seek information. One authority refers to the "go instructions" as the complexity pro-gram (Biggs, 1971). He sees information-seeking as nonspecific and as subsuming the various emotions. It is as if we were destined to monitor the environment to find its constancies and structuring. In other words, we *must* reduce uncertainty in order to decide how to behave.

Sensory deprivation experiments seem to indicate this. Well-paid subjects have undergone voluntary confinement, deprived of as much stimulation as possible. Room temperature was held constant, their vision was obscured, sound was blocked out, and they were cushioned to reduce tactual stimulation. The result was a tendency to hallucination and an impairment of the thinking processes. Few were able to endure the isolation for the contracted time (Heron, 1966).

Information in graphic communication reaches us through our eyes. The eye is often referred to as a "camera." But it's not. It does not cast a picture on the brain as a camera does on film. It feeds coded electrical signals to the brain for interpretation. Research by elec-trophysiologists has produced an understanding of what occurs within the eye and the brain. This can only be sketchily presented here.[1]

[1] It is, however, an interesting story and we suggest the reader will find it profitable to search out the following literature: Gregory (1970, 1972), Hubel and Wiesel (1962, 1963, 1965, 1968), Kuffler (1953), Lindsay and Norman (1972), Norman (1969), and Stent (1972).

Research by S. W. Kuffler and by D. H. Hubel and T. N. Wiesel involved the use of microelectrodes (less than a thousandth of an inch in diameter). These were inserted close to the ganglion cells behind the retina and close to the brain cells to record neural activity when the eye received light input in various patterns. By moving the electrodes about, it was possible to map patterns of neural activity. The subjects were principally cats and monkeys. Physiologists believe man's visual system operates in a similar manner.

We sense the environment — e.g., look at printed matter — when light energy impinges on the retina. Here it falls on receptor cells, rods and cones, which are called transducers because they change light to neural energy. The capacity of the eye is tremendous. The change occurs at a rate of about one million bits of information per second (Dixon, 1966).

Synaptic transfers carry the impulses from some 125,000,000 receptor cells to some 800,000 ganglion cells. Each ganglion cell receives information from a minute receptive field or portion of the retina. Each field is made up of off- and on-receptor cells (those 0's and 1's again). Light increases the "on-cell" impulses and decreases the "off-cell" impulses. The impulses reaching the ganglion cells represent an algebraic summation of on's and off's. The purpose of the receptor cells is primarily to establish light-dark contrast rather than to report amount of illumination. From the ganglion cells impulses are carried via the optic nerve to the brain. It might be noted that a process of selective destruction of information was started at the eye.

Information reaching the visual cortex of the brain is further processed at a number of additional levels of abstraction or selective destruction by cells arranged in a column positioned at a right angle to the cortical surface. At each abstraction level fewer and fewer neural cells are activated.

At the first cortical level of abstraction, cells were found that fired more intensely when a line fell on the retinal field in a particular orientation and position. These line detector cells monitor specific retinal fields.

At the next level the same basic features (dark or light lines and edges) are also analyzed by specific cells. However, each cell has a broader response. Its firing increases for lines in the same orientation as before, but position on the retina is not critical. Cells at this level cover a larger retinal area.

At the next level, the latest to be discovered, individual neurons respond to shapes (collections of lines). Analysis involves detailing prior information — line lengths are determined and angles are established.

How far does this convergence of information through ever-increasing selective destruction go? One could imagine a last cortical cell that fires intensely when a certain image falls on the retina. It seems unlikely. We can see an infinite number of patterns in a lifetime. It is now known that the cortical column cells relate to other sensory and memory information.

How the outputs of data from the visual system mechanisms that detect shapes, color, and movement are physiologically used to develop perceptions is not known. It is believed that the programs leading to feature analysis are "wired in." And it is theorized that memory data are involved in whatever physiological processes lead to perception. An explanation that neural activity patterns are integrated suddenly to form a perception is too simplistic, for at some point a decision has to be made: What do I perceive?

A visual object can be more than one thing. Figures 2-1 and 2-2 show several ambiguous shapes that can each be viewed as more than one object. It is as if when you look at them "the brain can't make up its mind."

At this point we must turn to theoretical explanations of how the final, conscious percept is achieved.

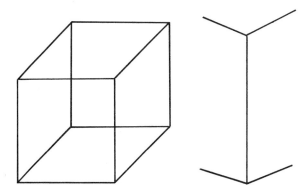

Figure 2-1. *Left: The Necker cube. Without change in perspective, this figure has reversing depths. Right: What is it? An open book you are holding? Or is it an open book someone facing you is holding?*

The data representing features (lines, angles, contours, and so on) of the original visual image interact on a two-way basis with data stored in memory from previous experience. Presumably all data (feature and memory) are in the same physiological code. The final percept is the result of successive decisions made after comparing incoming information and information in memory.

Consider what must be, in rough fashion, how we learn to recognize the letter *b* from the alphabet *a b c d e f g h i j k l m n o p q r s t u v w x y z.*

But first we must make a distinction between the terms "perception" and "recognition." As previously shown, we seem to be programmed to receive image features automatically. What seems to

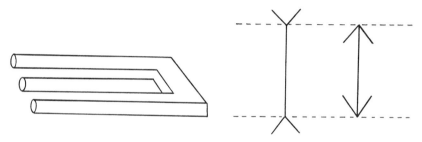

Figure 2-2. *Left: What about the middle prong? Does it even exist? This figure cannot be properly perceived. That is, your brain cannot make up its mind what your eyes see. Right: The broken parallel lines are drawn to prove to you that the vertical shafts are the same length. Do they look it?*

happen next is a testing of hypotheses of what is "out there," thereby answering the question of "What do I perceive?" Perception is thus seen to be an inferential process, a kind of inductive reasoning by which we arrive at a "best guess."

Lindsay and Norman see feature abstraction as a passive process, and perception formation, which they label "synthesizing," as an active process (Lindsay and Norman, 1962). Synthesis is a recall from memory of data stored from previous experience, setting up hypotheses and making comparisons of them with incoming data to reduce the number of alternatives from which to make a decision.

A "best guess" can be incorrect, or uncertain, as we saw in Figures 2-1 and 2-2. Have you ever stopped for a traffic light next to another car headed in the same direction? And as its impatient driver inched forward you got the distinct impression you were rolling backward? You may even have checked to be sure your car was firmly braked. You had a faulty perception; your "best guess" was incorrect.

Perception is thus the result of cognitive processes. A perception may be termed a cognition and as such be stored in memory.

Perceptual judgments tend to become fixed. As Cherry puts it, perceptions become "habits of inference" (Cherry, 1966). What we recognize today is what we perceived yesterday. Cognition is to know and recognition is to know again.

Now to our learning to recognize *b* . . .

Q. Does it have an oblique line?
A. No. (then it's not *k, v, w, x, y,* or *z*)
Q. Does it have a horizontal line?
A. No.
Q. Does it have a vertical line?
A. Yes.

Q. Does it have two vertical lines?
A. No.
Q. Does it have a curved line?
A. Yes. (then it's *b, d, p, q,* or *r*)
Q. Does the curve close to the vertical line?
A. Yes. (then it's *b, d, p,* or *q*)
Q. Is the curve positioned to the right of the vertical?
A. Yes. (it's *b* or *p*)
Q. Does the vertical extend below the curve?
A. No. (then it's a *b*)

To learn to recognize other letters additional features would have to be tested. For example, *t* contains right angles and *v* contains an acute angle.

Reading is, of course, more than proceeding along a line letter-by-letter. We do not understand a printed message or find meaning in an illustration by identifying lines, curves, angles, and so on.

A study by M. A. Tinker shows that the eyes make a series of short jumps or saccades along a printed line (Tinker, 1958). These occur four or five times per second. At each stop or fixation several words are "taken in." This would suggest that recognition attaches to whole words, perhaps even to phrases. But there's more to it than that. The context within which you view something is an aid to decision-making.

Let's look again at the hodgepodge of marks we asked you to interpret at the beginning of this section. It's repeated in Figure 2.3. We will put it in a context for you. It's a part of the title of this text.

Figure 2-3. *These are portions of letters forming one word in the title of this book. It is GRAPHICS.*

It is a tremendous aid to perception to know what the image must be. The percipient then has added information, which comes from context and thereby increases his expectations. The number of alternatives from which a choice must be made is thereby reduced.

Redundancy is another aspect of context and, like expectations, is an aid to decision making. A message is redundant if it contains more information than it needs to. This implies that a shorter message could have delivered the same information. For example, "He was a hard-working man until he passed away." The words "he" and "man" are repetitive; so are "was" and "passed away." Little meaning is lost in the phrasing, "A hard-working man died."

Information theory and information processing define reading as sensing a series of events (letters and words). Looking at illustrations is also sensing a series of events. The eye discerns various shapes and patterns, one after another.

To be nonredundant a sequence must be comprised of events independent of each other and equally likely to occur. Suppose you toss a die and get a six, then toss it again and get a three. The events are independent. Each number had a one-in-six chance of appearing. The sequence of two events was nonredundant.

Our language is not that way. Sequences of letters and spaces are redundant. Some letters show up more frequently than others. The letter *e* is most frequent, and *z* is rare. Does any letter other than *u* ever follow *q*?

Computers can be used to string letters together with varying degrees of redundancy. Nonredundancy would result from choosing from the 26 at random to build a series. It would most generally be unintelligible.

Selecting independently but with the chance of selection of a letter being based on its frequency in English introduces about 15 percent redundancy, which increases to 29 percent when selection of a letter is based on its frequency after the preceding letter.

Tests have shown that as redundancy increases, the ease of recognition of letters increases. Such experiments are made with tachistoscopes. These are projectors with precision control of length of exposure of any type of visual material—photos, printing, and so on.

In such tests, people were shown to be better able to recognize letters in a series structured at higher redundancy than at lower redundancy rates. Measurement was based on recall of letters shortly after exposure (Postman, Bruner and Postman, 1964).

It might be noted that after corrections for redundancy percentages were applied to the results, it was determined that while recognition increased with increased redundancy, intake of information in bits was constant over all exposures. In other words, redundancy increases the statistical probability of recognition but not necessarily meaning.

The English language is highly redundant. One could eliminate more than 50 percent of a printed message, paring nonessential words and many single words also, and still keep intelligibility.

What about redundancy in visual patterns? Now we are speaking not so much of letters and words as of illustrations.

As we have seen, redundancy serves the purpose of increasing predictability in order to minimize processing time. Predictable shapes—i.e., easy to perceive shapes—are characterized by one writer (Brown, 1966) as:

1. They tend to be symmetrical.
2. They involve straight lines or lines changing in regular manner.
3. They tend to involve few angles.

Studies of eye movements over photographs tend to reinforce Brown's contention. Mackworth and Morandi (1967) have reported on how subjects viewed a photo of Baja California taken by astronauts. Subjects concentrated examination on the more jagged portions of the coastline. The more even portions of the coastline were passed quickly over. So were the monotonously toned and textured interior areas of the peninsula.

Faw and Nunnally (1967) found substantially the same results. College students spent more time examining more complex and novel figures than the less complex and novel.

In both studies eye fixations were recorded. This suggests the possibility of testing the communication efficienty of such items as charts, diagrams, pictograms, prose, and possibly also photographs. Percipients might, after viewing such items, be tested for perception of content. Thereafter, scores could be divided by number of fixations to get an efficiency rating for the printed items (photographs also being considered as "printed").

Concept Formation

Man and animal alike seem to form and to test hypotheses to develop perceptions of things to avoid and to approach. Once established, perceptions are steady. One cannot unrecognize.

But here we part company with animals. The animal can be trained to respond to a triangle rather than to another shape. But the shape must be in his presence. He is, in a word, slave to his sensory perceptions.

But we can free ourselves of perceptual situations and think about them. Our ability to code information in symbol form (words and illustrations) and to use these images to arouse memory associations makes this possible.

Think of any word except a proper noun. The word you think of evokes meaning. Perhaps you have thought of "green." "Green" is not any single thing. You can say, "The grass is green" or "I prefer green."

Green is a label for anything possessing "greenness" along with other distinguishing characteristics. But you have never seen "greenness." "Green" is a concept. The process of analyzing events or objects to isolate common properties is concept formation.

Take a look at Figure 2-4. Can you determine the concept(s) revealed in the cards in the left-hand column? Work at it awhile before reading on. The four cards are positive instances of the concept. Some cards on the right may be positive but others are negative instances.

The eight cards are selected from a possible 16. They would repre-

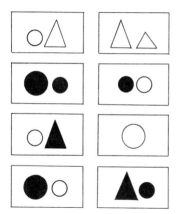

Figure 2-4. *What common features distinguish the cards in the left column from those in the right column? The cards on the left are positive or confirming instances of a concept. Some on the right may be, but not all are.*

sent combinations of four attributes, each with two values: shapes (circle or triangle), color (white or black), size (large or small), and number (single or double); $2^4 = 16$.

Feature analysis is an important aspect of both processes, perception and concept formation. In the former process, feature abstraction is automatic, as we have seen. In the latter, one has to focus one's awareness on the task of abstracting the relevant features and eliminating the irrelevant. One must determine whether a stimulus is a positive or a negative instance.

In the caption of the figure you are told that all cards on the left are positive, which considerably lessens your effort. But the mind is still involved in a hypothesize-and-test exercise until you discover the concept(s). There are at least three: all cards on the left have small circles, all have a large and a small figure, and all have two figures.

Perception "comes naturally," but man makes the decision whether or not to focus his mind and think conceptually. He can choose whether or not to concentrate his awareness on what is relevant and intelligible. Nature gives us the equipment for conceptual thinking, but the choice to utilize it is ours.

Some people prefer unawareness as a goal, since focusing awareness is "hard work." Many of us even purposely control our awareness, to avoid information we would prefer not to have to consider.[2]

The end result of conceptualizing is to set things into separate classes. Thus things divide, according to the concept of greenness, into classes of green and not green.

Many concepts can only be learned by definition. Called "relational concepts," they relate other concepts. "Under" and "between" are examples.

---

[2] For an excellent philosophical and psychological treatment of perception and conceptualizing, the reader will find Branden (1969) exceptionally interesting and informative.

Because feature analysis is an important aspect of both perception and conceptualizing, it is important that significant features be brought into proper focus graphically. For example, in the case of perception, special treatment of photographs may be necessary before reproduction to strengthen points of contrast to expedite proper recognition. Or again, care should be given to proper type selection to make sure that maximum understanding and legibility are possible.

Often the objective in communication is to place an idea or a product "in a class by itself." There are many means at the graphic designer's disposal to reinforce the defining attributes and uniqueness that set such an idea or product apart. We will have occasion to discuss the various techniques as they relate to expediting perception and conceptualizing later.

Memory Systems

Let us now consider memory structure and the part it plays in the human IPS.

Suppose you have just looked up a phone number. Before you can dial, you are interrupted. The delay may be brief, but you have to look up the number again. Or possibly you find you have forgotten the number and have to recheck even though there was no apparent delay. It would seem that there definitely is a type of short duration memory.

There seems to be another type, this of long duration. We can all recall things from years ago.

There's another way of looking at the situation. We process information serially whether reading or looking at illustrations. Suppose you are reading the sentence, "He turned to look out the win . . ." The preceding concepts leading up to "win . . ." must be held in storage until the remainder of the sentence is received. It's obvious what to expect. Long ago you learned the meanings of the concepts prior to "win . . ." These meanings were retrieved from a long-lasting storage.

We will call the two types STM (short-term memory) and LTM (long-term memory).

VISUAL STM

An important aspect of STM is the memory trace, also known as the preperceptual field and the visual short-term memory. It lasts at the most only a few seconds. Let us look briefly at a significant investigation of this aspect of STM by Sperling (1960).

Suppose you are exposed to a picture such as Figure 2-5. Tachistoscopic exposure lasts 50 milliseconds. How many letters will you recall?

Figure 2-5. *Suppose you saw this image for .05 second. How much could you recall immediately after exposure?*

Sperling first trained subjects to distinguish tones of high, middle, and low pitch. Then he made exposures such as those shown in the figure. After exposure he then signaled by tone which row should be repeated.

Subjects were able to comply by repeating the called-for row. But they could recall only occasional letters from among the remaining eight. Without a signal they could recall only four or five from the twelve.

The subjects must have read from a memory trace or icon, a sort of photograph. Performance was maximum when subjects were signaled up to a quarter-second after exposure. A two-second delay rendered subjects unable to reply.

These results are of interest to us because:

1. It would seem that feedback from a higher control designates what should be retained from incoming information—i.e., what is relevant.
2. Only a limited amount can be retained.
3. The graphic designer can control the selection of the design of type used in composing a message. We will examine this idea in detail later. For now, the reader can look briefly through a magazine or newspaper and find quite a variety of designs.

Perhaps the Sperling technique might be applied to a test of whether some type designs are better retained than others in the visual STM.

SHORT-TERM MEMORY

What happens to information that impinges upon the eye?

1. It is first recognized.

2. It may be in whole or in part forgotten. We do not act on everything we sense.
3. Significant or relevant portions move to STM.
4. Portions thought to be useful in the future are stored permanently in LTM.

We have already examined the visual STM. We now consider some other aspects of STM. In a now-famous study published in 1956 psychologist George Miller examined the limits within which our IPS operates. Communications engineers had thought of bits of information as channel capacities. Miller applied these concepts to his study.

Miller pointed out that man can make absolute judgments among "seven plus or minus two" alternatives. He cited studies in which subjects could easily classify the pitch of a musical tone as being in one of two categories. Correct responses were reliable among four categories.

The author reported studies in other areas of absolute judgment to reinforce his contention.

Accurate classification faltered when five categories were introduced. From beyond five classes performance weakened considerably, with most subjects able to use only six. As the number of categories increased so did the number of errors.

This would suggest a channel capacity for the human IPS of about 2.5 bits ($\log_2 6 =$ about 2.5), representing some 7 ± 2 items that can be held in STM.

However, Miller went on to point out that the span of STM differs from the capacity to make absolute judgments. True, STM seems to have a 7 ± 2 limitation on units but this does not necessarily represent about 2.5 bits.

For example, we may be able to recall seven decimal numbers presented in a random order. This represents 7 times 3.32 bits ($\log_2 10 = 3.32$) or 23¼ bits. Randomly presented, English words are worth at least 10 bits each. Remembering seven words represents 70 bits.

Norman (1969) points out this difference: making an absolute judgment is an attempt to encode information (classify it). When we hold word items in STM we are retaining previously encoded information.

Can you look at this number, turn away and recall it—35101217192426? There are 14 digits. That's beyond the typical STM span. But if you encoded it this way you could: (1) start with 3, (2) add 2 to get 5, (3) add 5 to get 10, and (4) alternate by adding 2 and 5. Now you can recall the number by applying a code of four items.

Miller concluded that we are constantly encoding into a verbal code to increase our capacity for handling information.

Much information, but by no means all, moves from STM to LTM. As its name suggests, it is long-lasting. In fact, some authorities believe it lasts throughout a lifetime and call it permanent memory. If items seem to be lost, it may be due to faulty retrieval.

Some writers believe information is stored in on-off patterns at synapses (Travers, 1970). Others feel it is stored in RNA molecules (Biggs, 1971). Although there are gaps in our knowledge of LTM physical structure, much is known of the part it plays in processing.

Precisely what information moves from STM TO LTM? First, information that is placed frequently in STM is likely to be remembered permanently. There is evidence that the transfer requires on the order of 20 minutes (Travers, 1970). Storage in LTM requires concentrated effort.

Second, information likely to be useful in the future is moved into LTM. Do you recall our suggestion for remembering the 14 digits? The four rules for reconstruction, if kept in LTM, would allow you to give the 14 digits at any future date. Such information "chunks" are referred to as codes as well as rules.

What happens to information transferred to LTM? (1) It may be used to add to or (2) to alter the structure of already existing codes. (3) It may be used to establish new categories and codes. In all three instances learning has taken place.

There is organization in LTM. If you're asked to recall something, you don't have to start a run through all that you know until you come upon it.

Recall is often more like problem solving with its attendant decision making than like retrieving from a vast storage bin; not always, though, because some things are used so frequently that you can respond at once. For example, you can answer immediately to, "What does 8 times 5 equal?"

On the other hand, suppose you are to answer the question, "Where were you at 4:00 in the afternoon a week ago last Wednesday?" You may have to engage in a reconstruction process, answering "Yes" or "No" to many secondary questions you pose to yourself before deciding where you were.

LTM holds a prodigious amount of coded information concerning concepts and events as well as relationships among them.

Suppose you ask somebody who knows a great deal about anteaters for the meaning of "anteater." He would probably respond with something like this paraphrased dictionary definition: "It's a tropical mammal that feeds primarily on ants. It has a long and sticky tongue and a long snout."

Now suppose you ask, "Do anteaters lay eggs?" Would he say, "No"? As a matter of fact, he would reply that some do. Found in Australia, Tasmania, and New Guinea, certain anteaters are among the few species of mammals in the world that do lay eggs.

There are two important points here. First, it may be "meaning" that is stored in a physiological coding. But an explanation of the meaning of a word requires the use of other words, which are themselves symbols for other meanings. Second, the relationship of one concept to other concepts is an important aspect of meaning.

The retrieval of information is facilitated by these relationships. They make possible more than one pathway to desired information. For example, in attempting to reconstruct where you were a week ago last Wednesday you were able to explore various possibilities. Meaning is the key to retrieval.

Thus far we have concentrated our attention on the memory of linguistic materials. What about pictorial or graphic memory? Haber (1970) has presented evidence that there are two types of memory—linguistic and visual.

He and L. G. Standing presented 2,560 photographs to their subjects at a rate of 1 per 10 seconds. The subjects were later shown the same pictures, each matched with a similar but not previously shown photo. The subjects were able to identify the previously seen pictures with 85 to 95 percent accuracy.

You can demonstrate visual memory to yourself. Imagine a visual scene from your past, perhaps sitting in the stands at a ball game. It comes back. But how many details can you read off?

Haber and Standing found their subjects, when asked to recall details of the photographs, frequently were not able to. After photograph identification, some were asked to list ten words. These words became the basis for word asssociation exercises. When these subjects were quizzed again, they were able to add details about the photos.

Haber's conclusion was that techniques for making connections between words and visual presentations would dramatically improve recall of the image.

Decision Making

It is time to bring together the things we have said about the structures and capacities of the IPS. We start with the premise that man is endowed with adaptive processes that allow him to adjust to his environment. If he cannot adapt, he cannot survive. Nature always has the final word.

The concept of adaptation presupposes problem solving and the latter presupposes decision making.

Information from the environment is the major determinant of what the problem will be. And what the problem is will determine how the IPS will set about solving it.

Figure 2-6 is a simplified flow diagram of information from its first sensing through to decision making. Information in Visual STM that is judged relevant to the situation passes through Set. The latter represents a physiological need or a cognitive set from the codes stored in LTM. The loop outside STM represents rehearsal of information ("saying it to oneself") to hold it in STM or learning before moving it to LTM.

DM represents the decision-making process, which involves matching information in STM with codes drawn from LTM. These codes are the result of previous decisions. The decision may be that codes in LTM should be changed or that new codes should be established. The decision may also lead to explicit behavior.

We have shown DM as integral with STM. This reflects the limited capacity of the STM. The following should make this clear.

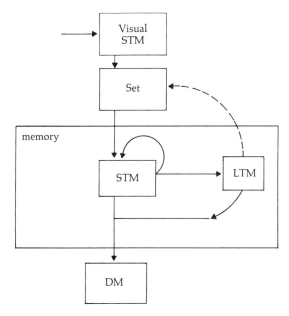

Figure 2-6. *Flow diagram of information in an IPS from stimulus to decision making.*

Suppose you are asked to multiply 34 by 4 entirely "in your head." Underlined terms represent information "chunks" to be held in STM.

1. $\underline{34 \times 4} = ?$ (3 units; these must be kept in STM through all steps)
2. $\underline{4} \times \underline{4} = \underline{6}$ carry $\underline{1}$ (3 original plus 3)
3. $\underline{4} \times \underline{3} = \underline{12} + \underline{1} = \underline{13}$ (3 original plus 5)
4. $\underline{13}$ affix $\underline{6} = \underline{136}$ (3 original plus 3)

   Response $34 \times 4 = 136$

Step 3 requires retaining eight items or chunks in STM. This is barely within the range suggested by Miller.

Now try visualizing the chunks to be held in STM while multiplying 3457 by 8 or 347 by 26. Either plot them as above or try working them in your head (no paper and pencil allowed). If you were to use pencil and paper you could do it easily. This shows that the limitation is in STM, not in mental capacity. It might be added that the protocol of DM involved in steps 1, 2, 3, and 4 is engendered from LTM codes.

The model we have suggested here can be imagined as implanted within the Socio-Cultural Environment circle at the extreme right in Figure 1-2 (page 11).

Emotion and Motivation

Up to this point we have emphasized man's reasoning power and his decision-making choice among alternatives. This basic attribute of man is often thrown out of focus by the way in which laymen and many psychologists view motives and emotions.

A frequent criticism made of communicators, particularly ad men and public relations people, is that "they play on people's emotions." The implication is that man is not only rational, he is also emotional. It is as if man were possessed of two natures — rational and emotional — which are in opposition.

The term "motive" is commonly used as an explanation for behavior. Why does Smith violently attack Jones? The answer, "Out of anger," is believed to be an explanation.

Treated this way, emotions and motives take on a psychological reality that divorces them from intellectual processes. Do motives explain behavior or attach labels to it?

Biggs (1971) argues that emotions and motives can better be understood within the context of information processing. If we are to say *why* Smith attacked Jones we must tell how Smith processed the information at hand at the time of the situation and what he decided to do. Biggs sees it as a case of "veridical and nonveridical data processing."

Man's reasoning power serves at least two basic functions: cognition and evaluation. Through cognition we decide what things are; through evaluation we decide their value to us.

The decisions concerning values—what is good and what is bad in terms of well-being and survival—is our free choice. But the fact remains that it is through values that man's behavior is guided.

An experiment by Schachter and Singer (1962) seems to indicate the relationship between cognition and emotion. They injected some of their subjects with epinephrine (adrenaline). In effect this activates the emotional (sympathetic nervous) system.

Some subjects were informed what the true effects would be— quickening pulse, a feeling of warmth due to increased blood pressure, shaky hands, and accelerated breathing. Other subjects were not told what to expect. A third portion of the injected group were incorrectly informed about expected reactions. They anticipated itching and headache. Still other subjects (called the control) were given placebo shots, which had no effect on the emotional system. All the subjects believed they had volunteered for experiments on the effects of a drug on vision.

Each of the various groups was then divided into two; one was placed in an environment in which a relaxed, happy atmosphere was promoted by paid attendants, the other in an atmosphere conducive to anger and aggression.

The misinformed and those not informed tended to pick up the provided emotion; those correctly informed and the control tended not to. Those expecting the reaction could account for their feelings; those not expecting the reaction could not account other than on the basis of the emotions of euphoria (in the pleasant atmosphere) or anger.

As we expand our cognitions we store the information codes in LTM. Cognitions become automatized. Learning to read was once a chore. Now reading is automatic. We are in effect self-programmed.

Value judgments too become automatic. The computerlike decision-making capacity of the brain can call forth these judgments as quickly as the judgments that you perceive from certain words.

Do you recall our mention of the "complexity program"? This gives the "go" instructions that arouse man to seek information in order to take action.

A high state of arousal is common to all emotion. The context within which arousal occurs supplies the opportunity to apply the label for a specific emotion.

The stimuli that arouse are themselves information. The latter occupies at least a portion of STM. Thus STM is not free for most effective decision making, a part of its limited capacity being occupied.

Many techniques for arousal are available to the graphic designer, as we shall see in later chapters. How he uses these techniques can either expedite or inhibit the effective reception of a message.

If the message is simple and not particularly challenging to the receiver, techniques of arousal may be an aid. If on the other hand, comprehension is more challenging, arousal techniques may be less necessary. They may, in fact, "clutter" the STM.

SECTION 2

VERBAL ELEMENTS OF COMMUNICATION

CHAPTER 3
Type and Type Faces

CHAPTER 4
Elements of Good Typography

CHAPTER 5
Using Type Creatively

CHAPTER 3 Type
and
Type Faces

Spoken and written words and the concepts
they represent are the prime moving force in shaping the destiny of
man.

With the invention in the mid-fifteenth century of printing from
movable type by Johann Gutenberg of Mainz, Germany, this force
was brought into focus. Before Gutenberg, duplication of messages
was from inked, hand-carved wood blocks or from the efforts of large
numbers of scribes who laboriously made copies by hand one at a
time.

As Thomas Carlyle put it, "He who first shortened the labor of
copyists by device of movable types was disbanding hired armies
and cashiering kings and senators, and creating a whole new demo-
cratic world; he had invented the art of printing."

Gutenberg developed a technique of casting individual letters
and other symbols from brass molds. Type was assembled within a
frame and wedged into position. The frame was then placed on a
press and inked. Next, pressure was applied to a piece of paper laid
across the type. The paper received the ink images from the type.

Much of today's printing is still done from metal type. The characters have a raised surface, similar to the letters on a typewriter. The
process of printing from such relief characters is termed *letterpress*.

There are several disadvantages for the graphic designer in this
method of reproduction. For one, composition of the message in
type and preparation of illustrations (termed *photoengravings*) are

relatively slow. For another, type and engravings must be *locked up* (we referred previously to the type being "wedged") in a rectangular *form* (which we referred to as a "frame").

Such mechanical restrictions tend to straitjacket the designer. Today he has more modern methods of type composition and printing at his disposal, which free him from the restrictions and give him greater flexibility in finding visual solutions to design problems.

These newer methods are based on the principles of photography and chemistry and will be discussed in greater detail later. The printing methods are *lithography* and *rotogravure.* The composition methods are referred to as *photocomposition* or *cold type,* in contrast to *hot metal* composition, which involves the use of cast metal type.

The photocomposition technique involves exposing letter negatives, one after another, onto photo paper or film at incredible speeds, far faster than the traditional hot-metal method. Moreover, because photography is utilized, type can be treated in many creative ways.

Type is the primary element in printing. Certain secondary elements, illustrations and decorations, supplement and reinforce type, but the latter can stand alone, capable of delivering a message.

In this chapter we will consider the nature of traditional, metal type. Today, of course, it is cast by machine rather than by hand and is available in a great variety of faces or designs. Later we will turn our attention to photocomposition. There are several reasons for considering hot metal first:

1. Letterpress printing will continue to be used for many years, even though it is giving ground to the more recent methods.
2. A knowledge of hot-metal techniques is necessary in order to understand the limitations of letterpress and to comprehend thereby the design opportunities offered by the newer printing methods.
3. Most of the printer's specialized language regarding type developed during the years when only the traditional methods existed. The jargon is also applicable to the newer methods.

For some time after the invention of printing, printers found one style of type in one size sufficient for their purposes. With the passing of time came an ever-increasing demand for additional sizes and designs to add variety to printed literature. As the expanding craft spread across Europe, changes reflecting the different cultures were effected by a sort of natural evolution.

In Italy, for example, letter forms were developed that resembled the graceful characters in manuscripts prepared by Italian scribes. The basic Roman form through the decades has undergone so many mutations that today there are literally hundreds of type-face styles basically Roman yet subtly individualized.

Estimates abound but, to guess conservatively, there are 1,200 to 1,500 different type faces. Counting variations in design and sizes, the number can reach several thousands. No single printer or typographer can supply all, naturally, but a search of various business firms will turn up any desired face.

The number continues to grow. New hot-metal and photo faces are constantly being introduced. Advertisers search eagerly for fresh designs to give their efforts a distinctive look. People in the media are also interested in new faces to improve legibility and at the same time to cut costs by devising ways to get many characters into small space.

The selection of a type face is an important step in planning how printing should look. If a man's typographic design activities are limited to a single newspaper, he may need to familiarize himself with fifteen to twenty-five different faces. On the other hand, a typography specialist dealing with large printers and typographic service houses (who compose type but do not print) may select from among many hundreds of faces.

Study and experience are the only means to becoming proficient. As the designer broadens his familiarity with different faces, he soon realizes that certain characteristics aid in distinguishing among them. As his capacity to recognize grows, his ability to make sound selection develops.

The fundamentals that aid in type identification appear later in this chapter. Needed first is a consideration of the physical properties of type and the way it is measured.

Type Materials

Type is made of metal or wood. The latter, generally maple or other hardwood, is called *poster type* because its major application is in the composition of posters. Metal, most commonly used, may be divided into two kinds: (1) foundry, and (2) casting machine metal.

Foundry metal is used in *foundry type,* also called *hand-set type.* Such type is cast by manufacturers known as type founders from whom it is purchased by compositors. Each letter and character is separately cast, except for *ligatures* — combinations such as *fi, fl, ff, ffi, ffl, æ*.

A printer's purchase consists of assorted letters and characters bought by the pound. He places them in cases that contain storage compartments. When needed, foundry type is taken from the case, a piece at a time, composed in lines, printed from, cleaned, and returned to the case.

The type wears and is nicked and broken in use; further, returning it to storage is time-consuming and hence expensive. Therefore, most metal type composition is done from type cast by the printer in his own shop from casting-machine metal. Several different kinds of machines are used for so-called *hot-metal composition*. They are discussed in Chapter 15. After being used in the printing process, such type is "melted down" and returned to its original metal form. The metal is then used again for casting other type. Thus "new" type is available for each printing and the returning problem is ended. Hot-metal composition is considerably faster than hand-set.

Measurement of Type

The *face* of a piece of type is that portion that receives the ink and makes contact with the paper. It is raised above the *body* of the type, as shown in Figure 3-1. Note that the body is longer than the letter itself. It is the length (from the upper end to the end nearest you) that determines type size and *points* are the unit of measurement. There are 12 points to a pica, 72 points, or 6 picas, to an inch (scant).[1]

Figure 3-2 shows the special ruler that decides type size and other printing dimensions. It is called a "line gauge" or "pica rule" or "pica gauge." Along the edges are various units of graduated measures needed by the printer and typographer. Usually inches by sixteenths are ticked off on one edge and *picas* and *nonpareils* (half picas) are on the other.

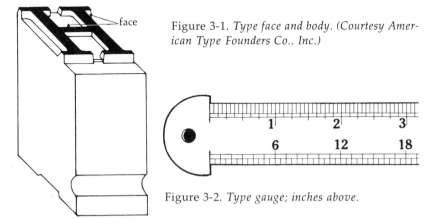

Figure 3-1. *Type face and body. (Courtesy American Type Founders Co., Inc.)*

Figure 3-2. *Type gauge; inches above.*

[1] Although 12 times 72 is 4 points less than 1 foot, printers say 72 points equal an inch for convenience.

Based on the point system, 1 pica equals 12 points; thus there are six picas to an inch. The pica is used to measure:

1. Length of lines; that is, from left to right (horizontally)
2. Width of columns (also a horizontal measurement)
3. Depth of columns; that is, top to bottom (vertically)
4. Size of margins
5. Size of illustrations

Illustrations are also measured in inches. Thus the reproduction of a photo, to be printed as 4½ inches wide and 3 inches deep, can be spoken of as either 4½ × 3 or 27 × 18 picas. Notice that width is always expressed first.

DETERMINING TYPE SIZE

Measuring the size of type with a line gauge is shown in Figure 3-3. In this case the type size is 5 picas, which translates into 60-points. Type height, except for wood type, is always expressed in points.

Figure 3-3. *Measuring type size.*

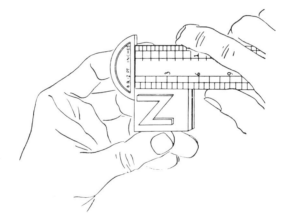

Note that the body is longer than the face. Different faces on bodies with the same number of points can vary in size because point size is the measure of body and not of face. For example, the type on the left in Figure 3-4 appears larger than the other, yet both faces are cast on 18-point bodies. One would say, therefore, "Both are the same size type."

Another variant among faces of the same size type is the length of the *ascenders* and *descenders*. The former is the portion of a face rising

This type face   a b c d e f g h i j k l m

Figure 3-4. *Both faces are 18-point, but one looks larger.*

above such center body letters as *a, s, c, e, i*. The letters *b, d, h* have ascenders. Descenders fall below the center body: — for example, *g, j, p*. The proportion of ascenders and descenders to center body is not standard and can differ widely from one type style to another. This can be observed in Figure 3-4.

Type sizes ranging from 4-point through 12-point are often referred to as *body, reader,* or *text* sizes (or faces); sizes ranging above 12-point are referred to as *display* faces.

WOOD TYPE SIZES

The size of wood type is measured by the actual height of the face, since the face fills the entire body with no space above or below. Wood type is used largely for placards and posters. Size is expressed in picas or more commonly in *pica lines*. Often size is stated simply as *lines*. That is, a 5-line type would be 60-point.

DETERMINING SIZE OF TYPE IN PRINT

Frequently it is necessary to determine the size of type in print. For example, you might be shown a printed piece and asked, "What is the size of the body copy used here?" You might measure with a pica rule from the top of an ascender to the bottom of a descender and make a "guesstimate."

This might indicate type size but not whether it had been *set solid* (without extra space between lines) or *leaded* (with extra space between lines). Even the pro would have difficulty judging 1- or 2-point leading (pronounced "ledding"). It would be best to identify the face and compare spacing with samples in a printer's *specimen book*. This is a catalog of available faces and samples are usually shown with and without various amounts of leading.

The Type Body

Helpful to anyone learning the art of typography is an understanding of the terminology relating to a piece of type (Figure 3-5). The *face* is the letter or character standing in relief atop the body.

The body stands on two *feet,* separated by the groove. The type must rest firmly on its feet when printing. If type is "off its feet," as the printer would say, it leans to the side and does not print properly, since only a portion of the face touches the paper.

The top of the body is divided into *counter* and *shoulder,* the areas within and around the face and the part of the top below the face.

The *nicks* are sections cut across the body. There may be one, as in Figure 3-5, or several on one body. The pieces of a given size and face have the same nick or combination of nicks, which provide a sort of identification code.

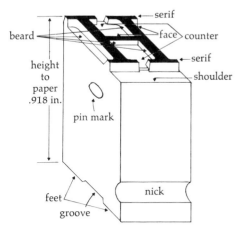

Figure 3-5. *Parts of a piece of type. (Courtesy American Type Founders Co., Inc.)*

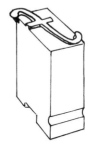

Figure 3-6.
Kerned letter.

Some faces are so cast that an element of certain letters overhangs the body. This part is called the *kern* (Figure 3-6). Usually found in certain italic and script faces (these slant right and will be discussed later in this chapter), kerns overlap the next letter in composition to allow for better spacing.

The words "height to paper .918 in." refer to the distance from the bottom of the body to the surface of the face. This measurement is referred to as *type high*. All printing materials — type, engravings, and auxiliary elements (border, rule, and so on) — must be at this height for proper printing.

It should be noted here that the term "face" can refer to the printed image on paper as well as to the raised surface on the body. Also, the term "counter" can refer to the blank space of the paper within and around the face.

Type Classification

Obviously, the qualified typographer should be able to identify type faces — but there are thousands available. To learn to recognize all — or any substantial number — would be a monumental task.

To facilitate recognition, the designer or typographer must learn how type faces are organized. Once he understands the system, he will be better able to locate the faces that will serve his needs. Moreover, a knowledge of the organization enables him — through the experience of dealing with different faces — to recognize many of the type designs.

Type is organized into: (1) groups or races, (2) families, (3) fonts, (4) series.

TYPE GROUPS

Authorities do not agree on how many groups or races there should be. Some indicate four, others as many as eleven. But, regardless of number, all are based on two considerations: historical development of the faces and their structural form. In this book, type is divided into the following five groups or races, some with subdivisions: Text; Roman; Gothic; Script and Cursive; and Decorative and Novelty.

Text

Today's type faces have their origins deep in the past. Early designers were inclined to fashion their faces on hand lettering. Gutenberg designed his type after the calligraphy found in German monks' manuscripts, and his adaptation, characterized by heavy, angular strokes, was used in the 42-line Bible (Figure 3-7).

Many designs have evolved from the Gutenberg style and become known as *Black Letter* and *Text* types, since their source was the German texts. Until more readable types were introduced in the twentieth century, Text types were widely used in German books and newspapers. The influence of Gothic architecture, too, can readily be seen in the Text type faces. But the typographer does not call them Gothic, although the letter form echoes this style.

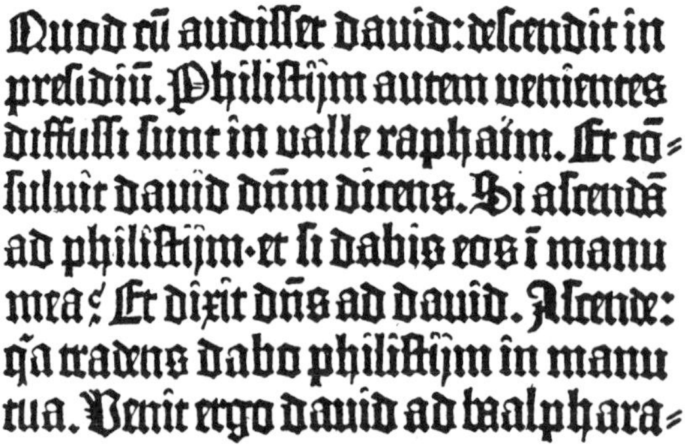

Quod cū audiſſet dauid: deſcendit in preſidiū. Philiſtijm autem venientes diffuſſi ſunt in valle raphaim. Et cō-ſuluit dauid dūm dicens. Si aſcendā ad philiſtijm· et ſi dabis eos i manu mea? Et dixit dūs ad dauid. Aſcende: qa tradens dabo philiſtijm in manu tua. Venit ergo dauid ad baalphara-

Figure 3-7. *Portion of the Gutenberg Bible.*

William Caxton (1422?–1491), the first English printer, used types fashioned after the German. For years thereafter these were the only faces used in England. There is, in fact, a Text face called Old English Text and it is not uncommon to hear Text faces referred to as Old English.

Figure 3-8 shows why a Text face, Cloister Black, is not widely used today and why only a few variations are extant: several lines are difficult to read. Therefore, it is often called on for special purposes where it is thought to be appropriate—for announcements, such as wedding and graduation, and in headlines short enough to be easily read and where the "feel" of the form befits the content. It is found in the latter situation, for example, in messages with religious over-

ABCDEFGHIJKLMNOPQRS
abcdefghijklmnopqrstuvwxyz

Figure 3-8. *A Text face, Cloister Black.*

tones. The use of Text elsewhere seems weak and out of place. Text should never be used in all caps. It is designed specifically for printing in upper and lower case. Note the poor legibility in Figure 3-9.

HARD TO READ

Figure 3-9. *Head in all-cap Text is difficult to read.*

Roman

Roman faces are a gradual development from Text based on manuscripts from Italian scribes, who wrote lighter, more graceful characters than the Germans. Another strong influence, from the inscriptions carved on ancient Roman buildings, is apparent in the capital letters of Roman faces. These stone-cut letters were in caps only, but, in copying them, the scribes developed a variation, a sort of lower case, in order to make their "writing" quicker and easier. These letters, known as minuscules, were adapted into the design of Roman faces.

A face cast in 1465 by two German printers who migrated to Italy, Sweynheym and Pannartz, is believed by some authorities to be the first Roman face (Figure 3-10). But it more closely resembles Text than does a face developed by Nicolas Jenson just five years later (Figure 3-11). Jenson learned the printing trade in Mainz, moved to Italy and set up shop in Venice. Which, then, was the first Roman

Murice iam croceo matabit uellera'tuto.
Sponte fua fandix pafcentefueftiet agnof.
Ipfe lacte domum referent diftenta capelle.

Figure 3-10. Adaptation of Text by Sweynheym and Pannartz.

face? We might say that the Jenson face was the first *pure* Roman. His type has been a model ever since.

The earliest type designers looked on printing as a method for giving wider dissemination to the work of the scribes. It was only natural that they emulated hand lettering. But in 1524 a French printer named Claude Garamond, who was also a type founder, produced a basically original face. He added subtle touches of beauty to the Roman and italic letters of the day that made his product preferred by most typographers. Garamond is still in wide use. A sample is shown in Appendix B.

William Caslon, an engraver, is also noteworthy for his contributions to the development of early Roman faces. Printing took its greatest step forward in England in the early eighteenth century when

VNC Autem teftimonia etiam exteriorum de ipfis diligenter citabimus. Illuftriffimi enim etiā græcorū nō imperiti omnino iudaicæ philofophiæ alii uitam eorū fcriptis fuis approbaffe uidentur:alii theologiā quantū potuere fecuti fūt.Sic eim difces nō temere fed abfoluta exquifitaq; ratione iudaicā philofophiā gentilibus nugis præpofitam a nobis fuiffe.Primum igit'ea ponā quæ de uita iudæorū præclariffimi græcorum teftantur.Theophraftum igitur audias:cuius nōnullos textus Porphyrius in his libris pofuit quos de abftinendo a carnibus cōfcripfit:his uerbis iudæi ad hæc ufq; tépora Theophraftus ait animalia quomodo facrificant? ut fiquis nos ad imitatione illorū hortaretur audire non pateremur. Non enim comedūt ex facrificatis: fed mel atq; uinum noctu infūdunt holocaufta facientes:nihilq; inde relinquentes:ut nec ille qui omnia perfpicit rem tam prauam ifpicere poffit:quod faciūt interim ieiunantes:ac quoniam philofophi natura funt de deo inter fe colloquétes noctu aūt ftellas afpiciétes oratioibus deum inuocāt.Primi enim ifti omninm hominum & bruta & fe ipfos offerre cœperūt:nulla neceffitate aut cupiditate id faciétes.Et i quarto eiufdé negocii hæc a fe ipfo fcribit Porphyrius.Effæi iudæi genere fūt: hi alter alterum magis diligunt q̄ cæteri homines faciant:& uoluptaté oém quafi uitiofam afpernant':continétiā & itegritaté animi ab omni perturbatione remotā præcipuā putantes uirtutem. Vxores nō ducūt:

Figure 3-11. Roman face developed by Nicolas Jenson.

Caslon began designing and casting type. His flair for lettering caught the attention of English printers who had been using imported types. Caslon's distinctively British touches soon gained wide acceptance. Caslon Old Style is still a popular choice in the United States and Europe. Its versatility is reflected by the rule still followed by many printers, "when in doubt, use Caslon."

Faces of Roman letter form are the most numerous of the five groups. Literally hundreds have been developed. While they are essentially similar in form, they may be divided into three kinds: (1) Old Style; (2) Modern; and (3) Transitional.

Roman faces have *serifs*. These short crosslines are placed at the ends of unconnected strokes of various letters. Close examination reveals that they differ broadly from face to face. They may be horizontal or inclined, generally the latter in lower case letters such as *m, n, u, r,* and *p.* Serifs may be heavy or light, bracketed or unbracketed (the bracketed serif is curved into the stroke to which it is attached), large or small.

Roman faces differ from Text in that they are lighter in tone and have greater contrast in the strokes within letters. That is to say, the counters are more pronounced. Certain refinements distinguish Old Style, Modern Roman, and Transitional.

OLD STYLE. Old Style is less formal than Modern Roman. Contrast between strokes is less pronounced. Compare Caslon O.S. (at the top) with Bodoni, an excellent example of Modern Roman, in Figure 3-12. Old Style serifs are rounded and bracketed.

ABCDEFGHIJKLMNOPQRSTUVWXYZ&
ABCDEFGHIJKLMNOPQRSTUVWXYZ&
abcdefghijklmnopqrstuvwxyz

ABCDEFGHIJKLMNOPQRSTUVWXYZ&
ABCDEFGHIJKLMNOPQRSTUVWXYZ&
abcdefghijklmnopqrstuvwxyz

Figure 3-12. *Caslon, an Old Style face (above), and Bodoni, a Modern face (below).*

MODERN. The most notable difference between O.S. and Modern is in the serifs. In the latter they are straight and thin, and unbracketed. In general the Moderns appear geometric, rather squared off and formal. They seem studied or mechanical in design. The O.S. face, in contrast, has a somewhat "artier," hand-drawn, less restricted look. It has a less precise appearance.

Giambattista (John the Baptist) Bodoni, an Italian, brought type design to what many consider the ultimate of perfection about the time of the American Revolution. He learned printing at an early age in his father's shop. Later he was apprenticed in Rome at the Catholic Church printing plant. Then he set up his own shop and his quality work won the attention and support of the Duke of Parma. The duke called Bodoni to Parma to direct that city's printing activities. The face we call Bodoni was developed there.

In its day, Bodoni was thought of as a classical face. The term "Modern" is meaningless in the real sense of the word. Bodoni was new nearly two centuries ago, but the term "Modern" persists.

TRANSITIONAL. These faces have both O.S. and Modern characteristics. Many authorities do not bother to classify them separately, some placing them in the Old Style and others in the Modern subclassifications. It is often difficult to distinguish Transitional faces from the other two. Historically, they were developed in an attempt to improve the legibility of Old Style faces by increasing the contrast between thick and thin strokes.

Baskerville is one of the most popular of the Transitionals. It was designed about 1752 by the Englishman John Baskerville, who reworked Caslon O.S. His design did not catch on at the time, but today the face is widely used. Can you detect the increased contrast in Baskerville? It is shown below in Figure 3-13; Caslon is the upper type. Now take a look at Bodoni again, in Figure 3-12. The contrast between strokes is less in Baskerville than in Bodoni.

Other popular Transitionals are Century, Scotch Bulmer, Bell, Bulmer, Nicolas Cochin, DeVinne, and Electra.

ABCDEFGHIJKLMNOPQRSTUVWXYZ&
ABCDEFGHIJKLMNOPQRSTUVWXYZ&
abcdefghijklmnopqrstuvwxyz

ABCDEFGHIJKLMNOPQRSTUVWXYZ&
ABCDEFGHIJKLMNOPQRSTUVWXYZ&
abcdefghijklmnopqrstuvwxyz

Figure 3-13. *Caslon (above) and Baskerville, a Transitional face (below)*.

Gothic

These faces are second only to Roman in both number and frequency of use. Their general appearance is not Gothic; as noted earlier, Text reflects the Gothic style. The name "Gothic" persists, however, in the trade, so we have to accept it.

Gothic faces are monotonal and skeletal. They are in stark contrast to Roman faces. They were introduced in the early nineteenth century as a symbol of protest against the traditional face of Caslon and the neoclassicism of Bodoni. Inspiration for development of the Gothic face came with the Industrial Revolution—the shift from manpower to machine power. A number of Gothics appeared between 1800 and 1850. Letterform for the Gothics was in the style of classic, ancient Greek characters, which bore strokes of uniform width. Thus, while the Gothics were "new" in their day, the origins of their styling lay in antiquity. What's that old saying, "There's nothing new under the sun"? It has been said that the roots of western civilization lie in our heritage from ancient Greece and Rome. Type of the Gothic and Roman races, the two most popular, symbolize the fact.

It was not until the 1920s that the simple purity of Gothic caught the fancy of designers. It became the face best capable of expressing the tempo of functional modernism in the arts. The term "Gothic" referred to, and still does, a "new" style of expression, independent of traditionalism.

The effects of functionalism, symbolized by Gothic, were brought to bear on typography by the Bauhaus Institute. Established in Germany in 1918, this was a school dedicated to revitalization of design in architecture, painting, sculpture, industrial design, and typography. The Bauhaus, a "think tank" of sorts, was dedicated to a break with tradition. Its advocates proclaimed the spirit of the machine age as against the age of handicraft.

One wonders whether the Bauhaus break with tradition was really that, after all. The mood of the twentieth century may be in Gothic, but the Bauhaus evangelists also favored Bodoni. Perhaps we can only conclude that each period in history produces a typographical style that bespeaks its own time.

There are several other labels applied to the Gothic group or race, used as synonyms for "Gothic." They are *Sans-serif, Block Letter,* and *Contemporary*. Sans-serif is French for "without serifs." Figure 3-14 shows Vogue, a typical Gothic face. Some Gothics have evolved that carry slight variations in strokes (see Figure 3-15), but note that the overall monotone effect is retained.

ABCDEFGHIJKLMNOPQRSTUVWXYZ
11112222333344445555666677778888999900000$$$$

Figure 3-14. *Vogue, a Gothic face.*

ABCDEFGHIJKLMNOPQRSTUVWXYZ&
abcdefghijklmnopqrstuvwxyz

Figure 3-15. *Futura.*

Gothic faces have long been popular in display or headline use, and, with the passing of time, their use in body or reader size continues to expand.

SQUARE-SERIF TYPES. There are a number of faces that might be described as Gothic with serifs added. They are something of a problem in classifying types. Because of the evenness of strokes and serifs, one might consider them a variation of Gothic. Figure 3-16 shows Stymie, one such face.

ABCDEFGHIJKLMNOPQRSTUVWXYZ&
abcdefghijklmnopqrstuvwxyz

Figure 3-16. *Stymie, a Square-serif Gothic face.*

Scripts and Cursives

Members of this group imitate handwriting by pen or brush; the most distinctive difference between Script and Cursive is that Cursive letters are not joined, while Script letters appear to be. The latter are carefully designed so that when two letters fall side by side, the gap between them is scarcely discernible. You get the idea in Figure 3-17.

ABCDEFGHIJKLMNOPQRSTUVWXYZ&
abcdefghijklmnopqrstuvwxyz

ABDCEFGHIJKLMNOPQRSTUVWXYZ
abcdefghijklmnopqrstuvwxyz

Figure 3-17. *Coronet (above) and Commercial Script (below), examples of Cursive and Script faces.*

Most of the letters in this group slant right. A few, however, are upright. Like Text faces, they are difficult to read if used for a long message. As a consequence, they are generally used for display, especially when an air of grace, charm, or elegance is desired. And because they tend to engender personal intimacy, they are often used on letterheads, social invitations, and calling cards. Like Text types, Scripts and Cursives should not be set in all caps.

Decorative and Novelty Types

This group cannot be so precisely defined that a face with the required characteristics can be placed in it. It is a catchall for faces that are not Text, Roman, Gothic, or Script-Cursive.

Some of these faces might be called "Mood" faces, since they give a period in time, a place, or a mood connotation. Examples in Figure 3-18 are Legend, P. T. Barnum, and Typewriter. What do they suggest to you?

ABCDEFGHIJKLMNOPQRSTUVWXY
Z   abcdefghijklmnopqrstuvwxyz

ABCDEFGHIJKLMNOPQRSTUVWXYZ&
abcdefghijklmnopqrstuvwxyz

ABCDEFGHIJKLMNOPQRSTUVWXYZ&
abcdefghijklmnopqrstuvwxyz

Figure 3-18. *Legend, P. T. Barnum, and Typewriter, examples of "Mood" faces.*

The remaining faces might be called "Novelty." Their features vary so widely that Novelty is about the only word one could use, except, perhaps, *potpourri,* but who could pronounce that? The faces in Figure 3-19 are Novelty. Many authorities prefer to call Lydian a Sans-serif. We prefer to classify it as Novelty because of the great contrast between strokes. It lacks the simple, skeletal structure of Gothic.

ABCDEFGHIJKLMNOPQRSTUVWXYZ&
abcdefghijklmnopqrstuvwxyz

ABCDEFGHIJKLMNOPQRSTUVWXYZ&
abcdefghijklmnopqrstuvwxyz

ABCDEFGHIJKLMNOPQRSTUVWXYZ&

ABCDEFGHIJKLMNOPQRSTUVWXYZ&

ABCDEFGHIJKLMNOPQR
STUVWXYZ&

Figure 3-19. *Lydian, Hobo, Cartoon, Neuland, and Broadway, "Novelty" faces.*

TYPE FAMILIES

As we've been discussing groups, we've been talking about families. Caslon, Bodoni, Baskerville, Century, and so on are all members of the Roman race or group. Likewise, we named several different Gothic faces.

How the various design elements, or parts of the face, are handled sets one family apart from another. Therefore, an adequate definition of family might be: a number of type faces closely related in design, such as the Caslon family or the Bodoni family.

Family Variations

Within families there may be a number of variations involving width, weight, and posture, but, regardless of these, the basic family design characteristics may remain. Width variations refer to the extension or condensation of letters and include *condensed, extra condensed,* and *extended* (or *wide* and *expanded*).

Several degrees of weight—that is, whether strokes are relatively light or heavy—range through *light, medium, demibold, bold,* and *extrabold (heavy).*

Types with postures that slant to the right are called *italic,* except those in the Script and Cursive group.

Because of these three factors, type faces are more specifically labeled according to their variations in the family. In other words, we might speak of a particular face such as Futura, as Futura Bold Condensed Italic. What about the normal face—that is, without any of these family variations? One would refer to it simply, for example, as Futura.

Some authorities list italic as a separate race; we prefer to call it a family variation. Its name was derived from Italy, its country of origin, and Aldus Manutius is credited with its first use. He designed it to make it possible to get more characters in a given space; italic characters compose closer together than upright characters.

Originally only lowercase letters comprised the italic alphabet and they were composed together with upright caps. Later designers gave the slant to the caps also and today the term "italic" is used to describe faces of either Roman or Gothic derivation, provided only that they be characterized by the slanting strokes.

Italics were considered as separate and distinct faces for decades. Today we call "italic" a family variation, since in nearly every case the italics have been designed by adapting already existing faces to make them slant. The term "oblique" is applied in some cases in lieu of "italic."

The upright version of a face is called "roman" by most printers. This is true regardless of group; that is, there may be a Cheltenham roman as well as a Futura roman. The latter would seem to be an inconsistency, since Futura is a Gothic. Trade practice dictates that roman is the opposite of italic. Thus one can say to a printer, "Set this in Futura roman," rather than have to say the confusing "Do not set in Futura italic."

All possible variations do not exist in any one family. The Cheltenham family has perhaps the largest number. Following are many faces that exist under this name:

Cheltenham Old Style

Cheltenham Old Style Italic

Cheltenham Old Style Condensed

Cheltenham Wide (Monotype)

Cheltenham Wide Italic

Cheltenham Wide (Linotype)

Cheltenham Medium

Cheltenham Medium Italic

Cheltenham Bold (Linotype)

Cheltenham Bold (Foundry)

Cheltenham Bold Italic

Cheltenham Bold Condensed

Cheltenham Bold Condensed Italic

Cheltenham Bold Extra Condensed

Cheltenham Bold Extended

Cheltenham Bold Outline

TYPE FONTS

A *font* consists of the assortment of letters, figures, and punctuation marks that constitute a branch of a family in one size. By branch we refer to a variation in the family. Thus the printer speaks of a font of Cheltenham Bold or Cheltenham Medium Italic, for example.

Occasionally a character from another font will appear in type matter, due to a mechanical error. Usually it is obvious, since its design is likely to be incompatible with the family with which it appears. The printer calls this "out-of-character" character a "wrong font" (or simply "wf"). The term denotes an error to be corrected.

The range of sizes in a family branch available from a printer or compositor is termed his "series." Thus, in Chelt. B.F. (Cheltenham Bold Face) he may say his series consists of 5-, 6-, 7-, 8-, 9-, 10-, 12-, 14-, 18-, 30-, 36-, and 60-point.

How to Identify Type

Pinpointing the name of a given face — that is, identifying it — is often a difficult task, even for an old pro. Yet, though faces may often seem to be alike, they really are not. The differences exist in the design elements of the faces.

Clues to identity may be found in any letters of the alphabet, and an experienced typographer will do so when necessary. But it is reasonably safe to make the generalization that a study of caps *T* and *A* and lower case *g, e, r, t,* and *a* will suffice. Simply remember *TAgerta.*

Serifs, too, are often a help. So are ascenders and descenders. The size of the *x height* (center body) of a face and the comparative lengths of ascenders and descenders are particularly significant in type identification.

The *set* of letters may also be helpful. Set is close when there is little space between letters in a composed line. This is due to the fact that letters fill — or nearly fill — the top of the body laterally. Some types have a wide set and at the same time a small face.

Contrasting the *thick* and *thin strokes* may be helpful. Note that the treatment of the *bowl,* the rounded portion, of *a* and *e* varies from face to face as does that of the two bowls in *g*. Also the position of the *hook* or *ear* on the top bowl of *g* may offer another clue.

Experience brings an increasing capacity to identify. There is no point in learning to identify simply as a feat of memory. But the typographer faces two situations where ability to identify is important. He may be asked to match a face previously printed or he may need to select faces that are appropriate to the message.

The Point System

To give instructions to the printer concerning his plans, the typographer must have a full knowledge of the measurement system standard throughout the industry. We have already been introduced to points and picas. We must now look at them in further detail.

All type measurement is based on the point system. The point is the smallest unit in the printing measurement system, about 1/72nd of an inch. Actually, it is 0.013837 inches, which means that 72.46 points equal one inch. It is sufficiently accurate to say 72 points equal one inch.

Two other units are part of the system. They are the pica (12 points) and the nonpareil, which is half the pica (6 points). We have already established their sizes.

THE EM

The *em* is related to the measurement system, although it is not, in the strict sense, a part of it. It is a unit of measurement of quantity of type, rather than a unit of linear measurement, as are the pica and the nonpareil.

An em is a square of the type size. There are 6-point ems, which are 6 points square; 8-point ems, which are 8 points square, and so on. The em quad is a blank type body—that is, it bears no face. And it measures the same number of points across each dimension of the top of the body, this measurement being the size of the type. Its basic use is for spacing within a line of type. It is often the amount of paragraph indention in body copy.

At one time printers commonly referred to type sizes by names. For example, 5½-point type was known as *agate* type; 6-point was called *nonpareil;* and 12-point was *pica* type. It was the *pica em* that became the standard unit of linear measurement. When speaking of measurement, one should say, "The column is 11 picas wide." However, printers and typographers often refer to the column as 11 ems wide. One simply has to realize that within the context of the situation they really mean 11 pica ems wide.

As stated above, the em can be used as a measure of quantity of type. This does not mean pica ems but ems of the type size being used, or, as they are sometimes called, *set ems.* Machine composition is often calculated and sold on the basis of so much per 1000 ems (set ems). One would calculate the number of ems in a space 15 picas wide and 7½ inches deep, 10-point composition, set solid, as follows:

$15 \times 12 = 180$ points wide
$180 \div 10 = 18$ (set ems in a line)
$7½ \times 72$ (points per inch) $= 540$ points deep
$540 \div 10 = 54$ lines (10-point, set solid)
$54 \times 18 = 972$ ems (set ems)

If there had been 15 inches depth, there would have been 1944 ems or 1.94 units of 1000 ems. The cost of composition would be cost per 1000 ems multiplied by .97 in the first case, by 1.94 in the second.

Set ems are also useful in copyfitting—calculating the space required for a given number of words when set in type. This will be discussed in a later chapter.

To summarize, the word "em" has two meanings:

1. The square of the type in question
2. A synonym for pica em when speaking about line measurement

THE AGATE LINE

Another unit of measurement used by the printer might be noted. It is the *agate line,* which appears on many line gauges. Sometimes simply called the *line,* this unit is a measure of advertising space. The cost of advertising is often quoted by the line. It can be defined as being 1 column wide and 1/14th of an inch in depth. The term "agate" comes from the name for 5½-point type. Although 5½ × 14 is more than 72, the number of points in an inch, the custom of computing 14 lines per inch prevails.

Be on guard against confusing agate lines and lines of type. When we refer to an ad of 28 lines, we mean either an ad 2 inches deep and 1 column wide—written 28 × 1—or an ad 1 inch deep and 2 columns wide—14 × 2, spoken of as "fourteen on two."

OTHER USES OF THE POINT

The point is also used to measure the size of *line-spacing* materials—that is, the nonprinting strips placed between lines of type to provide additional space, either to improve legibility or to bring a block of composition to a desired depth. Usually these spacing materials are metal. Leading of body copy is most often either 1 or 2 points.

The point also measures *rules* and *borders,* both of which are printing materials and therefore type-high. Rules print lines of various thicknesses. There are many styles—a single line, double line, multiple lines, and a dotted line (sometimes called *leaders*). Special rules with fine teeth may be used for perforating. These are slightly more than type-high and press into the paper during printing. Another special rule, known as a *scoring rule,* is available for creasing heavy paper to make exact folding possible. This rule presses into stock when it is run through an uninked press. It compresses the paper but does not cut, as does the perforating rule.

In designating the size of rules, the printer often refers to two measurements—the size of the printed line and the size of the body of the rule that supports the printing surface. Figure 3-20 shows that rule sizes remain constant. Different body sizes produce varying spaces between same-size rules.

The point is also used to indicate the size of *dashes, brackets,*

hairline—6 pt. body
1½ pt.—6 pt. body
3 pt.—6 pt. body
6 pt.—6 pt. body
hairline—2 pt. body
1½ pt.—2 pt. body
2 pt.—2 pt. body

Figure 3-20. *Various sizes of rules.*

parentheses, braces, ornaments, initial letters, special characters, logo-types.

Three types of dashes are shown in Figure 3-21. The *jim dash* is used to separate the decks (sections in a headline) and between stories or articles. The *30 dash (finish dash)* and the *ornamental dash* are used to separate unrelated items. The use of dashes is notably on the decline. The trend is toward single-deck heads, and white space is more and more being used to separate items.

Figure 3-21. *The jim dash. The 30 dash. The ornamental dash.*

Examples of brackets, parentheses, and braces are shown, left to right, in Figure 3-22. Many ornaments, among them florets and symbolic typographic embellishments, are available for printing, but few printers stock a wide variety because they are seldom used in modern typography. Decorative initials (Figure 3.23) are also seldom used today.

Figure 3-22. *Brackets, parentheses, and braces (left to right).*

Figure 3-23. *Decorative initial letters.*

Borders are more decorative than ruled lines (Figure 3-24). The measurement of a border rule indicates the thickness of the body.

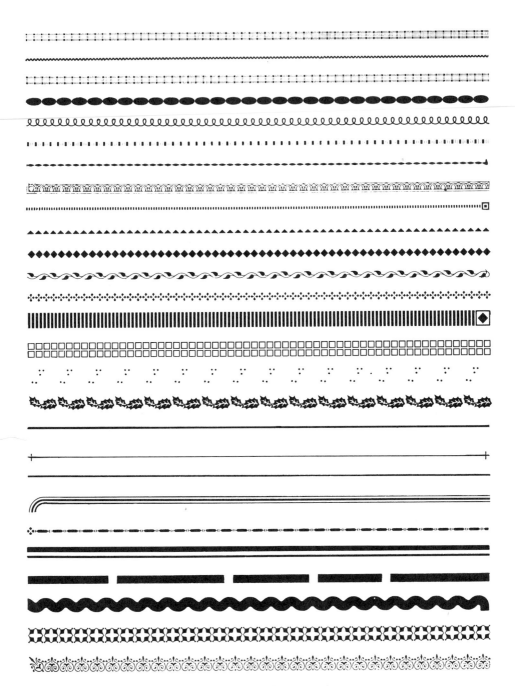

Figure 3-24. *Border materials.*

The term "special characters" covers a wide range of symbols. For example, advertising figures (large numerals), fractions, percent symbols, dollar and cents marks, prescription marks, and so on are stocked by many shops.

Logotype, or logo, refers to whole words on one body. Sometimes the words are combined with design to identify a product or business. The term also applies to the name of a publication, perhaps used on its cover or at various places inside. Naturally, the term is applied to a print from the type.

As a final observation concerning the point, the printer may refer to the thickness of heavy-weight paper as being so many points. In this application the term refers to 1/1000th of an inch and should not be confused with the point as used in type measurement.

Hand Composition

From the time of Gutenberg to the coming of typesetting machines in the last half of the nineteenth century, hand-set was the only method of composition. Today most composition is by machines (foundry or hot-metal or the relatively more recent photocomp). But hand-set remains important, because of the demands of advertisers and media designers for "out of the ordinary" faces. Consequently, many printers and composition houses carry wide selections of foundry type.

It should be borne in mind that the basic typographic rules and the terminology that govern machine composition—whether hot-metal or photo—are those established for hand composition.

The case in which hand-set type is stored contains *spaces* and *quads*. These are used to fill in nonprint areas within a line of type. Composition is done by assembling one at a time the needed characters and spaces. Earlier we mentioned line-spacing materials used to increase space between lines. Leads can be referred to as *vertical spacing*. Quads and spaces, used intraline, may be called *horizontal spacing* materials.

Spacing of Type

All lines of metal type must be of the same length. The process of making each line come to full measure (line length measured in picas) is called *justifying the line*. Rarely does a line come to exactly full measure at the end of a word or a sentence. Usually, the final word falls short or is too long for the remaining space.

In the former case extra space must be placed between words or occasionally within words (*letterspacing*). In the latter case space between words must be reduced or the last word must be hyphenated and continued on the next line. When a paragraph ends short of line length, the remaining space must be filled with spacing materials.

Spaces and quads are available in various widths (referring to east-west across the top of the body). The amount of spacing required for justifying is achieved with various combinations of horizontal spacing materials.

Lengthy composition requiring hyphenation is tedious. It can require as much as one-third of a compositor's time, even on hot-metal, line-casting machines, which set type four to five times faster than a hand compositor. The introduction of computer-controlled casting on machines — hot-metal as well as photo — has mitigated this problem. We discuss this aspect of typesetting in Chapter 15.

Proper spacing is an important consideration in hand or machine composition. It is an art, and a number of factors must be considered if the resulting print is to be pleasing to the eye. Let us look at some of these factors.

1. Spacing between words is better accomplished visually than mechanically. In Figure 3-25 the top line is spaced with common spaces, normally used between words. In the second line, spaces are reduced by 50 percent and the appearance is improved.

Figure 3-25. *Incorrect and correct spacing between words. (Figures 3-25–3-27 and "rivers of white" from* Typography, Layout and Advertising Production *by Edwin H. Stuart and Grace Stuart Gardner, courtesy Edwin H. Stuart, Inc., Publisher)*

𝕮𝖆𝖙𝖘 𝕮𝖆𝖓 𝕽𝖚𝖓

𝕮𝖆𝖙𝖘 𝕮𝖆𝖓 𝕽𝖚𝖓

If the face has a small center body (x height), less space is needed between words. The type in Figure 3-26 is Caslon 471. The top line in this 18-point sample is spaced with common spaces. In the second line, spacing is reduced and appearance improved. The third line shows Caslon 471, left, and Caslon 540. Though both are 18-point, the difference in overall appearance is striking. Extra heavy or "fat" letters usually require more than common spaces. In

Figure 3-26. *Incorrect and correct spacing between words.*

Cats Can Run

Cats Can Run

Caslon Caslon

Figure 3-27 the top line is Nubian with a common space. With 50 percent more space, the second line is more easily read.

NEW FAT

NEW FAT

2. The amount of space following a period is affected by the capital starting the next sentence. The period itself admits white space. If, then, the following letter is *T, W, V, Y,* or *A,* the space after the period should be less, since these caps also admit white space.

3. *Hair space,* one point or less, may be effectively used between a word and a period, colon, or semicolon. Question marks may similarly be spaced. Commas, however, should be flush against the previous word.

4. Some typographers decide on the between-word spacing that best suits the face and apply it throughout text composition. At the same time the composition is "ragged right," that is, the lines are not justified. They have an appearance similar to ordinary typewriter composition. Tests have shown this does not interfere with reading (discussed in Chapter 4). Those using the method point out that overall appearance is satisfactory and that the time required for justifying is saved. An example is shown in Figure 3-28. There is an increasing use of this technique.

Figure 3-28. *Ragged right composition.*

On the pages that follow, the reorganization and its effect on various banks are more fully explained in sections which include the photographs of the senior officers who are responsible for individual areas.

5. Words set all caps can be made to look less crowded if they are *letterspaced.* Note the two words below:

LETTERSPACING   L E T T E R S P A C I N G

Letterspacing of all caps in condensed type should be avoided.

The above applications can be supplied through machine and hand-set but the extra time and consequent cost are often foregone in favor of speed. It becomes a matter of weighing one consideration against the other. In any case, there is little excuse for what is referred to as *rivers of white,* shown below, left. More careful spacing eliminated the condition, right.

Among them were: Mr. and Mrs. Samuel Goldwyn, Mr. and Mrs. Florenz Ziegfeld, Mr. and Mrs. Louis B. Mayer, Mr. and Mrs. Irving Thalberg, Mr. and Mrs. Jack Mulhall, Dr. Harry Martin, Luella O. Parsons, Mr. and Mrs. Paul Zuckerman, Mr. and Mrs. Hugh Murray, Mr. and Mrs. Ben Jackson, Mr. and Mrs. Edgar Selwyn.

Among them were: Mr. and Mrs. Samuel Goldwyn, Mr. and Mrs. Florenz Ziegfeld, Mr. and Mrs. Louis B. Mayer, Mr. and Mrs. Irving Thalberg, Mr. and Mrs. Jack Mulhall, Dr. Harry Martin, Luella O. Parsons, Mr. and Mrs. Paul Zuckerman, Mr. and Mrs. Hugh Murray, Mr. and Mrs. Ben Jackson, Mr. and Mrs. Edgar Selwyn.

CHAPTER 4 Elements
of Good
Typography

Imagine someone browsing through a magazine. He may pause to glance over an ad for several seconds and then continue turning the pages. Again a pause, perhaps to read the headline over an article.

What is he paying attention to? You might say the magazine. But actually a tremendous amount of information impinges on all his sense organs: the visual certainly with the strongest sense impression and the aural and the tactual. Perhaps at some point a sound in an adjoining room may cause him to lay the magazine down and go to investigate. He may then return to his chair and take up browsing again. Not all sounds will interrupt his reading; nor does he pause over every item in his magazine or stop browsing when he shifts position in his chair to get more comfortable.

Many things compete for our attention; we do not attend to all of them. In fact, we may not even be conscious of them. Nonetheless, there seems to be some sort of monitoring of the environment and a selective control, for we can give attention when the need seems to arise.

An important neural subsystem, the reticular activating system (RAS), reacts to incoming information and arouses us to attention. In addition, it interacts closely with the cognitive processes, apparently monitoring and allocating the necessary analytic and problem-solving computations (Lindsay and Norman, 1972, pp. 622–627).

The printed message is made up of two elements: the verbal and the visual or the graphic. The term "verbal elements" refers, of course, to the words. "Visual elements" refers to anything printed other than words. An important component is the illustration. Both elements are means of transferring meanings; in other words, both are conveyors of information.

It has been said that we are in the visual age, and some observers go so far as to venture that the visual image will replace the word. We need to consider the contribution of each to effective communication. Man and animal have in common the capacity to respond instantly to the visual environment. Only man, however, possesses the facility to use words. In a sense words are also visual but their function is not simply to be seen. They are used for making statements and descriptions.

Many such statements are conditional and involve logic and inference. Language can be complex and difficult. Response is often delayed and time-consuming, in contrast to response to the visual.

On the other hand, illustrations are not capable of statements. As Gombrich (1972) put it, "The assertion that statements cannot be translated into images often meets with incredulity, but the simplest demonstration of its truth is to challenge the doubters to illustrate the proposition they doubt."

We can only conclude that the visual image is useful in arousing the physiological processes (emotions) and activating the cognitive processes. Without the aid of words the image is incapable of matching the statement power of words used alone.

People spend good money to get words and visual images into print. They want them to be seen and read. Thus the typographer or designer faces a dual responsibility: (1) utilizing visual elements to draw attention from competing messages and (2) choosing and arranging type to be as legible as possible.

During the past hundred years scientists, primarily psychologists, have studied communication via the printed page. Their findings have tended to confirm the standards or rules developed by typographers through experience—especially in the areas of selecting and using type (Burt, 1959, p. 31).

Although the conclusions of the psychologist must be viewed as provisional, they have value either as suggestions for procedure or as a recall to standards established by practicing typographers.

We will give most of our attention in this chapter to typographic practice in dealing with *body* or *text type*. This refers to type faces ranging in size through 12-point. These are the sizes generally used for composing the "guts" of a message. Faces in sizes 14-point and above are termed *display type*. We will deal with the typographic practices involving their use in later chapters.

There are two aspects of the use of body copy of particular interest to the designer: (1) legibility, and (2) appropriateness.

Legibility

The term "legibility" suggests a composition-reader interaction. It is therefore not enough to say that legibility means that the message is readily visible. The purpose of looking at composition is not simply to see it but to understand it—to grasp the meaning it carries. Comprehension is thus central to legibility.

There are other aspects to be considered. To be observed in the first place, type should be esthetically pleasing. That is, the face design should be consciously chosen, and letters, words, lines—in fact, the entire composition—should be so displayed as to invite and then sustain attention.

Let us return for a moment to comprehension. It comes as a result of processing information; thus it must be defined as units of understanding per unit of time. Comprehension determines the speed at which a reader moves his eyes across the composition. If all other conditions—including comprehension—under which reading is done are constant, the type that is read faster than another could be termed more legible.

A number of factors bear on legibility: face, size, boldness, leading, length of line, margins, even or uneven lines (justified or nonjustified), ink, paper, presswork, lighting, and the interest of the reader in the content.

The last factor is controlled by the selection of ideas, not by type, but is nonetheless important to the typographer. Tests indicate that reader interests are related to legibility and bear an effect on the use of type.

TESTING LEGIBILITY

Observations about the mechanics of reading are helpful to a discussion of legibility. Reading is done as the eyes make short jumps along a line. At each stop (fixation) several words are absorbed. Enough letters or words are perceived to fill in the gap between fixations.

Readers vary in proficiency. A skilled reader makes fewer fixations, has greater rhythm in eye movement and rarely has to make regressions—retrace to a previous point to pick up something missed.

The legibility of words or idea groups is more important than that of individual letters. Effective reading requires recognition of whole words, usually more than one. Content of the words (their meanings), clarity of expression, and absence of unfamiliar words are aids to rapid reading.

The following are the major tests used in measuring legibility:

1. Tachistoscopic tests. These measure the subject's reading accuracy by presenting letters and words in brief exposures.
2. The measuring of a reader's ease in distinguishing letters and reading words by presenting them at varying distances.
3. Studies of eye movements, blinks, and indications of fatigue. Specially designed "eye cameras" record movements over a printed area. Either a light ray is reflected from the cornea or a white spot is affixed to it. A tracing is made of the movements and laid over the printed material to determine the path of the eye.
4. Focal variation tests, which present messages as blurs slowly brought toward focus. The threshold recognition is thus established. Such tests, like distance tests, might be applied, for example, to poster and package design testing.
5. Binocular rivalry tests, which present a different image to each eye. A device called a haploscope, which is somewhat like a stereoscope, is used. The viewer will see one image as dominant or will vacillate between the two with an effect similar to that in viewing a Necker cube. If an image dominates, it is thought to be preferred.
6. Time-comprehension tests of prose reading followed by questionnaires to reveal the extent to which the content was retained and errors made.

Paterson and Tinker (1940), Tinker (1963), Burt (1959), and Zachrisson (1965), recognized as important contributors in testing, have used the last method as their principal technique.

Results from various types of tests do not always agree. A face may be found more legible by one procedure than another. But, in general, the findings have validated trade practices.

The student of typography should be on guard against confusing legibility testing with readability testing. The latter was developed by readability experts, most notably Rudolph Flesch, John McElroy, and Robert Gunning. They measure the relative difficulty of reading according to clarity of writing, ease of reading, and human interest. Briefly stated, they have found a message most readable when sentences are short and words are familiar and personal. Since such factors certainly influence reading efficiency, readability and legibility tests can easily be confused. Though both measure reader response, readability tests focus on content comprehension, and experts in this area have developed "readability formulas" to measure the level of difficulty in understanding written messages. Legibility tests, on the other hand, focus on the form of presentation of a written message.

Typographers have long contended that legibility is maximized by the use of the standard Roman faces. Tests to date have neither confirmed nor refuted the contention, although researchers have been inclined to conclude that it is valid. Typographers feel that familiarity and design factors render legibility to such faces. They point out that we learn to read from books printed in Roman and that the majority of what we read thereafter in books, magazines, and other literature is also printed in Roman. Further, the more irregular design features of Roman faces help the reader grasp word forms more rapidly in the reading process than in Gothic. Contrasting strokes give a rhythmic structure to words and serifs assist horizontal eye movement.

On the other hand, the monotonous sameness of Gothic faces, they feel, impairs reading. Gothic is often used for text material, especially when the number of words is not great; its use for display is well-established.

In earlier editions of this text we pointed out the following: "Advertisers in the large national magazines, who seek the best possible typographical advice, prefer Roman faces for text matter, a fact the student can readily verify by browsing through the pages of well-known publications." Try it today. While Roman may still show an edge, the fact is not nearly so certain.

Burt has offered evidence that among the Roman faces the modern designs seem less legible than the old-style, especially for children and older persons (Burt, 1959, p. 7). He concluded that legibility is reduced in modern faces because the design emphasizes the similar parts of the letter; old letters accentuate dissimilar characteristics. Contrast is the source of perception and meaning, as we discussed in information processing. Might this concept be applied to Roman vs. sans serif, where contrast is even more pronounced? Binocular rivalry tests show that people have a preference for Roman (Zachrisson, 1965, pp. 128–131).

One study of the legibility of Roman vs. Gothic (Robinson, Abbamonte, and Evans, 1971) attacked the problem on the basis of how the visual system is believed to function. We mentioned this in Chapter 2 when we spoke of Hubel and Wiesel.

Robinson et al. developed a mathematical model of the way in which neural components of the visual system are assumed to interact and abstract information to allow interpretation of what is seen. A testing of the model indicated that a computer, processing information according to the model, misjudged geometric illusions (such as Figures 2-1 and 2-2) in the same way as human beings do. Mathematical descriptions of these geometric figures were fed to the computer.

Information descriptive of Roman and Gothic type faces was given the computer and it was then asked to print out what it "saw." The results indicated Roman to be more legible in reader sizes but there was no legibility difference in the case of display sizes.

In research completed in 1974 under the auspices of the American Newspaper Publishers Association, Dr. J. K. Hvistendahl of Iowa State University found that a sample of 200 newspaper readers showed a marked preference for Roman type over sans serif type for newspaper body copy. The type faces compared were those in common use in American newspapers.

Further, Hvistendahl found that readers were able to read Roman type significantly faster in three out of four comparisons of type set in both ten and one-half and fourteen pica widths. In the fourth test the sans serif was read faster but the difference was not great. He concluded that newspapers should be ultra-cautious about changing from Roman to sans serif body copy.

What role does familiarity play? One noted authority, John R. Biggs (1968, p. 10), has indicated, "All the scientific experiments on legibility I have come across produced more or less the same results —that within obvious limits, people read most easily and with least fatigue those letter forms they are most familiar with."

Two attempts at measuring familiarity have been reported by Zachrisson (1965, pp. 85–90). People were asked in one test to select from among various printed faces the one that most resembled that in a book they had recently read and also the one that resembled one in a printed piece they had seen earlier the same day. The results led to the conclusion that typographers overestimate the impact of ordinary faces on the reader.

A second, two-part experiment compared the abilities of laymen (ordinary readers) and workers in the typographic field to recognize and reproduce the shapes of letters. The letters $a, f, g,$ and t were used on both tests. In the recognition version, a proper form was given along with six to nine incorrect alternatives. The subjects were to indicate the correct form. In the reproduction part of the experiment the four lines that demark lower case letters (to show the x-height, the ascenders and descenders) were presented with correct sample letters—other than $a, f, g,$ and t—in correct position. The subjects were to draw and position the test letters correctly. The results of the experiment indicated that both groups had a low level of ability to recognize and reproduce.

It would seem that, while people may perceive the total form, the structural detail is lost.

Typographers generally agree that, regardless of type face, caps and lower case are preferred to material set all caps. Paterson and Tinker (1940, p. 23) have shown that text matter set in all caps caused a 12 percent loss in reading time. This does not necessarily negate the use of all caps in display matter.

Like italics, the boldface variation of a type face serves well for emphasis. The families designed to give a heavier appearance when compared to others have been suggested by Burt (1959, p. 10) as useful for the very young and the elderly.

Typographers recommend 10-, 11-, and 12-point types for text matter for the average reader, and tests have borne out their contention. Burt (1959, p. 12), however, believes type may be too large or too small for some individual readers. He asserts that larger sizes are often preferable for both younger and older-than-average readers.

Logically, text matter presented in display sizes—as is occasionally done in promotional literature—risks a decline in legibility. It is apt to call attention to itself at the expense of the information it should be transmitting. Moreover, since few words fall within the eye span, more fixations are required of the reader with possibly the additional result of increased reading fatigue.

LEADING

Printers and typographers use leading primarily to enhance legibility. These are the rules they follow:

1. For ordinary text sizes, one or two points of leading are adequate.
2. For faces that are small on the body, 1-point leading is sufficient.
3. As length of measure is increased, the need for leading is greater for any face.

Burt (1959, p. 13) reported, "Little seems to be gained by 3-point leading; 4-point leading usually diminishes legibility; like excessive letter-size, it tends to increase the number of eye movements and fixation pauses."

LENGTH OF LINE

That length of measure influences legibility has been substantiated by research (Burt, 1959, p. 14). Short measures in a large type face require more frequent fixations, since the reader has more difficulty absorbing longer phrases. The number of hyphenated words at the ends of lines increases. Both decrease reading comfort and increase the time taken for perception.

Long lines, particularly in small type, also impair legibility, since the reader is slowed in picking up the succeeding line after swinging back from the end of the long line.

For many years charts expressing the limits for length of line relative to size of type have been available to printers and typographers.

The limits have generally been expressed in picas or inch equivalents.

Burt has suggested that since set of type (width of individual letters) varies from face to face, limits of measure might better be expressed by lengths of alphabet. The term "length of alphabet" refers to the space required for composing lower case letters *a* through *z,* with no extra space between letters. He has proposed that limits of two to three alphabets encompass maximum legibility and that alphabet length should correspond to body size (Burt, 1959, p. 14). That is to say, if the type face is set 10 on 12, or 10-point leaded two points, the alphabet length of 12-point type should be used.

The usual book faces in 7-, 7-½-, and 8-point are not considered satisfactory for newspaper editorial straight matter, partly because of the narrow column width, which is generally eleven or twelve picas. Special news faces have been designed for use in what is becoming the standard width, eleven picas. Such faces are usually 9-point and are set with half-point leading. They have an x-height as large as possible and are at the same time condensed to allow 28 to 33 lowercase characters (counting spaces and punctuation characters) per line.

Although the number of alphabets per measure falls below Burt's minimum, his studies were primarily concerned with book printing. Moreover, one need but give a hasty check to realize there are not an unreasonable number of hyphenations in the typical newspaper columns of straight matter.

There are a number of authorities who maintain that the 11-pica newspaper column is too narrow for easy reading. One study conducted under the direction of Professor J. K. Hvistendahl of Iowa State University indicated improved speed of reading with a 9-point news face on a 15-pica measure (Nelson, 1972, p. 195). The wider columns also reduce the number of hyphenations and allow for more even spacing between words. Several papers have adopted the 15-pica, 6-column page.

Many typographers find these rules of thumb for length of line useful: (1) minimum line length: one lowercase alphabet; optimum: one and one-half alphabets; maximum: two alphabets; (2) length of line in picas should not exceed twice the point size; thus 10-point type should not be set on a measure exceeding 20 picas; (3) lines should average 10 to 12 words.

These rules are not compatible. The words per line rule refers to average words, including such short ones as "the," "in," "on," "a," "by," as well as "Pennsylvania," "administration," "demonstration," and so on.

Printers generally consider the average word to be five characters plus one space. Lines averaging 10 words would thus accommodate 60 characters, somewhat in excess of two lower case alphabets.

MARGINS

Research findings vary widely regarding the effect of book-page margins on legibility. Burt contends excessively narrow margins may produce visual fatigue. Paterson and Tinker (1940, p. 109), on the other hand, found that the reduction of normal margins had no effect on reading speed.

Practitioners have long contended that ample margins invite reading, a belief that Burt (1959, pp. 14–15) seems to accept even while suggesting that reader preferences for margins are mostly a matter of esthetics. Considered ample are margins comprising about 50 percent of a book page.

In book work progressive margins are most frequently used; the narrowest margin is at the fold (inner margin), the next width at the top of the page (head margin), next at the outside (outside margin), and the greatest at the bottom (foot margin). These margins move clockwise on odd-numbered pages and counterclockwise on even-numbered pages. Thus they are held together by the narrow margins at the center.

The purpose of margins in all printing is to frame the type and other elements within a border of white space. Thus the amount of white space between elements within the printed area should be less than that of the margins in order to provide unity and coherence.

EVEN OR UNEVEN LINES

Most body copy is composed in even lines. But today more and more text is composed with irregular line lengths, the so-called "irregular right" or "ragged right." The left alignment remains even. The practice is often found in advertisements but is appearing more frequently in book work. Some newspapers are beginning to use the technique. Generally, if all lines are even, an occasional hyphenation at the end of a line is necessary. This is the most time-consuming operation in composition, and one purpose of the irregular right is to increase composition speed.

What of its effect on legibility? Zachrisson (1965, pp. 145–155) has reported an experiment in which it was established that uneven lines have no adverse effect on legibility.

OTHER FACTORS

The interaction between paper or printing surface and type face has an effect on legibility. The principal factor involved relates to the brightness contrast between print and paper.

Tinker (1963) has reported the following:

1. Black on white is superior to white print against a black background. When the message is short, white on black (so-called reverse printing) is useful for getting attention but text should be 10- or 12-point and preferably sans serif (p. 151).
2. Black on tinted paper under ordinary conditions is probably an unimportant factor (p. 140).
3. The legibility of different combinations of colored ink on colored backgrounds varies greatly. The best combinations have greater brightness contrast — e.g., dark ink on a light color.
4. Enamel paper should be carefully considered; glare may impair legibility.

Typographers follow several rules, which to our knowledge have not been researched. Old Style Roman faces were designed for letterpress printing on what was a relatively coarse stock in existence at the time of their creation. The combination of pressure printing on the coarse paper allowed the delicate hairlines to spread. Modern Roman faces with their fine lines print best on a smooth but uncoated paper. Highly polished paper tends to overemphasize the contrasts in such faces with a sacrifice in legibility. Transitional faces print well on a compromise between coarse and smooth paper.

There is no pressure in offset printing, for the image is transferred to the paper from a rubber surface. This printing method allows greater flexibility in selecting the type face.

The faces used in rotogravure printing must be able to withstand "screening," or breaking the image into a series of tiny dots. Typographers recommend avoiding hairline types, regardless of the nature of the paper. The density of the ink and the quality of the presswork are less under the control of the typographer than most of the previous factors. Their influence on legibility is obvious.

The typographer has no control over the lighting conditions under which the message is read, but, as suggested above, he can control the background against which the type is seen.

APPLYING LEGIBILITY FACTORS

There are three major reasons why the typographer must exercise considerable judgment in applying the principles of legibility:

1. Since testing has been primarily limited to book printing, adapting the principles to other areas requires care.
2. Researchers have noted a definite dependency of one factor on another. As Burt (1959, p. 30) pointed out, "assessments obtained

by varying just one characteristic in isolation may at times be highly misleading."

3. Considerations other than legibility should enter the selection of type and its arrangement. If legibility were the sole criterion, all printed matter would tend toward a monotonous uniformity.

What value, then, should the typographer place upon the principles? He should look upon them as flexible aids to judgment rather than as an end in themselves, realizing that no one combination of the individual factors gives an absolute, maximum legibility.

Appropriateness of Type

Appropriateness, or fitness, is the second aspect to be observed in the use of type. In the process of communication the message from source to receiver should fall within a field of experience or knowledge common to both. In other words, the message must be stated in terms that can express the ideas the sender wishes to deliver and, at the same time, be comprehensible to the receiver.

The reader's response is conditioned by the overall effect of the complete printed message. Recall the experiments reported by Haber? The subject matter is embodied, of course, in the words. How they appear plays an important part in their delivery. The selection and arrangement of elements should combine into a unified communication, appropriate to the message.

Appropriateness in this context has three meanings: it can be (1) the selection of faces according to the psychological impressions they bear; (2) the adaptation of legibility rules to fit the education and age levels of the reader; (3) the use of faces harmonious with the other elements and the overall design of the printed message. "Compatibility" would in fact be an appropriate synonym for "appropriateness."

PSYCHOLOGICAL IMPLICATIONS

The individual letters that comprise the upper and lower case alphabets of a given type face were designed to work together. The entire font is seen in infinite combinations within a block of type. From this comes a total visual impression that can be termed the "feel" of the face. It can suggest definite physical qualities in blocks of composition. For example, strength is conveyed by the Bodoni in the paragraph following. A touch of delicacy is suggested by the Caslon in the second paragraph. Both specimens are set in the same size type and leaded equally.

A block of copy set in Bodoni presents a "rough" texture somewhat like a corded material. This is caused by the vertical emphasis in the design of the face. Textural effect is due not only to the thickness of line but also to the amount of spacing between lines.

Copy composed in Caslon presents a "smooth" texture. The contrast between the vertical and the horizontal strokes is less pronounced than in Bodoni. The skilled typographer seeks a textural effect that is compatible with the nature of the message.

Touch or tactile experience plays a critical part in human behavior (Frank, 1957). It is, as Frank has indicated, the primary means of infantile communication and is crucial to learning later in life, yet its impact on communication has largely been neglected. The infant learns early to enjoy tactual contact, especially with textures. As sensory awareness expands, he establishes visual images to reinforce his tactile experiences; signs and symbols become surrogates for tactile communication and arouse responses originally made to tactile stimuli.

The patterns of printing elements are such surrogates and deserve the typographer's careful attention. The face used and the leading between lines can change the textural tone of composition in interesting ways.

Some writers have suggested that the various type faces, by reason of their design, can suggest different moods and feelings. Lists have been drawn giving a "personality" to each face, but these are no more than subjective evaluations. It will be far safer to depend on research to uncover the psychological associations with faces held by readers after more investigation has been done.

USING LEGIBILITY "RULES"

The typographer can temper the application of legibility fundamentals to fit specific kinds of readers. Large bold faces seem desirable for the very young and the very old. Generous leading helps beginning readers to move from line to line. Where the degree of reader interest is higher, greater flexibility is possible, since reading will be done despite reduced legibility.

HARMONY

For the total printed piece to present a unified communication, the type and other elements must be in harmony. The tonal-textural feeling of the type should blend with the border, the illustrations, and other printing elements and should be compatible with the paper and printing process used.

Overriding all these conditions is, of course, the nature or "feel" the message is attempting to impart. As Haber's tests have shown, the impression remains although details may not be evident.

Check List

To summarize, the real heart of a message is generally in its body copy. Headlines and illustrations serve to grasp attention; then, once the reader is caught, the body must be inviting to the eye and easy to stay with. Sound typography accomplishes this.

A checklist of typographical rules follows. The student must remember that they have to be applied with judgment in every individual case:

1. Long copy should be broken for easy reading. There are several techniques: indent paragraphs, or, if they begin flush left, add extra space between paragraphs. Normal indention is one em. Use subheads of contrasting face (different face) and/or contrasting weight; the bold face of the body type is good. Consider leaders and dashes, especially in advertisements. Relieve monotony by occasional italics and bold face at points of textual significance. Set copy in more than one column unless measures become so narrow as to impair legibility. Some paragraphs may be set on a narrower-than-text measure, centered in the column, especially in ads. Do not kill all widows (short line or a single word at the close of a paragraph) for they let in white space.
2. Set copy on the proper measure. One-and-a-half to two alphabets make a sound line length. As much as 60 characters and spaces (about ten words) may also be safe, especially in book work.
3. Do not use too many different faces in one body. Harmony and unity result with a single face, with its italic and boldface, for body and display.
4. Avoid reverses for long body copy; this is especially true in newspapers where ink tends to fill in the letters because of low-grade paper quality.
5. Avoid text over illustrations or tint areas, unless you are certain there is sufficient contrast.
6. Ragged right seems safe; consider twice setting text in ragged left or ragged left and ragged right; the eye is accustomed to returning to a common point after reaching the end of a line.

7. Roman type is preferred in general for body copy, although the use of sans-serif is becoming more popular.
8. Stay with 9-, 10-, 11-, and 12-point types for body copy. They are easier to read.
9. Consider leading as line length increases, or if the x-height is large. Don't overdo—3- and 4-point leading is seldom justified in text matter.
10. Margins should approach 50 percent of the page area and be progressive in book matter.

CHAPTER 5 Using Type Creatively

In the last chapter we were concerned with the handling of body type. Visibility—more specifically, legibility—was our major concern. Now we turn to the fundamentals of using type in design.

Design is basic to almost everything we do. There is design in such common activities as shining your shoes or scrubbing a floor; design also underlies the painting of a picture or the laying out of a printed piece. "A purposeful plan of action" is a satisfactory definition of design, except that for our purposes we should add the concept of "creativity."

Creativity suggests new and better ways of carrying out a purposeful action. When we need something—perhaps a machine to perform a certain function—if we are creative, we engage in purposeful action to invent it. But man's needs are for more than material things, such as machines. We also have spiritual or emotional needs—for joy, for happiness, for love.

Our museums contain many ancient artifacts the functional purposes of which we may not know; yet we find them a pleasure to look at simply because they express the joy, happiness, and satisfaction of those who designed them.

Thus any creative design is both functional and expressive. As Scott (1951) has put it, to *evaluate* or judge a design we must know its purpose or function. If we do not know, we can only *value* it, as in the case of the ancient artifacts mentioned above; that is, we can only say, "I like it" or "It seems to express the feelings of the man who designed it." In much of our everyday living we delude ourselves into believing we are evaluating things, whereas we react only to likes and dislikes. As Scott indicates, this is one cause of our poor judgments. One might say such judgments are "unreasoned."

Everything we have said so far directly involves the typographic designer. Since his work is an integral part of the visual communication, he has an obligation to the source of the message and to the receiver. He must know the source's intentions — in other words, the function. He must also understand how the receiver will react not only to the content but to the form the message takes. Form is the means of expressiveness, and meaning exists not only in the content but in the form as well. For a message to be received with maximum effect the two meanings must be compatible. It would never do for the typographer to use his design as a means toward expressing what he personally feels is "beautiful," at the same time ignoring the intent of the message.

Visual Syntax

As we have said, man communicates in print with verbal language and with visual form. Before we turn our attention to the latter, we should put both within the context of information processing.

Language is widely held by linguists to evolve naturally (Chomsky, 1968). Certain basic programs are "wired in," enabling man through exposure to a language to learn to use it. Stated another way, language is an innate structure in man. The languages of the world are similar in grammatical form, not in surface structure but in deep structure. This is because the enabling programs of language capacity are similar for all men (Chomsky, 1968, p. 50).

One naturally associates organized structure, syntax, and technical grammatical rules with any verbal language. All this leads too easily to a tendency to see the visual or formal as an unorganized, nonintellectual mode of communication (Dondis, 1973). Such is not the case.

Just as all human beings are endowed with language capacity, they also have a basic physical, visual perception system. What man looks at is structured by various constituent elements, just as verbal language is structured by spoken or printed words. And just as there are grammatical rules for composing effective verbal messages, there are rules for composing effective visual forms. Dondis refers to these rules as "visual syntax" (Dondis, 1973, p. 11).

Display Legibility

The body or text type is of little significance as impact value. Its purpose is not to attract the reader to a printed message. As a consequence the typographer can concentrate his efforts on making it as legible as possible. However, he must give special attention to the treatment of type used for display purposes. While legibility is also desirable for display, it is not so imperative because it has a primary function before reading speed. Its major use is to attract attention.

Although much literature is not illustrated, almost all of it has headlines or headings. In the remainder of this chapter we shall discuss the techniques for the imaginative use of type in display.

While legibility may be secondary in display, it must not be overlooked. For example, heads in all script or cursive (Figure 5-1) or set vertically and diagonally (Figure 5-2) become very difficult to read. In general, legibility of display is governed by the same principles as body type.

HARD TO READ

Figure 5-1. *Head in all-cap cursive is difficult to read.*

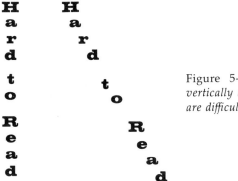

H
a
r
d

t
o

R
e
a
d

H
a
r
d

t
o

R
e
a
d

Figure 5-2. *Heads set vertically and diagonally are difficult to read.*

The New Typography

From the time of the early printers until the past century, type was displayed by centering each line on the measure. There were several reasons why this style prevailed for some 350 years. First, it presented a perfectly symmetrical effect. Man's orientation toward space depends on his sense of balance. Visual perception and this sense are closely related. Our need for balance has a major psychological effect on perception. Second, the avid desire of readers for the product kept the attention of printers focused on production rather than on design. Third, type can easily be composed this way by hand or by machine.

To understand the meaning of "The New Typography," a term often applied to the present-day use of typographical materials, let us briefly look at a few historical high points in the development of printing design.

The cutting of display faces in the nineteenth century introduced a new kind of typography. Often blatant, sometimes bizarre, these faces were designed for use in the increasingly competitive world of commerce. Posters, publicity bills, and cards printed with these faces had a look quite apart from that of a book.

With the twentieth century came the development of what has been called *Modern* Art, bringing new ideas and forms. A number of styles came into being in Europe and they had varying degrees of influence on typography there and later in the United States. Perhaps the most notable of these were Art Nouveau, Constructionism, and Dadaism.

Art Nouveau actually appeared in the last decade of the nineteenth century. In essence a style of decoration, its free-flowing lines and ornamentation were fashioned in wrought- and cast-iron furniture. Its effect on typography (see Figure 5-3) came with the free style of off-centered and counterbalanced lines and a more liberal use of white space.

Figure 5-3. *Art Nouveau influence on book design. Two pages from* The Canterbury Tales, *published by the Golden Cockerel Press, 1929; illustrated by Eric Gill. (Reprinted from* The Art Nouveau Book in Britain *by J. R. Taylor, by permission of The M.I.T. Press, Cambridge, Mass., and Methuen & Co. Ltd., London)*

Constructivism was an outgrowth of Cubism, the most controversial of the modern art styles. Cubism was based on analytical interpretation rather than on exact imitation of the subject. Decoration was eliminated and subjects were shown by means of geometric patterns involving cubes, squares, and rectangles.

The Constructivists continued the cubistic ideas of form and structure. The work of the Dutch painter Piet Mondrian is typical. He developed an asymmetrical style in which bold rectangular grid structures were counterbalanced. The Mondrian style has been somewhat subdued in The New Typography by elimination of the rigid pattern of grids. However, the counterbalancing of rectangular elements is still a popular technique. For example, see Figure 5-4. The large dark areas represent photos, the smaller illustrations are drawings. The dark area on the left is a headline. The remaining rectangles represent text type.

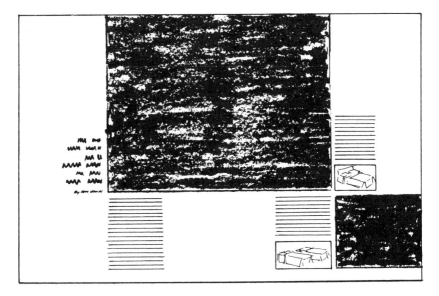

Figure 5-4. *Modern layout as affected by Mondrian art style. Grid structure of a two-page magazine spread.*

Dadaism contributed to the development of modern typography in a negative way. The very name of the movement—supposedly found by opening the dictionary at random—was a symbol of the confusion of the times. Dadaists worked directly in the typographic field. Their designs of printed messages were chaotic in appearance—lines of type using display and book faces running in various directions—even individual letters of words were positioned in completely unorthodox manner.

78 *Verbal Elements of Communication*

In post World War I Germany the Bauhaus, previously mentioned in Chapter 3, brought order to the chaotic movements preceding it. From this school have come these contributions, now evident in the New Typography:

1. Asymmetric design
2. Wide acceptance of sans-serif type
3. Relaxation of traditional (progressive) margination
4. Bold placement of illustrations
5. More interesting division of space with contrasting shapes of elements placed in interesting juxtaposition
6. Simplification and release from extensive ornamentation
7. Greater concentration on utilitarian use of typographic elements

APPLICATIONS OF THE NEW TYPOGRAPHY

Let us consider the applications of modern typography in two broad categories: (1) books and (2) ephemera. The divisions are based on the function of the material and reader attitudes toward the material.

Books

Books are generally intended for instructional or informational and entertainment purposes. Generally speaking, when a reader "settles down" with his book, his attention and interest are focused on its content. The designer must also remember that books are produced and bound for a more lasting impression. Convention and tradition have had a strong influence on book design.

Ephemera

All printing other than book production can be classified as ephemera. This material is less permanent and shorter than books. Included in this category would be newspapers, magazines, advertising matter, annual reports and so on.

These categories may appear to be loosely structured, but a brief examination of the theory of communication provides the reason for the classification.

Although effective communication is a matter of learning, there are different situations in which learning occurs, and these situations demand different presentations. For example, in a classroom the audience is predisposed to learn; the level of attention is high. In a mass communication situation involving ephemera quite the opposite is true. Therefore, the designer considers different approaches to effective presentation when he designs an advertisement or a magazine from those he uses when he designs a book.

In mass communication the attention of the reader is often low and his interest span short. Here the problem is to attract and to arouse attention. The message may be short and will be repeated in several contacts between the source and the receiver. As stated previously, book design is often governed by convention and tradition, and the methods of presentation are more established, although this is changing, as we shall see. Thus, magazines, ads, and newspapers follow one set of design principles and books another.

Book Design

The generally accepted standard for the book format until the influence of the Bauhaus made its impression was that of the classical page with its progressive margins and Roman type faces.

Figure 5-5, a spread of two pages, is typical of book margination. The page size illustrated is 6 by 9 inches, and the type page size is 26 by 42 picas. Margins are, progressively, 3½, 4, 6½, and 8 picas.

The spirit of the new typography suggests that we might deviate from the rigidity of the classical book page. Deviation is a safe step if we bear in mind the Bauhaus principle that design must be functional. It must not infringe on effective communication.

A striking departure from the traditional is the use of sans-serif for the entire text of a book. Traditionalists object to this, pointing

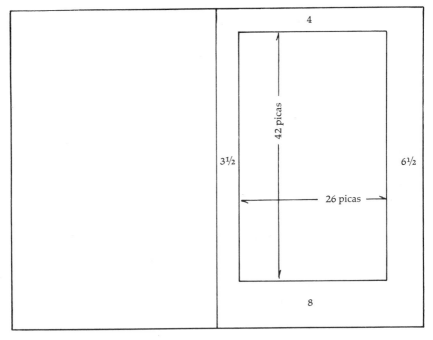

Figure 5-5. *Traditional progressive margins on a book page.*

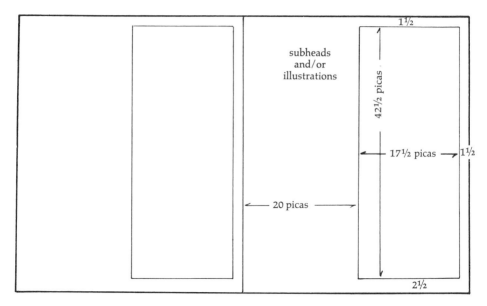

Figure 5-6. *New Typography book margin treatment.*

out a loss in legibility. Those willing to experiment point out that a somewhat condensed Gothic set on a measure that allows eight to ten words per line would be quite legible. A few magazines use this technique and more and more books are being so composed.

Another major departure from traditional book design is in the treatment of margins. Figure 5-6 shows a spread of 6½ by 7¾-inch pages with most unconventional margins. The text was set on 17½ picas. Margin sizes are marked in picas. The book was profusely illustrated; the wide margins were used for the placement of illustrations and subhead lines. However, many pages carried only white space to the left of the copy blocks.

It is not possible to discuss here in detail the increasing number of nontraditional book-design techniques. It is suggested that the student acquaint himself with them as they come to his attention. Illustrations, charts and diagrams, liberal use of white space, contrasting type styles, bleeds (running printed matter off the edges of the page), color, irregular type margins, and larger display faces are being applied more and more frequently.

Typographic design, like life itself, is an evolving process of change. It should not be changed for the sake of change but for improved function. The question becomes, "How interesting, typographically, should a book be?"

Design of the Ephemera

It is in the ephemera that the designer faces the fewest restrictions. This does not mean that wild experimentation is possible. The term "new typography" does not imply bizarre design but orderly and logical treatment befitting the content of the message. Experimentation is justified if there is a logical reason for it.

For example, examine the full-page advertisement in Figure 5-7. The white space across the middle seems to divide the ad into two parts. The technique attracts, although it would seem to violate the principle that a message should have unity. In this case, the advertiser depends on reader curiosity to bridge the white space gap. Note the strong contrast in tone between top and bottom of the ad; provocative contrast also exists in the content of the headline, urging the reader on.

Figure 5-7. *White space in ad center provokes curiosity. (Courtesy Lees Carpets)*

We shall deal with the use of pictorial elements in typographic design in Chapter 8. Let us now consider the use of type elements in design.

Symmetrical Design

The arrangement of type elements in symmetrical pattern has its origin in classical book design. While its applications today are limited, an understanding of its principles is basic to an appreciation of the more widely applied asymmetrical design.

You may recall from previous discussion that when we look at something we naturally perceive tone and shape. Manipulation of these two formal concepts arouses meanings in all of us, as we shall see. A single line of type parallel to the bottom of the page is seen as a pair of horizontal lines delineating the size of type:

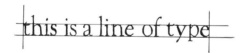

The tone of the type itself can be varied, for example, by using bold face, to give greater weight:

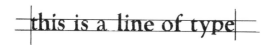

When several lines are composed in proximity, together they form a shape:

XXXXXXXXXXXXX
XXXXXXXXXXX
XXXXXXXX

If at all possible, the major weight should be above the center of the shape. Alternating long and short lines should be avoided if possible, since this makes it more difficult to sense the shape and thus the meaning.

It is one thing to arrange the lines of type in a display that forms a shape. Often, however, the designer must compromise when the sense of the content will be broken between two lines.

What is the best way to display "The Art of Growing Old" in three lines, all centered in the symmetrical style? Would the following suffice?

THE ART
OF
GROWING OLD

First, it would be preferable to have the two top lines longer than the third. Second, as here set, the relatively unimportant word "of" is emphasized by being given a line alone. This would then seem preferable:

THE ART
OF GROWING
OLD

The word "of" belongs with the word "growing." Further, there is now a more discernible shape.

Consider the design of the announcement card:

BINGO PARTY AND
DANCE
OLD MAIN CENTER
TUESDAY
JANUARY 8, 1974
8:30 P.M.
YOU ARE MOST CORDIALLY
INVITED

Note that there is equal spacing between all lines. Imagine a mono-tonal recitation of the message with pauses of equal length after each line. In essence, this is the same thing in print. Following is an improvement. Now the thought units are grouped and the spacing better fits the content.

BINGO PARTY
AND DANCE

OLD MAIN CENTER

TUESDAY, JANUARY 8
1974

8:30 P.M.

YOU ARE MOST CORDIALLY
INVITED

PLACING EMPHASIS

Even though the spacing is improved in the example immediately above, did you notice it seems to have too much of an overall gray tone? Certainly the simplicity and harmony satisfy the basic human urge for equilibrium and reduction of uncertainty. But don't forget the equally important need for stimulation.

It is possible to improve this situation. One might place emphasis on certain words, composing them in all caps and a larger size if other words are caps and lower case (Figure 5-8). If the other lines are all caps, perhaps the emphasized words might be set in lower case. In this case the lower case letters should be larger than the caps in the other lines (Figure 5-9).

Other possibilities exist, of course. Variations can also be effected by using small caps, italic, bold face, and color. It is also possible to mix type faces.

Remembering the designer's responsibility to meld the communication effect of the formal with the content, one should be careful to place emphasis on the key verbal elements.

Figure 5-8. *This hand-lettered layout shows emphasis by contrasting size and by caps vs. caps and lower case.*

Basic Considerations in
SYMMETRICAL DESIGN

Figure 5-9. *This hand-lettered layout shows emphasis by contrasting large-size lower case vs. smaller all caps.*

BASIC CONSIDERATIONS IN
symmetrical design

THE LAYOUT

The designer arranges the elements to center on a vertical axis in the middle of the type page, that area remaining after margins are subtracted from the page size. Generally, he lightly draws on layout paper the dimensions of page and type page together with the vertical axis. In addition, he draws a horizontal axis, approximately three-fifths up from the foot margin (Figure 5-10). The layout paper should be transparent enough to allow him to lay it over type specimens for tracing. The intersection of the axes marks the *optical center,* the position the eye prefers to the mathematical center.

In Figure 5-11 the major shape — major in content and form — falls over this point. Note that the lowest shape falls to the foot margin. In

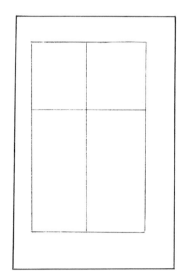

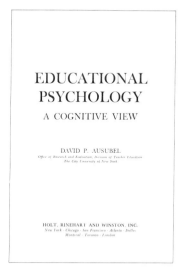

EDUCATIONAL
PSYCHOLOGY
A COGNITIVE VIEW

DAVID P. AUSUBEL
Office of Research and Evaluation, Division of Teacher Education
The City University of New York

HOLT, RINEHART AND WINSTON, INC.
New York · Chicago · San Francisco · Atlanta · Dallas
Montreal · Toronto · London

Figure 5-10. *Locating the optical center on a layout. Note that the horizontal axis is about three-fifths up the page from the foot margin.*

Figure 5-11. *Formally balanced all-type layout. (Copyright © 1968 by Holt, Rinehart and Winston, Inc. Reproduced by permission)*

Figure 5-12 the number of lines required to follow the heading force it toward the top of the page.

Figure 5-12. *Formally balanced all-type layout with major heading forced above optical center.*

Asymmetrical Design

There is a quiet dignity and elegance about symmetric display of type. Each line is centered with equal amounts of white space at either end of each line. The display is beautifully simple and logical.

One might suspect that "asymmetric" means abandonment of simplicity, balance, and logical arrangement. This is not true; the asymmetrical design achieves balance in a different way, is equally logical, and, as we shall see, is not more complicated.

Examine Figure 5-13. This is an asymmetrical type design. Compare it with Figure 5-11. In symmetrical design the space on the page serves only as background against which the type elements are displayed. The elements are more important than the space and the latter serves to frame the type display. In the asymmetrical situation space becomes an integral part of the design. This is more evident in Figure 5-14. Note how the left edges of the first four and the bottom three lines form a vertical axis as do the left edges of the three in the middle of the page. The left edge of the middle shape lines up with the "n" in "Edition." The groupings of lines form horizontal shapes which are placed on vertical axes. Figure 5-15 is a drawing depicting the various spaces established by the design.

THE MEASUREMENT OF MEANING

Figure 5-13. *Asymmetrical all-type layout. (Courtesy University of Illinois Press)*

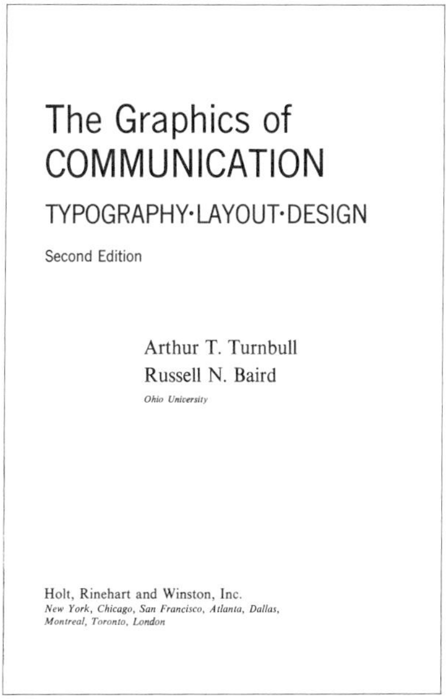

The Graphics of
COMMUNICATION

TYPOGRAPHY·LAYOUT·DESIGN

Second Edition

Arthur T. Turnbull
Russell N. Baird
Ohio University

Holt, Rinehart and Winston, Inc.
New York, Chicago, San Francisco, Atlanta, Dallas,
Montreal, Toronto, London

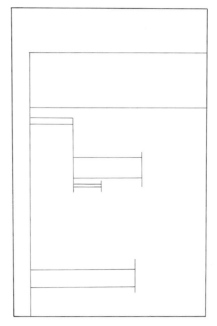

Figure 5-14. *Asymmetrical layout with dynamic use of white space. (Copyright © 1964, 1968 by Holt, Rinehart and Winston, Inc. Reproduced by permission)*

Figure 5-15. *Space division in an asymmetrical layout. The various relationships of the elements in the title page at left are immediately apparent in this sketch.*

Contrast is achieved within the type mass in symmetrical design by varying the features of the type face. In asymmetrical design contrast is achieved through the placement of masses. There are fewer variations within sans-serif alphabets than within Roman alphabets; consequently, the former is found widely used in asymmetrical design. This does not, however, preclude the use of Roman faces. In fact, a mixture of Roman and sans serifs within asymmetrical design is not uncommon.

In Figure 5-16 this is demonstrated. In (a) is sketched a symmetrical design of the title "Placement of Type in Design." In (b), (c), and (d) are shown asymmetrical variations. In (c) there is a combination of the two kinds of face design: "Type" being in an italic of Roman, the remainder of the message in sans serif.

Incidentally, note that the vertical axis in (b) falls along the stem of the capital T in the word "Type." In (c), because the T in "Type" is italic, the vertical axis is determined by a line that would be the center of gravity for the slanted letter. In (d) the axis is diagonal, established by the capitals T and D and this axis establishes the placement of the top two lines.

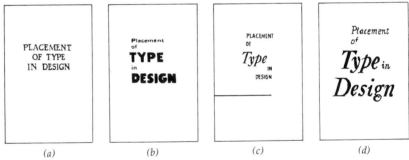

(a)   (b)   (c)   (d)

Figure 5-16. *Symmetrical layout, (a); alternate variations in asymmetrical layout shown in (b), (c), and (d). All are hand-drawn.*

Figure 5-17 shows an ad in which display and text are used in asymmetrical layout. Note that the left edge of the third display line establishes the margin for the text.

Figure 5-17. *Display and text in excellent asymmetrical treatment. (Courtesy Harris-Intertype Corporation)*

Headline Size

A number of considerations involving headline size are common to advertising and magazine editorial layouts. Many of these considerations apply to other forms of printing as well. The main heading should be sized large enough to stand out in competition with other elements of the page or ad and draw attention to the message. The main subhead should be large enough to attract attention to itself but not away from the main head. Beginning designers need to keep the function of the main head in mind, for they tend to undersize them.

Secondary subheads are often satisfactory if set in text size; it is important, however, that they contrast sufficiently with the body composition they accompany. This can be accomplished with boldface, italic, or a face of another type family.

These factors determine the size of the headline type:

1. Weights of other display elements.
2. Size of the space (page size or ad dimensions). Larger space calls for large sizes.
3. Amount of white space surrounding the head. A headline can be a smaller size when it is given emphasis with added white space.
4. Color printing of heads. Printing in color requires larger type sizes than printing in black.
5. Size of condensed type. A larger size is needed for condensed type than for standard width.
6. Length of the head. Longer headlines tend to force the designer to use a type size that is too small. The situation can be resolved by breaking the head into major and minor thought groups.

SPECIAL HEADLINE CONSIDERATIONS

Two other aspects of handling headlines deserve mention: headline form and headline typographic style. Because the head is both a graphic and a verbal element, it can generate interest through its form as well as its content. People will read what interests them. The form in which it is presented will invite them to read.

The simplest and most direct form is a single line. When content is of a high degree of interest, a headline presentation in a single line can be very effective. Often headlines are too long to fit in one line. When heads are set in two or more lines, form becomes a more significant consideration. Two or more lines are often centered one above the other. This is perhaps the most conservative possible treatment.

The designer's task is to make the form compatible with other layout elements. At the same time the form should offer minimum interference with reader comprehension of the content. It frequently becomes necessary to deviate from the centering of lines to satisfy the need of compatibility. Flush-left or flush-right headlines are, therefore, another common form.

Additional techniques accent form. We cannot make a detailed inventory here, but we may take a brief look at some of them:

1. Use of color
2. Combining rules or ornaments with the head
3. Reverse blocks containing heads
4. All caps
5. Mixing type faces
6. Printing the head on a tint block
7. Use of initial letters
8. Combining the head with art treatment
9. Use of hand lettering
10. Arranging the head in a special shape

Giving photographic treatment to headlines for unusual effects is also possible. Such a technique may be seen in Figure 5-18. A number of specialized businesses offer this service.

Many of the above treatments can be applied to entire headlines or to portions of them—and they may be used in combinations. Knowing the importance of the headline, the designer is often tempted to call attention to it through emphasis on its form. Caution, however, is well advised. As mentioned before, form should never overshadow substance or the content of the message. In processing theory, STM can only handle so much information at a time.

Accent on form may be justified under such conditions as these:

1. The special treatment adds to the understanding of the substance. That is, the headline, through form accentuation, is made *self-descriptive*. Examples are shown in Figure 5-19.

Figure 5-18. *Photographic headline treatment.* (*Courtesy Church & Dwight Co., Inc.*)

"There is nothing
so powerful
as an idea
whose time
has come."

If your NAILS

OR SPLIT

*UNCERTAIN
STOMACH

Figure 5-19. *Self-descriptive headlines.*

would
your tires
be
safe at
100 mph
?

The Dunlop Gold Seal is certified safe at 100 mph. So you're sure you're safe at 60, 70, or 80. And yet the full four-ply Gold Seal is still popularly priced.

And there's more safety to the Gold Seal. It has treads on the sides. Safety-Shoulders. They take the fight out of a tight turn, carry you smoothly up and over center lines or road shoulders without a lurch. They're patented*.

Then the Gold Seal has what tire men call a low profile. That means a 15% larger footprint area. More of the Gold Seal's wide tread is always on the road for better traction, greater safety, more miles of wear.

Doesn't the Gold Seal sound like a choice tire for a change? Drive carefully to your nearest Dunlop man. He's listed in the Yellow Pages.

Every new Dunlop tire meets or exceeds every official specification for safe performance.

*PAT. NO. 3,064,688

DUNLOP   ...means quality in golf, tennis, and tires.

BUFFALO, NEW YORK

72

Figure 5-20. *Headline integrated into text.*

2. The form treatment fits naturally with other layout elements. Photo treatment of the head in Figure 5-18 slants letters to the left to build the head around the Arm and Hammer trademark. In Figure 5-20 the head is shaped to integrate it into the copy or text.
3. Among smaller ads, where competition for attention is especially keen, special head treatments are often effective. Such techniques as shown in 5-19, as well as reversing the heads (printing white against black), are often useful.

The typographic styling of heads primarily involves spacing, letter alignment, and punctuation. In Chapter 4, we spoke of the need for spacing within all-cap lines of display. Between-line spacing in headlines set cap and lower case may often require visual adjustment, since ascenders and descenders may act to cause the lines to appear unevenly leaded.

The problem of letter alignment is shown in Figure 5-21. The example to the right is structured so that the letters at the right edges line up optically. The *W* is slightly to the left of the margin. For the most eye-pleasing appearance, *W, A, V, Y, X, C, O, G, Q,* and *S* should run past the margin, right or left.

WERLON WERLON
by Wedley by Wedley

Figure 5-21. *Left, normal letter alignment. Right, appearance is improved through visual alignment.*

In Figure 5-22 the punctuation is placed outside the left margin. The same may be done on the opposite margin. Imagine the irregularity of the margin line if the quotes were set flush on the line. The *T* would appear significantly out-of-line. Such treatment is common in display-sized type.

JOSEPHINE, TV'S LADY PLUMBER, SAYS:

"Try this test and see Comet get out stains other cleansers leave behind."

Figure 5-22. *Punctuation outside normal margin—"hanging punctuation."*

Not all designers follow this form. It is obviously more expensive. Yet it is in the best tradition of fine typography: Figure 3-7 shows such a style used in Gutenberg's Bible. Even today a few advertisers apply the treatment to body copy, as seen in Figure 5-23. But the style is seldom found in editorial columns, since its setting is time-consuming and hence costly.

Help heal the hurt with the new Johnson & Johnson First Aid Cream—the long-lasting antiseptic that helps fight infection, soothe the hurt, promote healing. Every minor skin break, from scrapes to scratches, from cuts to bites, needs Johnson & Johnson First Aid Cream.

Figure 5-23. *Note punctuation outside right margin.*

Initial Letters

We must mention the use of *initial letters* before leaving this chapter. These are display-sized letters integrated into body copy. They serve a dual function: first, to lend a spot of display to areas that are basically not display; and second, to bridge the gap between heads and text. There are two types: *rising initials* and *set-in initials,* shown in Figures 5-24 and 5-25, respectively. Note that with the former a word or two of the text is in all caps following the initial, which rests on the first line. In the latter, caps generally do not follow and the initial rests on a line of the text.

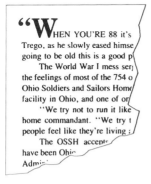

Figure 5-24. *Rising initial.*

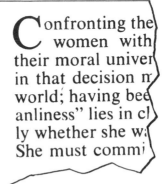

Figure 5-25. *Set-in initial.*

Conclusion

Typography is not a free art. Elements and space are not arranged for purely expressive purposes. Rather, there is a logical basis. Typography is a means to an end. Its function is to aid in effective communication. The most prosaic typographic presentation is probably better received than typographic trickery and distortion. But there is always room for a freshness of style and presentation so long as it does not inhibit clear exchange of information and consequently meanings.

SECTION 3   # VISUAL ELEMENTS OF COMMUNICATION

CHAPTER 6
Illustrations in Graphic Communication

CHAPTER 7
Color in Graphic Communication

CHAPTER 6 Illustrations in Graphic Communication

Although the hackneyed adage "One picture is worth a thousand words" defies proof and begs argument, the basic value of illustrations in graphic communication is beyond dispute.

Without attempting to put a relative value on illustration as compared with words, we can still be aware of the special effectiveness of images in accomplishing communication goals. The pervasiveness of images in our communication system is without question; we start to learn our verbal language from picture books and move on to maturity in a world of television, motion pictures, illustrated magazines and books, and newspapers.

Indeed, television seems to have launched us into an age of images, made us a nation of viewers rather than readers. All print media have responded to television's impact with more, bigger, and better illustrations. And an orator without "visual aids" to supplement his verbal presentation is swimming against the stream of imagery that seems to be flooding communication today. Even highway signs have been evolving from verbal to visual images to achieve instantaneous communication with motorists and to surmount the language barrier.

This increased emphasis on images for communication is not surprising. It comes merely as the result of technological innovations that have made the use of illustrations easier and more effective. The inventions of photography, photoengraving, motion pictures, and then television have each taken us one step farther toward our reliance on illustrations for communication. And if we look back to the early attempts of human beings to communicate graphically, we can see that pictures were the first message form. The caveman's pictograph demonstrated an appreciation of the communicative potential of illustrations at the earliest stages of graphic communication development.

Now, with our communication system in an advanced stage of development, we seem to be completing a cycle that places pictorial images again in a position of primary importance.

The Many Functions and Forms of Illustrations

Much of the effectiveness of illustrations comes from the variety of communication functions they can perform and the many physical forms they can take. Although a discussion of illustrations cannot totally separate function from form, let's at least place emphasis on their functions as we also discuss their forms.

As later chapters will explain in more detail, one of the basic functions of illustrations is *to attract and get attention.* Magazine editors, advertising designers, and other media users have long realized that a striking illustration is perhaps the best means for attracting a reader's eyes to a page or design. Although all forms of illustrations can accomplish this function, the *photograph* has been the primary choice. Photographs, because they are true-to-life duplicates of images that the human eyes see in the world about them, can compel attention quickly and forcefully. The emotions or reactions that are aroused as we view life about us can be aroused and catered to by photographs better than by any other means. The impact of television and motion pictures stems from this capability of reproducing true-to-life images, and the creators of print media are merely showing their understanding of it as they use photos as attention getters.

Photographs are also primary tools for the communicator when he wants *to inform* readers precisely of what took place at an event or happening. Auto accidents, sports action, parades, and other such news events can be shown to readers through photographs more effectively than with other kinds of illustrations.

The graphic communicator who wants *to instruct* his readers how to do something, however, will often find a *drawing* to be more effective. The editors of *Popular Science,* for example, often find it necessary to present step-by-step drawings to show readers how to assemble complicated objects. As shall be pointed out later, drawings can take many forms, ranging from simple stick figures to works of art

Figure 6-1. *Photos of human-interest subjects like this one of a boy and his new puppy can often appeal to emotions more effectively than words. (Photo by Mac Shaffer)*

Figure 6-2. *Tornado at Xenia: a photograph can effectively transmit information, as this photo indicates, with the aid of only a few words. In cases like this, words without pictures do not fully convey the message. (Courtesy Patricia A. Beck)*

Illustrations in Graphic Communication   99

containing a full range of tones and colors. It will suffice here to emphasize the point that drawings often are as vital or more vital than words in giving instructions to readers.

When the primary goal is *to explain,* illustrations can again be a primary tool. The understanding of complicated subjects can often be lost in a deluge of words but be clarified if explanatory illustrations come to the assistance of verbal elements. The presentation of virtually all statistical data can be aided by illustration. Consider, for example, budget figures—a *pie chart* showing basic allocations can clarify relations much more efficiently than statistics. So can *pictographs,* so called because relationships are shown by pictures. *Bar graphs* can serve the same function as pie charts; and *line graphs* can show trends (such as the ups and downs of Dow Jones Industrials for a year). On the other hand, *schematic diagrams* can explain the operation of printing presses and other machines better than photographs, words, or charts. And if the goal is to explain to readers how to get from place to place, a *map* can be indispensable.

As comic strips attest, illustrations can also be used *to entertain* the reader. Political cartoons, such as those drawn by Thomas Nast for *Harper's Weekly* a century ago and those created by Bill Mauldin for today's newspapers, have shown the effectiveness of illustrations when the objective is *to influence.*

Figure 6-3. *Pie charts are an old standby for presenting information showing relative amounts used or allocated from budgets.* (*Courtesy* Advertising Age)

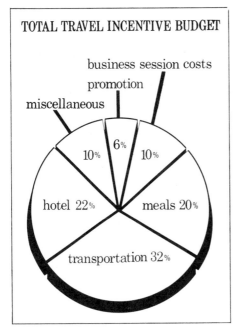

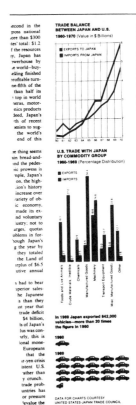

Figure 6-4. *In the illustration opposite, lower right, the editor used a line graph, a bar graph, and a pictograph to achieve communication. Line graphs have the special advantage of showing trends over time periods. Bar graphs are used to present statistical information when the relationship of amounts must be shown. Pictographs provide dual information of importance: a picture of the items being compared and a visual expression of the relative amounts involved. (Reproduced courtesy* The American Way, *inflight magazine of American Airlines)*

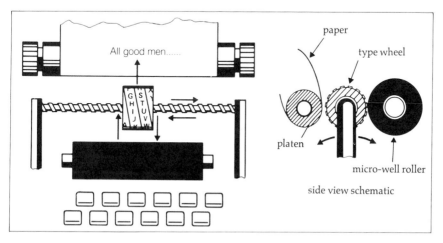

Figure 6-5. *Want the reader to understand a complicated device? A schematic diagram like this one is usually the best supplement to words in such cases. (Reprinted from* Product Engineering; *copyright Morgan-Grampian, Inc., 1970)*

Figure 6-6. *Verbal directions can be helpful, but a map can eliminate communication noise that verbal directions often create. Imagine the difficulty in trying to communicate verbally what this weather map shows in visual form.*

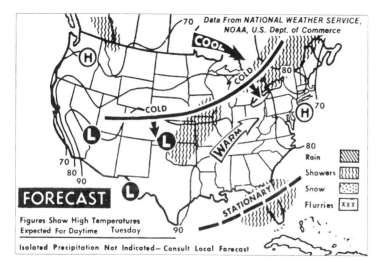

It should also be pointed out here that it may be necessary to combine types of illustrations for maximum effectiveness. For example, the line illustration used as a diagram of a football play and superimposed on a photo can be the only truly effective way to show how the action developed.

In thinking of the functions of illustrations — and types of illustrations as they relate to functions — we must keep in mind that illustrations work best in combination with words. The marriage of words and illustrations that makes them equal partners usually provides the most efficient communication.

The Production Aspects of Illustrations

So far we have looked at illustrations from the standpoint of the original form of the illustration as created by an artist or photographer. Before illustrations can be viewed by masses of readers, however, they must be produced in quantity by a printing process. As we consider illustrations from the production standpoint, different terminology, different categories, and different concepts emerge.

As will be explained in Chapter 12, many printing processes are available for the mass reproduction of words and illustrations. Some of the technicalities of the production of illustrations vary among these different processes. But for the two primary printing processes most production terminology and procedures are the same; these similar procedures will be discussed here and the technical differences will be explained in later chapters.

BASIC TYPES OF REPRODUCTIONS OF ILLUSTRATIONS

From the standpoint of their mechanical reproduction, there are two basic types of illustration each of which contains some sub-types. These two kinds of reproductions are *line* and *halftone*. They are best explained by briefly tracing their production steps.

Line Reproductions

Some drawings, such as pen-and-ink renditions, are composed of only solid tones, black lines on a white background. These are called *line drawings*. When printed, they are called *line reproductions*. Figure 6-7 shows a basic line reproduction. In order to reproduce Figure 6-7, the printer followed a relatively simple photographic procedure. The original art work, done with pen and black ink on a white background, is first photographed in order to get a production negative. During this photographing, the image may be enlarged or reduced, with re-

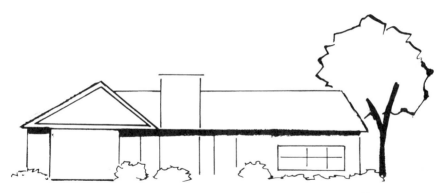

Figure 6-7. *A drawing that contains only lights and darks, no middle tones, is* known as a line reproduction *(for letterpress printing it is called a* line cut, line engraving, *or* line etching).

duction being most common. Line illustrations are usually drawn larger than the reproduction in order to minimize flaws that might be present in the original drawing. The negative that is created is then used to transfer the image to a metal surface for use on a printing press. This image transfer is possible because of the light sensitivity of the films and metals that are used.

For example, when the line illustration is mounted in front of the lens of a large camera (called an *engraver's* camera), light is beamed toward the illustration. That light reflects from the white background and strikes the film in the camera, making it black in the background. The dark lines of the illustration reflect no light, thus letting the film remain clear in the image areas. The developed negative therefore is dark (opaque) in the nonprinting area and clear in the printing area. The image it contains is a reverse image of the original drawing. This image is transferred to a light-sensitive metal sheet by beaming light through the negative to the metal. Light thus exposes the metal sheet where it is to carry ink but leaves the nonprinting area unexposed. The metal sheet can then be chemically developed or etched with acid for printing, depending on the printing process to be used. In either case, the light-exposed portion of the plate carries ink and the nonexposed area does not.

Halftone Reproductions

The reproduction of illustrations that contain tones between the extremes of white and black is more complicated and puzzling. These reproductions are called halftones, and they are necessary for all photographs, wash drawings, oil paintings, water colors, or any other original illustration containing *continuous tones.* The continuous tones that lie between white and black in a photo cannot really be carried to paper from a printing plate—either black ink is deposited on the paper or it is not. In order to create the impression of continuous tones in printed reproductions, an optical illusion is employed. The illusion of middle tones is created by breaking the printing image into tiny dots, each of which will carry ink from plate to paper; if the dots are small and widely spaced the area will appear to be light, and if they are large and closely spaced they will create a darker image. Figure 6-8 has been made with a coarse screen to make the dots visible at close range.

The dot pattern for halftones is created through the use of a screen in front of the film in the engraver's camera. The screen, either on glass or film, is composed of parallel lines that intersect at right angles. Although these lines are usually too fine to be seen by the naked eye, under a magnifying glass the screen pattern they create looks much like the screen used for a household door or window. The coarseness of the screen is dictated by the number of lines per linear inch, and the designation of the screen desired for halftone reproductions is of considerable importance. Figure 6-9 shows how a fine screen submerges the dot pattern in a halftone.

Screen coarseness varies usually from 55 lines to 175 lines per linear inch. Traditionally, the coarser screens have been used by newspapers and other media being printed on rough paper. Newspapers still using the traditional printing method are restricted to about 55 to 85 line screens. Media using other printing processes or finer paper (i.e., magazines) can employ the finer screens. Generally speaking, the finer the screen, the better the reproduction. Consequently, in specifying the desired screen, one must consider the printing process to be used, the smoothness of paper, and the quality level desired.

HOW HALFTONE REPRODUCTIONS ARE MADE. With the specified screen in his camera, the photoengraver places the copy on a copy board in front of the lens, puts the film behind the screen in the camera, and proceeds to make one or more exposures.

Halftone negatives may be made with only one exposure, like line negatives, but cameramen usually take a series of short exposures in order to get greater tone control and to retain detail in the extreme light and dark areas of the copy.

As the light is beamed to the copy, it reflects back through the lens opening and the screen to the film. Because the light that goes through the lens is reflected from the copy, it varies in intensity directly according to the lightness or darkness of the various areas of the copy. A photograph of a man with a white shirt and dark suit, for example, will reflect light strongly from the shirt and weakly from the suit.

When the light pierces the thousands of tiny holes in the screen, it is broken into thousands of small beams. The intense light spreads,

Figure 6-8. *This halftone, made with a coarser screen than the paper permits, contains a dot structure visible to the naked eye.*

Figure 6-9. *The basic reproduction of a photograph, oil painting, or other continuous tone illustration is called a* square-finish *halftone.*

as it goes through these apertures, breaking the screen lines into clear dots on the negative. The dots vary in size and shape and are connected or separated, depending upon the amount of light reflecting from the copy. It is because of this variation in the dot structure that all the tones in a photograph or other such illustration can be captured on film, transferred to a plate, and finally produced in the printing process.

The developed halftone negative looks to the naked eye like a standard photographic negative. With a magnifying glass, however, the thousands of dots created by the lines of the screen can be clearly seen. The image is composed completely of dots, both clear and opaque. One can readily realize how tiny the dots are by understanding that the number per square inch is always the square of the screen size: a 50-line screen produces 2500, a 100-line screen produces 10,000, and so on.

Halftone negatives are transferred to a plate surface by the exposure of light through the negative to the light-sensitized metal. On the finished plate, each of the dots that were clear on the negative becomes a tiny printing surface; the metal surrounding them has either been treated to repel ink or has been etched away so that it cannot receive ink. Areas that were dark in the original copy will have many relatively large and closely grouped dots to carry ink to the paper. Consequently, as the plate is printed, most of the paper will be covered with ink in these areas, and these areas will be dark to the eye. Light areas of the copy will contain relatively small dots widely spaced and will be light when printed.

THE MAGIC OF THE DOTS. One point about halftone reproductions should be emphasized. The dot pattern of a standard halftone, though it varies considerably, is present over all portions of the negative and consequently will be present over all portions of the finished plate. Therefore there are no pure black or pure white areas in a standard halftone. In areas that seem to be pure white in the original, some dots will stand to carry ink to paper. Areas that were pure black are marred by the presence of tiny clear dots. Figure 6-10 shows the picture of a cogwheel seemingly containing blacks, whites, and grays. However, the enlargement on the right reveals the presence of dots throughout.

In spite of the fact that halftones rely on dots to create the illusion of tones, when the proper screen has been selected the reproduction can be excellent. To the viewer, unaided by a magnifying glass, the dots on a halftone reproduction blend with the background to form a faithful reproduction of the original, as Figure 6-9 shows.

The principle of blending dots with the background can be easily illustrated by any student. By holding a newspaper at normal reading distance, all the letters and characters can be seen clearly. These represent the dots of a halftone. By pinning the newspaper to a wall and

Figure 6-10. *On the right, a portion of the silhouette halftone of the cogwheel (left) has been enlarged to show how the dot structure produces shades of tone. (Courtesy S. D. Warren Company)*

stepping back several paces, the letters and characters appear as masses of gray; the difference in tone created by columns of standard type matter as compared with areas of boldface type is the best illustration of how tones vary in halftones depending upon the size and the spacing of dots.

Tint (Tone) Blocks. It is possible, because of the dot magic of the halftone process, to reproduce areas of any given size in a uniform tint, or tone, of the color being used in a printing job. These tints can be produced in any percentage of the full density of the color.

For example, when black is being used, a 50 percent gray (just half the density of solid black) can be printed from a plate made to that specification. Other desired percentages, such as 20, 30, or 80, can also be obtained (Figure 6-11).

Figure 6-11. *Screen tints can serve to provide panels of color or tone, sometimes as background for type. Top, left to right: 10, 20, 30, 40, 50 percent tone values; bottom, left to right: 60, 70, 80, 90, 100 percent tone values.*

These "tint blocks," as they are called, are prepared through the halftone process. Instead of photographing an illustration, a white board is put in front of the camera and the desired tone is achieved by controlling the amount of light going through the screen to the film. Any screen, 55-line, 133-line, and so on, can be used.

Solid tints (100 percent of the tone) are made by exposing the plate area through clear, unscreened film.

The impression that an additional color was used in printing is often created by screened tint blocks. When red ink is used, for example, a tint appears as pink; when brown is used, tan results. Tint blocks behind type areas of another color are effective in drawing attention to areas that would otherwise be weak in display.

Creating Special Effects for Line Reproductions

REVERSING TONES.   When it is desired, the values in a line drawng can be reversed for reproduction; that is, the black areas in the drawing can be made to print as white and the white areas as black. Figure 6-12 shows the effect created by a *reverse line* reproduction. Figure 6-7 showed the same illustration reproduced in standard fashion.

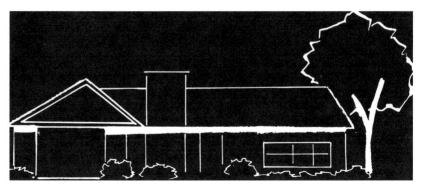

Figure 6-12. *The tone values of a line drawing may be reproduced as a* reverse line *illustration.*

To obtain a reverse line reproduction, a normal line negative must be made first. Then, by placing the line negative over another sheet of film and exposing it to light, a negative can be produced on which the values are the same as the original copy. The lines that were black on the original drawing are black on the negative; the other areas are clear.

When the second negative is transferred to the printing plate, the areas that were white on the original will be exposed on the plate surface and thus be made to carry ink to paper.

Common uses for reverse line illustrations are for signatures of advertisers or in other cases when an especially bold, black area is desired. It should be pointed out here that words in type can be line illustrations and treated as such for production, as shown by the reverse line reproduction in Figure 6-13.

OHIO UNIVERSITY

Figure 6-13. *Type can be treated as an illustration and reproduced with reversed tones, just like other line illustrations.*

CREATING MIDDLE TONES.   Line reproductions, as we have said, can be used only for illustrations that contain no middle tones — only the extremes. However, artists can produce illustrations that appear to have middle tones but in fact do not and are reproducible as line illustrations. Drawings done with a pen, as shown in Figure 6-14, can be produced as line illustrations when the shading is composed of hatch marks or other lines. Brush-and-ink drawings are also accept-

Figure 6-14. *Any pen-and-ink drawing, even if some tones seem to have been created by the artist, can be reproduced as a line illustration.*

able for line reproductions. They have a somewhat different flavor from those made with pen and ink, especially when the *dry-brush* technique is used. To create such drawings, the artist uses a brush that is virtually dry. To get ink coverage, he rubs the ink on the paper instead of flowing it on. By using rough illustration board for his surface, he introduces grays into the drawing because the ink does not seep between the high spots of the illustration board (Figure 6-15).

Coquille board, for example, has a surface composed of scores of small raised dots. By drawing on it with crayon or ink, the artist coats only the peaks of these dots. The dots then provide an illustration that looks like a halftone although no screen is used in its reproduction. Pencils used on a special velvety paper and charcoal on a rough paper expressly made for that purpose also create interesting effects without being reproduced as halftones, as shown in Figure 6-15. But

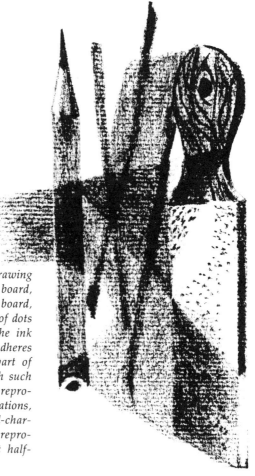

Figure 6-15. *A drawing made on a textured board, such as* coquille *board, gives the impression of dots and tones because the ink or other substance adheres only to the raised part of the texture. Although such drawings are usually reproduced as line illustrations, this one, a pencil-and-charcoal drawing, was reproduced as a highlight halftone.*

Figure 6-16. *Shading can be added to a line drawing (and it can still be reproduced as a line illustration) through a process called* Benday.

pencil, crayon, and charcoal drawings on smooth paper usually must be reproduced as halftones, or the grays and softness of tone that characterize these drawings will be lost in the reproduction.

APPLYING SHADING MECHANICALLY. The most common method for adding shading to line illustrations is a mechanical one called *Benday*. The method gets its name from the inventor of the original system used by engravers as they artificially added shading to the relief line plates needed in traditional printing. Now the term Benday more commonly refers to the shading sheets used by artists for adding tones to line illustrations. These shading sheets are available at most art supply stores in a wide variety of patterns; common trade names are Craftint and Zip-a-tone. They usually are adhesive-backed clear acetate sheets on which the patterns of dots, hatch marks, and the like have been printed. The artist applies the piece of patterned acetate over the desired area and then trims and peels away the excess, leaving the pattern precisely where desired. Benday shading has been added to our line illustration in Figure 6-16.

Another system employs drawing board (i.e., Craftone or Doubletone) that has been preprinted with shading patterns that are invisible to a camera until developed. The artist draws his line illustration on the board, then paints the areas to be shaded with a developer that brings out the preprinted pattern. With one kind of board (Doubletone) a second developer can be used to bring out a second, deeper shade of tone, thus providing the drawing with four tones: black, white, and the two added shades.

LINE CONVERSIONS. An interesting technique that came into vogue in the early 1970s is the use of a line reproduction for a photograph or other continuous tone illustration. To achieve this special effect, the original illustration is photographed as a line illustration would be—without a screen in the camera. All the middle tones are then lost and a highly contrasty representation (Figure 6-17) results. When the subject of the illustration is clearly recognizable without the middle tones, this treatment creates the impression of an artist's line drawing of the subject.

Figure 6-17. *A photograph reproduced as a line illustration ordinarily would not provide sufficiently accurate reproduction. Many photos are converted to line illustrations, however, in order to get the special artistic effect shown here.*

Types of Halftone Finishes

In addition to the wide variety of line reproductions available, the designer of modern pieces of graphic communication also has at hand an equally varied assortment of halftone treatments.

A basic halftone reproduction is called a *square-finish* halftone because it is a common rectangle (as in Figure 6-9). Any variation from a square finish requires special effort and time during production. This extra time and effort results in some added cost, the amount of which depends on the printing process that is involved as well as the amount of time and effort. In spite of extra cost, however, the use of a multitude of special finishes is common among all print media.

SPECIAL GEOMETRIC SHAPES. The simplest variations from the norm of a square finish halftone are special geometric shapes ranging from *circles, ovals,* and *triangles* to the most elaborate geometric designs.

The oval shape is used to create on "oldtime" impression for a photo, because photos often were framed as ovals in the early days of photography. Other irregular shapes can provide a directional em-

Figure 6-18. *The oval shown here is only one of an unlimited number of geometric shapes available for the reproduction of illustrations. This shape gives an "histori-cal" feeling to the photograph.*

phasis in a design; some are given rather bizarre dimensions to add to their attention-getting value.

VIGNETTE.   This finish provides a soft edge for a photo; instead of sharply delineated dimensions, the reproduction has an edge that fades into the background. The general shape of the vignette edge may be quite irregular or may be more standardized as it is with the oval impression created in Figure 6-19. A feeling of age or beauty is often being sought when the vignette finish is ordered. The removal of the dot pattern gradually from the edges creates the vignette; this work is accomplished partially by an artist but requires careful, detailed attention in production also.

SILHOUETTE.   Also called *outline,* this finish is as the name implies; the background of the photo is completely eliminated so that the central subject stands in sharp outline or silhouette against a blank background. The dot pattern that ordinarily is present in the background is completely removed from the halftone negative before it is exposed on metal for printing. This treatment serves to avoid distraction from the background and to give emphasis to the central subject by the sharp contrast between subject and surrounding area.

MORTISE. A *mortise* halftone is one containing a cutout (Figure 6-21). If the cutout is from the outside it may be called a *notch* halftone (Figure 6-22). Notches or mortises are usually rectangular cutouts; the most common is a rectangle cut from one corner of a square-finish halftone. In traditional printing, irregular mortises were difficult to saw from the metal engravings that were used; modern printing systems have afforded the opportunity for greater versatility in this regard. Now, for some printing systems any irregular shape can be masked out of a halftone negative with little difficulty.

Mortises are usually made to provide for the insertion, within the halftone area, of type messages or other illustrations.

HIGHLIGHT (DROPOUT) HALFTONE. Special care and handling of a halftone negative can give a reproduction that is devoid of dots (Figure 6-15) in some areas. A model's teeth in a toothpaste ad, for example, can be made pure white by painting out the few dots that ordinarily would carry ink to paper. Special attention given to exposure and development during the making of a halftone negative can virtually eliminate the dots in a highlight (light gray) area, but hand painting with an opaque fluid is usually required.

VELOXES. The use of a screened, continuous-tone photo called a *Velox* provides an efficient, versatile method for highlighting half-

Figure 6-19. *Softening the edges of a halftone creates a* vignette *reproduction.*

Figure 6-20. *Outlining or silhouetting the central subject can expedite the processing of information in a photo because competing background details are eliminated.*

Figure 6-21. *A portion cut out from the interior of an illustration is called a* mortise.

Figure 6-22. *If a cutout is from the outside into one or two of the dimensions of an illustration, the portion cut out is called a* notch.

tones and producing other special effects. The making of a Velox is identical to the making of a halftone printing plate except that it is made on photographic paper; this screened print therefore contains the usual dot pattern needed to reproduce the various tones. If a highlight effect is desired, the dots can be painted out with white paint on the photoprint. A Velox print can be photographed as a line illustration because each dot is copied just as if it were part of a Benday pattern.

Advertisers use Veloxes a great deal because they often want to highlight portions of an illustration in order to focus attention on particular features of their products; the Velox also makes it possible to paste all elements of an ad together to form a single line illustration ready for an engraver's camera. Any possibility of error in the arrangement of material in the ad is thus eliminated.

SPECIAL SCREENS FOR SPECIAL HALFTONE EFFECTS. Special halftone screens that will produce tonal variations while adding mood effects to reproductions have become a common tool for the designer of graphic communications.

There are screens made up of concentric circles, parallel lines, parallel wavy lines, thin irregular lines resembling old steel engravings, mezzotints, wood grains, and patterns of various materials such as twill and burlap. Each special screen pattern produces continuous tone reproductions with a special flavor (see Figure 6-23). Especially good for giving variety to subjects that must be shown repeatedly, these mood screens, along with line conversions and posterization, became especially popular with designers in the 1970s. Because they do not create reproductions with as much fidelity as a standard screen, they are best reserved for situations in which a desire for special atmosphere is greater than a desire for precise transmission of detail.

Figure 6-23. *An artistic flavor can be given to halftone reproductions through the use of special screens or special effects. Here is (a) a normal 110-line halftone; (b) is a line conversion; (c) is posterized using a 60-line wavy line screen; (d) uses a straight-line screen; (e) uses a mezzotint screen; (f) uses a cherry woodgrain. (Courtesy of the Bychrome Company)*

Figure 6-24. *The deliberate enlargement of the dot pattern of a halftone screen is sometimes employed for special effect.*

Also in vogue in recent years has been the enlargement of the dot pattern in a halftone reproduction to such a magnitude that the reproduction resembles a line illustration made with dots (see Figure 6-24, a small part of Figure 6-22).

POSTERIZATION. Posterization, another mood device, is especially effective when two colors can be used but it can also be effective without an added color (Figure 6-23). To achieve posterization, the wide range of tones between black and white are reduced to a single middle tone. This middle tone often is reproduced with one of the above special screens and/or in a second color.

All the above special screen effects for halftones tend to have one thing in common: they seem to convert standard photographs into artistic renderings. Effectively used, they add a desired dimension to a piece of graphic communication.

COMBINING LINE AND HALFTONE IN ONE ILLUSTRATION

It is possible, of course, for an artist to use his pen to create a line drawing on the face of a photograph thus combining a line illustration and a continuous tone illustration. This procedure, however, would result in a reproduction containing a screened line illustration because the drawing would be broken into a dot pattern by the screen used in the engraver's camera. (Remember: there are no pure whites or pure blacks in a halftone.) Letters (such as type in a headline) can be handled in the same way but with the same shoddy results.

To get sharp, clear line illustrations on the face of halftones, separate negatives are made for the line and halftone portions of the illustrations; these negatives are then exposed together on the printing plate to form what is called a *combination* illustration.

There are two kinds of combinations, one in which the line illustration appears in dark lines and the other in which it appears in white lines (Figure 6-25). The first of these is a *surprint combination*. To produce it, the halftone negative and the line negative are separately made as they ordinarily would be. The line negative is then exposed on the metal sheet, followed by the exposure of the halftone negative in the same position. Its name, surprint, comes from the fact that these two photo printings are necessary. The plate produced in this fashion will reproduce the line illustration in pure blacks while the

Figure 6-25. *On the left is a surprint combination. On the right is a reverse combination that has also been given an outline finish at the top and a vignette finish at the bottom.*

halftone takes care of the continuous tones. The other combination is called a *reverse combination* because it produces a reverse line illustration on the face of the halftone. To prepare a reverse combination, the halftone negative, the line negative, plus a reverse line negative (film positive) must be made. The two of these negatives that are needed (halftone and reverse line) can be placed together in position on a printing plate for a single exposure. The single exposure is possible because the background of a reverse line negative is completely clear and does not hold back any light.

A common use for surprints and reverse combinations is to get words across the face of a halftone. Figure 6-25 has been included here to show both types of combinations, plus some other treatments. Any and all of the special finishes can be used in concert in order to achieve a special communication goal.

Adding Color to Illustrations

Simply stated, color is added to printing by running a printing press with the desired color of ink in the press; for each color desired the paper must go through the press an additional time. Specifically, with regard to illustrations, the same thing can be said, with the addition that a separate illustration must be reproduced on a printing plate for each color. Therefore, line illustrations can be printed in as many colors as one might desire. Sunday comics are good examples of line illustrations in full color (the three primary colors plus black). Line illustrations in only two or three colors are also common. The preparation of artwork for multicolor reproductions is described in Chapter 7.

Halftones can be reproduced in color, too. It is even possible to reproduce a black and white photo in more than one color. Take, for example, the situation in which an editor has a black and white snow scene to be used on a page that will also be printed in blue ink. The editor can order the work necessary for a *duotone* reproduction that will appear in blue and black, a combination that would add a special chilly feeling to the reproduction. He will require two halftone negatives specially made to avoid the clashing of halftone screens that occurs unless the screen angle is changed as the two negatives are made. This clashing produces an undesirable *moiré* effect (Figure 6-26); it is because of this moiré that one cannot use clippings from printed material to serve as the original for halftone reproductions.

When two halftone negatives of the same subject have been properly made (one is usually toned down also) they can be used with excellent two-color results. Brown with black for desert scenes and green with black for forests and meadows are especially effective.

Figure 6-26. The "screen door" appearance of this halftone is caused by the clashing of two halftone screens. It is because of this clashing that a picture clipped from a publication usually cannot serve as original copy for a second reproduction.

Sometimes a color is added to a halftone area by printing a tint block with the halftone, thus adding a flat color uniformly across the surface. This method is easier and cheaper but produces less spectacular results.

Also, original artwork (i.e., paintings) done in two colors can be faithfully reproduced, but in a different manner. To reproduce original illustrations composed of blendings of more than one color, a color separation process is involved. The preliminary camera work is the same for the two basic printing systems. The following discussion, though it relates directly to the making of acid-etched plates for traditional printing, incorporates the principles of color separation common to both systems.

Process Plates for Full-Color Reproduction[1]

Originals for color reproduction include: all copy in which the subject is rendered in full continuous tone color, such as oil, watercolor,

[1] The section on full-color reproduction which follows is reprinted courtesy of the American Photoplatemakers Association.

or tempera painting; the color transparency; and the photoprint in full color, such as carbo, chromotone, dye transfer, imbibition, and wash-off relief.

Under discussion here are full-color originals where facsimile reproduction can only be achieved through the blending of the three primary colors plus black. Where an original is to be reproduced in one color only, the line etching or halftone is printed in that color; when a two-color original is to be reproduced, duotone halftones are employed; but, for full, four-color reproduction, it is necessary to make process color plates, one for each of the primary colors and one for black. Should the black plate be eliminated, the reproduction becomes a three-color process, still achieving the full blending of the primary colors but lacking the emphasis of black and its shades.

All full-color originals drawn or painted upon a material such as paper or canvas are reproduced by the light reflected from the original, whereas color transparencies are reproduced by transmitting light through the transparency. The color transparency is preferred over color photoprints because some loss of detail and color value occurs in prints or copies made from transparencies. Hand-colored photographs are inferior in reproduction because the underlying photographic image is recorded in the negatives and interferes with correct color separation.

THE COLOR PROCESS

In pigment, such as printing inks, the primary colors are yellow, red, and blue. By mixing these colors in correct proportions, any desired color can be obtained. In the same manner, superimposed printing of the process color plates in precise register causes a color-blended image with all the colors and values of the original. An artist can paint a picture using pigments of a score of different colors and hues, and a perfect reproduction can be achieved on the printing press using three halftone plates, each printing one of the three primary colors. In four-color process, a black plate is added to obtain strength in detail and to produce neutral shades of grays, which are difficult to make with the primary colors. The addition of the black plate also makes possible the use of red and blue printing inks in purer tones than those used in straight three-color process.

COLOR SEPARATION NEGATIVES

While it is true that the color principle of light differs from that of pigments, it is not essential to consider this distinction here. Photographic color separation takes a simple knowledge of the pigment primary colors and their complementary relationships.

In photographing a color original, the photoengraver first analyzes it for yellow, red, and blue color content. He then separates and records each of these colors on film. A color separation is accomplished by photographing through a color filter that absorbs or quenches those colors of which it is composed and permits the remaining color to be recorded.

To separate the yellow color in the original, a violet filter that prevents the photography of its component colors, red and blue, is used, and only the yellow is recorded. Similarly, to separate the red, a green filter deters yellow and blue and permits the red to be recorded; to separate the blue, an orange filter blots out the yellow and red and permits the blue to be recorded. To make the black separation, a specially modified filter is employed that limits color absorption and produces the required negative, eliminating the primary colors.

In the indirect method of color photography, the resultant negatives are in continuous tone (no halftone screen) and are called continuous-tone separation negatives. They are an accurate record of each of the primary colors in all their gradations of tones, plus black.

Color correction—that is, improvement of color rendition—is usually done at the time separation negatives are made, by a process of introducing photographic masks in the camera.

The separation negatives are then placed before the camera and rephotographed to produce positives; or they are placed in contact with a photographic plate, and a photoprint (positive) is made. It is necessary to make these positives so that they can again be photographed through a halftone screen.

It is also possible to employ a direct method of color photography, to separate the primary colors and produce halftone negatives in one photographic operation by placing the halftone screen in the camera at the time of color separation. The indirect method, however, permits greater photographic control of color separation, which would otherwise be performed manually by the etcher and finisher.

One of the newest and most promising devices for color correction should be mentioned before proceeding to halftone negatives. The scanner produces negatives or positives that are electronically color-corrected for color errors due to inherent characteristics of ink and color filters; it computes correct values for the black plate, removes the correct amount of undercolor, and carries out tone correction to compensate for gray-scale distortions. Mechanically, the time involved in color correction is reduced both in the camera work and in the attention given the plate by the etcher and finisher.

COLOR HALFTONE NEGATIVES

In order to print continuous-tone color, the metal plate must have printing surfaces capable of reproducing color gradations. This is accomplished with the halftone screen, which breaks up the image into minute dots varying in size, shape, and proximity.

In making halftone color negatives, each color positive is photographed through the same desired screen, but, for each color, the screen is placed at an angle thirty degrees apart from the other colors. This is so that in the printing no color dots will interfere with proper blending. Experience has determined that this degree angle will also keep a moiré pattern from forming.

This is the standard procedure for three-color process negatives. With the introduction of the fourth color, black, the screens for the black, red, and blue negatives are placed thirty degrees apart, and the screen for the yellow negative is placed between the black and red positions at an angle of fifteen degrees from each. The yellow dot being the least visible, the moiré is not offensive.

ETCHING, FINISHING, AND PROOFING COLOR HALFTONES

After the color halftone negatives are made, a photoprint of each is made on metal, as with standard halftones, and the resulting plates are etched, finished, and proofed.

For various reasons, photographic color separations are not exact. The task of final color corrections falls to the etcher and finisher — a task that, in addition to mechanical skill and artistic technique, requires a thorough knowledge of color composition. The color etcher must estimate the amounts of each color required and then etch the plates to produce that amount. Not until all four colors are combined on one proof can he see the results of his efforts.

Modern power proof presses simulate pressroom conditions, with specified inks and paper. Usually the yellow is printed first, followed by the red, blue, and black, in that order, although it is feasible to change this sequence if desired. The first proofing invariably shows that more etching, correcting, and reproofing are necessary.

CHAPTER 7 Color in Graphic Communication

W hat we see in the "real world" is in color. Yet, when we look at visual symbols of the real world (photographs or drawings or their printed reproductions), we recognize what is represented, and this is true whether the photos or drawings are printed in color or in black and white.

As we have seen, contrast is the source of all meaning; recall the "offs" and "ons," the 1s and the 0s, decision-making, and concept formation. We learn to recognize shapes because of tonal contrasts in space. We could not detect these shapes without light. We see something because of the light it reflects.

There must be something about the interaction between the visual system and light that allows us to accept black and white as a representation of reality. The two dimensions of light—brightness (wave amplitude) and hue (wave length)—are of significance here.

We are sensitive to all the hues (colors) in the color spectrum. When all our hue sensitivities are equally stimulated by light, we see white light. Remember from your science training that the light primaries equally mixed give white light. This we call achromatic light (light without color). When all our sensitivities react, but some more than others, we sense both the achromatic and the chromatic (light with color). Consider the difference between red and pink light. Both are chromatic, but the red is a heavy color saturation and the pink a light saturation. Hue may be thought of as white light with color added.

In summary, when we perceive light we sense differences in tone. The tones may be chromatic or achromatic. The differences in tone are the result of the relative brightness of the light reflected by what we look at. One can remove the color from a color TV picture, yet the tonal contrasts remain.

It is tempting to conclude from this that while color is useful, it is not necessary in printed communication. In a way this is so. In fact, much printing is black and white. However, color is an important tool in graphic communication. We shall consider some of its applications later.

The scientific aspects of color have been largely developed by physicists through their study of light. Their findings are of little *direct* help to most people involved in graphic communication, but inasmuch as they foster an understanding of the psychological effects of color, they are important and will be summarized here.

The Nature of Color

The source of all color is light. When we look at a red rose, we see it only because light reflects from it into our eyes, making the rose and its color discernible. But why are the rose and its surroundings, seen through the same source of artificial or natural light, not all the same color?

Light is visible radiant energy made up of various wavelengths. It is one of several electromagnetic waves listed in order of their frequency and length: long electric, radio, television, radar, infrared, visible light, x-rays, cosmic rays, and gamma rays. The longest waves are invisible. As waves shorten and their frequencies climb, they are felt as heat—infrared, for example—then reach visibility in a varying range we know as color. Magenta red is first as the longest; as the waves shorten they move from oranges, yellows, into greens, blues, indigo and violet. Beyond violet, at shortest lengths and highest frequencies, are invisible ultraviolet rays.

As the several wavelengths of light are separated—by raindrops, as in the rainbow, or by a glass prism—the colors appear. The white light of the sun contains all of them. When it falls on a surface that reflects all the white light, the surface appears white to our eyes. When it falls on a surface that absorbs all the white light, we see the object as black. When some of the rays are reflected and some absorbed, color is evident. The red rose reflects only red rays; in like manner, the color of everything depends upon which color rays are absorbed and which reflected.

Color, then, is a property of the light waves reaching our eyes, not of the object seen. The latter has the property of absorbing some wavelengths while allowing others to reflect.

THE PRIMARY COLORS

There are three colors in light and three in pigment called primary colors. The familiar pigment primaries are red (actually magenta), yellow, and blue (actually a blue-green referred to as "cyan"). The light primaries are green, red-orange, and blue-violet. All pigment colors are derived from mixtures of the pigment primaries; all light colors from mixtures of the light primaries. But the primaries themselves can be derived only one from the other. A pigment primary is caused by the reflection of two light primaries; a light primary by the reflection of two pigment primaries. This means a pigment primary is a secondary color of light, and vice versa, since secondary colors are the result of a mixture of two primaries.

Color Dimensions in Pigment

In order to apply color effectively, typographer, artist, engraver, and printer need a basic understanding of the various dimensions of color — hue, value, and chroma.

HUE

Hue is a synonym for color. We distinguish one color from another because of the quality of hue. For purposes of identification, hues are classified by arrangement in a circular scale (Figure 7-1).

The three secondary colors, orange, green, and violet, can be obtained by mixing the primaries to either side; for example, green is made with blue and yellow.

The intermediate colors result from mixing a primary with a secondary. For example, yellow and green make yellow-green. Intermediate colors can also be made by mixing adjoining colors; for example, yellow and yellow-green.

VALUE

Value refers to the lightness or darkness of a hue. A color can be lightened by being mixed with a lighter hue of the same color or by the addition of white. Lightening a color produces a *tint*. The printer can lighten a color by mixing the color ink with white ink or by screening the printing plate with a tint block.

A darker value is called a *shade,* achieved by adding either a darker hue of the same color or black. The printer can reduce the value by mixing a color ink with black or by overprinting the color ink with a screened black.

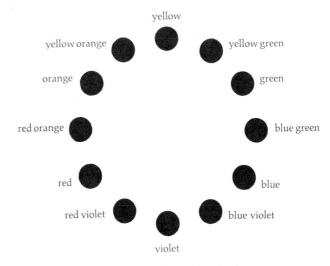

Figure 7-1. *The color wheel.*

CHROMA

Chroma refers to the purity or strength of a color. *Intensity* is a similar term. To alter chroma is to change the *tone* or to weaken, dull, or neutralize a color. This can be accomplished by adding the complementary color or gray. Gray is actually a color without hue and can be developed by an equal mixture of black and white.

Psychological Aspects of Color

As stated in Chapter 1, the three objectives in preparing graphic communication are: (1) to attract attention; (2) to be legible and comprehensible; and (3) to make an impression. The use of color is justified only to the extent that it contributes to the realization of these objectives.

Form and color are basic elements of visual stimulation. They have a vital share in man's emotional life. An object familiar in the daylight can seem to have a different form at night and becomes capable of arousing negative feelings.

The psychological impact of color has been researched primarily through several means of testing: (1) observation; (2) instrument; (3) memory; (4) sales and inquiry; and (5) unconscious-level. These tests also have been useful in developing many workable principles of advertising layout.

Observation tests study the reactions to color of subjects who are unaware that their behavior is being viewed and evaluated. The testers are often hidden behind one-way glass.

Instrument tests employ eye cameras, the tachistoscope, and lie-detector equipment. The psychogalvanometer is the best known of the latter. It measures reactions to color as revealed by somatic variations, such as pulse, blood pressure, and sweat-gland activity.

Memory tests involve questioning persons to determine how much and what they recall of items in print. These tests might show, for example, that advertisements using color rate higher than ads in black and white.

Sales and inquiry tests measure the effect of color on merchandise sales or on offers to the readers of advertisements. A common technique is to advertise items for sale through the mail, running some ads in black and white, some in color. Not only can color versus another, one color versus two, and so on. Inquiry tests seek the same information on offers of booklets, samples, and the like. The numbers of inquiries are considered indicative of the effectiveness of the different applications of color.

Unconscious-level, or indirect, testing uncovers attitudes that subjects cannot or will not reveal. People are not generally conscious of the effects of color. This is why the value of opinion testing — asking people directly how they react to colors — is questioned by most experts. Indirect testing, on the other hand, attempts to reveal unconscious reactions by depth interviews and projective techniques, such as word association.

Often the decision to use color is based on the assumption that it is better than black and white. The decision is never that simple. Many factors should be given careful consideration before the right color or colors can be selected. Once determined and properly applied, color can contribute substantially to effective communication.

The artist's knowledge and skill in the use of color are valuable aids in planning color printing. But it should be remembered that the end result of the planning should be the scientific application of color to the communications task and not a form of abstract expression in color.

Functions of Color

The functions of color in printing are:

1. To attract attention
2. To produce psychological effects
3. To develop associations
4. To build retention
5. To create an esthetically pleasing atmosphere.

Let us consider each function in turn, bearing in mind that they are interrelated and that they contribute to the three goals of graphic communication.

TO ATTRACT ATTENTION

This is the major use of color. Contrast is the basis of attention. Thus the addition of a bright color to a piece printed in black increases the attention-getting value of the piece.[1] Tests have shown conclusively that the number of people noting a printed communication is increased by the use of color.

When we say "attract attention," we refer to two separate responses from the reader. First he is attracted; then he pays attention if what attracted him holds meaning or interest.

Color should be applied to the elements of greatest significance. Since emphasis results from contrast, color should be placed with discretion. One color plus black offers the greatest contrast, for a color is always its most intense with black.

To effect contrast without black, several color schemes are possible. They are, in order of descending contrast: complementary, split-complementary, analogous, and monochromatic.

The *complementary scheme* uses colors opposite each other on the color wheel. Colors can be divided into two groups according to psychological suggestion — warm and cool. One complementary is warm, the other cool. Cool colors are blue, or predominantly blue. They are relaxing and recede on the page. Warm colors are red, or red and yellow. They are stimulating and advance to the foreground. Green and red-purple lie between the warms and cools and are thus relatively neutral.

Selecting colors takes care. Full-value complementaries can be disturbingly vibrant. A rampant hue can be controlled by changing its value or chroma, or by selective use in a limited area.

The *split-complementary scheme* contrasts three colors. A color is

---

[1] In printing terminology, anything printed in black plus a color is called a two-color job. Black is considered a color in the printing field.

used in contrast with the colors adjoining its complementary on either side. For example, the split complements of red are yellow-green and blue-green.

The *analogous scheme* uses colors that neighbor on the wheel — green, blue-green, and blue; or red-orange, orange, and yellow-orange. Related colors are either warm or cool. Analogous colors are less exciting than complementaries since contrast is missing.

The *monochromatic scheme* calls for the use of different values and strengths of a single hue. Generally in this arrangement weak, dull areas are the largest; small, bright areas provide the contrast.

Four helpful hints for planning color contrasts are:

1. The tint of a hue is stronger on a middle gray than on a full strength of the hue.
2. Warm colors are higher in visibility than cool.
3. Contrast in values—light versus dark—is greater than contrast in hues—blue versus yellow.
4. The darker the background, the lighter a color appears against it.

TO PRODUCE PSYCHOLOGICAL EFFECTS

The colors that predominate in an ad or other printed piece should fit the over-all mood of the message. The color suggestions of coolness and warmth in turn suggest formality and informality. Red implies life and many moods and ideas associated with life, such as action, passion, gaiety. Blue connotes distinction, reserve serenity. Green is nature; purple, splendor and pomp; white, purity.

TO DEVELOP ASSOCIATIONS

It is natural for people to associate certain colors with different products. Red is happily associated with cherries, while the thought of green with fresh meats is not pleasant. But many associations are not so obvious and research may be called for before a color selection is made. Personal judgment cannot always be trusted: although one might suspect that pink is preferable to blue for a face-powder message, an error could be made without a more tangible basis for the choice.

TO BUILD RETENTION

In describing something we are likely to refer to its color. This is because color has high memory value, a feature that the communicator can capitalize upon. A color should predominate because it helps the reader remember what he saw. Advertisers are, of course, particularly interested in reader recall of the message and repeat certain colors in their campaigns in order to establish product identification.

TO CREATE A PLEASING ATMOSPHERE

The misuse of color in a message is worse, from the viewpoint of the communicator, than the use of no color at all. Color may get the initial attention, but unless this is sustained and developed into interest, the reader will not spend time to absorb the message. Poor choice and application of colors can repel the reader immediately after his attention has been aroused.

Colors, including black, gray, and white, in the printed piece should be arranged in accordance with the same basic principles of layout: balance, contrast, proportion, rhythm, unity, harmony, and movement.

Balance comes from the judicious placement of the elements by weight. Color adds further weight to the elements. Bright colors appear lighter; dark colors, heavier. When used with black for a two-color job, the color should be given a relatively light weight so that it will not draw undue attention from the black. Normally, it should be run in large areas at a 30, 40, or 50 percent level; that is, screened to that amount. Solids of the color should be reserved for emphasis.

Contrast is necessary for legibility. Contrast in values is more significant than contrast in colors. For this reason, where color serves as a background, care should be given to its treatment so that it will not detract from other elements. If the latter are dark, the background should be light, and vice versa.

Proportion refers to the relationships between colors. Proportional arrangement calls for a pleasing balance of (1) dark colors and light colors, and (2) dull or weak colors and bright colors.

Rhythmic use of color is achieved through repetition at various points in the printed piece. Spots of a second color can be used effectively in this way to guide the reader's eye through the message.

Color, as well as form, can contribute to the unity of a printed piece. Misplaced, it can disintegrate the total effect, even cause the message to seem divided.

Harmony in its broadest sense results from abiding by the other principles of color use — balance, contrast, proportion, and so on. More specifically, harmony applies to the so-called color schemes. Thus one speaks of monochromatic, complementary, split-complementary, or analogous color harmony. Complementary colors are not automatically harmonious together, however, unless some consideration is given to their use.

Psychological tests have uncovered personal color preferences. Blue is highly popular, being *the* color preferred by men and second only to red by women. Tests also show that women are more color conscious than men and tend more to prefer tints and softer colors. Color preferences vary according to age, education, and geographic location of those tested. Bright colors appeal to young people, soft colors to older persons and to those with high levels of education.

Preference tests are of some value to the designer if he knows the specific group to which his message will be directed. But the value of general tests is questionable in view of the fact that researchers have also found that "favorite" colors can be unattractive in certain uses.

Types of Color Printing

Color printing can be divided into two types: spot color and process color. Process, meaning the various ways to reproduce color copy — photographs, drawings, or paintings — was discussed in Chapter 6 on photoengraving.

Full-color copy is usually reproduced with four inks by the *four-color process*. Occasionally, *three-color process* is used for full-color copy by eliminating the black plate. This effects a substantial savings, but not all copy lends itself to the treatment. Subjects in a light key, such as outdoor scenes, are adaptable, but portraits, people, and indoor scenes are better reproduced by four-color process, since the black gives the definition and detail needed for a more realistic effect.

Paintings or other copy done in two colors are subjected to camera separation and *two-color process printing*.

Spot color refers to multicolor printing (two or more colors), by methods other than process. The simplest form is *flat-color printing*. A message with text in black and headlines in red is an example. In this form, colors do not overlap to form new colors — red is red, blue is blue, black is black, and so on.

Flat tones can be used with solids. In addition to headlines in red, red tints can be placed behind certain portions of the type or perhaps behind halftones of photos printed in black.[2] If the flat-color spots do not touch, the entire ad can be prepared by the printer as if it were all one color.

In letterpress printing, at the time of lockup, the printer can

[2] To say that the color tint is "printed behind" the type does not mean that the color is necessarily printed first. Often the black is laid on the sheet, and the color is then printed. The one requirement is that the colored ink be transparent.

"break for color." This means that the elements to print black remain in the black printing form. The color elements are removed to the color form and are replaced with spacing material. If the printing is to be done with stereotype plates, two casts are made. The color elements are routed from the black plate; that is, removed with a rotating cutting blade. The black elements are routed from the color plate.

The lithographer can break for color by making two plates from a single flat or mask, allowing the proper elements to be exposed at the time each plate is burned. To indicate this type of color work to the printer, the layout can be done in the desired colors, indicating headlines and tints in red, for example, the remainder in black. Or the entire layout can be done in black. A thin transparent paper (an overlay) can be laid over the layout with the color indicated on it.

Much spot-color work calls for laying one color over another to form additional color. Tints and solids can be used in this way. The Sunday color comics are an excellent example.

Often *color register* is significant. The term "register" refers to the positioning of the impression on the sheet. For example, when a book page is viewed against a light, both sides should be aligned. If so, they are registered, or properly lined up. Color register refers to the alignment of one color with another.

If the colors do not touch and are not closely interrelated, the printer can break for color. This is called *loose register.*

When colors touch or overprint, the register is described as *tight, hairline,* or *close.* Modern printing equipment is capable of maintaining the position of impression at a tolerance of 1/1000 of an inch. An almost imperceptible lap can be given where spot colors come together.

There are several ways to indicate the necessity for color register to a printer. One technique of copy preparation requires the use of a clear acetate overlay. This is fastened over the *key plate,* which is a drawing of the copy to which other colors will be registered. This drawing is the copy for the black plate.

Art for the additional color is drawn on or pasted to the overlay, a separate overlay being used for each color. Register marks are added to key and overlay art and must coincide exactly when the overlay is positioned over the key. These marks being about the proper positioning of copy on the printing plates. Figure 7-2 shows key art, right, and an overlay for second color with register marks, left.

Another common method of copy preparation is the *key-line* technique. Black and color art are drawn on a single board or paper. Separation between colors is indicated by a key line. The areas to appear in color and in black are painted with black ink to within one-quarter to one-eighth of an inch of the key line.

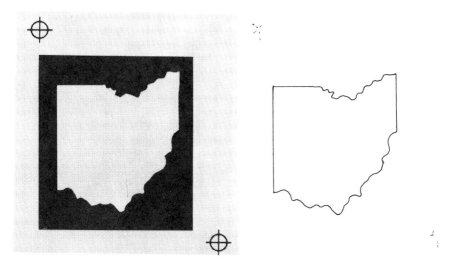

Figure 7-2. *Color copy prepared with an overlay (left). Register marks are shown on the key drawing (right) and on the overlay.*

When plates are made, the space up to the line is filled in for each color including black. The key line thus becomes the overlap. Figure 7-3 shows a key-line drawing for a circle, one side of which will be blue solid, the other side 60 percent black.

Figure 7-3. *Keyline drawing for color register.*

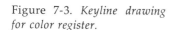

The Cost Factor in Color Printing

The added cost factor is usually an important consideration in the decision about whether or not to use multicolor printing. Expense piles up because the paper has to go through a single-color press as many times as there are colors. Between impressions, time must be taken for press wash-ups, changes of ink, additional make-ready.

Extra designing, camera, and plate charges are often involved.

Multicolor jobs can be run through two-, four-, and six-color presses. This can mean some savings, but such equipment is used only for long runs. The manner in which color is used adds little to the cost. A small spot or a more expansive spread of a second color applied to a sheet affects the total expense very little.

Designers and buyers of printing frequently hesitate to spend the extra money required for two-color or full-color printing. Yet there is abundant evidence everywhere of the significance of color in modern life. The market place is alive with it acting to sell products. The practical business world is under the influence of color now, as bright, warm reception rooms replace the austere, walnut-paneled ones of the past.

Color acts as a warning: do not park; stop; go. It promotes efficiency and safety through scientific application to work areas. It is used in modern architecture to an extent undreamed of a generation ago.

These are signs the communicator cannot well ignore. There are evidently plus values to be gained from the use of color, but he needs to know as precisely as possible what he gains from the extra cost.

Memory tests have shown that on the average readers increase with the addition of color. However, since there is no conclusive evidence that the ratio of increase is greater than the increase in cost, this may not justify the added cost. Other functions must account for the difference, but the dollar value of pleasing atmosphere, psychological effect, esthetics, and other intangibles cannot be appraised.

The communicator can solve the added cost problem only by resolving to apply the color allowable under his budget in the way that most efficiently accomplishes its particular functions.

Fidelity in Process Color

There are certain basic weaknesses in process color printing that mean the purchaser cannot expect exact reproduction or fidelity. These weaknesses occur because of: (1) differences between colors in light and in inks; (2) ink deficiencies; (3) the nature of halftone dots; and (4) the quality of paper.

PHYSICAL COLORS AND PIGMENT COLORS

The colors that enter the engraver's or lithographer's camera at the time of color separation behave according to the physical properties of light. The printer, on the other hand, must use pigmental or surface colors in his reproduction. To understand the difficulties this leads to, let us review the separation process. As explained in Chapter 6, a violet filter is used in preparing the yellow plate. As shown in Figure 7-4, this filter allows the red and the blue light to pass and record on the negative. Areas on the negative where these rays strike are dense. Yellow, the complement of the color in the filter, is held back. Thus the yellow areas become the most transparent on the negative. When the plate is made, a reversal of values occurs — yellows are the darkest, reds and blues are lighter.

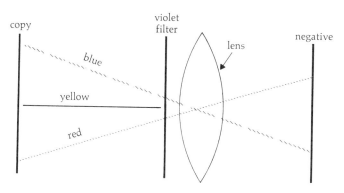

Figure 7-4. *Use of violet filter for making a yellow negative.*

The orange filter passes reds and yellows, holds back blue; the green filter passes yellows and blues and holds back red. These filters are used respectively for the blue and red plates.

The filters are analogous to the primaries of light in absorption and transmission, and they are complementary to the printing colors.

If art work could be submitted in standardized colors, the printer's chores would be much simpler. There is, however, no standardization, and there are countless colors available from many different sources. For example, the violet filter is used for all yellows, of which there is an infinite variety.

The printer's surface colors represent white light minus a color primary, since the three color primaries together represent white. Thus yellow is white minus blue, reflecting red and green. Cyan is white minus red, and magenta is white minus green. If a color in the art work, a certain yellow, for example, does not absorb all the blue light, the result on the plate is a distortion, a weakening, of the true value of that color. Similar distortions of other colors result in the separation process.

INK CHARACTERISTICS

The process inks used by the printer give rise to similar difficulties. Cyan is farthest from perfection, reflecting some red, which it should absorb completely, and absorbing much of the blues and greens, which it should reflect completely. For this reason colors requiring blues, notably purples and greens, suffer in reproduction. Magenta absorbs some of the blues and reds and reflects a high percentage of green. Yellow is the most effective of the process inks, since it absorbs nearly all blue and reflects green and red very effectively. True red, which should be effected by using magenta and yellow, also suffers in reproduction.

HALFTONE DOTS

The nature of the halftone process is a further obstacle to full fidelity of reproduction. Color photographs are reproduced with three layers of superimposed, continuous-tone primary colors. In an area of a halftone print where orange is being reproduced, for example, some of the magenta and yellow dots fall side by side, others overlap. The result is a variation in hue from the original.

EFFECT OF PAPER

Paper for process reproduction should absorb all colors equally — at least as nearly as possible. A pure white, which reflects all colors with a minimum of absorption, is preferred. Reflecting more light from its surface through the inks, it adds a brilliance to the reproduction.

Research, however, has led to the development of coordinated inks and papers to make process printing possible on pastel-colored stock with noteworthy results.

COLOR CORRECTION

Despite the above, it should not be assumed that process printing is ineffective. If straightforward separations were made, reproductions *would* fall far short of the original. However, the photoengraver's color-correction methods minimize the deficiencies by special treatments of negatives and plates.

Practical Pointers in the Use of Color

A number of practical pointers help the designer plan printed pieces with color. By no means an exhaustive list, the following cover many frequently overlooked considerations, applicable to monochromatic *and* multicolor printing:

1. When using more than one color, reserve the darkest for the basic message, using the additional color or colors for emphasis or for setting a mood.

2. Color used behind type should be light to insure easy legibility. In general the smaller the type, the lighter the color should be. This is accomplished, of course, by having the color screened.

3. Running type in color demands care. Some colors are too light ever to be so used on white stock—yellow, for example. If the type size is large, color has a better chance of supporting legibility. It is safest, however, to use color on type to emphasize a few words in a headline.

4. If four-color process and black-and-white halftones appear in the same form, the printer should be consulted before planning the layout or ordering engravings. If the black-and-white halftones are large and dark, they may require such heavy inking for satisfactory printing that, as a result, the black process plates will have to carry excess also, thereby muddying the color reproductions. Consultation with the printer and engraver in the planning stage can often solve this problem.

5. Care is required when running type in color (other than black) on a sheet on which process printing appears. Let us assume a red or an orange is desired. This necessitates printing type from two plates—magenta and yellow—in exact register. A satisfactory result is possible if the type is large. If it is small or light in weight, even the slightest imperfection in register will show.

6. Likewise, when printing in reverse is to appear on a color formed by overprinting two or more plates—for example, on a dark green formed by printing a screened black on a light green, the reverse printing must be on both plates. Unless they are printed in very close register, the type will not appear as a clean white. Naturally, the smaller the type, the more critical the problem.

7. Type printed in reverse should be within a fairly dark area to preserve legibility. As a general rule it is best to avoid reverses in a tone below 40 percent. If type is to appear in one color against a background of another—red on a black panel—the color on the type should be bright.

8. Often the artist prepares art for reproduction by overprinting one screened color on another and applies the screens to the art work, using screen tones on self-adhering acetate sheets. Improper angling of the screens must be avoided, for it results in an undesirable moiré pattern.

9. Several halftones printed on a page with a second color occupying the remainder of the space except for an even, narrow white

border around each photo will mean that even the slightest variation in register will be discernible, since the white borders become uneven.

10. It is sometimes possible to get full-color effect from two-color process plates made from full-color photos. This technique is not a substitute for full-color process, but startling results can be obtained under controlled conditions. The color photos should be composed of hues that are predominantly the same as those of the inks to be used in printing. For example, a color photo of a pair of dark brown shoes worn by a model dressed in a brown suit, posed against a red background might be effectively reproduced with process red and black.

11. Restraint must be exercised in the use of additional color. Because of cost, there is often a feeling that color ought to be applied lavishly to get one's money's worth. But overuse can defeat the reason for the extra expense. Often a single spot of color is sufficient; or two spots can be utilized, one to contrast with the other, and the two together to contrast with the basic color. Too much color, however, can create a weak communication.

SECTION 4 # DESIGN: COMBINING THE VERBAL AND VISUAL ELEMENTS

CHAPTER 8
Design Principles and Advertising Layout

CHAPTER 9
Principles of Magazine Layout

CHAPTER 10
Newspaper Typography and Makeup

CHAPTER 11
Planning and Designing Other Printed Literature

CHAPTER 8 Design Principles and Advertising Layout

In this chapter we return to the design of the printed message. We said a few basic things about the subject in Chapter 5. Now let us look at it in greater detail.

All design has structure. It will be remembered that the human IPS automatically seeks to impose structure on uncertainty. With this comes order and meaning, enabling man to cope with his environment. This is as true of typography and the other applied arts as it is of music, speech, writing, dance, or any of the fine arts.

Design can be effected in two ways. It can be created intuitively or through a logical and detailed plan. By either process it may emerge as an effective creation. This implies there are standards for evaluation. To discover these standards requires conscious effort. Once discovered they can be transposed into rules to follow in building an effective design.

Meaning in Design

The objective of the source of the printed message is the transfer of meaning from his mind to that of the reader. To this end he selects the elements, verbal and graphic, and arranges them in a structure.

Before we proceed, we need a clear understanding of "meaning." As Garner (1962, pp. 142–143) points out, two types of meaning exist in a structure. By signification, meaning exists in the elements. For example, we will, by association, find meaning in the words and illustrations. A separate kind of meaning exists in the structure—the relationships among the separate elements. As he puts it, in information measurement terms, one can distinguish one set of symbols as being better structure than another. That which is more meaningful is better structured.

Do you know what a self-embedded sentence is? Here is an example: "The man who said that a thief shot the housewife is a policeman." One sentence, "A thief shot the housewife," is embedded within another of the same grammatical form. This embedding follows a perfectly good structural rule in English. We do it all the time, perhaps intuitively, and without realizing it is a sound transformational rule.

There is no stated limit on embedding. It is possible to add a second embedding, a third, and so on; that such sentences are grammatically correct is indicated by the fact that they can be diagrammed (Miller and Isard, 1964).

Let's embed "the watchdog chased" after "thief"; "the family borrowed" after "watchdog"; and wrap the entire bit inside the sentence, "It seems more certain than not." This is the result: "It seems more certain that the man that said that a thief that the watchdog that the family borrowed chased shot the housewife is a policeman than not."

You can attach signification meaning to each word. But there is a crumbling of the over-all meaning when the reader comes to the string of verbs. Obviously the structure is at fault. One could find a better way to get across the information.

In information processing terms, the structure puts too much of a strain on STM. One is forced, when one reaches the verb string, to attempt to fit each verb with the proper preceding information. Miller and Isard reported frequent recursive eye movements from the ends of such sentences.

STRUCTURAL MEANING

To get a better understanding of structural meaning in the typographic design we can profitably continue our typographic design-verbal language analogy. Let's consider the matter of syntax. Here are four words and their paraphrased dictionary meanings:

1. anesthetizes—renders insensible to pain, touch, and so on
2. doctor—a person licensed to practice medicine
3. patient—a person under a doctor's care
4. frightened—filled with fright; afraid

These words can be arranged in 24 different orders. Some make little or no sense, even though we understand the meaning of each word individually. Consider three possible orders:

frightened patient anesthesizes doctor
doctor anesthesizes frightened patient
patient anesthesizes frightened doctor

Meanings are changed according to the ordering of the words. The way in which words combine in various structurings to give meanings is called syntax. Words come from the vocabulary of the user of the verbal language.

In Chapter 5 we spoke of visual syntax. The typography designer also has a vocabulary. From it he draws the various elements and arranges them syntactically to convey various meanings. Because we have grown up with it and are well experienced in the use of our verbal language, we can speak or write it with a high degree of competency in syntactical effect. To become effective in communicating graphically the typography designer must first acquaint himself with the vocabulary of design. After that he should learn the principles involved in its use. Then it's a matter of practice, practice, practice.

Design Vocabulary

We have been drawing parallels between verbal language and visual language. Let us not forget, as we pointed out in Chapter 4, that the visual cannot make conditional or logical statements. Its major function is to arouse the reader—to "tune him up" physiologically. But the visual form *is* a language, although primarily an "emotional" one. As a language it has a vocabulary, which consists of these elements: point, line, shape, tone, and texture. Selection from these elements and the arrangement of them lead to the visual statement.

THE POINT

This structural element is both imaginary and real. Either way it is a reference to a position in space and holds a strong attraction for the eye. The optical center is an example of the imaginary point. Initial letters act as points. Leaders are actual points; so are large dots used to attract the eye.

THE LINE

The line, too, can be real as well as imaginary. It is real enough when used to delineate shape, as in a line drawing or in figures or the letters of the alphabet. Words and sentences in themselves form lines. The line, real or imagined, shows direction and movement. It does not exist in nature. We "see" it as a demarcation between adjoining tones.

The imaginary line is vital in planning the position of the elements in typographic design. Look at Figure 8-1. An imaginary line is "seen" that begins at the left end of the names of the couple and falls vertically past the woman's face to the edge of the line reading "Call Toll Free" and is actually seen in the post holding the "Master Hosts Inn" sign. This direction of the eye to positions where important verbal information can be found is purposeful and controllable within the syntax of visual communication.

Figure 8-1. *Imaginary line suggests movement. Actual size: 10 inches high. (Courtesy Red Carpet Inns of America, Inc.)*

Figure 8-2. *Real lines suggest movement. (Courtesy Dancer-Fitzgerald-Sample, Inc.)*

Real lines can accomplish the same mission. Note the purposeful direction of lines in the male model's clothing in Figure 8-2. The lines, of course, take the eye to the verbal areas at the bottom.

You may recall the reference to Piet Mondrian in Chapter 5. In it we referred to his use of the line in the composition of visual elements. In Figure 8-3 is an example of an ad which shows the Mondrian effect with visible lines dividing the space.

This would suggest that the design space could be "gridded" with horizontal and vertical lines. Then, taking advantage of the fact that the eye moves left to right and top to bottom, the various elements could be so placed as to be seen in a certain order (syntax).

Figure 8-3. *Mondrian-style layout. (Courtesy Mr. Travel)*

Figure 8-4. *Visible grid lines in an ad. (Courtesy Pitney Bowes)*

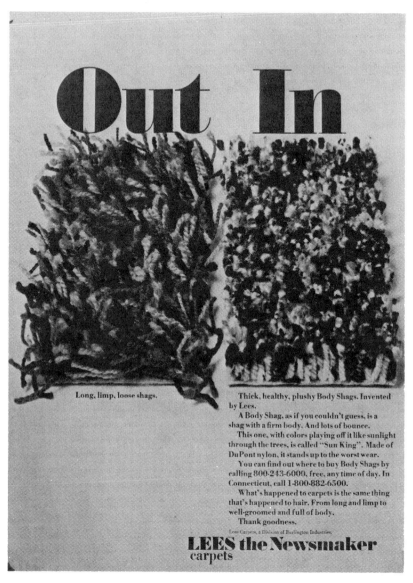

Figure 8-5. *Vertical axis is strongly suggested in this ad. (Courtesy Lees Carpets; agency: Doyle-Dane-Bernbach)*

This is done in Figure 8-4. In fact, the grid lines are visible. The ad in Figure 8-5 follows a grid structure but here the lines are only suggested. The grid structure is a common pattern in book and periodical design. You will see it in the magazine and newspaper design chapters. Figure 5-6 was also an example of a design to grid structure.

The brain-computer naturally processes information in horizontal-vertical terms. We sense our "feet-on-the-ground" stability in this manner without always being conscious of the fact. We are upright (vertical), feet on the ground (horizontal). The use of lines capitalizes on this basic fact.

SHAPE

Lines articulate shapes. Shapes may also be defined as tone, texture, edges (regular-irregular), and size. Groups of words can form shapes. The block of small type at the bottom in Figure 8-2 is a rectangle. Squint at it so that the words are indistinguishable; you can better sense its shape, weight, tone, and texture.

We impose on what we look at three basic shapes: square, circle, and triangle. There are, of course, endless variations of and combinations of these shapes and each shape psychologically suggests its own meaning. We call certain "dull" people (as we see them) "squares." We speak of the "love triangle," in which tension exists. The circle suggests peace, protection, safety.

TONE (OR VALUE)

If it were not for tone, we'd see nothing in the first place. The word "tone" refers to relative lightness or darkness. Only by this contrast do we visually sense points, lines, weight, and texture.

Our visual systems are set up to sense color, and that's what we see in nature. However, a black-and-white symbolization or representation—e.g., a black-and-white photograph—is perfectly acceptable and interpretable. One can change a color TV picture to black and white for instant and dramatic proof of this significant fact. Such a switch demonstrates the basic importance of tone to perception and consequently the acquiring of information. Relative lightness is called "value" whether one is speaking of chromatic (color) or achromatic (white) light. Thus value is synonymous with tone in this discussion.

TEXTURE

Any surface structure can be sensed visually as having texture. Thus we visually "feel." It is as natural to want to touch as it is to want to look. We referred to this in Chapter 5; texture is sensed not only in a block of type composition but in the surface of all shapes. An example was seen in Figure 8-2. Why the man wears a corduroy coat is obvious.

Putting It All Together

Now that we know the elements of the designer's vocabulary, let's see how he puts them together to make a composition. If the finished work is to be an ad, the composition he draws will be called a *layout;* if it is a page in a newspaper or magazine, it is termed a *page dummy.* The complete compilation of all pages is referred to as a *dummy.*

In the following discussion of composition, we will concentrate on layouts. Advertisers have been more active in researching the effects of composition than have printers or publishers. This is probably due to the high cost of ad space and the rough competition for attention they face. We will use examples of magazine layout where they are particularly applicable. However, more treatment in detail will be found in Chapter 10.

KINDS OF LAYOUT

The laying-out or ordering process puts the elements of vocabulary into a composition that, through syntax, delivers an effective message (transfer of meanings). Therefore, it must be carefully planned. The first step, *visualization,* is a thinking process from which come such decisions as:

1. The ideas (content) the symbols (verbal and graphic) will represent.
2. The number of elements to be used.
3. The relative importance of the information-bearing elements.
4. The order of presentation; this is what syntax is all about.

These decisions are influenced by the kind of product being advertised, the nature of the consumer, and the degree of his interest in and relationship to the product. The designer must know these things, for they affect his composition.

There are three kinds of layout, classified according to the care used in drawing them. This care is directly related to the purpose of each of the three kinds. They are: the *miniature* or *thumbnail sketch,* often made to aid in visualization; the *rough;* and the *comprehensive.*

The Miniature

This simplest of designs can be any size. It is generally smaller than the full-size, printed image, but it is usually proportional to it. Thumbnails have three advantages:

1. They are an economical way of testing the visual syntax.
2. Because they can be done quickly, the designer is free to try sev-

eral approaches, discarding those he doesn't like. Working full-scale would expend precious time and energy, perhaps leading to a hesitancy to discard a bad try.

3. The working of miniatures begets new ideas. The first and second sketches may miss the mark. But they warm up the creative, problem-solving process, leading to a flow of more productive ideas.

There is a strong parallel between editing verbal copy and visual copy. Experimenting with miniatures is really editing — defining and redefining the syntax and grammar of the visual statement.

In Figure 8-6 is a miniature of the ad seen in Figure 8-1. There are definite means of indicating the various elements in a miniature. Comparing the two figures you can see how the elements are represented. Note the treatment of headlines, illustrations, body

Figure 8-6. *Miniature layout of an ad.* *Actual size.*

Figure 8-7. *Rough miniature. Actual size.*

you'd be smart to think about Fall this Spring

$64

pre season coat sale

leader

Figure 8-8. *The rough layout. Actual size: almost 7 inches high.*

type, and the logotype or signature. Note that the weights of the units are roughly equivalent. Weight of elements is influenced by relative size, shape, and tone.

Miniatures can be prepared with any degree of finish. The example is done with reasonable care. Figure 8-7 is also a miniature of the same ad, drawn with less precision.

The Rough Layout

The miniature selected as best is redrawn as a rough, which is a full-size layout (Figure 8-8). This is more utilitarian than experimental.

Several drafts of a rough may be called for to take care of revisions and changes. The final rough bears a close resemblance to the printed ad. Headlines are lettered in to approximate their printed form. Illustrations are often hastily sketched. The position of the elements is precise enough to allow the printer to work from a rough in composing and making up the ad. In effect, the rough could be a "blueprint" for construction.

Designing layouts is simplified by the proper equipment. The best paper is a transparent bond known as layout paper, or a tough tracing paper will do nicely. A drawing board is a desirable work surface; a T square and triangle facilitate accuracy. Also needed are at least three black pencils—a 2H for light lines, a 2B for heavier lines, and a 6B for broader, heavier strokes. An Ebony pencil is also handy. A sandpaper pad is useful for shaping the leads to fit the kind of stroke you are using. Color pencils are useful in rendering color roughs. You may want to use the colored, wide felt pens for laying down colors in larger areas.

The beginner should learn early in the game to draw type faces in display sizes. Rule three light guidelines to indicate the x-height and the top of caps. Then lay the paper over printed specimens and trace. Be sure you make heavy enough strokes to suggest the proper density of letters in print. You'll be surprised how quickly you can get the "feel" of display lettering. And (would you believe?) it won't be long before you can draw guides and simulate letters without the specimen crutch. All it takes is practice. Music students practice. Typographers should, too. Your practice will reward you with unexpected proficiency.

The Comprehensive Layout

The so-called "comp" is very exact, rendered to show how the layout will look in print. Illustrations imitate their finished look and heads are precisely lettered in. Body type is usually ruled in. A type comp is drawn with proofs of type pasted in position so that the sponsor can get a still better representation of how the ad will look than is afforded by a rough.

Design Principles

The term "style" is often applied to the use of language. It refers to how one puts thoughts into words. If we say of a writer, "He has no style," we mean we don't like how he says it. His thoughts are not distinctive, and he expresses them poorly. "Style," however, can be more broadly applied. According to the dictionary, it refers to distinction and excellence in any artistic or literary expression.

There are standards of style in layout as well as in writing. In this section we will examine these standards—design principles—in turn: contrast, balance, proportion, rhythm, harmony, movement, and unity. It would be convenient to say they are listed here in order of importance. This can hardly be done, however, because they are interactive. You will understand how they interact when we discuss them.

Before we start, an important fact needs to be established. In a sense, this recaps some of the things said previously. They bear repeating.

The nervous excitation that takes place in the brain becomes a part of the visual design when we look at it. A simple do-it-yourself experiment will make this clear. Draw two parallel lines on a piece of paper, ¾ inch apart and 2½ inches long. Put a dot midway of their length and their distance apart. Draw straight lines fanning out from the dot as in Figure 8-9. Be sure these lines extend an inch or so beyond your parallel lines.

Now look at your drawing as you'd look at railroad tracks below you. Your parallel lines no longer look straight but bowed. Are they, really?

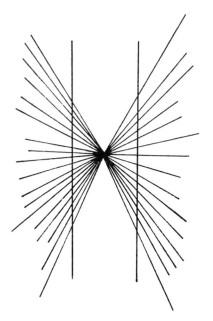

Figure 8-9. *What the eye sees excites the brain.*

Look at Figure 8-10. The two dark rectangles are ⅜ inch apart. They seem to belong together. Now look at Figure 8-11. The two are repeated, still ⅜ inch apart. But next to each at a distance of ⅛ inch is another, same sized, dark rectangle. The original two no longer seem to belong together. What happened?

The various layout elements interact. We feel these changes and call them attractions. Attraction refers to the "pull" resulting from these energy effects we project into the image. It is thus possible to attract the eye. But attention differs from attraction. This is more than a matter of semantics or verbal nit-picking.

Figure 8-10. *The two rectangles belong together.*

Figure 8-11. *The two rectangles of Figure 8-10 pulled apart.*

Attention comes after attraction — maybe only a few milliseconds after, but *after*. This idea is compatible with processing theory. Attention involves assigning meaning to what attracts. Perhaps an ad is merely intended to remind. The product is shown in large size. The verbal message is minimal. Meaning is quickly attached. This is the typical task of a poster or billboard. Simple ads of this nature in periodicals are often called poster ads.

On the other hand, some ads must do more of a selling job. Do you recall the discourse about concept formation? Before the reader can develop a sound brand concept — that is, discover its meaning — he must learn its positive instances or distinguishing features, as we labeled them in Chapter 2. Such an ad attempts to do this. More points of attraction must be placed in the ad. More attention is necessary. The reader must be held longer to learn the concept(s) involved.

CONTRAST

In any form of communication some materials (ideas) must be stressed more than others. The selection of these is, of course, a part of planning or visualization.

Contrast is the source of all meaning. Where is the understanding of "high" without the concept of "not high" or "low"? Contrast is, in fact, the only reason we see at all and explains why "see" may serve as a synonym for "understand."

IF YOU DON'T MIND PAYING LESS, YOU CAN GET A BETTER STEAK.

Some people still judge things by their price tags. If it costs more, they reason, it must be worth more.

To which Adolph's says, "Nonsense!"

Especially when it comes to steaks. Because the less-expensive cuts, like round steak, flank steak and sirloin tip steak are just as nutritious as the costly ones. They have a richer, beefier flavor. They have less fat, usually less bone. More protein, fewer calories. Pound-for-pound, they're a better value for your money.

In fact, the only thing they lack is natural tenderness.

And that's where Adolph's Instant Meat Tenderizer comes in. Use Adolph's on those less-expensive cuts and you can broil or barbecue a round steak to taste as tender and juicy as a porterhouse. You can barbecue a flank or sirloin tip steak deliciously tender enough to serve company.

And if you'd like to vary your menu, use Adolph's 15-Minute Meat Marinade instead. Then you can have the deep-down flavor and juicy tenderness of a delicious gourmet meal. And have it quickly too. Because Adolph's has taken the time and trouble out of marinating. It works in just 15 minutes!

So, next barbecue time, remember: If you don't mind paying less, you can get a better steak.

*Prices from U.S. Bureau of Labor Statistics. Average national meat prices, 1969.

Figure 8-12. *Contrast skillfully manipulated. (Courtesy Chesebrough-Pond's, Inc.)*

In Figure 8-12 there is masterful use of contrast, the designer's most potent tool for bringing meaning into sharp focus. Read the headline. There is a subtle contrast in meaning. The two steaks have been broiled, yet they still have their price tags—contrast because it's

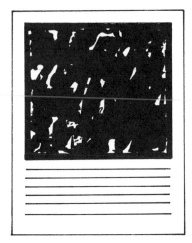

Figure 8-13. *Illustration and text of equal size, left, are less pleasing than when the illustration dominates, right.*

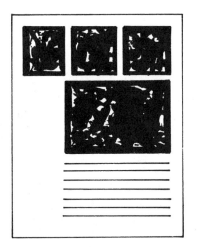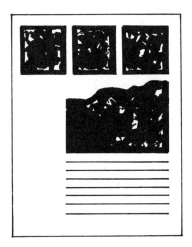

Figure 8-14. *Monotony of shapes, left, is relieved by a different treatment of the large illustration, right.*

unexpected. The one on the left is a more expensive cut; the one on the right is less expensive, according to the tags—contrast again, through a subtle visual treatment. Who wouldn't read the text after this invitation? The copy continues the contrast—less expensive cuts are as nutritious, have fewer calories and less bone; all they lack is tenderness and the product takes care of this problem.

Contrast can be achieved by applying polarities of size, shape, tone, texture, and direction. We use the term "polarity" advisedly. Hot–cold, high–low, and so on, represent polarities in meaning. In physical science, the term refers to contrary powers, and we are speaking in terms of physiological energy.

Contrast in Size

On the left of Figure 8-13 is a layout showing illustration and text of approximately equal size. On the right, the presentation is livelier because a dominant illustration supplies contrast.

Contrast in Shape

Although sizes contrast satisfactorily in Figure 8-14, a monotony of shapes exists. Attraction is enhanced on the right by the irregular shape. Note we speak of attraction, not attention.

Contrast in Tone

The dullness on the left in Figure 8-15 is brightened by tonal accent on the right. The headline at the top has greater attraction. The package has greater attraction. If the reader already knows what it is, it will have greater attention because of his earlier experience with it.

Figure 8-15. *Contrast of tone, missing on the left, "sparks" the layout on the right.*

Figure 8-16. *Color can be placed to direct eye movement. (Courtesy Fisher-Price Toys)*

Tone is also associated with color. Look at Figure 8-16. The first
pin on the left was blue in the original ad. So were the pin that is
tipped forward and the ball on the left. The eye follows these tones,
first pin to fifth pin, then back to the ball, which lines up with the
copy below. It is also interesting to note that these three items form
an inverted triangle pointing at the copy. An accidental arrangement?
Hardly!

Contrast in Texture

Look again at Figure 8-2. Contrast of the textures of his coat and her blouse serves an obvious purpose.

Contrast in Direction

The major aim in contrasting direction is to guide the reader's eye through the message. Figure 8-2 shows this. The horizontal headline is in contrast to the vertical models, backed up by the vertical lines in the man's garb.

BALANCE

Balance exists when the elements are placed with a sense of equipoise or equilibrium. That is, the weights of the elements counteract so that they seem settled where they are placed. The weight of an element is the result of size, shape and tone. Large elements, the other factors being equal, appear heavier. Irregular shapes bear greater weight than regular. Dark elements outweigh light ones, though a small, dark element can appear heavier than a larger but lighter mass.

We have already discussed the two kinds of balance: symmetrical and asymmetrical, mainly with respect to the placement of type elements. Let's consider again the asymmetrical, but now involving the placement of graphic as well as type elements.

You no doubt recall the seesaw or teeter-totter. To hold the board in balance, the heavier of two children must sit nearer the fulcrum than the lighter child. Weight times distance on one side must equal weight times distance on the other to achieve balance.

The same principle is at work in layouts. The optical center becomes the fulcrum. Figure 8-17 shows two similar weight units as elements in asymmetrical balance and Figure 8-18 demonstrates the

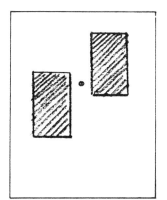
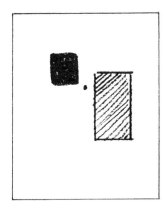
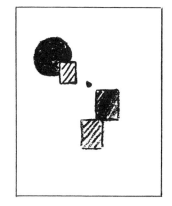

Figure 8-17. *Placement of two units in balance.*

Figure 8-18. *Proper placement of more than two units.*

proper placement of more than two elements. Figures 8-1 and 8-2 show asymmetrical balance in actual ads.

A major difference between the two kinds of balance lies in the use of white space. It is passive in the symmetrically balanced design. In the asymmetric, on the other hand, it becomes an active part of the visual presentation. Thus the layout becomes more exciting and dynamic, offering various points of attraction.

Symmetric balance — or perhaps balance with only minor variations — is found oftener than you might think. Skim through several national women's magazines. The standard content of large illustration, headline, copy block, and signature is not uncommon. Why should this be so in this highly competitive age? As you recall, the reader can process information in only limited amounts. If the ad is too complex, a stimulus overload could result. Better, such advertisers reason, to subdue form and concentrate on getting across a few major points. Context, we learned in Chapter 2, is an aid to processing. The reader in the women's magazine is within a context compatible with the message in such an ad.

PROPORTION

The range of visual stimulation approaches 180 degrees. However, one can focus on details only within about 3 degrees. Thus the eye moves in jumps over a layout. The calculating brain is constantly comparing the new information with the old in STM. Since contrast is the source of meaning, there is a constant measuring process going on. Compositional forces are being measured. This is larger than that; that is darker than this; that texture is smoother than this; and so on.

Proportion represents the results of the reader's decision-making. It refers to the relationship of one element to another or to the design as a whole in ratios reflecting size and strength.

Certain proportions are more attractive to the eye than others. The first task in layout is to select the size of the ad or its dimensions. A similar task exists in book work, of course, except that page or sheet size is predetermined.

Attractive dimensions are those in which the relationship of width to height is not obvious to the eye. Thus a square layout, with dimensions of 1 to 1, is less attractive. Proportions of 2 to 1 are too easily detected and to be avoided. Proportions close to 1 to 1 or 2 to 1 are weak because of their proximity to those just mentioned. Because they are less obvious, 3 to 1 dimensions are better. This applies to element relationships, involving tones, weight, size, and so on, as well as to ad dimensions.

Among the more interesting ratios are those evolving from the golden mean summation series: 2:3:5:8:13:21 and so on. Can you determine what number would follow 21? These suggest continuing ratios — 2:3::3:5; 3:5::5:8; and so on. Remember from high school algebra, "The product of the means equals the product of the extremes?" Thus 2×5 should equal 3×3. However, there is an error of 1 and it continues through the series, probably the result of Greek mathematicians' dislike of fractions.

Several things are of interest here. The 2:3 ratio is common in nature. For example, spirals in one direction on pineapples are in this ratio to spirals running in the opposite direction. The same ratio is found in flower petal arrays. To mathematicians these are known as logarithmic spirals, which evolve through growth and development in nature. As the summation series expands it exhibits a rhythmic pattern, suggesting the subtle interrelationship between proportion and rhythm. It is also interesting that the eye finds a point in blank space, the optical center, three-fifths from the bottom.

We suggest these things only to indicate that there is a beautiful logic in the design of the printed message, just as there is in all nature. Art is, after all, a reflection of order in the universe, a means of "telling it like it is."

There is an elegant contrast between a square and a so-called golden mean rectangle, the proportions of which are approximately 3:2. This contrast was common in Greek architecture. It is seen in an application in Figure 8-19 to the design of a magazine page. The rectangle above the square requires "closure" by the reader but there it is, standing in contrast. Note also the logically developed geometric patterns and the axis lines.

For the student interested in reading in more detail about the ways in which order in nature is reflected in man and his endeavors, we suggest reading: Hambidge (1926), Bragdon (1922), and Scott (1951).

RHYTHM

Rhythm is achieved through the orderly repetition of any element — line, shape, tone, texture. The eye will spot rhythm and follow its pattern. Rhythm is thus a vital force in movement. That was seen in Figure 8-16 where the blue tones carried the eye to the apex of the triangle pointing to the copy block.

Rhythm interacts with proportion, as we noted earlier. It is, like proportion, a manifestation of growth and development in nature. Look in a dictionary or encyclopedia for illustrations of snowflakes. Here you will find rhythm and proportion beautifully expressed. You will also find the other standards for judging effective design: contrast, balance, harmony, movement, and unity.

Examine Figure 8-20. Note the rhythm of the six rectangles. The ad, printed in full color, carried skin tones and dark brown back-

Figure 8-19. *Two units here are in 3:2 ratio: the extension of square into Golden Rectangle. (Copyright* Better Homes and Gardens; *reproduced by permission)*

grounds in all six rectangles. Note the subtle juxtapositioning of the numerals 1 and 2 in the squares versus the numerals in the bottom two rectangles.

HARMONY

It was previously stated that meaning lies in polarity—hot vs. cold; high vs. low; and so on. Harmony and contrast are bipolar. This

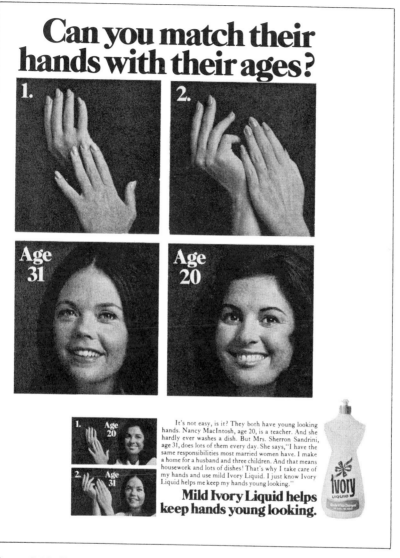

Figure 8-20. *Contrasting shapes, rhythm in color and tones skillfully matched to message intent. (Reproduced by permission of The Procter & Gamble Company)*

would seem to be a contradiction, for how can both be standards for evaluating a layout? The answer comes from processing theory. To find order and reduce uncertainty seems to be a basic force in man's nature. He is programmed to seek understanding. What would he be, where would he be if he were in a perfect state of balance, if all sensations were harmonious, and if he understood everything? Impossible, for contrast is the source of understanding.

Harmony exists in the mutual characteristics of the elements' tone, shape, size, texture. A book page printed in one face—with variations in sizes, the use of italic for folios and headings, and borders and decorative devices matching the weight and design of the type—is a good example. The principle is clearly evident in the design of this text. Only one type, Palatino, is used throughout.

Complete harmony is passive. Contrast, on the other hand, is active and vigorous. It produces emphasis and dynamic movement. It relieves monotony.

MOVEMENT

The very act of reading produces a sense of movement, even in the most prosaic, formally balanced presentation. The eye moves from left to right and from top to bottom. In other types of design, the control of eye movement becomes more of a problem. Inasmuch as the entire message is present at the same time (not true of TV or radio), the reader is free to look at any given point at any time. If the message is to be a cohesive whole, this must be discouraged. Manipulation of the elements—the syntax and grammar of design—is the means of eye movement control. The basic question in applying this standard is: "Does the movement that exists in the design carry the eye in the directions required by the content?"

UNITY

We refer you once more to the Haber study, covered in Chapter 2. The subjects recalled 85 to 95 percent of the photos previously seen, although they were fuzzy about details. The gist of a well-presented message should be remembered, although some of the details may not easily be recalled. Establishing the theme is the plus that unity should give to the message. Reconsider the Adolph's ad, Figure 8-12, and the discussion about it. We believe the ad did an excellent job of establishing the theme: Tenderize less expensive cuts and they will equal the costly cuts.

The individual elements must relate to each other and to the total design so that they effect coherence. Without this unity an ad cannot register a single, over-all impression. In the left of Figure 8-21 five rectangles are placed at random. In contrast to this confusion is the orderliness in the right-hand sketch. The five rectangles have been divided into two groups, one of three units, the other of two. A layout that lacks unity is likely to "fly apart." The beginner should remember to relegate white space to the outside rather than to allow liberal amounts to fall among the elements of the ad.

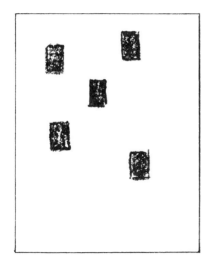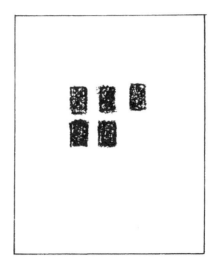

Figure 8-21. *Lack of unity, left, improved through proper grouping, right.*

Making Design Articulate

Structural relationships among elements in the layout should be accommodated to (1) the sequence of eye movements and (2) the order of absorbing the information the source hopes to impart. The latter is the prime function of form.

What we are considering here is organizing the elements. Organization presupposes a process of indicating to the reader (1) how some elements are related; (2) how others are different in their functions; and (3) which elements are most important in their function.

EYE MOVEMENT

The designer may devote considerable time to individual parts of his effort, but the reader tends to scan the total layout for an over-all impression. After that, assuming points of attraction engender attention, he may devote some time to details.

Thus it becomes important to consider the eye-movement tendencies of the reader as he scans a page, a spread of pages, or an ad. These tendencies have been revealed through lab experiments using the eye camera, with the following conclusions:

1. The eye tends, after leaving the initial fixation, to move to the left and upward.
2. The exploratory coverage of the space is from this point in a clockwise direction.

3. The eye prefers horizontal movement.
4. The left position is preferred to the right and the top position is preferred to the bottom. Thus the four quadrants of a space might be given communication values from one to four in descending order as shown in Figure 8-22.

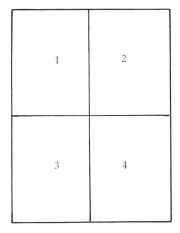

Figure 8-22. *Communicative value of layout space decreases from first quadrant to fourth.*

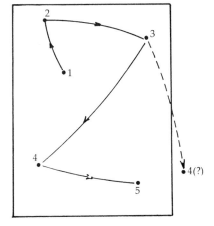

Figure 8-23. *Eye movement tendency moving from point 1.*

Figure 8-23 illustrates what we have said about eye-movement tendencies. Point 1 represents the initial fixation, *usually* at the optical center. The clockwise path from 2 through 3 is exploratory. Conceivably the eye may leave the space at 4(?) and move out of it.

The fact that these have been labeled "tendencies" means that this is not necessarily the path the eye will follow. The designer can influence the direction by the proper placement of elements. But if the eye is to be drawn to points 4 and 5 it is important that they involve content of interest to the reader.

If the reader will analyze a number of ads in several different printed media, he will notice that some are primarily illustrative with little verbal copy, while others are structured to highlight copy.

Copy should tend to be longer when the product is of exceptional interest because it is new or offers new features, when the need is more immediate, or when the product is technical in nature. If the advertiser is trying to solicit orders or convince nonusers of the product's merit, he is also likely to use longer copy. Copy is often shorter if the ad is a reminder, primarily reaffirming favorable attitudes, or if the product is of low inherent interest.

Admittedly these ideas are oversimplified. Their purpose is to point up the fact that the designer must consider the nature of the proposition and reader interests before he begins his work.

INDICATING ELEMENT RELATIONSHIPS

We have already indicated how elements can be associated by means of real and imaginary lines. There are several other techniques available. They include: (1) similar shapes, (2) similar tones, (3) similar size, (4) similar texture, and (5) enclosure in a portion of the ad by the use of borders, tints, reverses, and so on.

In Figure 8-20, most of these techniques are used. The question asked in the headline is the "hook" for getting reader interest. The four large rectangles emphasize the question. The answer is in the small rectangles. Sizes in the "question rectangles" are similar; sizes in the "answer rectangles" are similar. Tones and texture are similar in all six. All are interrelated through logical alignment. Note the subtle matching of numbers and ages in the answer rectangles in a sort of counterpoint. The reader can readily find examples of the fifth technique listed above.

INDICATING ELEMENT DIFFERENTIATION

If the need for relating elements exists, then means are needed for disassociating them. This is necessary in the interest of function. Differences can be made through shape, tone, size, texture, and by separating similar elements and differentiated elements with two enclosure techniques.

In Figure 8-20 we saw how the small rectangles were similar to the large ones and at the same time differentiated. It is through such subtle interplay that the designer manipulates visual forces for maximum effort.

CONTROLLING AMOUNT OF INFORMATION

Consider the following facts: the eye quickly scans the entire presentation, searching for points of interest; the capacity of STM, where points of interest are stored until they can be brought together in the total "visual image" is low; the output (decision-making) capacity of the IPS is relatively slow—on the order of 25–50 bits per second (Travers, 1970, pp. 79–83). Moreover, the reader has only a limited amount of time available for looking in this day of vast competition for his attention. As Travers (1970, p. 82) puts it, "If a person is flooded with more information than he can handle, his performance becomes quite ineffective . . . he does not separate out a little piece of the task for learning. He may learn nothing."

Here is a rationale for clean-cut simplicity. The number of visual elements should be held to a bare minimum. The way in which they are handled should lead to the tightest possible organization.

Look through ads in national magazines. Photographs of products are so treated that extraneous, distracting information is controlled. Perhaps the product is outlined—that is, it is shown alone. Not only does this focus interest but it offers the designer an irregular shape (nonrectangular) with which to work. Perhaps the product is shown in a square-finish illustration, but the background is plain, and either light or dark, thereby eliminating distraction; or the background may contain detail, but it is subdued or in softer focus than the product.

Newspapers offer numerous examples of techniques useful in presenting large numbers of elements, particularly in large department and discount store ads. The grid method or the enclosure of individual items to effect a sectionalizing of the total ad are the only feasible means.

There are occasions when reproductions of photographs do not give enough information. Perhaps vital details cannot be clearly seen and are ambiguous. In such cases the photo, before printing, is specially treated by an artist who *retouches* it—paints it with the necessary colors and values to bring out the details.

There are even occasions when photographs give too much information. The answer may well lie in the use of line drawings. Line drawings function in much the same way poetry does verbally. Both involve the use of highly abstracted information and state a message much more indirectly. The same message, if stated in full detail or directly, would lose its simplicity and thereby its effectiveness. Figure

Figure 8-24. *A few basic lines can deliver a message.*

Figure 8-25. *Simple line drawings detail construction features in this ad. (Courtesy of E. H. Titchener and Company, Binghamton, N.Y.)*

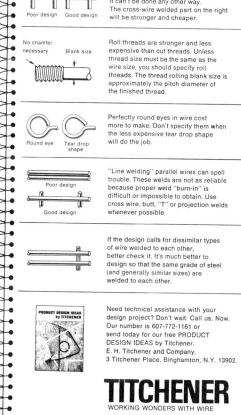

8-24, with a few simple lines, is capable of conveying a feeling of puzzlement and concern. The nose is only suggested and the eyes are missing. The viewer "sees" them, however. He knows from experience they are there.

In Figure 8-25 simple line drawings show wire constructions which, when separated from actual application, become much easier to visualize.

Pie charts, bar graphs, and line charts, as mentioned in Chapter 6, are effective means of summarizing information into visual form. Often their visual effectiveness can be enhanced by adding simple illustration to them, in effect creating *pictographs*. For example, rising prices might be indicated by high flying kites, with dollar signs on them. The pie chart might become a silver dollar or a bill cut into sections.

HANDLING ILLUSTRATIONS

The design of the printed piece starts with decisions concerning the handling of illustrations and headlines. This is due in large degree to the effects of newspaper, magazine, and television practice. Newspapers, in an effort to communicate quickly and efficiently, have developed the technique of giving the gist of the story in the headline, picture, and first few paragraphs. Magazines, reaching more selective readers and being produced under less pressure of time, have refined the basic newspaper formula and applied it to full pages and spreads. In a short span, using the picture as the basic component, supplemented by a concise verbal message, the TV commercial develops a basic concept with strong impact and dynamic movement.

It is usually best to begin the arrangement of the elements within a given space by the placing of illustrations. This is not necessarily because they are more important, but because the designer has greater latitude in placing headlines and subheads. Furthermore, through contrast with other visual elements, they play a major role in attraction.

If only one illustration is used, it can carry strong visual impact if it dominates the page. Additional emphasis can be given through bleeding one or more of its edges. A smaller illustration can be given added impact by surrounding it with extensive white space. Two illustrations can be sized equally and placed together and treated as a unit. Or they can be sized and shaped differently and placed in balance.

The problem of arranging several illustrations is somewhat more complex. One technique in solving the problem is to size illustrations equally and treat them as a unit. Another is to organize them into two or three groups and place them in balance. Both methods can be seen in Figure 8-20. A third technique calls for sizing one illustration much larger than others and using it as the focal point of interest. The illustration selected should emphasize the message and the interests of the reader. This is shown in Figure 8-26. A final solu-

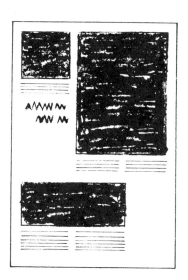

Figure 8-26. *One large illustration dominates.*

Figure 8-27. *Several illustrations treated as one large irregular shape.*

tion might be suggested. It is sometimes possible to gather several illustrations of unequal sizes into a group so that they appear as one single, irregular shape, as shown in Figure 8-27.

HANDLING HEADLINES

The headline is the most important of all printed elements that vie for reader attention. But even when a headline is not used—for example, in books or newspaper classified ads—chapter headings and classification titles serve a similar function by attracting the reader to the text of the message.

Nor are headlines always used in competitive reading matter, such as display ads, but when they are not used in such cases, the interest of the reader must be sufficient to bridge the gap and carry him from illustration to message.

In a broad sense headlines serve two functions: (1) they summarize or directly suggest the content of the message, or (2) they appeal primarily to a basic reader interest after which an attempt is made to present the source's message. The two headline categories can be classified as *direct* and *indirect*.

Direct heads are found on newspaper and magazine editorial pages. They are also found in advertisements when the reader's interest in the product or proposition is considered sufficient to carry him on to the message after he receives his cue from the headline.

Often the source considers the indirect head more effective, as in

Figure 8-28. *Indirect headline.*

When does an onion
have no smell?

SARAN WRAP

Figure 8-28. Note that the illustration involves the product but the head does not. In many ads neither head nor illustration relates to the proposition.

The headline is considered the most important element in competitive matter because seldom can the illustration alone complete the contact with the reader's interests. Illustrations may attract but they may be individually interpreted. Words are more consensual in meaning and are therefore more effective in completing the attraction-attention function.

A number of headline treatments were discussed in Chapter 5 and are pertinent within the context of this section. One matter remains for consideration here—positioning the headline.

The word "headline" suggests that this element should appear at the top of an editorial page or an advertisement. At one time this placement was common, but today more imaginative treatments are used. Even so, top placement is still widely used.

The student would do well to examine as many publications and ads as possible to analyze headline placement. For example, the main reason for varying the placement on editorial pages in magazines is to relieve the monotony that develops as the reader finds page after page with the headline at the top. How does the designer achieve this variation? The range of possibilities is limited only by his imagination. A wide search will reveal many interesting treatments.

Head placement in ads is somewhat more complex. Variation cannot be introduced simply to relieve monotony. Other considerations are involved. The importance of the head relative to the body copy will have a great deal to do with its placement. If the effectiveness of the ad depends on the readership of the text, the head must be so worded and placed as to carry the reader's eye from the initial point of attraction to the copy.

A common presentation to this end uses a dominant illustration with head immediately below, followed by the text. It is a format to which readers are accustomed. Placement of the head above a large illustration is also common. However, in this case, the head must be of sufficient type size to capture the reader's eye and compete effectively with the attraction power of the illustration. This can be seen in Figure 8-20.

Often the designer's task is to see to it that the headline, the major illustration, and the signature or a picture of the product be seen at a glance. When this is the objective, the text is very short or may not exist at all. This is true with reminder ads. Under these conditions the position of the head relative to the text becomes less significant than its relationship to the major attraction-attention illustration. Often head and package are combined with the major illustration to assure that the reader can grasp all the vital points of the message with minimum effort.

In Figure 8-20 we saw an ad that is completely of opposite nature. The headline is integrated into the relatively long text to achieve that desired unity. The text—and its persuasive power—is considered more important than in the case of a reminder ad.

An advertisement is a single thing—a single communication—a transfer of meaning or a concept. The ad must present a unified impression. It can do so via large illustration and headline, or it may invite the reader to delve into the text.

CHAPTER 9 # Principles of Magazine Layout

From the standpoint of both design and content, magazines are a hybrid form of periodical. They have some of the characteristics of newspapers, and in some cases actually are purveyors of news. But on the other hand they have a quality and a lasting value that would make them more closely akin to books. In fact, the common term for magazines among the professionals who design and produce them is *book*. Then, too, they resemble advertising in that great attention is given to their visual appeal, and they can, as in the case of house organs (public-relations magazines), go so far as to have basic goals resembling those of advertising.

This multicharacter aspect of magazines is illustrated in Figures 9-1 to 9-4: the newsmagazine employs standardized headlines in newspaper fashion; the scholarly magazine is in traditional book format; the public relations and consumer magazines have a flair that comes only from the application of special attention and artistic design principles that are characteristic of advertising. These differences point to a first principle for magazine design: A magazine's appearance should be functionally suitable to its basic editorial goals. The magazine that deals in spot news should look different from the one that is concerned only with abstract concepts, and the one that is headed for a scholar's bookshelf can be radically different from a magazine headed for a homemaker's coffee table.

But even within each of the many categories of magazines there are and should be substantial differences. Each individual magazine

Figure 9-1. *Newsmagazines often use basic newspaper headlines to attract readers to articles or departments. (Courtesy* Editor & Publisher)

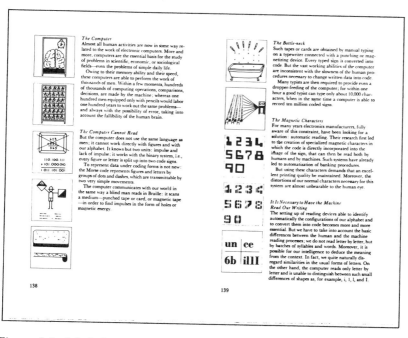

Figure 9-2. *Scholarly magazines often look just like books. (Courtesy* Visible Language, *formerly* Journal of Typographic Research)

Figure 9-3. *Some of the best magazine design is currently being done for public relations magazines such as this one.* (Courtesy Texaco Star)

Figure 9-4. *Consumer magazines are usually designed with obvious flair and sophistication — they have talented art directors.* (Reprinted by permission from Holiday Magazine, © 1973 The Curtis Publishing Company)

develops a character of its own, and physical appearance is a primary factor of that character. Magazines tend to take on human characteristics in the minds of their preparers and their readers. Editors become very sentimental about their books; one would think to hear them talk that their subject is their own child rather than a magazine. And many readers look forward to their favorite magazine as if it were a friend stopping in for his weekly or monthly visit for coffee and conversation. The layout of a magazine must, therefore, take into account the specific personality and character that its readers perceive it to have. The principle that magazine design must relate to a magazine's basic editorial role and to its own individual character serves as a foundation pillar for our discussion of magazine layout.

One other point, this one relating to the impact of graphics on magazines, must be made here. Visual appearance has been extremely important to magazines throughout most of their history. In the years since the advent of television, however, design has become increasingly valuable. Experimentation, some of it wild and bizarre, characterized some of the general consumer magazines as they entered their death throes in the 1960s and early 1970s. In these cases, it seemed that publishers were calling on graphics to be the life preserver for their drowning magazines. Although the rescue didn't work, the effort did put still more emphasis on magazine design.

The importance of layout for magazines is reflected in their staffing. Immediately following the editor, the first person listed in the masthead is usually the art director whose responsibility is the design and layout of a magazine. For many magazines, the art director and editor work as virtually coequal partners. The art director creates the physical external personality of the magazine, while the editor molds the "spiritual," internal character of the magazine. Obviously, both must work with full mutual knowledge and cooperation.

Volumes have been written about magazine layout and design, and this one chapter cannot present a depth discussion of that subject. In the space we have here we can, however, give some basic principles and relate the essentials of communication theory and basic design to magazine layout so that the journalism student, whether he be future newspaper reporter or magazine designer, can understand the "why" behind the skilled output of professionals.

The First Step: Break-of-the-Book

The layout of a magazine actually begins with an editorial job called "breaking the book." This task involves the allocation of the total amount of space among the ads, articles, departments, and other editorial material that is planned for the issue.

Because advertising determines the existence of a magazine, it is usually placed first, with consideration allowed for editorial-department needs. Although advertisers may request, pay for, and get special position, they are vitally concerned with the success of the editorial portions. As a matter of fact, their requests are often in connection with placement at or near certain portions of a magazine. Co-operation between business and editorial offices negates difficulties arising from advertising placement. It is common practice for ads to be located front and back with the center reserved for the main editorial section.

One of the minor layout problems associated with this practice is to alert the reader to the beginning of the content. The reproduction of the name plate is often used on the first editorial page to signal the reader.

Several studies have shown that a large percentage of readers peruse a magazine backwards. (This can be checked in a classroom survey.) Some magazines have, therefore, found it expedient to place some strong features as complete single-page units at the end of the editorial section. These serve as a starting point for the "backward" readers.

As the main editorial section develops, the pace should change frequently. Long articles should not be lumped together but should be relieved by single or fractional page articles.

Although the ads are placed first, the breaking of the book is primarily the responsibility of an editor; he is the one to make space decisions for editorial content.

But as he decides which articles get only one page and which get more, or which pages will get special color treatment and which won't, he must be aware of some basic production requirements.

These requirements stem from the fact that magazines are printed on large sheets of paper, usually big enough for 8 or 16 pages, and these sheets are folded into sections of the magazine. Each of these sections is called a *signature*. In order to let the printer work efficiently, the editor must complete pages in units corresponding to those that will be on the press at any one time. And, if he is to use color economically, he must plan color to fit in those same units of pages. This planning to meet production requirements is explained in detail in Chapter 16.

Magazine layout, therefore, is often the result of a team effort involving the advertising manager who places the ads, the editor who allocates space, the production manager who keeps printing costs in check, and the art director who designs the pages.

The Dimensions of the Stage: Format

As pointed out in the chapter on design principles, all graphic communications are restricted by certain visual limits just as an actor is confined to the limits of his stage. Every page designed must fit the proportions that have been set for it.

The graphics equivalent of the actor's stage is the *format,* the shape, size, and style of his publication.

The *format* of a magazine is a basic factor in its layout and is not subject to artistic whims. Magazines vary considerably in shape and size, ranging from small enough to tuck into a pocket to dimensions that equal the tabloid newspaper (Figure 9-5). Format is the result of one or more of three practical considerations: (1) ease of handling, (2) adaptability of content to format, and (3) mechanical limitations of printing-press sizes.

Ease of handling is the chief advantage of the pocket size of the *Reader's Digest* and many others. Easy to hold and to store, it is particularly suited to its contents, which consist mainly of text, with the illustrations secondary. The large sizes are best for emphasis on pictures, because the larger the photographs, the greater their impact. However, postage and paper costs have almost eliminated the larger "picture magazine" size.

Most magazines present text and illustrations on a relatively equal basis and use a format adequate for both — 8½ by 11 inches or about that size. Since this is the same size as standard typing paper, filing these pages is simple; also, the dimensions are familiar and comfortable for the reader.

Most magazines are vertical rectangles, a traditional shape substantiated by the difficulty of handling horizontal formats.

Some Theoretical Bases for Magazine Design

The design principles discussed in Chapter 8 and based on communication theory apply just as strongly to magazine pages as they do to advertisements. The end goal of magazine pages is to get information into the mind of the reader — to have the reader get meaning from the pages. Because magazines are usually more concerned with concepts than with straight transferral of specific facts, the role of graphics is especially important; more so than for the newspaper, for example.

The transferral of concepts requires the utmost in sophistication of visual presentation. Visual syntax must be clear and correct; the

Figure 9-5. *Magazine formats range from pocket size through the relatively standard 8½ × 11 to the large-format picture magazines.*

order and simplicity that are characteristic of any good design are especially important if magazine pages are to accomplish their communication goals.

Achieving Meaning Through Orderly Presentation

The orderly design of magazine pages starts with the margins that are used to frame the content of the page. Margins are important for two reasons. First, they are either the ending or the beginning marker (or both) for verbal copy. Try cutting the margin from both sides of a magazine page and note the reading difficulty incurred without the frame of white to set off the line endings. Second, they help make pages and spreads attractive and unified by wrapping the elements on a page into one package with a border of white margins. In this respect they act like the frame around a picture.

Margins are usually considered mandatory for type matter because of their contribution to legibility. But exactly what size they must be varies widely.

Many magazines follow traditional book margins because they are being designed in traditional fashion; most early magazines differed in appearance from the books of their day only because they had no hard covers. The scholarly magazine shown in Figure 9-2 is typical of booklike magazines.

Traditional book margins are progressive, with the bottom margin being the largest and the inside margin the smallest. The area inside the margins is called the *type page* because all type is required to be within that area. Type pages ride slightly high on a page because they are centered on the optical center which is slightly higher than the geometric center.

It is generally most important that the inside (*gutter*) margin be the smallest—ordinarily no more than half the size of the bottom margin. Gutter margins that are too wide destroy the order and unity of two facing magazine pages, and in most instances it is desirable to design facing pages as one unit. If each page is to stand separately, then extra white space at the gutter may be desirable.

As several of the illustrations in this chapter show, modern designers take great liberty with margins on magazine pages. Certainly no effort is made to have type fill out the full dimensions of the type page. But when there is extra white space available, most designers move it to the outside of the design, hence maintaining a white frame, however irregular it may be. Another common technique is

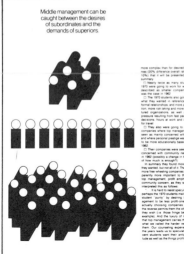

Figure 9-6. *In this layout, the panel of white at the top provides a directional movement in the design and helps tie the pages together. (Courtesy* Long Lines *Magazine, AT&T Long Lines Department)*

the use of large panels of white to create movement in a design (Figure 9-6).

If a magazine's policy is to give special emphasis to pictures, *bleeds* can be especially effective. A photo is said to bleed if it runs off the edge of the page. Bleeds are a good device for any magazine because:

1. They provide a change of pace in comparison with the pages with broken margins.
2. They give more room on a page by adding the marginal space to the content area.
3. Most importantly, they offer extra magnitude for pictures; without frames, photos seem to go on and on.

Balance and Simplicity Help Create Order

Probably the most important contributor to order in magazine design is balance, the feeling of equipoise that results from a relatively equal distribution of weights with respect to the optical center of a design area.

Symmetrical design is readily recognized, easy to obtain, and widely used for single pages or two-page spreads in magazines. Most commonly, symmetry is created by so placing a dominant illustration that it encompasses and rests on the optical center; the caption, title, and text that complete the page are also centered, thus assuring the perfect balance (Figure 9-7).

Figure 9-7. *Symmetrical balance can be achieved by having the illustration and title centered on the vertical axis.* (Courtesy Long Lines *Magazine, AT&T Long Lines Department*)

Placing duplicate weights on each side of the vertical axis will also achieve symmetry (Figure 9-8); in magazines, however, there is usually a strong element that is centered on the axis.

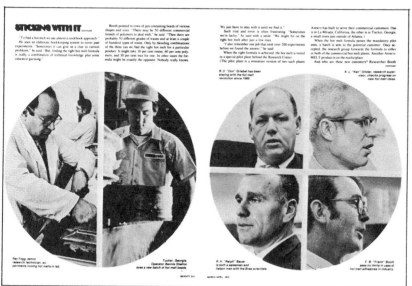

Figure 9-8. *Symmetrical balance can also be achieved by placing like elements on both sides of the axis.* (Courtesy Union Oil Company of California, Seventy Six *Magazine*)

Principles of Magazine Layout 185

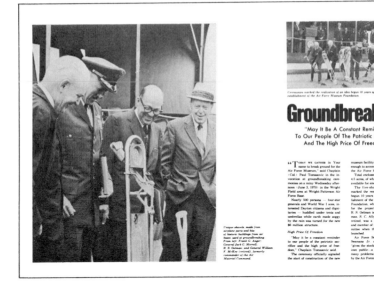

Figure 9-9. *Informal balance can be created by placing lighter elements farther from the fulcrum and larger elements closer to it. (Courtesy NCR World)*

For informal balance, weights are distributed at various distances from the vertical axis, with the lighter elements being put farther from the fulcrum in order to balance the heavier weights that are closer (Figure 9-9). Remember that weight comes from shape and tone as well as size.

For magazines, a page-to-page balance for spreads is also important. Readers, as they view a magazine, are almost always seeing two pages together. Except when they look at the front or back cover, the magazine is opened so that the eye can scan the two pages spread before them. These two pages thus form a design unit. Weights should be so distributed that balance exists between the two pages as well as on them (Figure 9-10). Also, the white space in the spread should be so assigned that the two pages hold together; the combined space of the two gutter margins must be overcome with any device that is available. Techniques for binding two facing pages into one design will be discussed later.

The handmaiden for balance in achieving the order in design that is so vital to communication is simplicity. We have long known from readability studies that simplicity in verbal language is essential for efficient communication; the same is true for visual presentation. Simple, straightforward visual syntax is important for magazines because of the conceptual nature of most magazine content.

Of first importance in visual syntax is a starting point that dominates all other components of the page or spread. In Figure 9-11 a large photo has been used for this purpose; the reader can be ex-

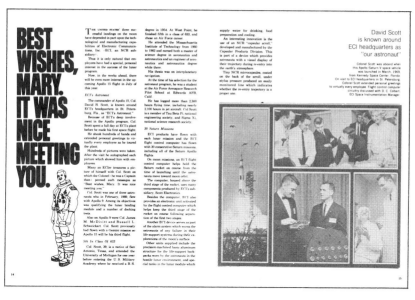

Figure 9-10. *Two-page spreads should be so designed that there is a feeling of equilibrium present, even if balance is not obvious. (Courtesy* NCR World*)*

Figure 9-11. *A large photo has been used here in the upper left of the spread to give the reader a strong visual starting point. (Courtesy* Monsanto Magazine*)*

pected to start there and then move to the title and the text. Pages with two or more equally prominent elements can create confusion because the reader may be misled into starting at a point in the design that would be equivalent to the middle of a sentence.

Figure 9-12. *An initial letter can help readers to find a starting place in a layout. (Courtesy* Long Lines *Magazine, AT&T Long Lines Department)*

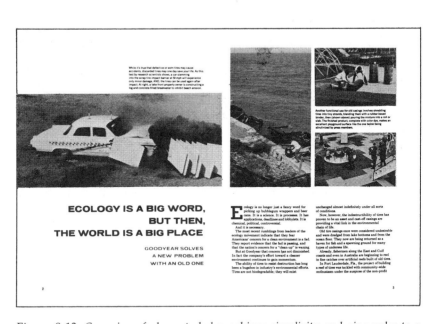

Figure 9-13. *Grouping of elements helps achieve simplicity and give order to a layout. (Courtesy of the Goodyear Tire & Rubber Company)*

Special care should be taken to be certain that a reader knows where the text of an article begins on a magazine page. One common typographical device for accomplishing this goal is the large initial letter, as shown in Figure 9-12. In the earliest days of printing, long before modern communication research, the value of special initial letters was realized, and they have not lost their value. Many magazine designers also have learned the value of what we might call an "end-of-design" graphic period. They place check marks, logotypes, star dashes, or some other typographical dingbat at the end of the text of an article. These dingbats emphasize the end of a magazine article just as the period signifies the end of a sentence. Otherwise readers may be inclined to turn a page or move to a facing page, falsely expecting the continuation of an article.

GROUPING, GRIDDING, AND ALIGNMENT

Simplicity becomes increasingly difficult to accomplish as the number of elements to be placed on a page is increased. This problem is solved primarily through the grouping of related elements. Note in Figure 9-13 how design elements, especially photos, are grouped to achieve simplicity. Note, too, how captions are handled to be essentially part of the photos they accompany. Captions, if placed too far from their photos, become design elements in and of themselves and can contribute to clutter and disorder. The same thing can be said about subtitles; they ought to be close to and part of their main title.

Another way to bring order to magazine pages in spite of the large number of elements to be displayed is by the grid method. In the grid method, the page is first divided into equal basic segments, halves, thirds, or quarters. Each segment is further divided into equal squares (Figure 9-14). Titles, photos, and copy are then forced to conform to these squares, or multiples of the squares. The rigidity of the grid system forces order and at least a relative simplicity to what otherwise might be chaotic pages.

The grid system requires careful preliminary planning and extreme accuracy in copy fitting and photo cropping because if elements slop over any of the grid divisions the orderliness is lost. Figures 9-15 to 9-18 show magazine pages that are in a grid pattern.

Alignment, which is a characteristic of gridding, is also helpful in creating order on magazine pages. Elements should be aligned as they are grouped so that the number of directions, as well as the number of elements involved on a page, is kept to a minimum. Analyze the accompanying illustrations to note how photos are aligned with each other and with titles; how lines of titles are aligned

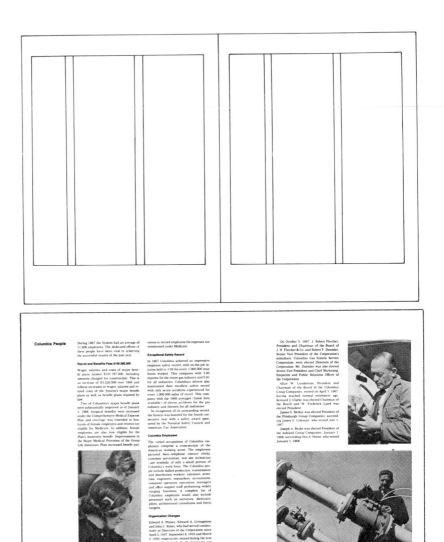

Figure 9-14. *The grid method calls for the division of a page into rectangles, which then serve as guidelines for the placement of elements on a page.*

with each other; how captions are aligned with the edges of photos or the edges of a column of type. Alignment of an element within a photo is even considered by skillful designers (Figure 9-19).

Before a beginner places any element on a magazine page he should ask himself, "What should this line up with?" because the odds are that it should be in alignment with at least one other element.

Figure 9-15. *Gridding can produce effective page designs when there are several elements to be used, above left.*

Figure 9-16. *With only title and text to place, the grid system can still produce a good effect, above right.*

Figure 9-17. *Another result of gridding, left. (Figures 9-15, 9-16, 9-17* copyright *Better Homes and Gardens. Reprinted with permission)*

Controlling Direction

Once a reader has been directed to a starting point, he must be guided through the remainder of a magazine article until he has received the entire message. This guidance involves the use and placement of elements that create visual motion in desired directions. As pointed out in Chapter 8, this eye movement comes from

Principles of Magazine Layout   191

New Discoveries
In Sumatra

Exploring for new reserves takes oilmen deep into the sweltering jungles of Sumatra. In the relatively cool shelter of a tent, a CPI seismic crew adjusts its sensitive instruments (facing page) while other members of the team slog through the jungle to find the site of the next test shot. Top to bottom: left, workers and their families live in modern housing and enjoy a swim in the club pool at the Duri field; an oilman digs into a plentiful meal at a remote jungle location; trees are felled to use as foot bridges to cross swampy areas. The aerial view (above) shows a typical Sumatran riverside village. The red section of the map (top, right) indicates the area where P. T. Caltex Pacific Indonesia (CPI) has production; a helicopter (above, right) moves a portable housing unit for a drilling crew to a new jungle location.

Continued on Page 4

Figure 9-18. *Gridding produces a semblance of Mondrian design. (Courtesy* Texaco Star)

Figure 9-19. *Note in this example that the designer has carried alignment to the extent that the caption is aligned with an element in the photo. (Courtesy* Texaco Star)

reader habits but it can also be directed by lines, both implicit and explicit.

With horizontal flow generally preferred to vertical, magazines have an advantage because of their two-page spreads. The proportion of the 17-by-11-inch area formed by two facing pages of the standard magazine format is ideal for the display of visual material. In order to get linkage between the two pages, however, the vertical gutter formed by the two interior margins must be overcome. An obvious line, created by a series of dots or an uninterrupted line, either full-tone or shaded, can produce horizontal movement between pages very easily (Figure 9-20).

Figure 9-20. *Horizontal alignment and eye movement can be obtained with an obvious line. (Courtesy* The Trading Post, *Timken Roller Bearing Company)*

Photographs that have been grouped to form a horizontal line can also give horizontal direction (Figure 9-21). A regularity in the placement of illustrations can produce a sense of rhythm as well as directional movement (Figure 9-22).

Pages or spreads must always be designed with the realization that Americans have been doing their reading in a left-to-right fashion since the first day their first-grade teacher unveiled the magic of reading to them. The visual syntax must take this custom into account, and the starting point should ordinarily be in the upper left. Other elements should follow movement to the right and/or down. In most of the illustrations in this chapter, it can be noted that the starting point is in the upper left and normal reader eye movement is followed from that point.

Deviations from that pattern should be looked upon in much the same fashion as a writer looks upon incomplete sentences and other grammatical variations from the norm: they should be used only for desired special effects, and they should make the overall communication more efficient.

Figure 9-21. *Linear placement of illustrations or other elements can achieve the same effect as a line. (Reprinted from DuPont* Context, *published by the DuPont Company)*

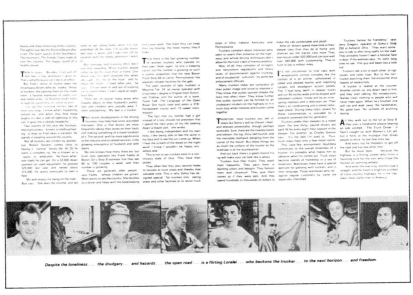

Figure 9-22. *A regularity of placement of layout elements in some instances can seem to create a rhythmic pattern. (Courtesy The Sohioan)*

194   *Design: Combining the Verbal and Visual Elements*

Controlling Contrast to Achieve Harmony and Unity

To give the reader a starting point on a magazine page, we make one element stand out from all others and place it in a reasonable location, usually upper left. To get the reader to move along at the end of the message, we provide other "stand out" elements at intervals. In these and other instances we are employing *contrast* to get our communication job done.

Contrast, as explained in Chapter 8, comes from differences: differences in size, shape, tone, or direction. Contrast is essential in magazine layout as it is for all layout because contrast makes each element discernible as an individual entity. Contrast can, however, be overdone. Too many elements shrieking for attention prevent or delay the reader's getting meaning from a message. All shrieks and no whispers can obviously mean that nothing will be heard. And, in the final analysis, it is hoped that each magazine article will be related in a single voice, not a multitude of shouts.

Therefore, contrast must be controlled. On each spread or page it must be controlled so that the overall message will be communicated in harmony and with unity.

Harmony results from controlled contrast; it comes from using types and other elements that are different enough to be seen but similar enough to blend well with each other. It also comes from the selection of visual elements that are in keeping with the subject or readers of the message that is being communicated.

With regard to magazines, harmony between the subject and its presentation is of primary importance. Considerable effort is invested in trying to have title type and design reflect an article's subject. Figure 9-23 shows how type selection and basic page design can reflect an article's content.

Once a design mood is set for an article on its opening page, it should carry that mood through to its conclusion. A six-page article that starts out with old-fashioned type dress and 1890 layout style should carry that dress and style throughout all six pages.

It is not necessary, however, for any magazine to carry the same typographical or design mood from cover to cover. There should be some standardization throughout all its pages, but each article can take on its own personality, especially in a magazine that is trying to present highly varied content. The two parts of Figure 9-24 are from the same magazine; each spread is in harmony with its subject, and they differ from each other quite substantially.

Figure 9-23. *Type selection and page design can reflect the content of an article.* (*Both above courtesy* House Beautiful, *copyright 1972, 1973, The Hearst Corporation; below courtesy* Long Lines *Magazine, AT&T, Long Lines Department*)

Figure 9-24. *Both these spreads are from the same magazine; they are quite different, however, because they were designed to be appropriate to their subject matter, not to each other. (Courtesy* Gulf Orange Disc)

197

A Word About Special Pages and Problem Pages

Front covers and table-of-contents pages require special layout attention — covers because they are so important; contents pages because they tend to be dull and uninspiring.

THE FRONT COVER

A magazine's front cover is like a store's front display window, a building's entrance, an automobile's exterior styling. It should encourage attention and create the desire to go inside.

The functions suggested by these comparisons are vital, and there is the additional need for the instant identification of the magazine from its competitors and of its issue, as distinct from its previous issues.

Covers consist of type display alone or of type and illustration combined. The latter is employed most frequently today. The principal identifying characteristic is usually a distinctive name plate, but design or color or both may be used for the same purpose. A name plate must be unique and large enough to merit quick recognition. Design, as an aid to recognition, should be flexible so that nec-

Figure 9-25. *Magazine covers vary widely in design and approach; some are all type, some emphasize a drawing, and others are photographic.*

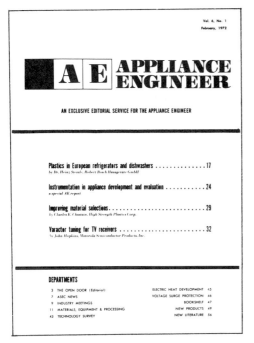

essary variations in the shapes of illustrations can be accommodated from issue to issue. Cover illustrations selected from the interior content can entice a reader into the magazine, but type is needed as well to direct the reader to specific articles inside. Reference to page numbers is an added lure.

Issues may be set apart from each other by changes in color, design, and the use of volume and issue numbers. No cover is complete without the latter, of course, but such information is usually so subordinate that instant issue identification must be aided in other ways.

Because some magazines sell their front covers to advertisers at a premium price, the editorial department is compelled to create covers so valuable in maintaining readership that the business office will not appropriate this vital part of a magazine to add to income. This pressure, plus the cover's important functions, makes cover designing especially important.

THE CONTENTS PAGE

Any magazine large enough for the reader to have logical difficulty in locating material should have a table of contents. Its information may consume only a portion of a page but must have sufficient display to be found instantly, which usually necessitates placement well forward in the magazine.

Paid-circulation magazines using second-class mail distribution are required to include certain basic information regarding entry as second-class matter, office of publication, and so on, somewhere within the first five pages. Since such masthead data is commonly on the table-of-contents page, the position of the latter is more or less predetermined.

The combination of masthead information and a long list of titles can mean a dull page. Therefore, many magazines now (1) make an effort to use illustrations on the page, (2) give special typographical display to some listings in the contents, and (3) bury the mailing and masthead information where it can be found when necessary but where it does not represent a major element on the page.

Small photographs, taken from important articles in the issue and used adjacent to the listing in the contents table, can help spruce up the layout and point the significant features.

Checks, bullets, and other typographical dingbats can be used (perhaps in color) to give variety to the listing of titles and tempt the eye. Whatever the device, monotony caused by a long list of items equal in display should be avoided.

Special display should be reserved for what is new in each issue; material that appears regularly, such as mailing information and titles of content departments, should not be emphasized.

PROBLEM PAGES

Advertising on split or fractional pages creates layout difficulty for magazines as well as for newspapers. These pages are not a serious problem if their editorial portions are treated as separate design areas. They can be made attractive and functional by realizing that their shapes may be quite different from the ordinary page shape.

The extreme vertical often left after ads have been placed cannot be laid out like a two-page spread, but its dimensions can be exploited. Titles, illustrations, or other layout elements must simply be made to conform to the area. Two facing verticals can be brought together in the center of a spread by ads located on the outsides. Or, with ads spread across the bottom, the upper portions of two pages can be linked for a horizontal layout field. In such cases, the techniques used for spreads are applicable.

Many fractional pages are used for carry-over material, but continuations are being avoided more and more. Most magazine articles can be confined to full pages up front, by adjusting the space for display (titles, and so on) to make the text fit. Fractional pages can then be used attractively for short items of various kinds that have adequate reader interest.

Figure 9-26. *Most designers do everything they can to add interest to a magazine's contents page. (Courtesy Union Oil Company of California, Seventy Six Magazine;* Friends *Magazine; B. F. Goodrich Company,* Tempo *Magazine)*

CHAPTER 10 # Newspaper Typography and Makeup

Newspaper design traditionally has been so different from all other printed literature that even a different term, "makeup," has been used to describe the process of putting together newspaper pages.

Until very recently the term "makeup" has indeed been much more accurate than design in describing the creation of newspaper pages because those pages were put together without any particular attention to the basic precepts of design or legibility; they were just "madeup" of the parts that were available. In fact, in some cases newspapers seemed to have been put together in direct contradiction to the rules of good design.

For many reasons, this situation is changing, and ever-increasing attention is being paid to legibility, functionality, and attractiveness in newspaper pages. But inherent problems in newspaper design have served to keep progress at a rather slow rate.

Problems associated with newspaper design have stemmed from many causes. The large size of a newspaper page, for example, presents an immediate design problem. A page size approximating 17 by 22 inches was not meant to be functional or inherently attractive. Add to the unwieldy size the necessity for displaying 15 to 25 items on the page, as has been newspaper custom, and you have an almost impossible design situation. The speed with which a page must be made up also has never permitted the attention to detail that good design requires. And always in the background has been the knowledge that high reader interest in news has made physical appearance much less crucial for newspapers than for magazines, advertisers, or other users of print media. Editors have known that a newspaper's main product is the news. How reliably and thoroughly it presents the news should be *the* factor by which to appraise its performance. But a newspaper's appearance is important, too. Its typography and design have become increasingly important factors in determining whether or not it can attract and hold readers.

In the preceding chapter on magazine design, we pointed out that magazines are like people in that each has its own personality, and physical appearance is an important part of that personality. Such is also the case with newspapers. Like people, whose habits of dress reveal age, background, and associates, the appearance of a newspaper also reveals these very same factors.

Some papers are more than a century old, and their typographical dress shows their age. They are likely to be more concerned with showing their conservatism and reliability than they are with projecting any personality traits. Other newspapers came into existence to fight for a particular cause or to appeal to a special class or reader, and the circumstances of their founding may still be apparent in their typography and design.

Unfortunately for the contemporary reader of some of these newspapers, the physical characteristics that are present because of tradition are not necessarily the characteristics that make for easy reading or functional design by modern standards. Small type, narrow columns, restrictive headline patterns, and other newspaper practices stemming from bygone years came into existence without deliberate planning. Like Topsy, they just grew.

Some newspapers have broken free from the restrictions of tradition and are now designed to take advantage of new knowledge and new techniques. Although these innovators are still in the minority, several factors have been at work in the 1960s and 1970s to bring about some drastic changes. These factors include:

1. The new printing technology, which permits much greater freedom of design; century-old mechanical restrictions have fallen by the wayside.
2. The changing role of the newspaper, caused, primarily, by the influence of television. Rather than chase every fire engine and include every item from a police blotter, many newspaper reporters are concentrating on depth coverage of significant events. Thus a front page that formerly contained 20 display items now may have only four or five.
3. The successful trend in newspapers to resemble magazines in content and approach — an offshoot of the newspaper's changing role.

4. Greater knowledge of human communication and information processing, which has an influence on legibility and design considerations.

These factors pressing for change are important to all future journalists as are the changes that have been resulting from the pressures. But on the other hand the majority of today's newspapers still follow traditional procedures. These procedures, firmly rooted as they are in newspaper history, must also be known and understood by all future journalists.

Let us first take a look at newspaper makeup traditions — what they are and how they came into existence. Then, in the latter part of this chapter, we can discuss current trends and analyze some case examples of newspapers that have discarded tradition in an effort to get maximum effectiveness in visual presentation.

Influence of Heritage and News Policy on Makeup

The typographic dress of the *New York Times* bespeaks the character that its news policy substantiates. Its headline patterns are holdovers from a bygone era; they tell readers that the *Times* is an institution of long standing. There is nothing in its makeup to lure the great mass of readers who are more interested in film stars than foreign policy. Instead, the balanced, dignified, and dull arrangement of material on its pages seems to say, "Here is all the news *if* you have the intellect, the sophistication, and the time to dig it out."

A comment that the makeup of the *Times* is on the dull side is actually not a significant criticism, of course. The *Times* is the *Times,* a valuable newspaper property with one of the most precious reputations in the world. And, although it may seem to be paradoxical, the *Times* can be cited as an example of the good application of at least one sound typographical principle despite its quiet mien that breaks many "rules" devised by experts in graphic communications. If there are cardinal precepts in newspaper typography, this is one: *a newspaper's appearance should appeal to its selected public and should truthfully reflect its own character.* The loyalty and support of its followers are proof of the *Times'* success in following this precept.

Other newspapers, such as the members of the Scripps-Howard group, appeal to a different audience and are quite different in character from the *Times.* Their typographic dress reflects this difference, as it should. As crusading and fighting newspapers appealing mainly to the masses, most Scripps-Howard publications use a bold and vigorous makeup featuring strong headlines.

Still other newspapers—members of the Hearst group are notable examples—use massive display that shouts their wares loudly enough to attract even the most unattentive reader. They give the impression of having so much shocking news that it is difficult to get all of it on their pages. Day in and day out they seem to be in the position of the circus master who must keep three rings going in order to squeeze all his good acts into one show.

In many cases, the direction a newspaper is taking today was determined years ago. The *Times,* for example, was founded during the era of the penny press. At that time, penny papers such as James Gordon Bennett's *Herald* were offering New Yorkers a steady story diet of murder, sex, and violence. These papers had come into existence to provide the new audience of factory workers, created by the industrial revolution, with daily newspapers at a price they could afford. Henry J. Raymond and his cofounders of the *Times* recognized another need of these new newspaper readers for a daily publication higher in tone but at the same low cost. Thus the *Times* was founded with the definite intent of drawing discriminating readers away from other penny papers. Later in its history, when it was on the verge of bankruptcy, the *Times* was given the motto "All the news that's fit to print" by Adolph S. Ochs and was rededicated to its philosophy of appealing to a select group of readers.

E. W. Scripps set off on his own in 1878 to start his first newspaper of typical penny-press character but with special emphasis on bold crusades to improve the status of the mass factory laborers. In the first issue of that paper, the *Penny Press* (now the *Cleveland Press and News*), he set the tone that has been characteristic of most subsequent Scripps-Howard papers.

The Hearst newspapers still show the effects of their roots in the yellow journalism days of newspaper history. In the 1890s, William Randolph Hearst led his *New York Journal* and other papers into a raucous journalism that flourished on sensational news announced by sensational typographical display.

Kinds of Headlines and Their Importance

Headlines are perhaps the greatest outward manifestation of a newspaper's personality. They are its most striking facial characteristic and have several jobs to do in addition to contributing to a newspaper's personality. They help sell newspapers, index the news, grade stories according to importance, summarize the news for hasty readers, and help to make the paper more attractive.

The first newspapers in the United States used no headlines because there was no need for them. Colonists lucky enough to get a newspaper could be expected to read all of it without the salesmanship urging of display type. Newspapers were extremely small, and readers had a built-in interest in everything that could be put on their pages.

As newspapers grew in size, it became apparent that readers needed some help in selecting which portions to read and in getting the gist of stories quickly. Headlines then became fixtures. The physical appearance of these early headlines followed no scientific plan; they were created without any real thought about their appearance. These, for want of a better term, are called "traditional patterns" in this text.

TRADITIONAL HEADLINE PATTERNS

There are four basic traditional headline patterns: (1) *bar line;* (2) *inverted pyramid;* (3) *hanging indention;* and (4) *step lines* (sometimes called *drop lines*).

The first typographical pattern for headlines was the *bar line* (Figure 10-1), a single line of type centered over the story. To tell more of the story in a headline, several bar lines separated by dashes were used.

As the editor-printers of pre-Civil War days set bar lines, they often found that what they wanted to say would not fit into a single line. In these instances, they usually carried over the extra word or two to a second line and centered that line under the first, thus creating an *inverted pyramid* (Figure 10-2).

The Civil War gave editors news of unusual importance, and the subsequent need for greater headline display. Using the two headline patterns known to them, they gave more display to big stories by adding more decks to the headlines. Bar lines and inverted pyramids were usually alternated as the headlines were constructed.

The *hanging indention* joined the other headline forms during the latter part of the Civil War and took its place in the multideck headlines prevalent at the time. It is composed of a top line flush to both sides, and usually two additional lines uniformly indented from the left (Figure 10-3). Like the inverted pyramid, it is seldom used today except as a subordinate deck.

For years the bar line merited undisputed claim to the top spot in headlines. Perhaps a few more bar lines were mixed with inverted pyramids and hanging indentions as the headline progressed down

RULING IS 6 TO 1

Figure 10-1. *Bar line.*

The Proceedings
In Washington

Figure 10-2. *Inverted pyramid.*

Producers Schedule 570,000
Assemblies; June Activity
Up 1% Despite Ford Strike

Figure 10-3. *Hanging indention.*

the column, but the top deck was always a single bar line. In this position, it was given the greatest display—the largest type size. Consequently, it was impossible to get more than one or two words in the top deck, making it a mere label that told little about its story.

The desire to tell more in the top deck resulted in the introduction of the *step line* in the late 1800s. By adding a second line set flush to the right and moving the top line flush to the left, editors created a new pattern that quickly became popular (Figure 10-4). It gave editors a neat, orderly arrangement and enabled them to get more information into the top deck. The step line is still used by both newspapers that have redesigned their makeup in recent years and by papers retaining their traditional appearance.

Wall St. Hails
Action by U.S.

Figure 10-4. *Step line (drop line).*

In order to show some grading of the news on their pages, editors in the early years of headlines had no choice but to add more decks to stories of importance. These were the days of the Hoe type-revolving machine, a rotary press that depended on wedge-shaped column rules to hold the pieces of type in place on a rotating cylinder. It was impossible to break across columns without having type fly everywhere as the cylinder rotated.

This problem was solved with the introduction of curved stereotype plates by Charles Craske at the New York *Herald* in 1854, but multicolumn headlines did not become common until the heyday of yellow journalism.

NEWER HEADLINE PATTERNS

When William Randolph Hearst and Joseph Pulitzer engaged in their monumental struggle for circulation during the Spanish-American War, typographical display took on a new significance for newspapers. Street sales, on a cash-per-copy basis, had grown in importance since the method's introduction by the penny papers several years earlier, and it did not take long for publishers to realize that headlines sold newspapers.

As direct salesmen, headlines received more attention in newspaper offices and greater size in each day's issue. *Banner* lines (headlines spreading across every column of a page) became common. Many banners during the Spanish-American War were two-line step lines.

Although newspaper make-up became more conservative and restrained again after the war, the use of headlines spreading over more than one column had become an accepted practice. Some papers preferred the vertical impression created by single-column heads of several decks, but even these put spread headlines over particularly important stories.

During World War I, editors again made extensive use of banner lines because of the extraordinary importance of the news resulting from the conflict. They became so much a fixture for many papers that after the war some papers continued to use a banner on page one regardless of the news value of the day's top story.

The banner line is, of course, simply a bar line that extends over all the columns on the page. In that sense it is a traditional pattern adapted to modern needs. There are some typographical patterns of relatively recent vintage, devised for two reasons: (1) to make headline writing easier, and (2) to put more white space around headlines so that each will have better contrast and readability.

The basic form for these newer healines is *flush left*. All lines are started at the extreme left side of a column, and substantial variation in line length is tolerated (see Figure 10-5). Flush-left headlines are easier to write because of the greater variation permitted in line length and because each line has the potential of going to the full column measure. Drop lines, in order to allow room for the step, must always be shorter than full measure.

A common variation of the flush-left headline is the *square indention,* often called *modified flush left* (Figure 10-6). Instead of starting at the extreme left side, all lines are indented uniformly.

Charter Suit Asks State Redistricting

Figure 10-5. *Flush left.*

Representation Called Unfair And Unequal

Figure 10-6. *Modified flush left.*

To get more white space around headlines, many newspapers use a short line above the main deck of flush-left or square-indention head-lines. The line is usually in smaller type, may be flush to the left or centered (Figure 10-7), and is usually underlined with a thin rule. This headline form goes by many names, including "astonisher" and "kicker."

Estes Investigation Continues
New Witnesses Found

Figure 10-7. *Kicker headline.*

SOME SPECIAL HEADLINE USES

When portions of stories are carried over (*jumped*) to other pages, headlines must be placed over the continued portion of the story.

These are called *jump heads*. They may take any typographic form as long as they are in harmony with headlines throughout the rest of the paper. Jump heads were originally scaled-down versions of the headline at the top of the story, but most newspapers have simplified them as much as possible. Figure 10-8 shows some representative jump heads.

U. S. Seeking Information On Steel Men

Continued from First Page

Department is not at liberty to disclose them."

JET CRASH

Continued from Second Page

the eve of an air show to celebrate the introduction of a

MINISTERS' TALKS ON BERLIN HINTED

Continued From Page 1, Col. 1

standing of United States attitudes on iseaes conncected with the European economic and political union that is expected to

Feud

(Continued from page one)

approximately existing levels. But this provided no money for planned new undertakings — the labor retraining program,

Figure 10-8. *Some representative jump heads.*

A *folo head* is used over a story related to a main story above it. A national weather round up, for example, may be followed by one or two items giving details about regional weather. Some newspapers use rules to set off their folo heads.

Boxed heads take several forms (Figure 10-9) and are used to give special display for small stories. They provide effective contrast when they are placed between two headlines of larger type size.

Editors like special headlines to signal a feature or humorous story. Italic type formerly did well at this but has been used so generally for all types of news that it no longer serves. Headline arrangements employing double kickers, stars, asterisks, and other decorative devices, now perform as *feature heads*.

Standing heads appear in issue after issue over columns, departments, or other regularly repeated features of a newspaper. Many newspapers use both a standing head and a working head for this purpose. The standing head identifies the feature, while the working head is supposed to attract readers to that day's output. It is common for the standing head to be of the kicker variety (Figure 10-10).

Who's News

Management—
Personnel Notes
* * *

* * *

dent engineering, of Formica Corp., a sub-

Jet Helicopters Slice Travel Time Between New York, Airports
* * *

They Cut Local-Service Line's Cost; New York-Philadelphia 35-Minute Service Planned

Dividend News

G.C. Murphy Proposes 100% Stock Dividend; Plans Rise in Payments

Figure 10-9. *Typical boxed heads.*

DEAR ABBY

An Extra Burden on Mailman

BY ABIGAIL VAN BUREN

DEAR ABBY: When our
Joh⌐   ⌐me h⌐

TV REVIEW

A Test of Faith in 'Jacob and Joseph'

BY KEVIN THOMAS
Times Staff Writer

"The Story of Jacob and
Joseph," appropriately air-
ing (Palm Su⌐⌐⌐⌐) at 8:30

'THE STORY OF
⌐R AND J⌐⌐

The Gallup Poll

Public Opinion Closely Split On Abortion in 1st 3 Months

By George Gallup

PRINCETON, N.J. — The
·blic is clos⌐l⌐   ⌐ded—
⌐4

hibiting and restricting a
woman's right to obtain an
abortion during her first
three ⌐   ⌐ pregnancy

survey, by key demogra⌐⌐
breakdowns:

Figure 10-10. *Standing heads can be used as kickers for working heads.*

HEADLINE SCHEDULES

Headline schedules (*hed skeds*) are a collection of all the headlines to be used by a particular newspaper. They are relatively inflexible, although on some papers editors are permitted to concoct an occasional special headline. A headline schedule gives a newspaper continuity of character; readers can recognize their paper day to day by the uniformity of the appearance of headline display issue to issue. The hed sked also saves time on the copy desk and in the composing room.

A well-planned schedule provides headlines for every purpose. Banner lines, *top* heads (headlines for the top of columns), secondary, spread, folo, feature, and departmental (sports, society, and so on) headlines are specified. From the schedule, headline writers can find for each headline the number of decks, the unit count for each line, the number of lines, the style and size of type, and any special typographic treatment. Rather than spell out each characteristic, the writer can simply mark his copy with a number, letter, or other symbol to identify it for the composing room. A "#1" label, for example, may tell the composing room that the headline is flush left, capitals and lower case, with a top deck of three lines, 36-point Erbar, and a second deck of two lines, 24-point Erbar indented one em.

HEADLINE CAPITALIZATION AND PUNCTUATION

Uniform capitalization and punctuation are as essential for headlines as they are for the text material of a newspaper. The headline schedule, the style sheet, or both should set the rules to follow.

Of course, all-cap headlines give the writer no problem with capitalization. But when there are capitals and lower case, considerable variation occurs. Most newspapers use capital letters to begin all words in a headline; some make an exception for certain prepositions.

One of the most interesting recent developments in this regard has been the growing acceptance of standard sentence capitalization for headlines. Edmund C. Arnold, professor of journalism at Syracuse University and author of *Modern Newspaper Design*, has been a vigorous leader in the movement. In his book and in clinics he conducts throughout the country, Mr. Arnold has advocated "down-style" headlines because "They are easier to read by eyes accustomed to down-style in all our text material. They are easier to write because of the extra units saved by fewer caps" (Arnold, p. 64). His opponents argue that capitals are needed for emphasis, that their long strokes enhance readability by setting the words apart, especially when the spacing between words is tight.

Figure 10-11 shows some down-style heads. Their practicality has brought them into the same general use that the standard capital-and-lower-case headline traditionally enjoyed. The old and extensive debate of "all-caps" versus "c. & l.c." has also virtually been resolved in favor of the latter.

Council selects Taylor as temporary chairman

Stolen tombstone brings
probation to two students

Figure 10-11. *Some typical down-style headlines.*

Punctuation of headlines differs from text punctuation in these ways:

1. Periods are not used at the ends of headlines.
2. Semicolons are used instead of periods to indicate the end of a skeletonized sentence within the headline.
3. A comma is often substituted for "and."
4. Single, instead of double, quotation marks are usually used.

Other Makeup Components

In addition to headlines, there are a number of other components of newspaper makeup. Some, such as body type, name plate, ears, column width, column separators are more or less constant. Other decorative devices are called upon for special occasions. No decision on the typography or makeup of a newspaper is more important than the selection of body type, for most of what a newspaper has to say is said in the small 8- or 9-point type used for body copy. Selection should be based entirely on practical considerations. It is doubtful that any newspaper reader has ever given any real thought to the esthetic properties of a body type, but all are concerned with its legibility.

Some aspects of the mechanical production of newspapers have direct bearing on type selection. The coarseness of newsprint, the need for stereotyping by the large dailies, and the highly fluid nature of newspaper inks create special problems.

Before 1900, the most commonly used type for this purpose was a face called "Roman No. 2." It retained its popularity after the turn of the century and was joined in 1904 by Century Expanded as a widely used news body face. These served adequately until dry-mat stereotyping and faster presses became common. The increased pressure to which type was subjected by the new stereotyping method caused the fine lines of Roman No. 2 and Century Expanded to break down. With the rough newsprint traveling through presses at greater speed, ink had a tendency to fill up some areas of letters.

After extensive research and experimentation, the Mergenthaler Linotype Corporation produced a face designed especially to surmount the problems of newspaper printing. The new face, called "Ionic No. 5," immediately became popular when it was introduced in 1926. It was followed by other specially designed news-body faces: Excelsior in 1931, Opticon in 1935, and Corona in 1940. In each case, maximum attention was given to the special mechanical requirements of newspapers and the desire to get maximum viewing area with greatest space economy. These faces (and Paragon) are shown in Figure 10-12.

The Intertype Corporation has also produced efficient and popular news faces, including Ideal News, Regal, and Rex. No matter what his composing machines, the newspaper publisher has the choice of several excellent faces for body type. Photocomposing machines make available a wide range of good news faces.

Sizes of Body Type

The early newspapers in America were set in agate or 6-point type. Although some newspapers or portions of them (the classified section, for example) are still set in such small sizes, the trend has been toward the larger. Several factors have increased the pressure for the better legibility of somewhat larger sizes. Competition from other media, increasing numbers of elderly readers, and a greater realization of the physical effects of eyestrain have caused most newspapers to go to 8- and 9-point sizes. An increasing use of extra white space (leading) between lines has accompanied the movement toward larger type sizes.

The average newspaper page is set off in eight columns 22 inches long. As this standard size originally developed, so did the tendency to settle on a column width of 12 pica ems. But the rising cost of newsprint in the 1950s brought about a trend toward narrower columns. Soon 11.5 ems became commonplace, then 11 ems. Changes to narrower columns, compounded by mat shrinkage, brought on a number of problems.

There is an appealing touch of human nature in the story of this stolid English merchant, who in his fiftieth year turned aside from his prosperous undertakings to devote himself to learning and practising the new-born art of printing. Caxton was living at Bruges, so well thought of by his compatriots that he had been elected "Governor of the English Nation in the Low Countries," when, to please his pa-

IONIC NO. 5

There is an appealing touch of human nature in the story of this stolid English merchant, who in his fiftieth year turned aside from his prosperous undertakings to devote himself to learning and practising the new-born art of printing. Caxton was living at Bruges, so well thought of by his compatriots that he had been elected "Governor of the English Nation in the Low Countries," when, to please his pa-

EXCELSIOR

There is an appealing touch of human nature in the story of this stolid English merchant, who in his fiftieth year turned aside from his prosperous undertakings to devote himself to learning and practising the new-born art of printing. Caxton was living at Bruges, so well thought of by his compatriots that he had been elected "Governor of the English Nation in the Low Countries," when, to please his pa-

PARAGON

There is an appealing touch of human nature in the story of this stolid English merchant, who in his fiftieth year turned aside from his prosperous undertakings to devote himself to learning and practising the new-born art of printing. Caxton was living at Bruges, so well thought of by his compatriots that he had been elected "Governor of the English Nation in the Low Countries," when, to please his pa-

OPTICON

Figure 10-12. *Linotype's group of newspaper legibility faces. (Courtesy Mergenthaler Linotype Company)*

There is an appealing touch of human nature in the story of this stolid English merchant, who in his fiftieth year turned aside from his prosperous undertakings to devote himself to learning and practising the new-born art of printing. Caxton was living at Bruges, so well thought of by his compatriots that he had been elected "Governor of the English Nation in the Low Countries," when, to please his patroness the

CORONA

For example, national advertising often did not fit the number of columns for which it was designed. Publishers usually were forced to give away space in these instances. Some newspapers using the teletypesetting (TTS) system had to face up to the issue of making their column width coincide with that of the lines set from the perforated tape used in the system or use a particular size or set of type to accomplish the same end. For the public, however, perhaps the most important facet of the move to narrower columns was the increased difficulty in reading that resulted.

Judge Extends Air Strike Ban

NEW YORK—(/P)—A federal judge has ordered a 10-day extension of his temporary ban against a strike by Pan American World Airways' 500 flight engineers.

Daniel Kornblum, counsel to the engineers' union,, said he would seek an immediate review of U.S. Dist. Judge George Rosling's action by the U.S. Court of Appeals.

Rosling ordered the extension Tuesday 20 minutes before the expiration of his order which last Saturday ended a strike against Pan Am four hours after it started.

Rosling called counsel for Pan Am and the union back before him again today for continued argument on the airline's application for a full-fledged injunction.

Eastern Air Lines — shut down since Saturday when

Juvenile Correction Assailed

CLEVELAND—(/P)—Ohio is failing to rehabilitate its youthful offenders despite its

Figure 10-13. *A two-column lead is used to separate and give contrast to headlines.*

Varying Column Measure for Special Effect

For newspapers with the standard eight columns, some of the advantages of wider columns can be attained by varying column width, which also creates special effects. Even with teletypesetting, the width of columns can be manipulated to good advantage for locally punched tape.

Often type is set to a one-and-one-half or two-column measure on editorial or other special pages. Type size usually increases in wider columns, and the result is a pleasing and readable page.

Also common are the so-called *2-10 leads,* an effective makeup device. "Spread leads" is a more general name, but the term "2-10s" is used because they are generally set two columns wide in 10-point type. They can be carried across more than two columns and can be in a different point size. They serve well to separate headlines (see Figure 10-13) so that each gets good display.

Extending the column measure for body type also creates a horizontal flow of layout masses, a characteristic sought by many newspapers of modern design.

Column Separators

Columns are traditionally separated by a hairline rule on a body sufficiently thick to provide adequate white space on each side of the line. A 6-point body is most common. Debate persists on whether the black line created by the hairline rule is needed between columns. Many designers prefer white space to do the job. One of the interesting aspects of the debate is that the opposition calls column rules old-fashioned. However, the first newspaper in the United States used only white space. Ben Harris separated the columns of his *Publick Occurrences* with white space, and James and Ben Franklin did the same with their *New England Courant* of the early 1700s. Other early newspapers including the second newspaper in the colonies, the *Boston News-Letter,* used rules. Ample precedent for either course of action exists. As far as appearance is concerned, the question is moot; but there are some mechanical factors worth considering.

Column rules present somewhat of a problem because they must be carefully cut and mitered so that they form neat joints with other rules. The smaller papers that must reuse column rules also have a problem with nicked, bent, or blunted rules, for they can make a sloppy appearance. Many weekly papers have abandoned column rules for that reason.

Regardless of the means, column breaks must be adequate to give the reader a place to start and end his reading. Generally, one pica of space is considered the minimum without rules; with hairline rules at least a 6-point body is needed. To conserve newsprint during World War II many newspapers used less, but not with good results.

Most newspapers without column rules have found it necessary to return to rules for separating some advertisements. Borderless ads run together in confusing fashion without some means of specific demarcation. Confusion also exists for the reader unless rules and dashes cut across columns properly. There is a tendency to eliminate these devices when there are no column rules, but some layout problems cannot be solved without them. Most common are the *cut-off rules, "30" dashes,* and *jim dashes.*

As the name implies, the cut-off separates layout units in any instance where the reader might not otherwise know where to stop. A picture and cutline must be cut off from the unrelated story below it. Headlines of more than one column need cut-off rules to direct the reader into the column where the story begins.

Cut-off rules ordinarily extend to full-column measure and form a plain, light, single line. Wavy rules, oxford rules, parallel rules, and decorative devices, such as star dashes, are also used depending upon the newspaper's "layout personality." The type of rule and the extent of its use should harmonize with other makeup practices.

The "30" dash is appropriate in traditional makeup to signify the end of a story. It is usually plain, centered in the column, and long enough to be more than half but less than two thirds the column width.

The jim dash is shorter than the "30" dash and is used to separate the decks of headlines or items within stories. Both the jim and "30" dashes are being replaced by white space in newspapers of modern design. They are available in decorative forms also, but plain, light lines are most common.

THE NEWSPAPER NAME PLATE, OR FLAG

Every newspaper needs a quick means to identify itself. The *name plate,* or *flag,* performs this function. Its basic component is the name of the newspaper; its traditional position is at the top of page 1. It should not be confused with the *masthead,* the statement of ownership and other pertinent information that usually appears on the editorial page.

Because it is in a prominent position in every issue and has a specific job to do, the name plate is an important part of a newspaper's makeup. Originally they were hand set in a large size of the body-type style because that was all the printer had. Today they can be highly decorative since they are electrotypes made from type proofs or artist's drawings. Unless a paper goes through a wholesale redesigning, name plates do not change in order to maintain their primary function of immediate identification for the newspaper.

When a new name plate is being designed, these factors must be considered:

1. It should have enough display or boldness to get instant recognition.
2. It should be appropriate for the newspaper and the community it serves.

Many newspapers use Text (Black Letter) for name plates. Its boldness and its impression of reliability stemming from its traditional association with religious printing are desirable characteristics.

Figure 10-14 shows some typical name plates. Note that some have *ears* (display elements at the sides of the name plate). Ears can draw readers' attention to inside features, give weather news at a

Figure 10-14. *Some typical nameplates with and without ears.*

glance, state price for newsstand sales, and so on, but many newspapers have dropped them.

Name plates formerly extended fully across the top of the page, but that practice is no longer followed by many newspapers. Smaller name plates, some only two columns wide, are now common. Their chief advantage is that they can be moved to different positions to permit greater variety in top-of-the-page display. Many newspapers have name plates in several widths for maximum flexibility. Whether a paper retains its name plate in traditional width and position depends upon its willingness to adopt this and other modern changes designed to make design more functional.

Small newspapers often use an electrotype until it is so worn that the name plate is no longer sharp and crisp. Duplicate electros should be kept on hand so that replacements can be made before wear is noticeable. Another fault is the undue separation of the elements of the name plate (name, ears, slogans, datelines) so that each stands apart instead of in one unit. The result is a distracting busyness.

Photographs and illustrations are more important to newspapers today than ever before; in all likelihood this emphasis will continue. Types of illustrations and plates have been discussed in earlier chapters. There are a few other typographic devices available to makeup editors that need attention. Some are merely decorative, others have more specific functions. In general, they complement photographs and headlines by adding tone variations to a newspaper page.

Subheads, special *paragraph beginnings,* occasional *boldface paragraphs, boxes* and *simulated boxes, thumbnail* cuts, large *initial* letters, and numerous types of *dingbats* (stars, asterisks, and the like) can add spice to dull layout areas. Some of these are shown in operation in Figures 10-15 and 10-16. Occasional boldface paragraphs add a touch of life to long gray columns of type. These paragraphs are often also indented to make them stand out still more. Many newspapers have stopped using boldface paragraphs recently, primarily because of production problems they create.

Boxes can break the gray tone while displaying small interesting items that might otherwise be lost among stories of greater length. A true box is ruled on all sides, but seen more today are boxes simulated by rules at top and bottom only. The text is usually indented for boxes; if side rules are used, the indention is necessary to allow space.

Photographs and line drawings of half-column width occasionally provide a spot of boldness in columns. These *thumbnails,* as they are called, present a problem because type must be specially set to run around them. Their most frequent use is to present a likeness of the author of a column.

Behind the Flood Wall

Harold Martin, machinist in The Times composing room and oldest printer in terms of service, was

mission. He charged he had been turned down on racial grounds.

MANY DELAYS

After many delays, the case was tried on its merits last Jan-

what the employees believe."

Missouri 'Climate' Changed

John R. Thompson, executive vice-president of the Missouri State Chamber of Commerce,

IT'S surprising to see Williams inconclusive and hesitant where always he has been certain and direct, no matter

Figure 10-15. *Cut-in, flush left, and centered subheads and boldface paragraph beginnings are used to brighten gray areas.*

Vet's Book On 'Patients' Entertains

PARK AVENUE VET, by Louis J. Camuti and Lloyd Alexander; Holt, Rinehart and Winston, 184 pp., $4.

WHOLLY CATS, by Faith McNulty and Elisabeth Keiffer; Bobbs-Merrill, 208 pp., $3.50.

By WALTER B. GREENWOOD

CENSUS FIGURES on the matter are unreliable, but there is general agreement that in the last decade the cat has become the most popular of household pets. Remarkably independent and adaptable, they adjust better to the teeming uncertainties of urban life.

Novel Loss Was Gain

From Famous Fables, by E. F. Edgar

SHORTLY after he took up writing as a career, Sir Arthur Conan Doyle dashed off a novel and mailed it to a publisher. The amateurish effort was lost en route and never was recovered.

Years later, when he was an established author, Doyle was asked how he felt about the loss.

"Are you still worried by the thought that it will never be found?"

"No," replied Doyle, "I am worried that it might be."

Humor Lost When Novel Is Too Long

LEARNER'S PERMIT, by Laurence Lafore; Doubleday, 308 pp., $4.50.

LAURENCE LAFORE, a professor of history at Swarthmore College, has a good joke going in "Learner's Permit" but he suffers from interminabilia, a disease invented for the express purpose of classifying people who don't know when to stop.

The scene is Parthenon College in Acropolis, N. Y. This college doesn't

ning or a new series of atmospheric tests.

The new flurry of activity at this desert proving ground coincided with the recent

---

A mighty underground blast—most powerful set off in the United States and the first announced use here of an H-bomb type device—shattered the desert calm today.

---

resumption of testing in the Pacific and with announcement of plans to lob a dum-

counties, cities, and city school districts thereof." Another statute designates the Personnel Board of Review as the agency to enforce civil service.

So it is hard to see how the board has any choice but to investigate the union's charges and, if it finds them true, to order the cities to comply with the law.

Some politicians of the old school still prefer the patronage setup that was common in Ohio before 1912, but

Figure 10-16. *Boxes, large initial letters, half-column cuts, and boldface paragraphs are also used as page brighteners.*

Available dingbats are so numerous that they cannot all be described here. There are stars, asterisks, bullets (like large periods), squares, diamonds, and many special designs. Dingbats in the form of dashes act as paragraph separators; singly, they often serve as spots to draw attention to items in tabulated matter.

Large initial letters begin a major segment of copy in many books and magazines, but are also found on some editorial or other special newspaper pages. They may be either *set in* so that the top of the initial lines up with the top of the body matter or they may be permitted to rise above the text. The latter method is used more in newspapers, because it poses no lining-up problems.

Makeup: Putting the Parts Together in an Attractive Package

The student, armed with a knowledge of the components of makeup, is ready to put the parts together in attractive, functional page units. As was said at the beginning of this chapter, physical appearance is extremely important to a newspaper. Makeup is the art of creating the desired appearance for a newspaper; it conveys a certain personality that in turn directly affects the makeup practices a paper will follow. All editors, therefore, work within certain limitations as they design each day's pages. By so doing they give continuity to their newspaper's appearance.

Makeup has other functions. First and foremost, it should help the reader get the maximum amount of information in the shortest possible time. It should grade the news — let the reader know which stories are most important and least important, which are serious and which are light in nature. It should help him move easily from one item to another and provide quick and handy summaries of the news at a glance.

In theory, it seems necessary to put various front-page layouts into specific categories; whether this is done in practice is questionable, to say the least. Although a few makeup men may have definite patterns in mind as they decide a front-page format, most of them approach their task with only two objectives: *function* and *attractive design*. Seldom do their pages meet the specifications of any prescribed category.

Each front page is, and should be, somewhat different from that of any other day because its news is somewhat different. When the makeup editor is doing his job well, his page design naturally evolves through the sound application of basic design principles and without regard for stereotyped patterns. How he does this is explained in the following paragraphs. Specific categorizing is purposely kept incidental, rather than primary, to the discussion.

PREPARATION OF A DUMMY

Like a pattern for the dressmaker, a *dummy* is the first step for the makeup man. In its preparation, he assigns a page position to each story and illustration. A copy schedule supplies all the information he needs. It is an inventory of the day's news and identifies each story, describes each headline, gives the length of each item, and lists each piece of art (photograph or illustration). To a degree, the news has already been evaluated by copyreaders who have weighed the importance of items and assigned headlines accordingly. A few of the stories competing for top ranking are sometimes without head-lines and page position awaiting last-minute developments to deter-mine placement.

Main Focal Point on Front Page

The makeup man's first job is to decide which story is to get "top play." He then dummies in his main story in the front-page focal point – the upper-right corner. The importance of this position is traditional, based upon the usage of banner headlines. It is logical for the reader to trace a banner from column one to column eight and follow the story down column eight. The key position for inside pages is the same as that for all other printed designs – the upper left. It is covered in detail later in the text.

On the front page, the upper left is usually considered the place for the number two (second-in-importance) story. From that point on, stories are placed according to their worth as indicated by the headlines assigned to them. A rule of long standing is that large heads go high on the page. In other words, the largest single-column headline is used higher on the page than other single-column heads; the largest two-column headline is higher than all other two-column heads, and so on. Boxes, because they are treated as illustrations, are used contrary to this rule, as are some feature heads that stand out because of special typographic dress.

To Jump or Not to Jump

As main stories are put into position, the makeup man must decide how much of each story is to run on page 1 and how much, if any, is to be jumped to another page.

Most newspapers have a basic policy regarding jump stories. Some insist that all front-page stories be complete (see Figure 10-17), some merely try to keep jumps to a minimum, and others insist that most major stories carry over to provide complete coverage. It is agreed that the "no-jump" front page is an ideal worth seeking because readership loss comes with any carry over.

CREATING AN ATTRACTIVE DESIGN

On some newspapers, the makeup man dummies in only a few of the day's main stories. The remaining spots are filled while he directs the

Figure 10-17. *A no-jump front page. (Courtesy* Cincinnati Post)

forming of the page on the stone. Generally speaking, makeup is improved with thorough dummying.

After the main stories are in position, the other items are arranged on the page according to the dictates of good design. For a newspaper page, these are basically the same as they are for any other printed matter: *contrast, balance, harmony, unity,* and *motion.*

HOW TO ACHIEVE DESIRABLE CONTRAST

Contrast comes from opposites: light and dark, large and small, tall and short, fat and thin, straight and crooked. It is the element that makes graphic communication possible: contrast between lightness and darkness makes type and illustrations visible.

Because we start with a field of white, it is easy to fall into the trap of thinking that contrast automatically comes from dropping large dark areas onto this field. It is true that the first of these will give maximum contrast, but what happens with consecutive additions? Contrast is steadily reduced, of course.

Contrast Among Headlines

With this in mind, two rules of contrast apply to headlines.

1. *Headlines should be separated by white space, gray matter, or illustrations.* Some newspaper makeup men put teeth into this rule by insisting that two headlines never be placed together on a page. There are a number of ways to separate them. Spread leads provide gray matter between spread headlines and the headlines of stories below, as shown in Figure 10-13. Photographs, illustrations, and boxes serve likewise. Most makeup men, by the way, treat boxes as if they were illustrations because they perform the same functions in layout.

Separation of headlines on a horizontal plane is especially important. If two headlines of like size and style are next to each other horizontally, they form a so-called *tombstone.* As can be seen in Figure 10-18, tombstones reduce the contrast for each headline so much that the reader can be tricked into reading the two headlines as one. Obviously these should be avoided.

2. *If headlines must be together, they must be individually distinctive so as to retain some contrast.* Their difference can be in type size, type style, or the typographical pattern of the headline.

Two spread heads in large type can be separated by a single-column head in smaller type. An italic head may be placed next to a roman, or a lightface next to a boldface. Boxed heads or feature heads can stand out from adjacent heads by white space and size-difference. Spread heads with a broad horizontal sweep are distinct

GUIDO EXPECTED | U.S. SPACECRAFT
TO VOID PERONIST | FIRED AT MOON;
ELECTION GAINS | 229,541 MILES,
IN ARGENTINA | 60 HOURS AWAY

Navy Decides to Back	10-Story Rocket Takes
Army in Pressuring	750-Pound Ranger IV
President — Military	Aloft, With Televi-
Leaders at Midnight	sion and Scientific
Conferences.	Apparatus.

Figure 10-18. *A tombstone.*

from single-column heads in a vertical shape, but again difference in type size or style helps (Figure 10-19).

Contrast in Body Areas

The practice of changing the line measure for editorials is a good example of contrast in body areas. With lines in single-column measure on the rest of the page, editorials two columns wide get special visual attention.

Change of measure for contrast is not restricted to the editorial page, of course. Front-page feature stories and major interpretive efforts displayed under a *skyline* (a banner on a story above the name plate) or a spread head at the bottom of the page are frequently given the additional eye appeal of wider columns.

Indention of lines, quite often accompanied by dropping the column rule in favor of white space between columns, is often put to similar purposes. The boldface paragraphs, special paragraph beginnings, and other typographical decorative devices shown in Figures 10-15 and 10-16 represent other methods of acquiring contrast in body areas.

A Word of Warning

Contrast is essential to good design, but it can have undesirable aspects. Imagine a page with every headline set in a different face,

Chamber Declares Economic Growth Hinges on Tax Cut	Probe Spreads to Boston In $100,000 Swindle Case	U. S. ASKS SOVIET JOIN IN LOWERING BARS TO TOURISTS

Chamber Declares Economic Growth Hinges on Tax Cut

By the Associated Press
WASHINGTON, July 7—The
U. S. Chamber of Commerce

Probe Spreads to Boston In $100,000 Swindle Case

Brooklyn Realtor Tells of Introducing
Parties in Mexico Gold Refining Deal

By the Associated Press
NEW YORK, July 7 — New name was rented in Mr. Schermond's

U. S. ASKS SOVIET JOIN IN LOWERING BARS TO TOURISTS

WASHINGTON, July 7 (UPI)
—The United States advised Russia Friday it is lifting its travel ban for Soviet tourists and exchange visitors, and invited the

SOVIET VETO KILLS U.N. KASHMIR PLAN

Salan Calls for End Of Algerian Terror But Attacks Resume

A FARM STOPGAP IS SENT TO HOUSE

Dissent, 100th in Council,
Stirs a Wrangle Between
Stevenson and Russian

By **ROBERT C. DOTY**
Special to The New York Times.
PARIS, June 22—Raoul Salan, serving a life sentence for
leading the Secret Army Organ-

Would Extend Emergency
Plan—Freeman, Beaten,
Looks to Next Year

Figure 10-19. *Tombstones can be avoided if adjacent headlines are varied.*

and body copy varying widely among stories. There would be plenty of contrast, but the overall result would be distasteful. Effective contrast makes each component stand out on its own without destroying the equilibrium, harmony, and unity necessary for good design.

Newspaper makeup that concentrates so much on contrast that it neglects other parts of good design is called "circus makeup." It is characterized by spread headlines, often in excessively large type, all over a page with little or no thought to the total picture. There is no doubt that circus makeup creates an impression of action and noise — but so much from so many directions that the reader can barely see or hear any of it.

Balance is primary in the makeup of some newspapers and purely secondary for others. Newspapers trying to project a conservative, steady, and reliable personality are inclined to make balance dominant in their page design. "Shouters" may deliberately try to subordinate balance lest their readers think the day's news a trifle dull. Most newspapers try for a middle ground.

Balance on a newspaper page is acquired by placing relatively equal weights on both sides of an imaginary line splitting the page into vertical halves. Balancing opposite corners is also considered. When these weights are virtually identical, the makeup is in *formal balance,* or *symmetrical.* When they are only relatively alike, the balance is *informal.*

Headlines and illustrations have the most inherent contrast, which means they exercise the strongest influence on equilibrium; therefore, their placement is especially important. A formally balanced newspaper page has every headline and illustration on one side of the page perfectly matched in weight and position by others on the opposite side.

Figure 10-20. *A front page with only minimum balance, above left. (Courtesy* Denver Post*)*

Figure 10-21. *A front page with rather obvious balance, above right. (Copyright 1974* Los Angeles Times. *Reprinted by permission)*

Figure 10-22. *A front page with such pronounced balance it is almost symmetrical, right. (Courtesy* Columbus Dispatch*)*

But because makeup acts to grade the news for readers, formal balance demands that news stories develop in importance by pairs. Naturally, this is rare, and as a result formal balance is relatively uncommon in newspapers.

Functionally, in newspaper makeup, headlines are balanced by pictures, headlines of one pattern by those of another, lighter elements by heavier elements placed closer to the center, like the heavier child sitting closer to the center of a teeter-totter.

Newspaper front pages with varying degrees of balance are presented in Figures 10-20, 10-21, and 10-22.

HARMONY IN NEWSPAPER MAKEUP

The makeup man is concerned with three kinds of harmony as he lays out newspaper pages: (1) the general appearance of the pages with the character or personality of the newspaper, (2) typographic, and (3) special pages with their subjects and readers.

Harmony of Appearance and Character

Because harmony in a paper's personality concerns the basic character, it is usually controlled by specific management policies. Only minor decisions on detail are made in this respect from day to day.

The range of headlines, the emphasis on illustration, and the preferred makeup patterns are a matter of policy. The makeup man must simply translate his news judgments into assigning headlines, display for photographs, and page arrangements that do not depart from the predetermined paths.

Typographic Harmony

Newspapers have more difficulty achieving typographic harmony than the other printed media do. The large size of the pages and the great number of individual units of type display almost require that the selection of display be *monotypographic* within any *section* of a newspaper. Some newspapers still have headlines in two or, at the most, three type families, but their ranks steadily decrease. Restricting the use of display type to one family assures harmony, and the numerous variations within any type family offer many ways to avoid monotony.

Type families can and should change from department to department. One family may be used for basic news pages, another for the sports pages, and perhaps another for the editorial page.

Harmony with Subject and Reader

Type families can be changed in different sections because their subjects and readers differ. The heavy sans serifs of a sports page may be inappropriate for an editorial page. Compare the typography of the sports and editorial pages of Figures 10-23 and 10-24; these pages have display faces that are completely different, but each is harmonious with subject and reader.

Figure 10-23. *Editorial pages are often given a different typography in order to give the page a special character. (Figures 10-23, 10-24 copyright 1974* Los Angeles Times. *Reprinted by permission)*

Figure 10-24. *This sports page is from the same issue of the* Los Angeles Times *as the editorial page shown in Figure 10-23, but it has been given a sans serif headline treatment which results in somewhat bolder display.*

UNITY RESULTS FROM HARMONY

A page with harmony also has unity. If all its components are compatible and in keeping with the paper's character, the makeup of a page will be harmonious unless the following factors creep in:

1. The design breaks pages into sharply defined sections.
2. Individual components have so much contrast that they stand separately and not together.
3. The design creates a feeling of movement that directs the reader off the page.

230   *Design: Combining the Verbal and Visual Elements*

It is difficult to know just how much the arrangement of display elements on a page contributes to the reader's eye-movement pattern. Some precaution is taken to put headlines and other display elements in lines intended to give the reader a directional boost. This effort is most apparent in a kind of makeup called "focus" or "brace." When one story dominates a day's news, it is given heavy display top right. To focus attention on that story, headlines are staggered from the lower-left corner to the upper-right. The resulting line leads to the main story and forms a brace for the heavy weight that has been given to it, in much the same way that a triangular brace gives support to shelves.

Modern Trends in Newspaper Design

The makeup practices described in the foregoing pages are solidly embedded in tradition. Although a few newspapers have completely discarded tradition in favor of complete new faces, most have either resisted change or have been selective in accepting new practices.

TRENDS IN HEADLINE PATTERNS

One of the most basic areas of change has been in the typographical design of headlines. In revamping their headline schedules to keep pace with modern developments, even traditionally designed newspapers have tended to include some or all of these principles:

1. The number of decks in a headline should be kept to a minimum. The tendency has been to eliminate secondary decks except for occasional use with banners and other large heads. Even then, one secondary deck is usually considered sufficient for a gradual scaling down in type size to make an easy transition from large display type to body type.
2. To compensate for the reduction in number of decks, headlines are spread across columns for additional display, thus creating a horizontal rather than vertical impression.
3. Jim dashes (short, plain, centered dashes) should not be used between decks; they are superfluous and disturbing. Use of rules of all kinds is kept to a minimum because white space performs the usual functions of rules more efficiently.
4. Capital-and-lowercase heads are better than all caps. They permit the headline writer greater unit count and are easier to read.

5. Decks should not exceed three lines; they become confusing as more lines are added.
6. Flush-left headlines are preferable to other patterns because of their flexibility of unit count. They also save time in the composing room because spacing is no problem; it is not necessary to center the middle lines as in three-line step lines.
7. Headline capitalization should follow standard sentence capitalization rather than the traditional practice of capitalizing each word.

COLUMN WIDTHS THAT ARE MORE LEGIBLE

From the reader's viewpoint, one of the more important changes made by some newspapers recently is a change to wider columns. Newspapers like the *Louisville Courier Journal* (Figure 10-25) and *Los Angeles Times,* which have gone against the trend toward narrower columns, have reported strong benefits from their switch to a six-column format. The *Christian Science Monitor* (Figure 10-26) went still further, changing from eight to five columns with excellent results.

Of perhaps most importance among the benefits derived from fewer columns is the improvement in readability. The constant eyeball jumping necessitated by the short 11- to 12-em lines was always recognized as a hindrance to readability. The 14-plus ems in the lines of a 6-column paper represent an excellent length for readability of 8-point type; the *Monitor's* five columns, 16¾ ems wide, in 9-point Excelsior are ideal on this score.

Readers have also benefited from more descriptive headlines because of the increased room in a column; headline writers who have struggled to summarize a story in a one-column headline have cheered the extra freedom, too.

Wider columns also offer mechanical and cost advantages. Hyphenation, the curse of typesetting, is reduced sharply. Fewer lines mean fewer justification problems and faster typesetting. Paste up of pages is also easier with wider columns.

The main stumbling block in the move to six columns per page has been the national advertising problem. Ads prepared for standard eight-column pages must be redesigned for wider columns or permitted to "float" in the extra white space. The *Louisville Courier-Journal* met this problem by eliminating the differential between local and national rates, thus making it possible for advertisers to get the extra width without increased cost. Advertisers responded by generally floating their ads; the additional white space was welcomed as a device for giving greater display for their copy. And the *Louisville Courier-Journal* has reported that the increased linage from

Figure 10-25. *A pioneer in the move to wider columns was the* Louisville Courier-Journal. *(Courtesy* Courier-Journal*)*

Figure 10-26. *The* Christian Science Monitor *gets excellent legibility by using five columns per page. (Reprinted by permission from the* Christian Science Monitor; © *1972 The Christian Science Publishing Society)*

national advertisers has compensated sufficiently for the drop in revenue per square inch that came with the change. Local ad problems related to the switch have also been solved.

It is to be hoped that other newspapers will go to wider columns in the future; in spite of problems that arise, other benefits make the change desirable.

CONTEMPORARY CHANGES IN PAGE DESIGNING

In earlier chapters we have emphasized some theoretical principles as a basis for good design of printed material. Much of this discussion centered on such things as *simplicity, order, modules, grids, line, point,* and the like.

It is interesting to speculate what a newspaper would look like if it were designed completely without regard for traditional makeup practices — if it were designed by a creative art director with only design and communication principles to guide him.

Some indication of what such newspaper pages might look like can be seen in an experiment conducted by an executive of Foote, Cone & Belding, an advertising agency. Dan Kelly, a senior vice-president and creative director of the agency, asked his art directors to redesign some newspaper pages. Some of their results are shown in Figure 10-27.

The art directors who participated in the experiment, though they admitted that their suggestions were not necessarily practical, were unanimous in the belief that much can be done to improve newspaper appearance.

This belief has been shared by many other media design experts and through their efforts and those of others some notable advances have been made. These improvements have included:

1. Virtually a complete break from the vertical appearance typical of many traditional newspapers and a change to a horizontal appearance.
2. Much more individuality in headline treatment, giving newspaper headlines as much opportunity to be as different as the titles are in a magazine. This requires a greater flexibility in head schedules, or a halt to their use.
3. A more simplified treatment, keeping the number of visual units on a page to a minimum and consequently giving each much greater emphasis.
4. More departmentalization as an aid to the reader, and a resultant de-emphasis of the notion that headlines must grade the news —

Figure 10-27. *Examples of what newspapers might look like if designed by art directors.*

Figure 10-28. *Examples of contemporary design in modern newspapers. (Courtesy* National Observer; The Advocate, *Newark, Ohio;* Detroit News)

eliminating the idea that big stories need big headlines and small stories must get small headlines.

5. Modular design that geometrically creates the feeling of order sought in all good designs.
6. Greater emphasis on illustrations — and larger illustrations.
7. Much stronger use of white space again, much in the way that magazine designers have used it throughout the years.

Several contemporary newspapers can be singled out as excellent examples of these design improvements; some of these are shown in Figure 10-28. The newspaper most often cited as an example of what a well-designed newspaper format can be is the *National Observer*. Note that most, if not all, of the principles enunciated by designers have been put into practice by the *Observer*.

MAKEUP OF INSIDE PAGES

The same principles of functional, attractive design that apply to the makeup of front pages should carry over into inside pages, but there is one restraining influence there: the advertising.

Although the editorial staff may not like it, advertising governs the size of any issue and to a great extent controls the appearance of most inside pages. Its effect on size is readily discernible when one looks at the large Wednesday and Thursday editions and the tissue-thin Saturday issue. The grocery store ads in midweek produce a big issue, and the Saturday issue is small because fewer stores buy space on that day, and not because it is a slack news day. As a matter of fact, sports and other department editors often find that on their biggest news days their space allotment may be at a minimum.

With regard to appearance, one need only look at the stacks of ads on inside pages to see an immediate design problem. Advertising departments usually get first crack at page layout; the ads are placed before the editor gets his space allocation. Makeup men can only do their best to make the page look as attractive as possible by sound planning of the space that remains.

Advertising is usually arranged in one of three basic patterns: *pyramid to the right, double pyramid,* or *well*. Shown in Figures 10-29, 10-30, and 10-31, these arrangements are used in order to get as many ads next to news matter as possible. Advertisers do not want their messages buried beneath other ads.

As mentioned earlier, the key focal point on inside pages is the upper left, and, with ads pyramided to the right this portion of the page is left for news display. Consequently, the pyramid to the right arrangement has been traditionally preferred by news departments.

Figure 10-29. *Ads arranged in pyramid to right.*

Figure 10-30. *Ads arranged in double pyramid.*

Figure 10-31. *Ads arranged so news must fit into a well.*

At least one designer has insisted, however, that newspaper inside pages cannot really be made as attractive as possible until the custom of arranging ads changes to permit the creation of a simple rectangle for the news area at the top of the page (Nelson, 1972). Even without a news hole with better proportions, however, inside pages can be made more attractive if:

1. Simplicity, balance, contrast, and harmony are sought as strongly as they are for front pages.
2. A sufficient number of multicolumn spread headlines are assigned, along with illustrations, boxes, and other major display items to provide at least one visual "stopper" for each page.
3. The display effect of the advertising at the bottom of the page is considered as the editorial content at the top is being displayed.

TABLOID MAKEUP

In addition to bemoaning the arrangement of ads on newspaper inside pages, designers have consistently criticized the large size of the standard newspaper as also being detrimental to good design.

Nelson listed a change to a smaller format as the first requirement for newspapers to achieve really good design. He and others consider the *tabloid* size (half the usual newspaper size) to be much better. A greater ease in handling has been considered an advantage of tabloid format for years.

Figure 10-32. *Inside pages are adaptable to modern design practices, too. (Courtesy* Times-Democrat, Davenport, Iowa, *and* National Observer)

Figure 10-33. *The* New York Daily News *and* Chicago Sun-Times *are very popular tabloids. (Reprinted by permission of New York* News Inc. *and* Chicago Sun-Times)

The one factor working against tne increased use of tabloid format has been its association with sensational journalism; to some, the word tabloid is synonymous with sensational news policy. This association resulted from the sensational tactics of the new tabloids of the 1920s, but it is no longer justified.

Hundreds of good suburban papers, as well as such excellent metropolitan dailies as the Long Island *Newsday* and the *Chicago Sun-Times*, have been presented in tabloid form for years. The newspaper with the largest circulation in the country, the *New York Daily News*, is a tabloid.

From the standpoint of design, the tabloid size has several advantages. As can be seen in Figure 10-33, it is readily adaptable to magazine techniques; fewer elements per page make simplified, orderly design much easier to accomplish. The merits of the tabloid format are so strong that it seems inevitable that eventually many more newspapers will convert to its smaller dimensions.

CHAPTER 11

Planning
and Designing
Other Printed
Literature

Some factors involved in producing effective
graphic communications are beyond the control of the designer who
is preparing materials to appear in the established media. He has to
fit his layout to prescribed size limitations; he must use the printing
process by which the medium is produced; the paper is predetermined as well as the ink, and this in turn affects his use of continuous-tone art work.

It is in the printing field outside the media that the communicator
finds fewer restrictions and can exercise the fullest creative use of the
principles of graphic communications. Here he controls the selection
of: (1) printing process; (2) color; (3) paper; (4) nature of the fold; (5)
size and shape.

Because this product goes directly to readers, it is referred to as
direct literature. It may be mailed, distributed by individuals, or
placed at convenient locations where readers can help themselves.
The most common means is by mail, and, when so handled, it is
referred to as *direct-mail literature*.

Kinds of Direct Literature

Such printed pieces take many forms. The scope of this text cannot
include them all. In broadest terms they divide into two groups: (1)
booklets and (2) flat or folded sheets.

Generally, the printed piece of direct literature comes from the printing press as flat sheets of paper. They may be folded and trimmed to become booklets. For example, in Figure 11-1 is shown a flat sheet with the folios (page numbers) as they would fall on one side. Take a sheet of paper, write the folios on it as shown, and fold it in the two directions indicated by the dotted lines. Folded properly, it should look like Figure 11-2. You can now carefully lift the leaves and place the folios 2, 3, 6, and 7 on the proper pages.

Now refold the sheet and imagine staples driven through the "backbone" at the points indicated by the arrows in Figure 11-2. The staples should clinch parallel with and on top of the fold between pages 4 and 5. Next, imagine that the entire unit is compressed and that knives trim on the dotted lines as shown on the top and bottom edges and the fore edge in Figure 11-2. You can do this on your folded sheet, using two staples that you force through the backbone with your fingers and then taking scissors to the edges. You will wind up with what is shown in Figure 11-3, a folded and trimmed eight-page booklet.

What you have just produced is a *self-cover booklet*. An alternative is possible. A four-page cover can be printed (usually on a heavier paper) and the eight-page unit can be inserted before stapling and

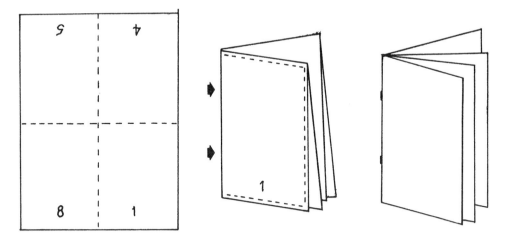

Figure 11-1. *Flat sheet that can be folded to make eight-page booklet.*

Figure 11-2. *Folded sheet that forms eight-page booklet.*

Figure 11-3. *Folded and trimmed eight-page booklet.*

trimming. Then you have a *separate-cover booklet.* If the cover stock is so heavy that it makes folding difficult, it may first be processed with a scoring rule (see Chapter 3).

Booklets are sometimes called "pamphlets" or "brochures." Essentially the booklet is a small book and is made up of eight or more pages bound together, usually stapled. The booklet ranges in number of pages up to 36 or 40 and the number of pages must be divisible by four. The format itself may be either vertical or horizontal.

Books usually have more pages and are bound with more permanent covers. Books, moreover, are of a literary or scientific nature, whereas the content of booklets is more likely to reflect promotional interests.

Book format is traditionally standardized. It has roughly three main divisions: (1) the preliminaries, or front matter; (2) the text; and (3) the references, or back matter.

The preliminaries include the *half title,* the book's first printed page on which appears only the book's title; the *title page,* which includes the title and the names of the author and the publisher, and the place of publication; the *copyright page;* the *preface;* the *acknowledgments;* the *contents;* the *introduction* when it is not a part of the text proper; and, often, a second half title. Tradition governs the order of these pages and whether they fall on a left- or a right-hand page. *Folios,* or page numbers, are in lowercase or small cap roman numerals, appearing first on the opening preface page, although the actual numbering starts from the half title.

The text section contains the chapters; the reference section consists of appendixes, bibliography, glossary, and index. In text and reference sections folios are in arabic. They may be either at the top or at the bottom of the page. *Running heads* usually appear at the top of each page, and the content is often different on the right- and left-hand pages.

Throughout, the progressive margins remain consistent although text on facing pages may run a line or two long or short depending upon makeup.

What we have said here about books refers to traditional formatting. We saw (Chapter 5) that book design may be altered considerably in the new typography.

In the design of booklets, too, tradition and formality may be applied in varying degrees (see Figures 11-4 and 11-5). Because of their usual promotional nature, booklets are more often of an informal design. Because a message unfolds through succeeding pages, as in a book, a continuity of style must be maintained by the designer, who works with units of individual pages or units of facing pages.

calendars to obtain wider and more consistent display of his business announcements. In 1869 George Coburn of Hartford, Connecticut, began printing calendars which carried advertising, and in 1879 a newspaper editor in Coshocton, Ohio, produced advertising specialties in the form of candy boxes and school bags.[2] These may very well have been the first advertising specialties other than calendars to be made and distributed in the United States. However, without library files, in contrast to newspapers and magazines, and with the records of many old businesses long lost or destroyed, there exists little possibility of establishing an exact and undisputed date or place of origin for this method of advertising. However, this is of small consequence since it is the present position of specialty advertising and its potential for future development that are important both to businessmen who sell and use it and to students planning careers in advertising.

SPECIALTY ADVERTISING OF TODAY

Specialty advertising industry sources estimated 1970 sales at $871 million. The industry employs some 250,000 people in its many phases. Of the approximately 4,400 companies in the field, some 900 are suppliers, 3,200 are distributors, 10 are direct selling houses. Also associated with the industry are a number of firms and individuals engaged in the manufacture and/or sale of machinery, equipment, materials, services or supplies to other members of the industry.

Within the industry itself, the terms **supplier, distributor** (often referred to as a specialty advertising "counselor" or "agency") and **direct selling house** are defined as follows:

"A **supplier** manufactures, imports, converts, imprints, or otherwise processes advertising specialties, calendars or business gifts for sale through specialty advertising distributors."

"A **distributor** develops ideas for the use of specialty advertising products, buys these products from suppliers and sells them to advertisers under his own company name."

"A **direct selling house** combines the functions of supplier and distributor within one organization. It primarily manufactures its own products and sells them directly to advertisers through its own sales force."

The industry is served by Specialty Advertising Association International which was formed in 1964 by the consolidation of two existing trade associations. SAAI and its predecessor organizations have served the field since 1903. It publishes a monthly newsletter, conducts two trade shows each year, and works in general to advance and promote the welfare of the industry as well as its member firms. SAAI also performs a number of special services for its members which include, in part, a comprehensive public relations program, annual Executive Development Seminars, Management Practices Conferences, a Sales Training Manual and fact sheets on various types of advertisers, and an annual

[2] Estelle Carpey, "The History of the Ad Specialty Industry," **The Advertising Specialty Counselor**, May 1954 (Philadelphia, Pa. The Advertising Specialty Institute, Inc.)

8

Awards Competition for outstanding use of specialty advertising in business promotion. The Association maintains a Washington-based counsel.

Also serving the industry is The Advertising Specialty Institute, a privately owned business organization, which operates as a central source of information for many industry firms. It publishes **The Advertising Specialty Register** and the semi-annual **Market and Credit Report**, the standard directories of specialty advertising suppliers and distributors, respectively. **The Counselor**, a monthly trade journal devoted to the industry, also is published by the Institute.

For much of its history, the specialty advertising industry was concerned primarily with products, and its sales tended to be highly seasonal. But operations and orientation have changed greatly during the past two decades. Although there is still some seasonal peaking toward year's end because of the calendar business and the use of other types of advertising specialties and gifts as Christmas remembrances, on the whole sales are spread more evenly throughout the year than they once were. This has been due in large part to a marked change in the level of selling in the industry and type of sales representatives engaged in this function. The "peddler," whose interest never went beyond making a sale when making a sale meant little more than displaying a variety of merchandise and letting it sell itself, is being replaced among the more progressive distributors by the specialty advertising counselor. These counselors are trained to sell an advertising or sales promotion idea rather than selling merchandise. They are consultants and advisors to their clients, helping them with their individual advertising problems and fitting the advertising specialty to the specific job that confronts each client.

SAAI's annual Executive Development Seminars contribute to the advancement of this trend toward improved and more scientific procedure with the specialty advertising industry. The Seminars run for eight days and include, among other things, courses in marketing problems, advertising media, employee selection and training, and written and oral communications. These Seminars, conducted by midwestern universities, are more than refresher courses and permit those attending to earn the title of Certified Advertising Specialist (C.A.S.) upon successful completion of the program.

9

Figure 11-4. Formal page layout of spread in booklet published by the specialty advertising trade association explaining the nature of their industry. (Courtesy Specialty Advertising Association International)

Figure 11-5. Informal balance of two pages in a combination informative-promotional booklet. (Courtesy nuArc Company, Inc.)

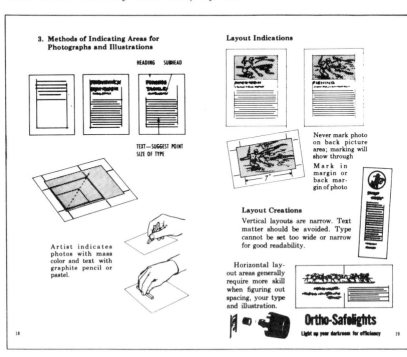

The arrangement of elements in a booklet can differ from page to page. Cuts can bleed; copy block widths and margins can be varied; display and color can be used with a free hand.

The front cover, often referred to as the *OFC* (outside front cover), will receive one of two types of treatment. In the case of an informative or literary booklet, it will be more conservatively handled with only a title set in type and placed formally or informally (see Figure 11-6). If the nature of the booklet is more promotional, display treatment of the cover may be more extensive, incorporating both visual and verbal elements (see Figure 11-7).

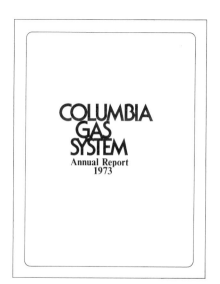

Figure 11-6. *Conservatively designed booklet cover. (Courtesy Columbia Gas System)*

Figure 11-7. *Display treatment of booklet cover. (Courtesy nuArc Company, Inc.)*

FOLDERS

The printed flat sheets delivered from the press do not always take the form of books or booklets. Many printed jobs are known as *flat pieces.* Perhaps several are printed together on a large press sheet and then trimmed (cut) from it. Such flat pieces take many forms. There are letterheads, cards, announcements, posters, fliers, business forms, instruction sheets, envelope stuffers, and so on. These are often printed on one side only. The principles of design we have previously discussed apply to planning the message they carry.

We are, however, more interested here in those printed messages that are not finished flat but are, instead, folded. Such pieces are known as *folders*. The subject of folding will be given a comprehensive treatment in Chapter 16, but there are certain implications in the folder that have a direct bearing on information processing. This is due primarily to the fact that, like booklets, folders consist of pages. The serial ordering of these pages is not so rigid, as we shall see in a moment, as it is with booklets. Thus the design of folders presents some unique problems.

Human information processing is basically serial. When we present a message on one flat area, we hope we can control information intake by guiding the eye through the message by means of visual syntax. Nonetheless, the reader may still look at any part of the total message at any time he wishes. This is not so when he reads a booklet. But the problem arises again when we consider the folder.

Let us examine why this is so. Broadly speaking, the piece can be given any of several kinds of the so-called *letter fold*. Such pieces are usually about 8½ by 11, 9 by 12, or 8½ by 14 inches. A letter fold takes such pieces down to a size that will fit the No. 10 envelope, which is 4⅛ inches deep by 9½ inches wide. In addition to these more common-size folders there is the *broadside,* which is a jumbo folder, usually 19 by 25 inches up to 25 by 38 inches when it is flat (before folding). It unfolds to a smashing spread concentrated on one idea.

In Figure 11-8 are shown some common letter-fold pieces. Note that they result in 4-, 6-, 8-, and 10-page folders. We are presenting

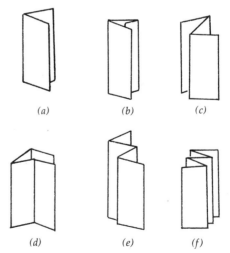

(a)   (b)   (c)

(d)   (e)   (f)

Figure 11-8. *Common letter folds: (a) 4-page single fold; (b) 6-page standard or wrap-around; (c) 6-page accordion; (d) 8-page standard, double parallel fold or fold within a fold; (e) 8-page accordion; (f) 10-page accordion.*

here only a few of the many possible treatments. Our concern is their effect in information processing. Try making these folds yourself with pieces of paper. The drawings indicate vertical formats, but the folder could also have a horizontal format.

Folder (a) presents no particular problems. Page 1 could be treated as a separate page, 2 and 3 separately or as a spread, and page 4 as a single unit. But folders (b), (c), (d), (e), and (f) offer more interesting possibilities. Consider, for example, (d). Take the folder you have made. Close it by swinging the left half to the right. When the reader opens it, he comes to a two-page spread; another opening reveals a four-page spread. The design of the same folder could be treated in other ways. Turn it back for front. Now consider what was the back as the front. Now it unfolds in a different manner. The order of the message and the designs given the pages may call for different treatments from folder to folder.

These considerations do not exhaust the possibilities. Look at Figure 11-9. Take a piece of paper. Fold it as a six-page accordion. Before doing so, cut off a piece diagonally as shown. Note the step-effect that allows portions of page 3 and page 5 to be seen from the front.

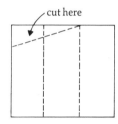

Figure 11-9. *Angle-cut accordion fold.*

Folds do not have to be equal as seen in Figure 11-8. Figure 11-10 shows what are known as a *short fold* and an *off-center fold.* To do the latter, lay a sheet in front of you. Bring the left edge toward the right but let it fall short, then crease; repeat and crease. As with the diagonal-cut accordion fold, an interesting tab or index step is visible.

Figure 11-10. *Short-fold, 12-page, left; off-center 8-page double parallel fold, right.*

What Kind of Printed Piece?

An important creative decision is the kind of printed piece to be produced. The following factors favor the use of a booklet:

1. Lengthy copy requiring continuity of presentation.
2. Need for a number of illustrative examples.
3. Highly technical material.
4. Catalogue material.

The folder, on the other hand, lends itself when these conditions exist:

1. A series of illustrations is to be presented, as the number of different models of a product.
2. Short but crisp text is offered.
3. The unfolding naturally builds a climactic impression.
4. Production speed and economy are required. Booklet production means time-consuming, extra folding-and-binding operations, while folders can be *self-mailers*. With the latter, one section is left open for addressing and for the printing of postal *indicia,* an indication that the sender has a permit to pay postage at time of mailing in lieu of affixing stamps. Booklets are usually mailed in envelopes, thereby entailing the dual expense of envelopes and insertion.
5. *Imprinting* of, for example, various dealer names is called for. Such work can be done economically on the flat sheets before folding.

Standard Unit Sizes

An early step in planning the printed piece is the preparation of the dummy. At this point the designer must remember that the size of the piece has a significant effect on final production cost because manufacturers, in the interest of economy, produce certain standard sizes of paper, available through printers. Thus only certain-sized pamphlets and other forms of direct literature can be cut advantageously from these stock sheets. Following are these standard sizes:

Bond: 17 by 22 (basis), 17 by 28, 19 by 24, 22 by 34, 28 by 34, 34 by 44 inches.

Book: 25 by 38 (basis), 28 by 42, 28 by 44, 32 by 45, 35 by 45, 38 by 50, 19 by 25, 23 by 29, 23 by 35, 36 by 48, 41 by 61, 44 by 66, 45 by 68, 50 by 76, 52 by 76 inches.

Cover: 20 by 26 (basis), 23 by 35, 26 by 40, 35 by 46 inches.[1]

Suppose an 8-page booklet, 4½ by 6 inches, is being planned. What size stock can be used? Remember these points before solving this problem:

1. One-half inch should be subtracted from the short dimension of the stock to allow for press grippers, which hold the paper as it goes through the press. This is three-eighths of an inch on some presses. Printing can extend to but not beyond the grippers.
2. One-eighth inch should be allowed for bleed trim on every edge of the piece.

Thus we can determine that 64 pages can be printed on a 25-by-38-inch sheet, 32 on each side, as shown in Figure 11-11. This means a total of eight 8-page booklets per sheet of paper.

The finished booklet should be 4⅝ by 6¼ inches to allow trim of one-eighth inch on top, bottom, and outside to open the pages. The fractions along the right side of the sheet in Figure 11-11 indicate trim allowances. As long as the print area falls at least one-half inch below the top of the sheet, 25 by 38 inches is adequate.

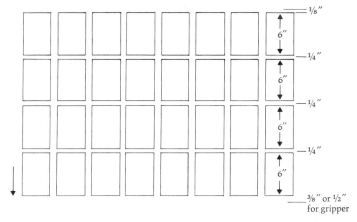

Figure 11-11. *Thirty-two 4½ x 6-inch pages imposed on one side of a sheet.*

But when bleed pages are in the design, the printed booklet should be 4¾ by 6½ inches. When trimming is done, the cut to make the finished 4½ by 6 inches is then deep enough to insure inclusion of the bleed art. The piece should be printed on a 28-by-42-inch sheet for bleeds.

[1] The basis size of cover stock (20 by 26 inches) is slightly larger than 19 by 25 inches, one half of the basis size of book paper (25 by 38 inches), to allow for *overhang covers;* that is, covers with dimensions larger than the inside of the booklet.

COMMON SHEET SIZES

Size of piece (in inches)	Sheet size for trim	Sheet size for bleeds	Number of pages
3⅜ by 6¼	28 by 42	28 by 44	96
3¾ by 5⅛	32 by 44	35 by 45	128
4¼ by 5⅜	35 by 45	38 by 50	128
4½ by 6	25 by 38	28 by 42	64
4 by 9⅛	25 by 38	28 by 42	48
5¼ by 7⅝	32 by 44	35 by 45	64
5½ by 8½	35 by 45	38 by 50	64
8½ by 5½ (oblong)	23 by 35	25 by 38	32
6 by 9⅛	25 by 38	28 by 42	32
7¾ by 10⅝	32 by 44	35 by 45	32
8½ by 11	35 by 45	38 by 50	32
9¼ by 12⅛	25 by 38	28 by 42	16

A piece can be printed from other than standard-sized paper. Manufacturers make paper in special sizes, and quantities in excess of 5000 pounds can be purchased economically. For small amounts, extra costs usually dictate fitting the design to a standard size.

Presses and envelopes are made to accommodate all of the standard-sized pieces. Special envelopes can be made to order. Both standard-sized letter and *booklet envelopes* are available through the printer.

Special Paper Considerations

In addition to size, certain other aspects of paper need the attention of the designer. These are: (1) kind; (2) color; and (3) weight.

KIND OF PAPER

Bond lends itself well to folders because of its good folding quality. It is strong and durable. Offset prints well on its hard surface, but it should be avoided for most letterpress work. Common weights in use are 20- and 24-pound, equivalent to the book paper weights of 50- and 60-pounds. Weight means the *basis weight*, the weight in pounds of a ream (500 sheets) of paper cut to its basic size.

Coated book stocks are high-priced and tend to crack in folding. Letterpress reproduction is best, but coated stocks are available for offset.

EQUIVALENT BASIS WEIGHTS OF STOCK

Book paper Basis: 25 x 38	Cover paper Basis: 20 x 26	Bond paper Basis: 17 x 22
30	—	—
35	—	13
40	—	16
45	25	—
50	—	20
60	35	24
70	40	28
80	45	32
90	50	36
100	55	40
120	65	—
150	80	—

Uncoated book stocks are less distinctive than coated — and less expensive, enough so that in a long run the cost savings is substantial.

Offset stocks, which are also book paper, fold excellently and are thus particularly adaptable to folders. The weights of 60-, 70-, and 80-pound are most used.

Cover stock is particularly useful for the addition of separate covers to booklets and is also used for folders and pamphlets. Weights above 80-pound usually require scoring before folding.

Cover stock is also available in 90-, 100-, and 130-pound weights. No paper is made in weights above 150.

COLOR

White has been the traditional color for paper since the earliest days of printing, and black ink on white paper will probably continue most popular in the future. But for some time interest in color stocks has grown. There are several reasons for this:

1. The contrast of color stock to white. With the bulk of printing done on white paper, messages on color stock get attention.
2. Increased understanding of the psychological effects of color. As discussed, color stimulates positively and negatively. Skillfully used, color stock creates atmosphere and builds retention. Because black and white are in a sense the absence of color, they lack the psychological impact of printing in color ink on color stock.
3. Research in developing compatible inks and papers. Paper and

ink manufacturers, with the assistance of psychologists, ophthalmologists, and lighting engineers, have uncovered pleasing combinations of color ink on color paper. Four color-process printed on a color stock has proved startlingly effective when the key color black is substituted by a dark color ink compatible with the paper.

The reading task is simplified when the message is printed color-on-color. There is less reflection than black-on-white. Many experts contend this reduction in contrast is a welcome relief for the reader. Because the cost of color-on-color is not much greater, the continued improvements in paper and ink manufacture will no doubt mean expanded use.

It is possible to match the color of some text stocks with cover stocks when this is desired. If a perfect match cannot be made, the designer would do well to consider a definite contrast between the two.

If a color stock is used for folders, all pages must, of course, be of that color. In the case of booklets, however, it is possible to use color stock for some of the pages, the number of such pages being divisible by four.

Even when a stock of one color is used throughout a booklet, it is possible to give some pages a different color by laying the color on the pages with ink. Offset printing is particularly adaptable to this technique. The same thing applies to the printing of folder pages as well.

WEIGHT

The weight of the stock used must be considered primarily because of its effect on mailing costs. This factor alone cannot, however, determine the weight. The nature of the message and the effect of the paper on the reader may require a stock of such substance that higher mailing costs can be justified. If a booklet carries a self-cover, consideration must be given to durability, which means that a substantial stock may be called for. Self-mailer folders likewise call for heavier paper.

Other Design Considerations

If the decision is made to maintain margins from page to page in a folder, the two side margins and the top should be about the same and the foot margin slightly larger. Such a decision is likely when the

Figure 11-12. *Margination on folder pages. (Courtesy South Carolina Electric &*
Gas Company)

message is primarily verbal, as in Figure 11-12. Incidentally, on the
four pages on the opposite side of those shown were the Income
Statement and the Balance Sheet, each spread across two pages. What
letter fold do you think was given the piece? The treatment of three
equal margins and a larger foot margin may be given to booklets of
eight or twelve pages. If the booklet contains more pages, progressive margins are often followed throughout.

Rarely are folios placed on folder pages. Unless they are an aid to
the reader, they are not used in booklets. If they are used, a table of
contents is generally included.

Whether or not to print on the *IFC, IBC,* or *OBC* (inside front
cover, inside back cover, outside back cover) of booklets is often determined by the nature of the contents. If the content is informative
and the layout formal, these are often left blank, particularly if the
piece carries a separate cover. If the booklet is promotional and the
design less formal, the covers are often printed, particularly if the
piece carries a self-cover.

Whether the folder or booklet is vertical or horizontal is a matter
of option. Nonpromotional booklets that are formally designed are
usually vertical in the tradition of the book. Promotional materials
may be presented in either format. A particular advantage of the

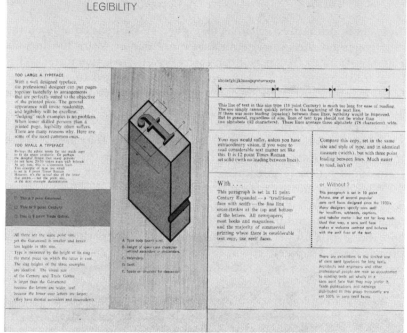

There are, then, two typographies, as there are two worlds: and, apart from God or profits, the test of one is mechanical perfection, and of the other, sanctity—the commercial article at its best is simply physically serviceable and, per accidens, beautiful in its efficiency; the work of art at its best is beautiful in its very substance and, per accidens, as serviceable as an article of commerce. The typography of Industrialism, when it is not deliberately diabolical and designed to deceive, will be plain; and in spite of the wealth of its resources— a thousand varieties of inks, papers, presses and mechanical processes for

Stand at a distance from a building, and a sign a hundred feet long can be read without a twitch of an eyeball. But a newspaper headline held at arm's length not only requires that the eye move, even the head may have to swivel slightly.

The reading process is one of identifying the patterns created by words and phrases in type. The eye moves along the line, relaying these composite visual forms to the brain, where the abstract forms are decoded into meanings.

It becomes obvious that for continuous text, the proper length of line is that which enables the eye to grasp the units of pattern in the line with a minimum of eye movement; the muscles of the eye share with other parts of the body the reaction of fatigue from over-exertion.

Experience has resulted in general agreement that eight to ten words constitutes a basically readable line of type; this represents a line of roughly two alphabets or 52 characters in length. When a line goes longer than this, leading must be introduced between the lines to facilitate the eye's identification of the letter forms without confusion with the adjoining lines.

Lines which are shorter than this standard will obviously involve even less eye-strain; but they present a technical problem to the typesetter, for as the number of words diminishes, the fewer are the spaces in which he can distribute the necessary space to fill out his line. Where there are long words that are impossible to break (like 'stretch'), this often results in the uneven spacing that impedes legibility.

Figure 11-13. *Bridging the gutter: with art and headline, left above; with white space, left below; with headline, above. (Both on left: courtesy Mead Corporation; above: © Westvaco Corporation)*

folder is that vertical and horizontal layouts are possible within the same piece. Consider the wrap-around, six-page folder, for example. Page 1 may be a vertical. Upon opening it, the reader may see a horizontal spread over pages 2, 3, and 4.

By bridging the gutter in a vertical format book, the designer can also present horizontal designs. Some of the techniques for doing this were shown in Chapter 9. In Figure 11-13 are shown spreads from booklets in which some of the techniques are applied.

Checking Press Sheets

Once a message is released to a medium, the opportunity for controlling the printed result fades. In the case of direct literature, however, there is a chance to check the printed piece as it comes from the press. At this point it is possible to find and correct *fill-in* or *plugging* of halftones and fine lines; streaks, slurs, and other blemishes; improper makeready and inking.

Press sheets, or *press proofs,* are marked by an arrow that indicates change of position. It is drawn to point out where type or art is to be moved. A circle is drawn around areas where makeready is faulty or where some other imperfection is spotted, and the proofreader's delete symbol draws attention to the circle.

One cannot be too careful in searching for errors in either verbal or visual copy before releasing it for publication. Information processing theory tells why. Things that we look at are usually within a familiar context which aids us in perception. Sometimes we see things that aren't there; at other times we don't see things that are there, all simply because of our expectations, which are guided by the context. Thus it is easy to misperceive.

One interesting study of proofreading (Corcoran, 1967) confirms this interpretation. Subjects were asked to cross out each letter *e* in passages of prose. Analysis of results showed that subjects were more likely to miss the silent *e* than the pronounced one. Further, the *e* in the word "the" was more likely to be missed than other pronounced *e*s. Corcoran also found that the absence of an *e* that would have been silent is less likely to be discovered than the absence of an *e* that would have been pronounced.

Such results suggest that there may be some interrelationship in memory between information received visually and aurally. In any event, a highly focused awareness is a necessity in the search for errors in the message.

SECTION 5   # PRODUCTION OF GRAPHIC COMMUNICATION

CHAPTER 12
Graphic Reproduction Processes

CHAPTER 13
Preparing Verbal Copy for Production

CHAPTER 14
Preparing Visual Copy for Production

CHAPTER 15
Machine Composition and Presses

CHAPTER 16
Paper: Selection, Folding, Binding, Finishing

CHAPTER 12 Graphic
Reproduction
Processes

For today's user of printing there exists a
veritable smorgasbord of technical processes from which he can
select one or more systems precisely suited to his needs.

There is, for example, the old standby invented by Johann Gutenberg in the fifteenth century. For hundreds of years this system of
printing from movable type, called *letterpress* because it carried ink to
paper by pressing raised letters against the paper, was the only commercial system available.

But now there is also a photochemical system called *photo-offset
lithography* that is, for many purposes, a much more efficient and
capable method for reproducing mass numbers of verbal and visual
images on paper. The quality potential and the efficiency of offset, as
it is usually called, are so great that it has pushed letterpress aside as
the basic system for much of the printing that is being done today.

And *gravure,* a printing method that lifts ink from recessed pools
onto paper, has been combined with photography and fast presses to
create *rotogravure,* a system used to produce millions of catalogues,
newspaper Sunday supplements, and many other media.

Although these three systems are the basic methods (Figure 12-1)
accounting for most of the current printing volume, there are numerous other specialized processes ranging from *silk screen,* a relatively simple procedure, to *electrostatic,* a system relying on photoconductivity and electrical charges to put images on paper.

This availability of many competing processes has made the
knowledge of printing systems an essential first step in the under-

259

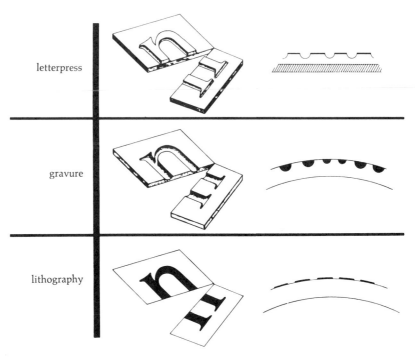

Figure 21-1. *The three basic methods of printing. (Courtesy Lithographic Technical Foundation)*

standing of printing production that is essential for any prospective graphic communicator. Whether a student is planning a career with newspapers, magazines, public relations firms, or advertising agencies and departments, he will find such knowledge essential for carrying out his work. All aspects of planning, editing, and the production of printed media have a direct relationship to the characteristics of the printing process being used.

Basic Principles of Common Graphic Reproduction Processes

To understand the specific reproduction systems in commercial use today, it is necessary to give some attention to their basic mechanical or chemical principles. One or more of the following five principles serve as the basis for each printing method with a modern commercial application:

1. Inking obtained by pressure against a relief (raised) surface.
2. Inking obtained by chemical action from a *planographic* (flat) surface.

3. Inking obtained by lifting ink from an *intaglio* (engraved or depressed) area.
4. Inking obtained by seepage through a stencil or screen.
5. Images created on light-sensitive surfaces through *photography* and/or *electrical attraction.*

Relief, or Letterpress, System of Printing

Because it is the traditional system of printing, letterpress perhaps requires less explanation than other methods. There are, however, a number of characteristics and ramifications of the system that must be noted.

It takes only a moment's thought to realize that letterpress can be defined as a direct, mechanical system of printing from raised surfaces. But the words *mechanical* and *raised* point to characteristics that are of considerable significance to anyone either preparing material for reproduction by letterpress or considering the system's quality and cost levels.

PRODUCTION STEPS IN THE LETTERPRESS PROCESS

For printing to be done directly from a raised surface, words and illustrations must, in some way, be "carved" or molded in relief in a substance sufficiently hard to withstand wear from constant applications or pressure. It should also be apparent that equality of pressure for all elements against the sheet being printed becomes a matter of necessity for a high level of quality in this process.

These two requirements point directly to five matters of importance to users of the letterpress process:

1. Traditionally, words and letters have had to be cast in metal to be reproduced.
2. Illustrations must be separately manufactured in plate form to be reproduced.
3. For fine quality of reproduction for photographs, a smooth, coated paper is required.
4. Time and skill are required in "making ready" a press form so that the pressure of each element against the paper is equal, thus giving an even application of ink.
5. Traditionally, letterpress has required the casting of curved metal plates as a duplicate of an original page of type and engravings in order to use presses with higher speeds.

Let us look at each of these items to see how they are of importance to the journalist who works with the letterpress process.

Type Composition

In traditional letterpress shops, the mechanical preparation of copy starts with a skilled technician, the *compositor*. He may operate a machine, such as the Linotype, Intertype, Monotype, or Ludlow typecaster, or he may even set by hand the pieces of type stored in *cases* (drawers). Type cast from molten metal is called *hot type* and its use has been fundamental to letterpress printing for centuries. Compositors of hot type have served extensive apprenticeships, are strongly unionized, and are relatively well paid. Thus hot type composition has been a costly part of letterpress printing for many years.

Automation of hot type composition has been effected in many plants through the use of tape-driven machines; tape that is punched by a typist drives the casting machines much in the fashion of the old player piano. Perhaps of most importance, however, has been the introduction of computerized *photocomposition* or *strike-on* methods of typesetting for letterpress. These systems are explained thoroughly in Chapter 15. It suffices here to point out that some newspapers and other periodicals have eliminated the use of hot type; the hard, raised surface necessary for letterpress printing is created by etching complete-page plates. Type that has been set photographically on film or paper (or struck on a sheet of paper as with a typewriter) is pasted into position to form a page. The *page pasteup* is then converted to a metal or plastic relief plate.

Plates for Illustrations

The need to have a raised surface for printing all kinds of illustrations by letterpress has also been an important factor in any comparison with other processes.

The traditional letterpress method for reproducing illustrations is to create acid-etched metal plates on which the nonprinting area is cut away in acid baths, leaving the image area in relief. Even the simplest pen-and-ink drawings require the manufacture of separate metal plates called *line* engravings; photographs or other illustrations containing continuous tonal variations require a complicated procedure of breaking the image into dots on the plate surface, plus the subsequent complicated acid etching that makes the dots stand in relief and thus be able to carry ink to the paper. These plates are called *halftone* engravings.

The special plates needed for all illustrations are one of the costly aspects of letterpress printing; they also tend to restrict somewhat the use of illustrations. Because each line drawing or photograph is a separate added cost and because the cost for each illustration increases with the size of the illustration, there has been a tendency to use fewer and smaller illustrations than otherwise.

Procedurally, photoengravings in letterpress require working with still another production specialist, the engraver. The time allowance for the engraver's work has to be coordinated with the printer's deadlines. In some operations, notably those of newspapers, the printer also operates an engraving department, thus reducing scheduling problems.

Some electronic machines are now in use that make plastic or metal plates for letterpress illustrations without acid etching. Most of these employ the principle of an electric eye scanning the illustration and sending electronic impulses to a hot needle that etches dots or lines on the plate surface. Some of the restrictions in size and number of illustrations tend to be reduced in situations where these machines are installed; the cost of their operation tends to be fixed, thus making the unit cost less with added use.

Paper Requirements

The relief characteristic of letterpress printing necessitates the use of extremely smooth paper in order to get good reproduction of photographs. For high fidelity in reproduction, the dots in a halftone engraving must be extremely small; these tiny raised dots are lost or smudged in the hills and valleys of the coarse surface of cheaper papers. Consequently, the hard, smooth finish of more expensive papers must be provided for fine photographic reproduction. When coarse papers must be used because of cost, the engravings are made so that their dot structure is much larger, with a resultant loss of quality. Many magazines offer excellent examples of the beautiful reproduction of photos that can be achieved in letterpress printing on smooth papers; newspapers, because they are printed on the cheapest kind of paper, offer examples of poorer picture quality.

Importance of Makeready in Letterpress Printing

Theoretically, type set for letterpress printing is *exactly* 0.918 inches high, and all plates are mounted at *exactly* the same height. Perfect impressions depend on this exactness. But perfection, of course, is seldom attainable. Compensating for the imperfections in type and plate height, as well as other factors affecting pressure, is accomplished through a procedure called *makeready*. Makeready is vital to letterpress printing because it establishes the level of reproduction quality. Fine presswork can be obtained only by carefully adding tissue paper under low areas and by cutting away packing where impressions are too heavy. This work on the press cylinder is time-consuming and costly, but it makes possible the finest kind of printing. Other printing systems that do not rely on a raised surface for putting ink on paper do not require a makeready operation.

Special Requirements of "Rotary" Letterpress

The fastest of printing presses is the *rotary* press, so called because plates and/or type rotate on a cylinder as they carry ink to paper.

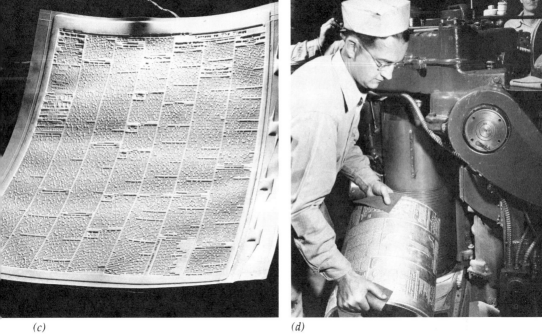

(c)   (d)

Figure 12-2. *Steps involved for rotary letterpress. (a) Text and illustrations are cast or engraved in metal, then placed in a page form. (b) Papier-mâché mat is positioned over the page form, which will then receive intense pressure from roller to create mold for stereotype plate. (c) Finished mold. (d) Curved printing plate being removed from casting machine. (e) Stereotype plates being positioned on rotary printing presses. (© by The New York Times Company. Reprinted by permission)*

(e)

Until recently the only way to use the rotary principle in letterpress was first to put the type and plates together in a flat form, then duplicate that form on the surface of a curved plate that would fit around a plate cylinder. This was usually done through *stereotyping*, a method of duplicating that used a papier-mâché or fiber board mat to serve as a mold for a casting in molten lead. In stereotyping, the mat is placed over the page form and subjected to great pressure, forcing the relief areas of the form to be depressed in the mat. When molten lead was put on the mat in a cylinder-casting box, the lead would contain, in cylindrical form, the relief printing image of the original form. It was stereotyping that made modern newspaper production possible; the speed with which modern metropolitan newspapers are printed would not be possible if printing had to be done from a flat form.

The necessity of stereotyping, although it has been a boon to newspaper printing for decades, has been somewhat of a hindrance to letterpress printing in competition with other processes. Some loss of quality that occurs during the duplicating process, plus the need to maintain a stereotyping department, have served as disadvantages. However, new techniques to permit rotary printing by letterpress without stereotyping have come to the fore in recent years. The most significant of these techniques are those that permit the use of cold type as well as eliminate the need for stereotyping. In these systems, page pasteups are photographed and the negatives thus created are used to expose the printing image on a single thin, flat sheet of magnesium or other metal, or plastic. The metal sheet is then shallow etched to create a relief image. This lightweight, pliable plate can then be wrapped around a "saddle" and used on the printing cylinder of a rotary press.

One of the more spectacular systems for making these plates involves the use of laser beams. The Gannett Company, the publisher of a large chain of newspapers, announced in 1973 that it had successfully tested such a system. According to Gannett, its system successfully passed field tests under normal operating conditions. A series of multiple laser beams, directly from photo-composed pasteups, produced lightweight, combination metal and plastic plates at the rate of one every two minutes and performed satisfactorily in runs of up to 200,000 impressions.[1]

Plate-making systems such as these seemed to be an indicator that many newspapers would continue to be produced on letterpress presses much longer than had been forecast by many experts in the 1960s. Not only do they enable the use of the latest photocomposing systems, but they permit the owner of expensive rotary presses to forego purchasing offset presses.

[1] "Gannett Confirms Testing of Laser-Plate," *Graphic Communications Weekly,* October 9, 1973, p. 3.

Uses and Capabilities of Letterpress Printing

Many observers and prognosticators in the printing industry have concluded that letterpress is suffering from a terminal illness that is certain to bring death in a short while. The great rush to offset as a basic means of printing has served to give credence to this diagnosis. Although there is no doubt about the ills now being suffered by letterpress, there is considerable doubt about any prospective death for the process.

Although the traditional type composition methods for letterpress are rapidly becoming obsolete, innovations in the system are making new composition methods feasible. These innovations, plus the need of many publishers to retain expensive letterpress equipment, would seem to insure a long life span for letterpress printing. Projections by *Inland Printer/American Lithographer* in 1973 about the decade ahead indicated that letterpress would still be accounting for 35 percent of the printing in this country by 1983.[2] For the newspaper industry, the American Newspaper Publisher's Association predicted that while 88 percent of the newspapers in the United States would be offset-produced by 1979, the remaining 12 percent would be consuming 80 percent of the total newsprint. In other words, the larger newspapers, because of their bulk and their circulation, would still be using letterpress methods.

It would seem, therefore, that many basic printing tasks will continue to be accomplished through letterpress on into the foreseeable future. The continued use of letterpress, and the fact that it is the traditional system of printing, which has been responsible for many of the customs and practices now accepted for all systems of printing, makes this system of considerable continuing importance to the student.

Photo-Offset Lithography

Photo-offset lithography, of increasing interest to everyone in the field of communications, differs from letterpress because it is: (1) *photographic*; (2) *planographic* (printing is done from a flat surface); (3) *chemical* in nature rather than mechanical; and (4) usually *indirect* rather than direct. Each of these differences can have an effect on editorial, as well as on mechanical, procedures.

For example, the fact that it relies on photography for the preparation of copy before actual press operation means that offset can employ several systems of type composition. Anything that can be

[2] "Printing, Where Have We Been, Where Are We Going," *Inland Printer/American Lithographer,* October, 1973, p. 33.

photographed can serve as copy for offset lithography. Hence a type-writer or similar machine can be a composing machine; material so composed is generally called *cold type* because it did not have to be cast from molten metal. The traditional hot type may also be used, but only if a *reproduction proof* is pulled to be photographed.

Why this feature is preferable for some editorial operations should be obvious; instead of being done by a skilled craftsman at some printer's shop, type for offset may be composed in a publication office. As machines resembling typewriters become better adapted for such work, this feature becomes increasingly significant.

Combined with its photographic characteristic, the planographic nature of offset has a direct bearing on the use of illustrations. When an offset cameraman takes a photograph of copy, he is not concerned if line illustrations are on the same sheet with type material. Therefore, such illustrations can be used in any quantity with no resultant effect on cost.

Other illustrations, such as photographs, must be handled separately because they have shades of tones and are not merely made of line (full tone) or white (no tone) areas. Halftone negatives, made by exposing the original illustration through a screen onto film, must be made, but the planographic characteristic eliminates the need for etching separate metal plates with acid as is done for letterpress. This separate handling means some additional cost, but generally less than that for letterpress plates. Special treatments (unusual shapes, silhouettes, and the like) also can be achieved with greater ease. These and other characteristics of the offset process should become clear to the student as he understands the various steps in this system of printing (Figure 12-3).

STEPS INVOLVED IN THE OFFSET PROCESS

The work of the offset printer may start with any one of several stages of copy preparation. For simplification, we shall assume, until a later chapter, that all artwork and copy preparation prior to the photographic step have been completed by the buyer. Camera-ready copy for offset usually consists of line material and halftone illustrations.

Making Line Negatives

The line work includes all headlines or titles, body copy, captions, and any line drawings or decorative devices. These items, applied with wax or pasted with rubber cement to a piece of white cardboard, go to the cameraman. Each item is in its proper position on the page or pages included in the pasteup. The halftone areas are marked by guidelines blacked in with india ink, or indicated with

(a) Line copy is pasted up.

(b) Pasteup and halftone copy are photographed separately.

(c) Negatives are developed.

(d) Negatives are opaqued to eliminate undesired clear spots.

(e) Negatives (line and halftone) are stripped into flat (goldenrod).

(f) Plate is cleaned.

(g) Plate is coated (steps f and g are eliminated when presensitized plates are used).

(h) Flat is placed over plate and plate is exposed to light (burned) through negatives.

(i) Plate is developed.

(j) Plate is covered with special ink that makes image area accept printing ink.

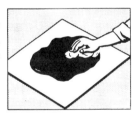

(k) Plate is put on press cylinder.

(l) Paper goes between rubber blanket and impression cylinder to receive ink.

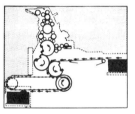

Figure 12-3. *The principal steps in offset lithography. (Reprinted from* Printer 1 & C, *Navy Training Courses, U. S. Government Printing Office)*

red acetate or paper. The pasteup is then ready to be photographed in the same size, enlarged, or reduced.

Cameras used to make negatives for offset are the same as those used by makers of photoengravings for letterpress printers. To photograph a pasteup of line copy, the cameraman simply loads the camera with film, puts the pasteup on the copy board in front of the lens, and makes his exposure. Thus a full page or pages, minus photographs, can be produced as a negative in a matter of seconds. The negative is then developed and dried.

Making Halftone Negatives

The photographs or other illustrations that must be made as halftones are treated separately, but in much the same manner as the line negatives. Before halftone copy can be photographed, a screen must be placed in the camera between the lens and the film. The screen breaks the image on the film into dots. One exposure is needed for line copy; halftones require several. The timing of the exposures and the development of the film are critical; it takes considerable skill to make halftone negatives that will give a clear, accurate reproduction of the subtle gradations of tones.

Preparation of the Flat

Once the halftone and line negatives have been made, they must be *stripped* into position in a sheet of opaque, ruled paper usually called a *flat* or *goldenrod*. An opening large enough to accommodate the line negative is cut from the flat, and the negative is fastened in place with cellophane tape.

At this point it should be recalled that the areas to be taken up by halftones may have been blackened on pasteup. If so, they appear as clear spaces on the negative, for black reflects no light onto the negative, and, when developed, the film remains transparent. Therefore, the halftone can be taped into position behind these "windows," as they are called, completing the final step toward platemaking. If only guidelines are used to designate halftone areas, two other alternatives can be followed. The halftone area may be cut out of the line negative and the halftone taped in the hole. Or, if there is no room for tape around the window, a separate flat may be used for the halftone. In that case, the opening in the separate flat must be perfectly positioned so that the halftone will be in its proper place on the plate.

Making the Plates

Platemaking is the next and final step before material goes on the press. Flat metal plates, usually of aluminum or zinc and about the thickness of tin cans, are used in offset. They are made light sensitive by either the manufacturer or the lithographer. The flat is fastened to the plate with cellophane tape and then "printed" in the photographic sense. The plate is exposed to light through the negatives in the flat. If halftones are in a separate flat, the plate must be "double burned" by exposing one flat onto the plate after the other.

The burned plate is then developed. Any of several techniques may be used, depending upon the type of plate, but in principle the process is much like developing a photograph. Rubbing the plate with chemicals hardens the emulsion in the exposed areas and causes the image to emerge.

For *deep-etch* plates, a special type of offset plate designed for long press runs, a somewhat different procedure is followed. Instead of working with negatives in a flat, the lithographer uses film positives. Thus, light penetrates the plate in the nonimage areas, hardening them and leaving the image areas soft and able to be removed during plate developing. The hardened areas around the printing portions are called the "stencil" and they provide protection from wear on the printing area. The fact that the printing areas are somewhat recessed causes them to receive a thicker coating when developed. This, in turn, permits a much longer press run without noticeable wear.

For still longer press runs, plates combining copper with aluminum have been put into use. In some cases, chromium plating is also used. These *bimetal* and *trimetal* plates are so made that the printing area will be of long-lasting copper and the nonprinting area of aluminum, steel, or chromium. Runs of 500,000 or more are then possible.

The simplest of all offset plates is the *direct image* master — a short-run plate usually made of paper or plastic. As the name implies, the image is typed, drawn by hand, or in some other method applied directly to the plate surface. Machines that, without any of the photographic steps, transfer original images to these masters have increased their use immensely. These machines, operating in the manner of office copiers, can thus duplicate pasteup pages of type or any other original material in seconds. The grease-receptive image that has been applied to the plate surface will accept the ink of an offset duplicator; the nonprinting area accepts the water and rejects the ink. These direct image masters are inexpensive and easy to prepare, but will provide only short runs. Consequently, they are used mainly for office purposes and not by commercial printers.

Xerox and other photocopying machines can also be used to prepare master plates for offset presses. These simplified methods of plate preparation have been influential in causing the rapid increase in the office use of offset duplicators.

Offset-Press Operation

Offset presses are rotary in nature and use the principle that grease and water do not mix to deliver the desired impressions on paper.

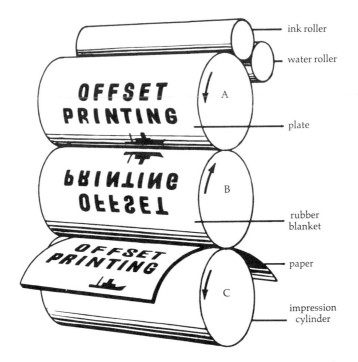

ink roller

water roller

plate

rubber blanket

paper

impression cylinder

Figure 12-4. *Principle of offset-press operation. As plate cylinder A rotates, it is coated with water in the nonimage area and greasy ink in the image area. The ink image is transferred to the rubber blanket on cylinder B and then to the paper as the paper passes between the blanket and impression cylinder C. (Reprinted from* Printer 1 & C, Navy Training Courses, *U. S. Government Printing Office)*

The printing section of the press includes a *plate* cylinder, a *blanket* cylinder, an *impression* cylinder, inking rollers, a moisture system, and a plate-adjustment (registration) device (Figure 12-4). In addition, of course, it has a *feeder* system to move the paper into the press and a *delivery* system for the finished work.

That all material to be printed is on one thin, flat, and pliable plate is one of the virtues of the offset process. Make ready is no problem, and the plate is easily wrapped around the plate cylinder much in the way that a mimeograph stencil is applied.

Once the plate is on the press, the operator must apply the moisture (water plus an additive) to the surface of the plate. The water adheres to the nonimage area of the plate and is repelled in the image areas. When ink, a grease, is applied, it adheres only to the image area and is repelled by the water-wet portions. Because of the water–grease action and its photographic nature, offset lithography is considered a chemical process. It is called an *indirect* process because impressions are not made directly from the plate. The plate never touches the paper; instead, it deposits the inked image on the blanket cylinder with each revolution. The paper receives the image from the blanket as the sheet or web goes through the press between the blanket and impression cylinders. The impression cylinder is simply the surface backing up the paper as the blanket squeezes against it, serving the same function as the platen in a typewriter or the bed of a traditional flat-bed press.

To summarize, the original copy for an offset job is first converted to a negative, then to a positive image on the plate (type reads from left to right), then to a reversed image on the blanket, then to a positive image on the paper. Each revolution of an offset press therefore consists of:

1. Application of water to the nonimage area of the plate
2. Application of greasy ink to the image area of the plate
3. Transfer of the inked image to a rubber-blanketed cylinder
4. Pickup of the paper by the feeding system of the press
5. Insertion by the press of the paper between the blanket and the impression cylinders
6. Deposit of the image from the blanket to the paper
7. Delivery of the sheets or web of paper

Although this may seem to be a lengthy series of details, all is accomplished instantaneously. Because offset presses operate on the rotary principle, they are capable of extremely high speeds. In general, their speeds are basically determined by the efficiency of their feeding and delivery systems; the cylinders can rotate as fast as an electric motor can turn a drive shaft.

The most frequent problem in offset-press operation is the maintenance of a proper balance of moisture and ink. Changes in humidity sometimes give pressmen a great deal of difficulty in keeping this balance.

Advantages of Offset Printing

The explanation of offset as presented in the preceding pages and as illustrated in Figure 12-5 should suggest these specific advantages of the process:

1. Anything that can be photographed can be used as composed type. Letters and characters typed with an ordinary typewriter can serve as the "type" for offset; so can those that have been exposed on photographic film or paper; for that matter, even handwriting can be

(a)

(b)

(c)

274

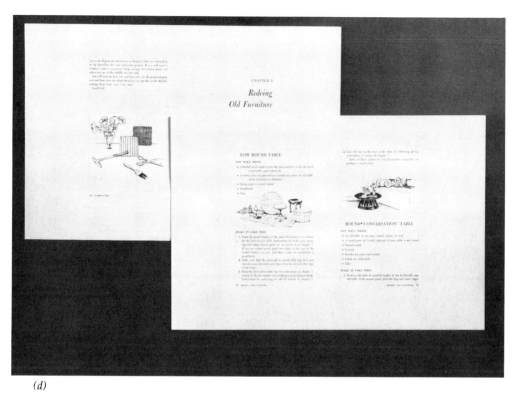

(d)

Figure 12-5. Steps in photo-offset lithography. (a) Manuscript being set on perforated tape and being fed into Linasec computer. (b) Tapes from the computer are fed into this Linofilm machine and copy comes out in galley form. (c) Skilled proofreaders read galleys against original manuscript. (d) Pasteup copy ready to be photographed. (e) Camera and automatic developer.

(e)

(f)

Figure 12-5 (continued). *(f) Stripping negatives into a flat in preparation for making a plate. (g) Burning the plate: exposing it to light through negatives. (h) The plate ready for the press. (i) A 77-inch Miehle press. (Courtesy Vail-Ballou Press)*

(g)

(i)

used. The use of cold-type composition eliminates the need for the skilled technicians ordinarily involved in typesetting.

2. Line drawings, charts, diagrams, and similar illustrations add absolutely no cost to a job printed by offset. Once positioned in proper relation to any accompanying type matter, they are photographed along with it.

3. Photographs, paintings, and other continuous-tone illustrations can be reproduced at lower cost. The exposure of such illustrations on photosensitive plates without having to use an etching process to obtain relief surfaces creates this cost advantage. Special shapes or effects for illustrations are less expensive for the same reason.

4. A major cost and quality advantage is introduced because rougher papers can be used and quality illustrations can still be produced. For some printing jobs, the requirement of a smooth-surfaced paper can add considerably to the expense. It can also restrict the designer when he wants a textured surface to add to or create a particular mood for his product. The "squeezing" of the inked image from a rubber blanket onto the paper makes it possible for quality printing of photographs to be obtained by offset on a wide variety of surfaces.

5. Elimination of *makeready* results in a cost advantage. The planographic characteristic of offset produces a good printing job with the uniform pressure exerted as a blanket cylinder and an impression cylinder make contact. In letterpress printing, a need to raise or lower the level of type or plates to get an even impression is time-consuming and costly. This adjustment, requiring skill and time, is not needed for offset.

6. The flat, paper-thin plates used in offset are easier to store than the type and plates used in letterpress. Further, masks and original pasteups can be easily maintained for future use.

7. Duplication of complicated, previously printed material, such as inventory forms, is simplified. Where the letterpress printer would have to spend time setting type and putting it together with column rules, a lithographer can simply photograph the entire printed form, put the negative in a mask, and expose it to a plate.

8. The rotary presses used in offset are fast and efficient when compared with the common flat-bed cylinder and platen presses used in much letterpress printing. An offset plate, because it is pliable, can be wrapped around a cylinder. Printing from a rotating cylinder is much faster than printing from a flat surface.

9. Paper can even be used for offset printing plates. This method often costs less than a mimeograph stencil and can produce a much neater product.

10. Lifelike color (four-color process) is often producible at lower cost by offset. Quality can approximate that of competing processes, and the sensitive acid etching required to produce letterpress color plates is avoided.

This list of advantages of photo-offset lithography represents more than a set of specifics to be memorized by students for test purposes. Along with other mechanical developments to be explained later, these advantages have served to revolutionize the printing industry. In so doing, they have had a profound effect on our ability to educate, inform, and entertain people of all ages and in all walks of life. Every printed medium of communication has been affected by the offset revolution. Books, magazines, newspapers, brochures, booklets, and all other kinds of printed material have profited from it. In the case of each medium, one or more of the above advantages of offset has been especially appealing.

The Big Switch to Photo-Offset Lithography

The big switch from letterpress to offset by the nation's newspapers represents perhaps the most drastic evidence of the growth of offset as a printing method and its importance to society's communication needs. This change is especially dramatic because of the capital investment involved. Publishers with millions of dollars invested in letterpress equipment naturally are reluctant to discard that equipment while it is still in working order.

Nevertheless, the number of daily newspapers being offset printed went from 10 in 1960 to 264 in 1966 and 976 in 1973. Thus 55 percent of the nation's dailies were offset printed in 1973 and numerous other conversions were also in process at that time. The journalistic trade publications rarely had an issue in the early 1970s in which they did not report another newspaper plant converting to offset. For a lengthy period of time, considering both daily and weekly newspapers, an average of a newspaper a day was converting to offset. It should again be pointed out, however, that a tendency for the largest newspapers to retain letterpress meant that, in gross production of newspaper pages and circulation, letterpress maintained a leadership position.

The magazine industry has felt the effect of offset, too, especially in the small-to-medium class. By 1972, for example, 94.6 percent of the company and institution publications in the United States were offset-produced. When these "house organs," as they are called, entered their period of greatest growth following World War II, only 19 percent (in 1946) were printed by offset; by 1966 the majority (61.43 percent) were using the process, and by 1973 the nonoffset industrial magazine was a rare exception. These magazines, with relatively small circulations, found that cost reduction, particularly as applied to the reproduction of illustrations, was a primary advantage.

In the specialized business magazine field, the shift to offset was also spectacular. By 1970, about two out of three of these magazines were products of offset and McGraw-Hill, the largest publisher of business magazines, had converted all its output (about 40 magazines) to offset. While many mass circulation consumer magazines were still able to use rotogravure and letterpress advantageously because higher initial costs could be countered by other advantages, even for these circulation giants the advantages of faster presses, improved cold-type composition, and more durable plates have resulted in the increasing use of offset.

The textbook field also gives dramatic evidence of the growth of photo-offset lithography. In the years immediately following World War II, an offset textbook was a rare exception. Based on offset's performance during the 1960s, authorities predicted that the process would eventually dominate all levels of textbook production. By 1970, more than nine out of ten elementary school books were offset-produced. At the college level, offset was accounting for more than 80 percent of the textbook production. In all cases, the trend was continuing in offset's favor.

What factors have caused offset's phenomenal increase in textbook production? Obviously, the answer to this question is complicated—factors are interrelated and overlapping. Most of them could, for simplification, be reduced to one factor—lower cost—but this would not really be accurate. The one cost factor that does stand out, however, is offset's ability to provide quality illustrations at low cost. Books for the primary grades, where illustrations often transcend text in importance, were the first to show offset's advantage in this regard. The increased use of this process for books at higher education levels has closely paralleled the need for strong illustrative support for verbal exposition. The offset process provides a means of achieving excellent reproduction of photographs on relatively rough paper at small extra cost, and the reproduction of charts, graphs, and diagrams at no added cost has opened new vistas for authors and publishers. Rather than planning on a minimum number of illustrations, concentrated in a few inserts on smooth paper, authors and publishers can now provide the profuse illustrations throughout that are demanded by modern educational needs. And this can be done on a softer, less reflective, cheaper paper.

The spectacular increase in offset production for all media has been caused also by new developments in type composition methods. As a matter of fact, the ability of letterpress to retain much of its business has related directly to its ability to adapt these new composition methods to letterpress production. Full discussions of these composition developments are presented in Chapters 13 and 15, but a brief reference to them is in order here. Machines essentially similar to electric typewriters, but capable of producing from punched tape a variety of type faces similar to those of letterpress type, were the beginning. Photocomposing machines that produce type on photographic negatives or paper have given an added push. Then the introduction of keyboarded input devices to supplement the composing machines made it possible virtually to eliminate type composition in the traditional sense. When these systems are used, the writer's work can go directly from manuscript typing into type proofs without the use of human typesetters.

The emphasis on the increased use of offset lithography presented in the preceding few paragraphs is there for a very good reason. For both student and practitioner in the graphics of communication, there has been no more important development since the invention of photoengraving and machine type composition. It is important because it means that in working with any medium—newspaper, magazine, book, pamphlet—offset lithography must be understood as a basic means of production. It is more important, however, when considered in connection with the new developments in computerization and type composition, because of the effects it will have on the nonmechanical aspects of graphic communication. Writing, editing, and visual techniques are all undergoing change and must continue to undergo change to take advantage of this emerging process. Consequently, it rates special emphasis. But on the other hand, letterpress printing will continue to be important to the printing industry. It will be in common use in years to come and must also be given adequate attention. Other processes, descriptions of which follow, will continue to have their specialized niches.

Gravure Printing

The terms "gravure" and "intaglio" are used to describe the printing process in which images are transferred to paper from ink-filled depressions in a surface rather than from inked lines in relief or material on a flat surface.

A typical application of the process in its simplest form is the engraving of calling cards or formal invitations. The lines to be printed are cut into the surface of a plate, the plate is coated with ink, then wiped clean, leaving ink only in the depressed areas. When paper is pressed against the plate, it picks the ink out of the depressed areas, thus coating the image in relief on the paper.

The simple engraved invitation can be considered only a distant relative, however, of the fine reproductions of works of art achieved by gravure printing. These are the result of adding photography to the process (*photogravure*); the ability to make these reproductions with high speed has come from the adaptation of the rotary-press principle to the process (*rotogravure*).

Photogravure is not as commonly used as letterpress or lithography because of the high initial cost for plates, but for long runs with a demand for great fidelity of reproduction of photographs and similar artwork, it offers unique advantages. Generally speaking, the use of photogravure is not feasible for runs of less than 5,000; for rotogravure the quantity needed should ordinarily be 100,000 or more.

PRODUCTION STEPS IN GRAVURE PRINTING

In some respects the steps involved in photogravure printing are similar to those of photo-offset lithography, at least in the early stages when photographic procedures are followed.

Making Negatives for Gravure

The first step in preparing gravure copy is to photograph the original. Different films are used for line copy and for halftone copy; a film that provides maximum contrast for line copy and solids; a minimum-contrast film for continuous tone copy. The negatives are then combined to form a film positive — a reproduction of the copy on a clear piece of film.

Transferring the Image to the Plate

In photogravure printing, a sensitized gelatin transfer sheet called *carbon tissue* is usually used to transfer an image from the film to the plate. The carbon tissue is prescreened; that is, it is exposed to light through a screen in a contact printer before any attempt is made to transfer an image to the plate. The prescreening points up the difference in the function of the screen in gravure as compared to that in offset or letterpress platemaking. Here the screen performs only a mechanical task: It creates walls between wells of ink to be etched on the plate and has no part in producing tonal qualities.

Screens used for gravure plates may vary in the number of lines per square inch, as do offset and photoengraving screens, but for gravure the lines are transparent. The screen pattern made on the carbon tissue is, therefore, composed of opaque lines.

After this pattern has been exposed on the carbon tissue, the screen is removed from the contact printer, the film positive is put in its place, and light is directed through it. The gelatin surface hardens to the degree of the intensity of light that strikes it. The exposed carbon tissue then has ridges of completely hardened gelatin in the pattern of the screen (light of full intensity went through the transparent screen lines in the preprinting) and other raised areas of gelatin of varying hardness according to the amount of light released through the film positive.

The gelatin deposits on the carbon tissues are transferred, in position, to a copper plate. The plate is then etched with acids that eat into the metal at depths determined by the hardness of the gelatin. The plate surface is thus composed of uniform rectangular wells of ink formed by the thin walls created by the screen pattern. These wells are shallow for light tones, deep for dark.

The plates described are conventional; some gravure plates are now made so that the ink wells vary in size instead of depth or, through a process called *News-Dultgen,* in both size and depth. The latter process has been used particularly for color work.

Gravure Press Operation

High-speed rotogravure presses work on the same principle as that used in making simple calling cards or invitations. Basically, it is a matter of filling the wells with ink, scraping the excess ink from the surface, and applying paper to plate with pressure (Figure 12-6a).

The rotary press plate is cylindrical and receives a watery, fast-drying ink as it revolves in an ink bath. The plate is scraped clean by a steel knife known as a *doctor blade* before it receives the paper, thus leaving ink only in the wells of the image area. Gravure presses are both sheet-fed and web-fed and have considerable variation in press size and speed of operation.

Figure 12-6. *Production steps in gravure printing. (a) Basic principle of press operation. Doctor blade scrapes excess ink from cylinder before ink is carried to paper from depressed areas.*

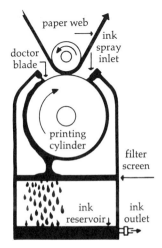

(b)

(c)

(d)

(e)

(f)

Figure 12-6 (continued). *These photographs show the plant where 3.2 million copies of the* New York News *Sunday magazine and comic sections are printed each week by rotogravure. (b) Laying down carbon tissue on a copper-plated cylinder. (c) Staging: applying asphalt paint to areas not covered by tissue, to keep acid from raw copper; staging begins in foreground; in background, a finished cylinder, ready for etching. (d) Etching a cylinder. Etching depths range from 5 microns for light tones to 35 microns for dark tones. (e) A Motter press with 13 units, showing bridge crane and tracks for handling the 3,000-pound cylinders. This press is 160 feet long, 30 feet high, and 18 feet wide. (f) These two 4,000-gallon ink storage tanks hold red and blue ink. Black and yellow inks are stored in 8,000-gallon tanks. (Courtesy the* New York News; *photos by David Leventhal of the* News)

The picture sections of Sunday newspapers, magazines, reproductions of paintings, and a great variety of product containers and wrappings are among the items printed by the gravure process. The chief asset of the process, reproducing highly faithful copies of photographs and paintings (both monotone and color), is possible because the thin ink in the wells of the plate spreads enough during printing to virtually eliminate any screen or dot pattern. In addition, variations in tone result from the thickness of the ink deposit instead of from a dot pattern, and photographs are reproduced with a special quality than cannot be otherwise achieved.

Type reproduction by photogravure is another matter. As pointed out earlier, type matter and illustrations are transferred together from a prescreened carbon tissue to the plate. Type matter is screened at the same time. Because of this and the watery consistency of gravure inks, the text material of a gravure job is less sharp than it would be if prepared by other systems. As a matter of fact, one of the means of discovering whether or not a piece has been printed by gravure is to check the fuzziness of the type matter.

The use of gravure in commercial printing has expanded with the call for more printing on materials like cellophane, new plastic films, and foil. New composition methods, a boon for offset, have also aided gravure. Expected improvements in plate-making also promise much for gravure's future. One of these improvements is electronic engraving, which skips the chemical etching step in plate-making. The process, developed in Germany, is coming into increasing use in Europe and the United States. This system involves scanning of color separation prints and electronic activation of a diamond stylus which mechanically engraves the copper plate. *Inland Printer/American Lithographer* predicted in 1973 that the 10 percent share of the country's printing business then held by gravure would increase to 20 percent by 1983.[3] But to the prospective journalist, gravure's special forte in printing remains the quality reproduction of photographs, usually in extremely large runs.

Silk-Screen Printing

Based on a principle completely different from the three commercial printing methods discussed so far, silk-screen printing is relatively new. All the equipment needed for the most elementary kind is a wooden frame, some stencil silk, a material to block the pores in the

[3] Ibid., October, 1973, p. 33.

silk, a squeegee, and paint or ink. Figure 12-7 illustrates these basic processes.

The silk, stretched tightly over the bottom of the frame and fastened, constitutes the printing form. A solid area is printed by putting paper under the screen and forcing ink through it with the squeegee. To form any desired image besides a solid, it is necessary only to block up the pores of the screen in any of the areas where ink should be withheld. A silk screen so prepared is called a *stencil*. It can be prepared in several ways.

PREPARING SILK-SCREEN STENCILS

The most common method involves the use of transparent paper which has been bonded by a film of lacquer. This can be used as a tracing medium by placing it over the material to be reproduced. A cutter traces the outline of the material with a knife, cutting and stripping from the paper the lacquer film in the areas that must be printed. The sheet is then bonded with a solvent to the silk screen, and the backing paper is pulled away, leaving the lacquer film to plug the screen in all nonprinting areas.

The main advantages of the lacquer-film method of stencil preparation are durability (runs of up to 20,000 are possible), ease of preparation, and relatively high quality.

Some stencils, however, are prepared by hand painting with a brush, by photographic development, and with lithographic crayons

Figure 12-7. *Silk-screen printing. (a) Basic process: Stencils are cut by hand or done photographically; stencil is adhered to underside of stretched fabric and backing sheet is peeled off; squeegee forces ink through stencil to paper underneath. (Courtesy Masta Display, Inc.)*

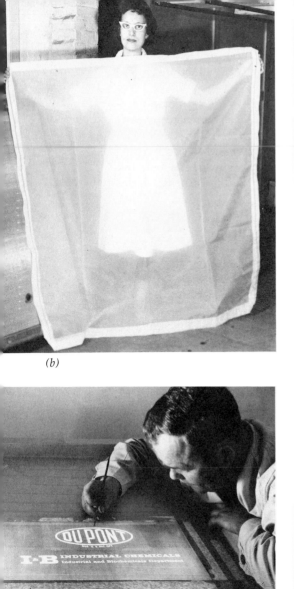

(b)

(e)

(c)

(d)

(f)

(g)

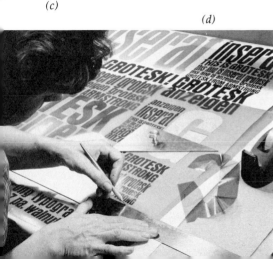

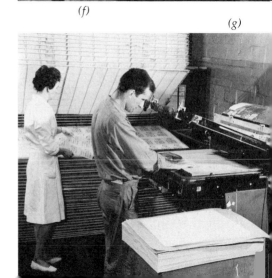

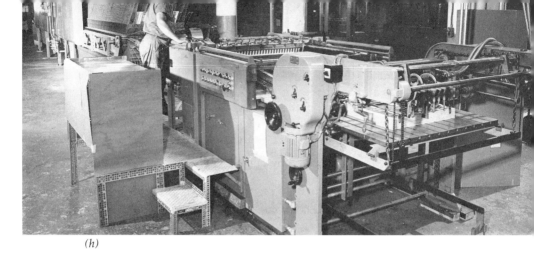

(h)

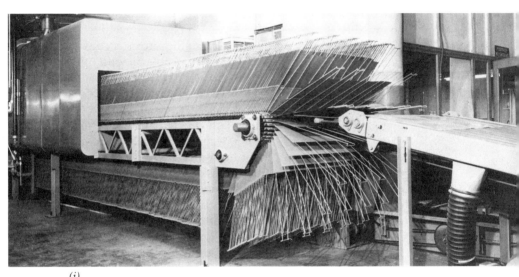

(i)

Figure 12-7 (continued). (b) A screen of porous silk. Various metallic-wire materials also are used for screens. (c) A photographically produced stencil has been applied to a screen and nonprinting areas are being opaqued by a skilled craftsman. (d) Here a stencil is being hand cut—open parts will become printing areas. (e) Screen-process ink—often called paint— has the consistency of syrup. An ink man is shown measuring to a precise color formula. (f) A simple screen press. Ink in frame is pressed through silk by a hand-drawn squeegee blade. (g) A semiautomatic screen press requires positioning of paper by the operator, but actual printing cycle is automatic. Note drying rack. (h) A 30- by 44-inch fully automatic screen-process press capable of printing up to 3,000 sheets an hour. Unit is more than 60 feet long. (i) The 30- by 44-inch press delivers printed sheets into a wicket dryer. Sheets can be air dried or baked dry in the heat tunnel through which the wicket passes. (j) The heart of the 30- by 44-inch screen press is the frame and squeegee, similar to the simple hand press in principle but fully automated. (b, e, g–j: courtesy Kaumagraph Company, Wilmington, Del.; c, d, f: Photo-Art pictures)

(j)

289

and materials. The first is especially suited for stipple and drybrush effects and requires a great skill from the painter. The second is the most complicated of the methods but is particularly effective for halftone and fine line reproduction. Lithographic materials are used mainly by artists for self-expression and for fine art reproductions; stencils so prepared result in beautiful work but are not suitable for long, commercially feasible runs.

USES AND CAPABILITIES OF SILK-SCREEN PRINTING

Posters, displays, and fine art reproductions are perhaps the best-known uses of the silk-screen process, but it serves many other purposes. Because virtually any surface of any thickness may be printed on by this process (bottles, decalcomanias, machinery dials, wallpaper, and fabrics, to name a few), silk screen is considered whenever a printing job presents difficult problems with other processes.

The process has decided limitations. Although halftones can be reproduced by silk screen, the other processes offer much better results. One of the basic advantages of silk screen is that heavy opaque layers of ink can be laid down. This, however, produces a disadvantage because drying becomes difficult. The overall slowness of production is still one of the process's drawbacks, but it is being overcome through recent improvements. New heavy presses have capacities up to 6,000 impressions per hour, and supplementary equipment will feed this production automatically into wicket, jet-air, or oven-kiln dryers that greatly reduce drying time.

Silk screen printing is growing rapidly, especially in the packaging field, and owes its increasing use to its versatility. So-called impossible printing jobs often become completed screen-process jobs.

Photogelatin Printing

Although photogelatin printing differs from photo-offset lithography because it does not require a screen for the reproduction of halftones and is a direct process, it is similar in that it is photographic, chemical, and planographic.

PRODUCTION STEPS IN PHOTOGELATIN PRINTING

Except for the omission of the screen as continuous-tone negatives are made, the first steps of photogelatin production are the same as those of photo-offset lithography.

Line work and photographs are handled separately and then stripped into position in a mask. After any needed retouching or opaquing is completed, the mask is placed over the plate in a vacuum frame and light is directed through the negatives. Plates used in this process are coated with a thin film of light-sensitive gelatin. As the light goes through the negatives and strikes the plate, the gelatin coating undergoes a chemical change that makes it moisture-repellent according to the amount of light received. It is this characteristic that makes photogelatin unique.

Instead of achieving variations of tones by a dot pattern or by the depth of ink receptacles, photogelatin gets its tonal range according to how much water the plate repels. In clear areas (not light-struck) the plates take a full coating of water that completely repels the thick ink. In areas struck by full light, all water is repelled and all ink received. Exact reproduction of the tones between these extremes is obtained as varying amounts of ink adhere to varying exposures on the plate.

USES, CAPABILITIES, AND LIMITATIONS OF THE PHOTOGELATIN PROCESS

Photogelatin printing is equal to or better than any of the other processes for the exact reproduction of photographs, paintings, and the like. Because it is a screenless process, it can produce true duplicates of the original. This is especially apparent, for example, in copies of old documents made by photogelatin — every flaw or symptom of age is faithfully reproduced. Photographs duplicated by photogelatin and glossed with varnish cannot be told from the original and can be used as original copy for the other printing processes.

Advertisers who want to show their products in the very finest detail consider the photogelatin process. Book publishers who want especially good reproduction of illustrations in a quality book turn to it. Some catalogues and sales or public relations presentations are also done by this process. In fact, photogelatin becomes an alternative to other printing methods whenever faithful reproduction of photographs or works of art is essential. Its use is restricted mainly because it is slow and because plates cannot be carried over from one day to another, thus limiting the number of impressions. The cost involved in making a new plate daily for a long press run tends to make other systems cheaper for large jobs; with other printing systems the cost per copy goes down substantially as the number of copies increases.

Most photogelatin presses in the United States accommodate large plates (40 by 60 in.), but they produce only about 800 impressions an hour. Although the rate of turning out small printed pieces can be increased by putting several on one plate, the photogelatin process is still slower than other systems.

Electrostatic Printing

Xerography, a dry system of printing based on electrostatic principles, was demonstrated publicly for the first time in 1948. Although its early commercial applications were mainly restricted to office photocopying machines, the process still represents a revolutionary concept that may have considerable importance in the future.

Xerography uses no ink, no pressure, and no chemicals for getting reproductions on paper or other surfaces. Instead, a dry powder and the principles of photoconductivity and electrical attraction are used to create the duplicate images (Figure 12-8). Plates made of an electrically conductive material, such as sheet metal or foil that have been coated with a photoconductive material are used to transfer images to paper. Sprayed with electrons, these plates become electrically charged and light sensitive. They are exposed to an image pattern

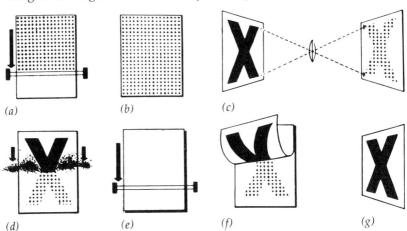

(a) (b) (c) (d) (e) (f) (g)

Figure 12-8. Principle of xerography. (a) The surface of a specially coated plate is charged as it passes under wires. (b) Plate, when charged with positive electricity, has coating. (c) Copy X is projected through camera lens. Positive charges disappear where light strikes but remain where the X holds back the light. (d) A negatively charged powder adheres to the positively charged image. (e) After powder treatment, a sheet of paper is placed over the plate and receives a positive charge. (f) Positively charged paper attracts powder from the plate to form a direct positive image. (g) The print is heated for a few seconds to fuse the powder and form a permanent print. (Courtesy Xerox Corporation, Rochester, N.Y.)

under a projection lens or in a camera or contact printing frame in the same way that standard photographic film or paper is exposed. Whenever light hits the plate, the electrostatic charge is discharged; wherever light is withheld (in the printing area), the charge remains. Powder is then applied to the plate, adhering to the charged area and falling away from the nonprinting (discharged) area.

The transfer of the image from plate to paper is accomplished first by charging the paper; as it contacts the plate, it attracts the powder; then heat is applied, melting the powder and fusing it to the paper. Thus the desired image is transferred (printed).

The xerographic process makes it possible to photograph a subject on a plate, develop the plate, and produce a positive print in less than a minute. It has been applied especially to machines for copying letters, documents, plans, charts, and other such material.

Fascinating possibilities lie ahead for Xerox's Magnafax Telecopier, a device that transmits printed and pictorial documents over an ordinary telephone line. Using this equipment, a sender puts his document on the drum of a Telecopier, plugs his telephone into a base outlet and presses a button. Inside the device the document is scanned and the visual signals thus picked up are converted to electrical impulses and then to sounds. At the receiving end of the telephone line, a Telecopier receives these sounds and converts them back to print. The process takes about six minutes from the start of transmission to delivery of the facsimile.

Xerox announced another breakthrough in 1973 when it introduced its 6500 color copier, a machine that would copy full-color originals onto ordinary paper and transparency material. The time necessary to produce a copy was 33 seconds for the first one and 18 seconds for each additional copy.

An electrostatic process developed by the Stanford Research Institute has been applied commercially in dramatic form by the Electrostatic Printing Corporation of America. Because the system does not depend on pressure for printing, even such resilient surfaces as egg yolks and piles of sand can receive the printed image.

This versatility is electrostatic printing's primary advantage, and it has been used commercially to print on the surface of fruit and vegetables and other unlikely surfaces such as welding rods. Wherever pressure would be a problem, for example, glass bottles or medicine capsules, electrostatic printing is expected to gain wide use.

Printing by this method is accomplished through the use of a stencil backed by a finely meshed metal screen that is electrically charged. The paper or other printing surface is backed by a metal plate carrying an opposite charge. A powdered ink picks up the screen's charge and then jumps through the screen into the areas left open by the stencil to the negatively charged printing surface. The powder then is fused to the surface with heat.

Thus, this electrostatic process resembles both Xerography and basic screen printing. Electrostatic charges are used instead of squeegees to get ink through the paper, and the ink is in powder rather than paint form.

The system's low cost (press costs are expected to be half those of conventional presses) and versatility give promise of a bright future for electrostatic printing.

Jet Printing

Another pressureless, plateless system closely related to the electrostatic systems mentioned above is *jet printing,* a method still in its developmental stages as this book was written.

In jet printing, the ink is squirted through a nozzle (A. B. Dick Videojet System) or several nozzles (Dijit system), then charged electrostatically and controlled by a computer to form patterns of characters.

Plateless, noncontact printing was deemed to have enough potential for the American Newspaper Publishers Association to contract with the Massachusetts Institute of Technology for the development of such a system for newspapers. The high speed and simplicity of jet printing make it a fascinating possibility for the future.

SOME MISCELLANEOUS REPRODUCTION PROCESSES

The preceding reproduction processes represent only a few of the total number, although they account for the bulk of large-quantity printing.

The term "printing" in its broadest sense includes the work of the photographer who turns out photographs from negatives and of the typist who uses carbon paper to make six copies of written material. These and other activities are often ignored or treated separately because their production capacity is minimal. But actually, any person who engages in communication through graphic means should view these and other limited processes as integral to the whole field.

Mimeographing, for example, is a duplicating system of considerable potential. A stencil process fulfills many communication needs, such as newsletters, high school newspapers, instruction manuals, sales pieces, and interoffice communications.

Spirit duplicating is also used for similar purposes. It employs an aniline-dye carbon paper beneath a sheet of coated paper to make master copies that, when moistened with an alcohol-base liquid, deposit impressions on paper.

Used within their natural limitations, all duplicating processes are important means of transmitting messages. Choosing a process for any situation is a vital step because both effectiveness of communication and resultant cost are affected.

Selection of the Process

The wide range of processes would seem to make the selection a rather difficult chore. In most cases, however, there are factors that immediately pare down the possibilities. These include: (1) availability, (2) cost, (3) deadline, (4) number of copies, (5) type of paper, (6) use of photographs, and (7) quality level.

Many items are mimeographed simply because a machine is available and the job can be turned out in a short time. Letterpress printing is used on occasion because it is the only process available locally for a job requiring top quality in both words and pictures. Offset lithography is used in a given instance because good quality reproduction of photographs on a textured paper is a necessity, and the press run is large. A newspaper publisher continues to use letterpress printing when a shift to offset might seem feasible because the change-over would require a greater investment than he can afford.

These examples merely give an indication of the various factors that influence process selection; they are not intended to represent a complete list of possibilities by any means. Nor can this chapter make the student professionally adept at deciding a process for a publication or a major printing job. It is hoped, however, that it has provided the descriptions essential for a communicator to work effectively with any of the processes. The special meaning to students of the technological revolution in printing is that many of the processes of printing have moved from the "back shop" to the "front shop." Editors instead of printers may now find themselves supervising production of type as well as page layout. The compositor of type may be entirely bypassed; as editorial material is created on a keyboard it is automatically produced in type. Therefore the editorial journalist in fact becomes the printer as well. For that reason it has become more important than ever that those entering the communication industry understand the entire process from the idea to actual printing of messages.

CHAPTER 13 Preparing
Verbal Copy
for Production

Copy preparation is a primary factor in implementing effective printed material. It is the last line of defense against error, against misunderstanding by the printer and the readers, and against sloppy appearance.

When the printer receives copy, it must be accurate in every detail, or errors will certainly mar the final result. Furthermore, without specific and detailed instructions, its appearance in type may not even resemble what was desired. And, as every novice who has been sent in search of a "type squeezer" knows, copy must fit prescribed areas: lead type slugs or lines of phototype cannot be compressed.

On the other hand, it takes only one instance of less copy than is needed to fill the space requirements to show that too little is as bad as too much. There are two solutions to this problem — extra leading (white space) between lines or writing additional material. Either solution will require more work for the printer and will increase costs.

Therefore, three important aspects of copy preparation that must be understood are: copy correction, copy marking (with printer's instructions), and copy fitting. The traditional methods for getting words ready for printing will be discussed first; the techniques involved when computer-related technology is used will also be explained.

COPYREADING SYMBOLS

Correction Desired	Symbol

1. Change form:
    3 to three. . . . . ③
    three to 3. . . . . (three)
    St. to Street. . . . . (St.)
    Street to St. . . . . (Street)

2. Change capital to small letter . . . . ℓ

3. Change small letter to capital . . . . d̲

4. To put space between words. . . . . the|time

5. To remove the space. . . . . .news paper

6. To delete a letter and close up . . . . .judgment

7. To delete several letters or words . . . . .shall ̶a̶l̶w̶a̶y̶s̶ be

8. To delete several letters and close up . . . . . . .superintendent

9. To delete one letter and substitute another. . . . .receive

10. To insert words or several letters. . . . . .of ‸the time

11. To transpose letters or words, if adjacent. . . . .recieve

12. To insert punctuation, print correct mark
    in proper place:

comma	⟋	parentheses	(
period	⤫	opening quote	⤷
question	?	closing quote	⤶
semicolon	⟓	dash	—
colon	⤫	apostrophe	ⱽ
exclamation	!	hyphen	=

13. To start a new paragraph. . . . . ¶ or |It has been

14. To center material. . . . .⌉Announcements⌊

15. To indent material. . . . . The firs⌉
                                                   ⌊day's work

16. Set in boldface type . . . . The art of

17. Set in italic type . . . . The art of

18. To delete substantial amounts of copy, draw
    an X over the area and box it in.

19. To set several lines in boldface type, bracket   (The first
    the lines and mark bf in the margin.   bf(day's work

Figure 13-1. *Copyreading symbols.*

Copy Correction

Fortunately for the student, the basic techniques of traditional copy correction are the same for all media—whether copy is being prepared for newspapers, magazines, books, promotion pieces, or advertising. A universally accepted set of symbols makes this task relatively fast and efficient. These symbols are easy to learn because they are functional and are based on common sense.

Copy to be set should be typed double- or triple-spaced. All corrections can then be made at the spot of error, either on the line or above the line. Figure 13-1 shows both the symbols for correcting errors in typewritten copy and those used for typesetting instructions; the latter are discussed in more detail later. Figure 13-2 shows a story that has been edited, using these symbols.

Figure 13-2. *A copy editor has used symbols to correct this story before giving it to the compositor for typesetting.*

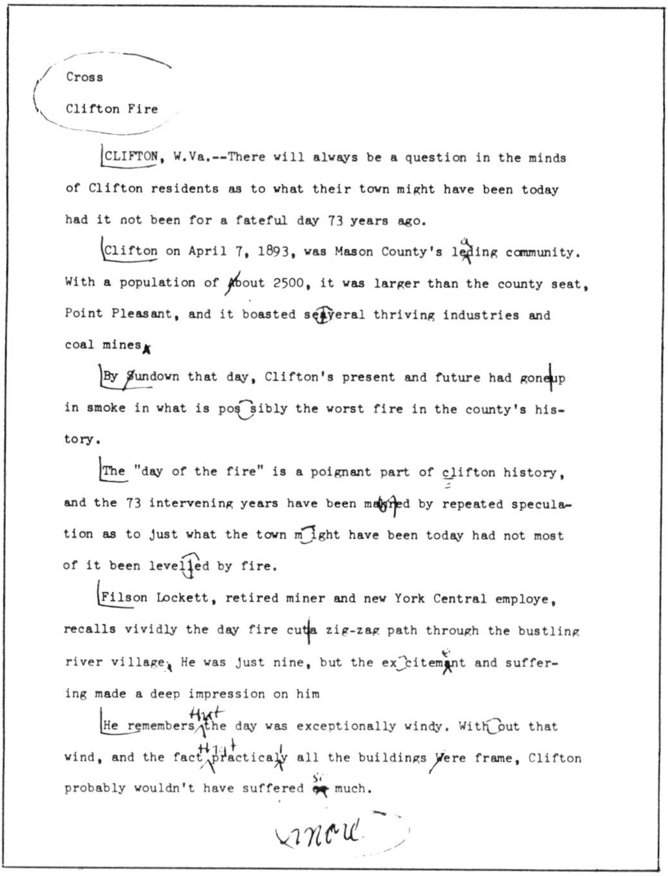

The correcting process does not end with typewritten copy, of course. When the copy has been set into type, galley proofs are read to detect and eliminate errors made by the typesetter. There is seldom enough space between the lines on a galley proof to enable a proofreader to use any of the symbols shown in Figure 13-1 at the point of error. Even with enough room to do so, the typesetter would have to read through complete proofs to find the symbols instead of being able to see each correction at a glance. Therefore, special *proofreading* symbols are used *in the margin* to correct material that has been set in type. A mark may also be made at the point of error. Many proofreaders for newspapers and magazines draw a line from the point of error to the correction in the margin; most readers for book publishing firms do not. When guidelines are drawn, care must be taken to avoid obliterating the remainder of the line to be corrected. The symbols for marginal marks (Figure 13-3) are basically the

---

Page 2

Cross

Clifton Fire

The fire broke out about noon in a structure around a salt well, near the bank of the Ohio river. It spread quickly to a salt storage shed. The blustering wind fanned flames and embers into the furnace section of the salt works, and across the road where a small plant was destroyed.

Townspeople quickly rallied to shrieks of plant whistles and church bells, but they were pitiful with their bucket brigade as fire roared through the timbers.

A call for help was sent to Middleport, across the river. Middleport possessed one of the few fire engines in the area. It was modern for its day, but inadequate for a blaze raging with the intensity of the Clifton fire. The fire engine was loaded on to a ferry boat and started toward Clifton. Winds raised such high waves on the Ohio that water broke over the deck of the ferry.

Middleport's fire engine did some good. Stationed at the corner of Mason and olive (Sts.) the Middle port firemen managed to save the Woodrum home, which stands today.

At that point *then* the flames veered eastward a long Olive (at.) to Columbia and High and out Columbia. At one point *they* burned all the homes between a saloon and church, causing one wag to remark "she burned from hell to heaven."

⋀ Make correction indicated in margin.

Stet Retain crossed-out word or letter; let it stand.

.... Retain words under which dots appear; write "Stet" in margin.

X Appears battered; examine.

≡ Straighten lines.

✓✓✓ Unevenly spaced; correct spacing.

// Line up; i.e., make lines even with other matter.

run in Make no break in the reading; no ¶

no ¶ No paragraph; sometimes written "run in."

¶ Make a paragraph here.

tr Transpose words or letters as indicated.

𝒮 Take out matter indicated; delete.

𝒮 Take out character indicated and close up.

¢ Line drawn through a cap means lower case.

9 Upside down; reverse.

⌒ Close up; no space.

Insert a space here.

□ Indent line one em.

[Move this to the left.

] Move this to the right.

sp Spell out.

⌐ Raise to proper position.

� Lower to proper position.

w.f. Wrong font; change to proper font.

Qu? Is this right?

l.c. Put in lower case (small letters).

s.c. Put in small capitals.

caps Put in capitals.

c.+s.c. Put in caps and small caps.

rom. Change to Roman.

ital. Change to Italic.

≡ Under letter or word means caps.

= Under letter or word, small caps.

— Under letter or word means Italic.

⩰ Under letter or word, boldface.

⋌ Insert comma.

⋌;/ Insert semicolon.

:/ Insert colon.

⊙ Insert period.

/?/ Insert interrogation mark.

(!) Insert exclamation mark.

/=/ Insert hyphen.

⋁ Insert apostrophe.

ⅤⅤ Insert quotation marks.

⋎ Insert superior letter or figure.

7/ Insert inferior letter or figure.

[/] Insert brackets.

(/) Insert parenthesis.

⊬ One-em dash.

$\frac{2}{M}$ Two-em parallel dash.

bf Boldface type.

⍦ Set *s* as subscript.

⍦ Set *s* as exponent.

Figure 13-3. *Proofreading marks and symbols.*

same for either system. A marked proof is shown in Figure 13-4.

Many errors creep into printed material because someone fails to follow through after galleys have been corrected. If errors are detected at the first reading, revised proofs with corrections should be checked, for a compositor can err as he sets a correction in a line or as he substitutes corrected lines. Instead of pulling the line containing an error, he may take out another one and replace it with the one he has corrected. The result is double-talk that can destroy all meaning for the material.

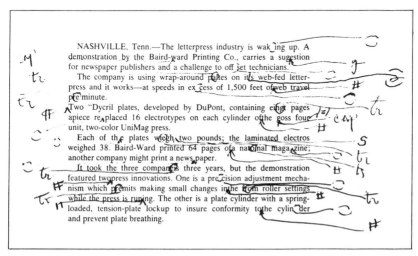

Figure 13-4. *A specimen galley proof marked with proofreading symbols. The number of errors has been greatly exaggerated here to show the widest possible variety of symbols. Actual proofs have very few errors.*

It is true that there is usually another opportunity for corrections to be made even if revised galley proofs are not called for, but this final reading should not be used for detecting errors in typesetting. These last proofs are made in the form of pages or, in the case of advertising, of the completed ad. They provide a chance to check if material is positioned properly, headlines are with the right story, captions are with the correct picture, and so on. To delay typesetting corrections to this point is wasteful because it takes more time to unlock a form or alter a pasteup to exchange lines than it does to make the change when type is still in galleys.

Printers accept responsibility for the errors of their compositors, but charge for the time spent correcting errors that were not detected in original copy or remaking lines for an editor or author who has merely changed his mind. These revisions become more expensive as material moves into the advanced production stages.

Publications with their own mechanical departments can hide the cost of author's alterations or other laxities because there is no bill that must be paid by the editorial department. But the cost remains nevertheless.

Some letterpress publications require duplicate sets of galley proofs, one for marking corrections and one to be cut apart and pasted on layout sheets. The set to be corrected is usually on white paper; the other is often on colored stock. Proofs for pasteup bear markings across the type area to identify the storage location of the type. This helps the printer's makeup man find the type as he puts pages together. The same is true for offset publications if the camera-ready pasteup is done by the printer with this preliminary pasteup as a guide.

Press proofs are also obtainable, and in some cases this additional safeguard may be warranted. But if the person who must check the proofs is not on hand when the material first goes on the press, expensive press time can be wasted, since the time the job is on the press must be paid for whether the press runs or not.

Regardless of precautions, errors occur. Absolute vigilance from the beginning of the typed copy to the final production steps keeps them to a minimum. Nothing can be taken for granted; it is amazing how easily errors seem to occur in such obvious places as headlines and titles in large display type.

Marking Printer's Instructions

Before a printer can set a single line of type he must have at least eight basic points of information:

1. Type size (expressed in points)
2. Type family (Century, Cheltenham, . . .)
3. Family branch (bold, condensed, extended, . . .)
4. Letter posture (italic or roman)
5. Letter composition (caps, lower case, . . .)
6. Leading
7. Appointment of space (flush, centered, . . .)
8. Line length (expressed in picas)

Theoretically, then, the instructions for setting a line of type would read like this: "8/10 Bodoni Bold Italic caps and lower case, centered on 21 picas." However, much of this information does not have to be written on every piece of copy. Depending upon the circumstance, it can be taken for granted that some of the instructions are understood by the printer.

In body copy, for example, it is assumed that the appointment of space is to be flush left and right. Only exceptions must be marked. Letter composition is considered to be as shown in the copy; that is, typed capitals are to be set as capitals, lower case letters are to be set as lower case. Printers also set copy with roman letter posture and with no leading unless there are indications to the contrary.

The marking of copy for titles and headlines is also simplified because of the following assumptions mutual to editor and printer: that (1) posture is roman unless marked; (2) machine leading is not needed unless marked; (3) line length is to be "line for line"; and (4) letter composition is to be as shown in the copy.

But whether by mutual understanding or by specific copy marking, a line of type cannot be set unless the printer has the eight points of information. This is especially true of "transient" material, as distinguished from periodical copy. Procedure for periodicals differs because the regularity of issue permits considerable uniformity.

NEWSPAPER PROCEDURE

Marking copy for the mechanical department of a newspaper is simplified by several factors. Selection of type sizes, style, and leading is a decision of management and is seldom subject to change. Column widths (line lengths) are standard, although there may be some variation on the editorial page for by-line columns or special features. Speed in processing copy is essential and time is at a premium. Because headlines have such a direct effect on the character of a newspaper, they are standardized as much as possible.

Copy is channeled through one central (universal) copy desk, a number of departmental desks, or both. These desks are directed by people who are expert in the English language and versed in the newspaper's style and its composing and pressroom procedures; they prepare copy quickly and efficiently for the mechanical department.

Because body type specifications do not change, much of the copy is sent to the composing room with no marked instructions other than those for exceptions (multicolumn leads, special treatment for editorials or columns, and so on). Standardization applies to headlines too. A comprehensive schedule that visualizes all possible headlines and gives all the information a headline writer may need is prepared by the editorial department for the composing room. Each headline is keyed by a number or letter; to give the composing room all necessary information about the final appearance of a headline, the writer simply labels the headline with any agreed-upon designation, such as "#1" or "AA," and this immediately refers the compositor to the type size, face, and so on, similarly marked on the comprehensive schedule.

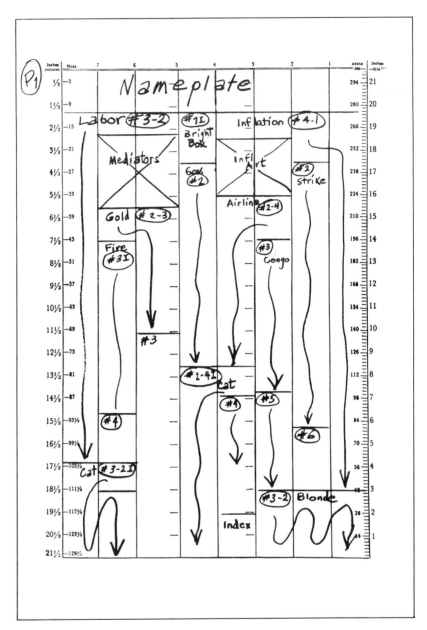

Figure 13-5. *A typical newspaper page dummy.*

Body and headline copy are usually sent to the composing room on separate sheets. For the most part, the display sizes of type are composed on the Ludlow or Linotypes and Intertypes reserved for display, and the body sizes are set on Linotype or Intertype straight-matter machines. If body copy and headlines were on the same sheet, the compositors would not be able to set both at the same time.

To place a headline over the proper story when pages are made up, a "slugging" system is used. The body copy is slugged with a word or two to identify the story — most newspapers use the first two words of the headline. As the text type is put in place, the slug line is replaced by the headline it identifies.

Other special problems for the newspaper are handled with equal efficiency. Continuing stories (which are set in type in intervals as they develop during the day), stories that must be changed slightly between editions, and stories that must be set before a headline has been written require special markings. These vary from newspaper to newspaper, but are always conveyed by techniques that simplify the communication of instructions from the editorial department to the composing room.

Newspaper Makeup Instructions

A newspaper must be put together in a hurry. Virtually every step of the makeup process is based on approximation, rather than exact calculation. As stories are processed, their length is estimated and each is recorded with pertinent data on an inventory sheet usually called a *copy schedule.*

This information is used for page dummies. As the makeup man prepares the dummy, he writes the slug for each story in the position on the page that he believes the story merits. He indicates the probable length of the story with an arrow and shows the placement of illustrations by drawing an X through the space. The dummy then serves as a pattern as the stories and headlines are put in a form prior to stereotyping or printing. Figure 13-5 shows a typical newspaper page dummy marked up.

ADVERTISING AND BROCHURE PROCEDURE

The marking of copy for advertisements is quite different. In most cases a full *markup* (Figure 13-6) is used for communicating instructions about typesetting and makeup to the printer. It is best described as a drawing of how the ad is to look when printed. All display lines are lettered in exact position, illustrations are sketched in, and body type areas are indicated by drawn lines. Instructions for type sizes and style are written with colored pencil and circled next to each bit of display type or in the margin. The body type areas are identified by letter — A, B, C, and so on.

Body copy is provided in typewritten form, is marked with

Figure 13-6. *An ad layout marked with printer's instructions is called a markup; it serves the function of a dummy.*

typesetting instructions, and is slugged with the corresponding letter from the markup. By following these instructions and checking with the markup, the mechanical department or printer can create an exact replica of the ad as designed by the advertiser or his agency. The same procedure is followed for flyers, handbills, direct mailing pieces, and other brochures.

MAGAZINE PROCEDURE

The preparation of magazine material is usually a cross between those used for newspapers and for advertisements. Sometimes articles are prepared with full markups by an art department; or the editor may follow a fast course like his newspaper counterpart. But in most cases a middle ground is followed.

Often there is no headline schedule; titles follow no set typographical pattern. They are lettered in position on a dummy, with typesetting instructions entered as in advertising markups. The relative stability of column measure and other aspects of body copy permits the use of minimum marking for such material.

Because there is usually sufficient time between issues, a magazine dummy is made by pasting galley proofs of text material or specimen copy of body and caption type in position, with the titles lettered in by hand (Figure 13-7). Rough layout sketches in miniature or full-size often precede the pasteup dummy.

Figure 13-7. *A magazine dummy with galley proofs pasted in position and the title lettered in position and marked for the printer.*

The procedures described above are based on the assumption that copy is being prepared in customary typewritten form for typesetting in a traditional printing shop.

Such procedures are still in use for most of the printing being done today, especially by the public relations or advertising designer who prepares transient material for reproduction in one of the thousands of independent printing establishments in the country. But for some large magazine publishing firms, and especially for newspaper news services and many newspapers, new technology has necessitated some changes.

These changes have stemmed primarily from new computer-related typesetting systems. These systems are explained in detail in Chapter 15, but we must look at their relationship to copy preparation here.

Optical Character Recognition

One of these systems is called *Optical Character Recognition* (OCR). It involves the use of devices called *readers* or *scanners*, which convert typewritten copy to tape or memory for driving computerized photocomposition machines.

With OCR, a sheet of copy, typed double- or triple-spaced, is simply put into the machine's hopper. The copy is scanned at tremendous speed (hundreds of words per minute) and with remarkable accuracy.

To use OCR devices:

1. Copy must be typed on a typewriter that produces letters or a bar code that can be recognized by the system; IBM Selectric with the Courier 12 type font and a carbon ribbon are often specified.
2. Because the system depends on character recognition, all corrections and instructions must eventually be made on the proper typewriter.

In order to keep copy flowing when some OCR systems are first installed for newspapers, the traditional copyreading symbols shown in Figure 13-1 are still used by editors. These marks, however, are made with a pen using colored ink that is invisible to the scanner. Special typists convert the editing marks to typewriter changes that the scanner can read (Figure 13-8).

OCR devices have become amazingly accurate and flexible. Some of the earlier machines could not handle crumpled paper, lines slightly awry, and other such imperfections. Now most scanners can tolerate substantial irregularities and still be highly accurate.

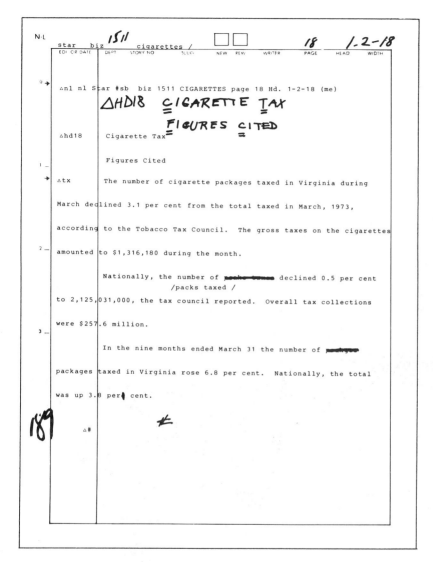

Figure 13-8. *A sheet of copy ready for an Optical Character Recognition device. The headline and the traditional corrections in pen were made in a color not visible for the scanner, then the corrections were typed in place for reading by the scanner. (Courtesy* Richmond Times-Dispatch*)*

Many scanners also are equipped to use almost human logic in some cases where character identification presents a problem. Some machines stop completely when a character cannot be identified, and the operator must "tell" the device what the character is. In others, however, the machine will try several times and finally make the "best guess" based on logical factors, just as people do (see Chapter 2).

OCR devices can be used separately from or in conjunction with machines called *video display terminals* (VDT) or *cathode ray tube* devices (CRT).

The Use of Video Display Terminals

A video display terminal consists of a typewriter-like keyboard and a television picture tube. It can be used "on line" with a computer; that is, material typed on the keyboard can be fed directly into a computer for later recall, or it can be used for punching the tape that runs a computerized phototypesetter.

Figure 13-9. *A modern newsroom where editing and reporting are done on video display terminals (also called cathode ray tubes). (Courtesy* Detroit News)

Figure 13-10. *An editor, working at his VDT, can make editing changes simply by hitting the appropriate keys on the keyboard. (Courtesy* Detroit News)

The adoption of VDTs to replace typewriters by both the Associated Press and United Press International has made them important gadgets for the future journalist. In AP or UPI bureaus stories are typed on VDTs. An editor may make corrections immediately or the copy may first be stored in a computer and recalled later for editing. Editing changes can be made on the keyboard (or perhaps right on the picture tube with a light pencil—a pencil that writes with a beam of light). Coding done in the same fashion channels the story to the computer and from there to any kind of distribution system selected for it; it may be coded to go on the state wire, a regional wire, a national wire, or any specialized wire.

In newspaper installations, VDTs may be used by reporters just as they are in AP and UPI bureaus. They may also be used as basic editing tools, however. If a story is stored in a computer after it has originally been typed on a VDT, it can be recalled for viewing and editing on the same VDT or perhaps one of a full bank of terminals provided for editing personnel. Or, if the story was originally typed on a Selectric or other scannable typewriter and then fed into an OCR scanner for computer storage, it can also be recalled for viewing and editing on a VDT.

The mechanics of editing on a VDT are relatively simple. The editor views the story, or a portion of it, on the television screen above his keyboard. If the screen is not large enough to hold the complete story, the editor can "scroll" the story by hitting the appropriate key. Scrolling "rolls" the story upward across the face of the screen in much the same fashion that the words for a song are displayed in a "sing-along" film. The viewable portion of the story can be stopped for editing at any time.

Most editing changes are then made in connection with a cursor key. This key controls a blinking light dot that can be moved anywhere on the screen. The dot is moved from its home position (upper left on most machines but at the bottom left on others) by pressing the appropriate left, right, up, or down key. When the cursor is positioned at the spot where a change is to be made, other keys are used to add or delete a character or characters, delete sentences or paragraphs, transpose letters, and so on.

After a story has been corrected or changed as desired, the editor replaces it in the computer memory or puts it into type by simply touching another key. The fact that no other human being handles the story has two major advantages: (1) cost savings are substantial because the editor and/or reporter is in effect the typesetter; and (2) the possibility of error is considerably reduced.

OCR devices and VDTs, in combination with computerized photocomposition of type, have almost eliminated the human element in typesetting. They have, however, introduced one complication: the necessity of coding typesetting instructions into language that a machine, rather than a human being, can understand. For example, to tell a human being to set some copy in 9-point Times Roman in lines that are 30 picas wide, we write "9/10 TR x 30." To tell a computerized system the same thing, the instructions might be "WCSAS.000Y100" or "SMUA-LJCS9LR" (Romano, 1973, p. 59). These "command codes" increase in complexity as the complexity of the job increases. Marking these codes on copy is the job of a "markerupper," as he is called in many printing establishments. A markerupper is to typesetting what a programmer is to data processing. Unfortunately, coding and markup are not uniform among typesetting systems. Therefore, anyone marking copy for computerized photocomposition must learn the peculiarities of the system with which he must work.

For commerical printers, the need for markup represents a cost item they have been unaccustomed to. Consequently, there has been some variation in charging customers for this cost, but in general the custom has been to add about 5 percent to the time charged to a printing job. Compared to the nonproductive costs involved in earlier typesetting systems (i.e., changing magazines on a hot metal linecasting machine), and taking into account the great speed of computerized systems, this added complication and cost is an unimportant detail.

For newspapers and other periodicals the complexity of command coding is greatly reduced. For obvious reasons, the typesetting itself is highly simplified in publication situations, and in addition the systems are engineered to have much of the coding wired into the machinery, leaving only a very simple instruction process for human operators.

As this edition was being prepared, adjustments and experimentation with the new technology were still under way in print shops and publication offices all across the country. Exactly what will finally emerge as standard operating procedure is a matter of conjecture. But there is no doubt that in the future, especially in the newspaper field, the letters OCR, CRT, and VDT will become about as familiar as ABC.

Pasteups for Lithography

It is possible to provide a lithographer with a dummy, the written copy, and all illustrations as is done in letterpress printing. The lithographer can then assemble all the elements in page form himself. This procedure, however, does not provide the full cost advantage of this process.

It is customary for users of lithography to prepare page pasteups, thereby doing for themselves what is equivalent to the composing-room page makeup of letterpress printing. All line material, including text and display type and any illustrations that would be reproduced as line engravings in letterpress, are pasted in position on a suitable white cardboard. Photographs or other continuous-tone illustrations must be treated separately. Although the pasteup must be done accurately, anyone using a T square, triangle, and drawing board with care can do the job so well that none of the elements are out of line. Type proofs must be handled carefully so that the ink does not smear, because any smears and blemishes will appear in the final copy. These page pasteups are then photographed by the lithographer and the resultant negatives are stripped into the mask.

All photographs and continuous-tone illustrations must be scaled and cropped for lithography just as they are for letterpress printing. They are photographed separately from line copy, through a screen in order to reproduce their tonal variations. Each is then separately stripped into the mask.

Figure 13-11. *A pasteup being prepared for offset lithography. (Courtesy New York Lithographing Corporation)*

One of the most exacting details in doing a pasteup is the indication of the space for illustrations that are to be stripped separately. For square-finish halftones, the space is usually indicated by accurately ruled lines or by a rectangle of black or red paper pasted in place. Lithographers will usually indicate their preference for either of these methods.

When line and halftone matter are to be combined (as in letterpress combination plates) an acetate overlay containing the line work is usually registered over the halftone as if for color application (see Chapter 7).

Other special halftone finishes, such as silhouettes and vignettes, can be specified through the use of tissue overlays as indicated earlier for letterpress. To make sure they will be positioned properly on the plate, the pasteup techniques are commonly used. In one of these, a *camera lucida* is employed. This device projects art work at desired scale to a drawing surface on which the subject can be outlined. This outline can then be accurately positioned on the pasteup. Otherwise a photostat to size is used on the pasteup to show the location of the illustration.

Copyfitting

The planner of any kind of graphic communication is vitally concerned with copyfitting. It is important to the editors of newspapers and magazines, the advertising designer, and the public relations man who puts together booklets and brochures, for, without it, unnecessary costs are incurred, or attractive layouts are destroyed, or both. If more type than needed is set, the payment for the *overset* is wasted cost. Titles that cannot fit a given space must be rewritten and reset with unnecessary loss of time and money. Areas of text type that fail to fill their allotted space can jeopardize the effect of a good design.

Depending upon the circumstance, copy fitting may be rough or extremely accurate. There are several methods, each suitable to its purpose. For body-type sizes, these include an estimation based on numbers of words per column inch, an *em* system, a *square-inch* method, and a *character-count* system. For display sizes, a *unit count* is used.

COPYFITTING FOR NEWSPAPERS

The fast pace of newspaper production allows no time for complicated copyfitting methods. Stories are written so that they can be cut from the bottom with destroying meaning. When they do not fill a space, filler material is supplied.

Consequently, estimation based on the number of words in a column inch is sufficiently accurate. Depending upon point size, column width, and leading, this figure usually ranges from 30 to 40 words per column inch. When reporters use a uniform setting for line lengths on their typewriters, this figure can be converted into lines; that is, four typewritten lines equal a column inch.

It only takes a second, for example, for an experienced copy editor to gauge a story's length to be 20 typewritten lines (four lines equaling a column inch) or five column inches. Other systems take more time, but offer greater accuracy when called for.

EM SYSTEM OF COPY FITTING

The *em* system of copyfitting is reasonably accurate and is useful for estimating space requirements during the preliminary stages of production. It is also useful in determining which type size will squeeze a prescribed amount of copy into an allotted space. (Any copyfitting problem can be solved by this method, but it is ordinarily not used when a type face and size have already been selected; a more accurate result can then be obtained by considering the space characteristics of the selected face.)

A knowledge of printing measurement is mandatory for an understanding of the em method. The following must be committed to memory:

1. A point is one 72nd of an inch (72 points equal an inch) and one-twelfth of a pica
2. A pica is 12 points (one-sixth of an inch)
3. An em is the square of the type size (an 8-point em is 8 points wide, a 10-point em is 10 points wide, . . .)

The system also depends on the following estimations:

1. For type sizes 10-point or smaller, three ems equal one word
2. For type sizes 11-point or larger, two and one-half ems equal one word

Because the em system is based on averages for word length, spacing between words, and type-design characteristics, it is accurate only to a limited degree. It should not be used for computations involving condensed or extended faces.

How to Use the Em System in Typical Situations

To find the space needed for a given amount of copy when the type size and length of line is known, first determine:

1. The number of words in the copy
2. The number of ems in each line, and subsequently the number of words that will fit in each line
3. The number of lines of type necessary for the copy
4. How much vertical space these lines will occupy

For a typical situation, follow these steps to determine the amount of space needed for the body copy of a direct-mail promotion piece. Once the space requirements are known for all of the copy, an appropriate size can be selected for the folder. Assume that the lines are to be 18 picas long, and the type is to be either 8-point solid or 8-point leaded 2 points.

STEP 1. Estimate the number of words in the copy quickly by counting the words in five or six lines and dividing the total by the number of lines. Multiply the average number of words in these lines by the number of lines to find the number of words in the copy:

> total number of words in six lines: 72
> average number of words in one line: 12
> total lines (150) times average number of words in line (12) equals 1,800 words in the copy

All typewritten lines are counted as full lines, including those that begin and end paragraphs because there will be an equivalent number of short lines when the type is set.

STEP 2.   To find the number of words in a line, first divide the length of the line (in points) by the type size. This gives the number of ems in the line; divide the number of ems by 3 (if type size is 10-point or smaller) or 2.5 (if type size is 11-point or larger) to get the number of words.

> 18-pica line times 12 points per pica: 216 points per line
> 216 points divided by 8 (point size of type): 27 ems per line
> 27 ems divided by 3 (number of ems in word):
> 9 words per line

STEP 3.   The number of lines required for the copy is computed by dividing the number of words in a line into the number of words in the copy.

> 1,800 words of copy divided by 9 words per line: 200 lines

STEP 4.   The amount of vertical space needed for these lines can be found by multiplying the thickness of each line times the number of lines. Remember to be concerned with the thickness of the body of the type; if the type is leaded, leading must be taken into consideration. For example, if 8-point type is leaded 2 points, the line thickness is 10 points.

> for 8-point solid: 200 lines times 8 equals 1,600 points
> for 8 on 10: 200 lines times 10 equals 2,000 points

The measurement of type areas is usually expressed in picas, so the answer is converted:

> 1,600 points divided by 12 points per pica
>   equals 133⅓ picas
>   or
> 2,000 points divided by 12 points per pica
>   equals 166⅔ picas

Knowing that the body type area must be 18 picas wide and either 133⅓ or 166⅔ picas deep with leading, the sheet size for the mailing piece can be decided. Copy can be broken into any number of columns, and space must be allowed for illustrations and display type also; these factors, in addition to standard paper sizes and other elements discussed in other chapters, result in a sound decision.

To find the number of words to be written when an ad, brochure, or booklet has already been designed and space has been designated, determine:

1. The number of lines of type that will fit into the designated area
2. The number of ems and subsequently the number of words that will fit into each of these lines
3. The total number of words

For this example, assume that an ad has been designed with a copy area 21 picas wide and 28 picas deep. The copy is to be set in 12-point type leaded 2 points.

STEP 1.   Find the number of lines by dividing the line thickness into the area depth (in points).

> 14 points divided into 336 points (28 picas times 12 points per pica) equals 24 lines

STEP 2.   Figure the number of ems in the line by dividing the point size of the type into the length of the line in points.

> 12 points divided into 252 points (21 picas times 12) equals 21 ems

(Note: In this example, because the type is pica size, it was not necessary to have completed this step.)

Find the number of words by dividing the average number of ems per word into the total number of ems in a complete line.

> 2.5 into 21 ems equals 8$\frac{2}{5}$ words per line

STEP 3.   Find the number of words to be written by multiplying the number of words in a line times the number of lines.

> 24 times 8$\frac{2}{5}$ equals 201.6, or 201 words needed to fill the space

In writing to fill, it is a good idea in most cases to write a few lines less rather than more. It is usually easier to expand copy with a little extra leading between lines than it is to shorten it by editing after it has been set.

To find the size of type to use when the space and number of words are known, follow the same procedure with one exception. First decide a feasible type size, with or without leading, and then work the problem as if to discover the number of words to be written. If the answer is smaller than the number of words already written, the type size is too large or some leading must be eliminated. If the answer is considerably larger, the size selected is too small or some leading can be used. Through trial and error, a solution is reached.

SQUARE-INCH METHOD OF COPYFITTING

Although it is somewhat less accurate than a word count, the *square-inch method* is useful for the preliminary planning of all printed matter. Its chief advantage is simplicity; answers can be found quickly. It is based on the following table showing the average number of words per square inch in each common body type size, solid or leaded:

SQUARE-INCH TABLE

Type size in points	Number of words per square inch if set solid	Number of words per square inch if leaded 2 points
6	47	34
7	38	27
8	32	23
9	27	20
10	21	16
11	17	14
12	14	11

The ease with which common copyfitting problems can be solved by using this table is shown by these examples:

Example 1. Finding the number of words to write to fill a given space. Designed is an eight-page booklet, plus cover, with type to occupy an area 5 by 7 inches on every page. There are 35 square inches of type on each page (found by multiplying 5 by 7); multiplying 35 by 8 (the number of pages) yields that the booklet will accommodate 280 square inches of type. Assuming the type to be 10-point, leaded 2 points, a check of the table reveals that 16 words will fit into each square inch. Multiplying the number of words per square inch (16) by the number of square inches (280) reveals that approximately 4,480 words must be written to fill the booklet.

Example 2. Finding the size of type to use. On hand is an area 4 by 7 inches into which must be put 560 words. Dividing the square inches in the area (28) into the number of words (560) gives 20 words in each square inch. Thus the table indicates that 9-point type leaded 2 points will enable 560 words to be set in the space.

CHARACTER-COUNT METHOD

For maximum accuracy, the *character-count method* of copyfitting is used. It is the only practicable system for the precise work of preparing copy in the final stages of production for magazines, advertisements, and most promotion pieces.

It is the most accurate system because the unit of measurement is the character instead of the word and because it takes into account the widths in type designs. Words vary greatly in length, and any copyfitting that depends on an average for word length can achieve only limited accuracy. Type designs—even those considered standard, not labeled as condensed or extended—vary considerably in the number of characters that will fit into a line. If specific information about type design were not necessary for this method, there would be no need for any other system. But, before the character-count method can be put to use, the number of characters that will fit in each line must be known.

The manufacturers of type-casting machines provide such data in accurately compiled tables. Printers relay the information to customers, either with type-specimen catalogues or upon request. Sometimes the number is expressed only as "characters per pica," in which case it must be multiplied by the measure of picas in a line to get the total characters for each line. Usually, however, this bit of computation has already been done, and character counts for pica measures ranging from 10 or 12 to 30 are given, as in the table below. Using this information, some representative character-count problems that follow can be worked out.

SAMPLE CHARACTER COUNT SCALE

10-point Kennerly

Line length in picas	12	14	16	18	20	22	24	26	28	30
Character count	27	34	39	45	51	57	62	68	74	79

10-point Vogue

Line length in picas	12	14	16	18	20	22	24	26	28	30
Character count	28	34	40	46	52	57	62	68	73	79

Courtesy Lawhead Press, Inc., Athens, Ohio.

Finding the Amount of Space Needed

When the type face and size have been selected and line length is known, the amount of space needed can be found by:

1. Computing the number of characters in the copy
2. Finding the number of characters that will fit into each line from the table
3. Dividing the number of characters per line into the total number of characters to find the number of lines needed
4. Converting the number into any desired unit of measure

Example: A magazine article is to be set in 10-point solid Kennerly. The columns are 20 picas wide. How much space should be allowed in these 20-pica columns for the article?

1. Find the number of characters in the copy by counting the characters in a few lines and deciding an average. Multiply that figure by the number of lines to get the total. For this example, assume that there are 100 lines of 70 characters, or a total of 7,000 characters.
2. A check of the table shows that 51 characters will fit into a 20-pica line.
3. Dividing 51 into 7,000 yields 137 and 13/51 lines. Since there is no such thing as a fraction of a line of type, space must be allowed for 138 lines.
4. The depth of 138 lines can be converted to any unit of measurement. Each line is 10 points thick, so the depth is 1,380 points. If a line gauge is used in preparing the dummy pages for the article, the answer may be needed in picas. Dividing the 12 points per pica into 1,380 points reveals that 115 picas of space must be left in the 20-pica columns of the magazine.

Finding the Amount of Copy to Write to Fill a Given Space

When space for copy has been prescribed, the amount of copy that will fill the space can be found by:

1. Checking the table to find the number of characters per line
2. Dividing the point size of each line into the depth of the area (in points) to find the number of lines to be written.

Example: An advertisement has a copy area 18-picas wide and 22-picas deep. The type to be used is 10-point Vogue leaded 2 points. To know how much to write for the message to fill the desired space:

1. Check the table. Forty-six characters will fit into each line.
2. Because each line is 12 points thick (10-point type plus 2 points of leading), 22 lines will fit into the 22 picas of depth. If each line were not 1 pica in thickness, the number of lines would be found first by multiplying 22 picas by 12 points to get the depth in points, and then by dividing by the line thickness (12 points) into the area depth. The writer can set the marginal stops on the typewriter so that each line written contains 46 characters and equals a line of type.

If there were a need to find the total number of characters, a third step of multiplying the number of lines (22) by the number of characters in a line (46) would suffice. There is seldom a use for this information.

Some of the work of copyfitting can be reduced by cooperation among writers, editors, and layout men. The time needed to determine the number of characters contained in articles is cut by writers using consistent typewriter settings so that the person doing the copyfitting knows in advance that typed lines always average a certain number of characters.

The copy paper used by a magazine can be ruled to show line lengths of typewritten copy that correspond to lines of type in the publication's columns. By typing within these lines, the writer helps the copyfitter find the space needed for the material almost instantly.

Fitting Display Type to Space

Even the most accurate copyfitting method described is inadequate for computing the space requirements of headlines, titles, or other lines of display type.

The character-count system, sufficient for type sizes as large as 12-point, requires some modification before use with larger sizes. For body copy, the character-count method depends upon averages for the width of characters, an allowance being made in the scales for wide letters (*m* and *w*), narrow letters (*f, l, i, t*), and capitals according to their normal frequency in text material. But the large size and limited application of display types create a possibility of intolerable error unless specific attention is paid as each individual letter in a title or headline is fitted to space.

UNIT COUNT FOR DISPLAY TYPE

For near-perfect copyfitting of newspaper headlines, magazine titles, and the like, a *unit-count* system is used. It is similar to character counting except that instead of counting every letter as one character, the letters are assigned units according to their width. Some degree of accuracy is sacrificed to keep the system from being too cumbersome. Letters are assumed to fall into one of four categories: *thin, normal, wide,* or *extra wide.* Normal letters are assigned one unit, thin letters one-half unit, wide letters one-and-one-half units, and extra wide letters two units. Therefore, for display type containing capitals *and* lowercase letters, the following allotments are usually made:

all lowercase letters and numbers 1 unit
> *except*

m and w   1½ units
f, l, i, t, and 1   ½ unit

all capital letters   1½ units
> *except*

M and W   2 units
I   ½ unit
spaces   1 unit
punctuation   ½ unit

Depending upon the design of the type, occasionally *j* and *r* are assigned only a half unit. Other variations can be made, but the assignments above meet most situations.

The unit count for headlines of *all capitals* is different from that of both capitals and lowercase. For simplicity in counting, the basic capital letters are assigned one unit in all-cap heads. The unit allotments in all-capital display lines are:

all letters 1 unit
> *except*

M and W   1½ units
I   ½ unit
spaces   ½ unit
punctuation   ½ unit

Note how the two headlines in Figure 13-12 are counted.

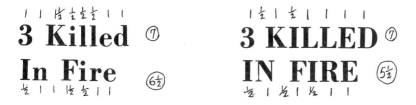

Figure 13-12. *Unit count for headlines. Note that unit values assigned to letters and spaces differ between all-cap and cap-and-lowercase headlines. The fact that the first line totaled seven units in both cases is only coincidence.*

Virtually all the work connected with display types involves writing lines to fit a given space. It is therefore a matter of ascertaining the maximum number of units for the line, and then writing within that limitation. In newspaper offices these maximums are shown on a headline schedule. Originally, they are derived by setting lines composed of a normal assortment of letters and spaces and counting the units in these lines. Character counts shown for display type in printer's type specimen books may also be used as line maximums.

Whatever the source, the maximum count per line has to be observed. The temptation to squeeze an extra half unit may be strong if the wording of the title or headline seems especially good — and occasionally such fudging on the count pays. But when it fails, the waste of time for the writer to rewrite and for the compositor to reset the line is inexcusable. The gamble is not worth the effort and expenditure.

CHAPTER 14 Preparing
Visual Copy
for Production

Photographs and other illustrations are copy to the photoengraver and lithographer, just as text and titles are copy for any printer. As copy, they require the same careful editing and preparation that is taken for granted while working with words for printing, but is too often neglected while processing illustrations.

Essentially, the processing steps for illustrations are the same as those for verbal copy. Drawings and pictures can and do contain errors, both mechanical (smudges, creases, chemical spots) and qualitative (poor tones, faulty backgrounds). Such errors should be corrected, or the work should be redone. With regard to the marking of instructions, it should be obvious that information about size and shape must be given. And a picture that is too large or too small for its space causes as many problems as overset or underset type.

Processing illustrations is essentially the same for both traditional printing and offset lithography. The slight differences that are present will be pointed out in the following discussion.

Cropping Photographs

Photographs, like news stories or magazine articles, are sometimes verbose, poorly constructed, too large, or too small. They must be edited to tell only what they are supposed to tell, reconstructed to give emphasis where it is needed, reduced or enlarged to fit space.

Figure 14-1. *Grease pencil was used to place the four crop marks on this photo. The marks indicate the dimensions of the photo; only the area inside the marks will be included in the reproduction.*

The basic part of picture editing is called *cropping*. It is the figurative cutting of the original photograph to eliminate the abovementioned faults when it is in plate form on a printing press.

Cropping is "figurative" cutting because portions of a photo will rarely be cut away with scissors or blade; marks made with a grease pencil are used to indicate the finished dimensions. These are usually placed in the white border around the photograph, or on the mounting board used for backing.

Every photo that enters production should contain four crop marks. These marks set the dimension of the photo; two of them mark off the width and two mark off the depth. Without crop marks the production people will naturally assume that the entire image surface is to be reproduced.

Figure 14-1 shows typical crop marks for a photo.

CROPPING FOR CONTENT

As photographic prints come from a photographer, they often contain shortcomings that should be corrected. Unnecessary or disturbing detail should be removed, attention may need to be shifted to the important feature, composition may need improvement.

In most cases judicious cropping can eliminate these weak points. To decide what should be cropped, it is helpful to use two L-shaped pieces of cardboard that can be moved over the face of the photograph until they frame the most desirable portion. Crop marks corresponding to the inside corners of this frame, but drawn on the white margins of the photograph, later direct the platemaker to use only the portion of the photograph that is enclosed in the frame.

CROPPING TO FIT SPACE

Commercial photographs usually come in one of two standard sizes: 8 by 10 inches or 5 by 7 inches, but editors often have to work with snapshots in a multitude of sizes. However, in spite of the wide variety of photo sizes, only rarely can a picture be used for publication in its original dimensions.

Platemakers can make enlargements and reductions with their cameras. But, because enlargements and reductions are done photographically, platemakers have no magical way of changing the *shape* of a photograph. If the original forms a wide horizontal rectangle, the plate will be in the same shape. In other words, the plate is a *scaled* version of the original.

Therefore, the depth of a vertical photo that must fit into a horizontal rectangular spot on a page must be cropped sufficiently to fit into such a shape.

There are two basic systems of finding how much must be cropped in such instances, one involving arithmetic, the other the measuring of lines. Working these is called scaling, or proportioning.

Scaling Illustrations

The scaling of illustrations is the equivalent of copyfitting. Common problems include finding: (1) the depth of a reproduction when the width is known; (2) the width when the depth is known, (3) the amount to cut (crop) when both depth and width of the reproduction are known. These problems are most often encountered in reducing photos to smaller plate sizes, because platemakers get better quality with reduction than they can with enlargement. Scaling provides the information for either enlargements or reductions.

ARITHMETICAL SYSTEM

A rectangle is shaped by the relationship of its adjoining sides. For example, a photograph 4 inches wide and 2 inches deep is the same shape as a rectangle 2 inches wide and 1 inch deep. In both cases the width is twice the depth.

This relationship in a photo can be expressed as a fraction: photo width/photo depth. The same can be done with a reproduction: reproduction width/reproduction depth. By setting up these fractions as an equation, any missing dimension can be found by simple arithmetic. The following are typical examples.

Example 1. Finding the reproduction depth when the width is known. Assuming a photo to be 8 inches wide and 10 inches deep and the cut to be 2 inches wide, the equation is:

$$\frac{8}{10} = \frac{2}{x}$$

To solve, cross multiply 8 by x to get $8x$, and 10 by 2 to get 20. If $8x = 20$, then x (engraving depth) $= 2.5$.

Example 2. Finding the reproduction width when the depth is known. Assuming a photo to be 7 inches wide and 5 inches deep and the reproduction is to be 3 inches deep, the equation is

$$\frac{7}{5} = \frac{x}{3}$$

By cross multiplying, $5x = 21$. The reproduction width is then $4\frac{1}{5}$.

Example 3. Finding how much to crop from a photo to give it dimensions that will reduce to fit the size and proportions of a specific layout area. Some students seem to have difficulty with this kind of problem — they fail to visualize which of the four dimensions in the equation is the unknown. In fitting a vertical photo into a horizontal space, it is the reproduction depth that is unknown; in fitting a horizontal photo into a vertical space, it is the reproduction width that is unknown.

If a photo is 8 inches wide and 10 inches deep and is to be made into a plate 5 inches wide and 4 inches deep, the depth of the photo must be cropped, for it is the unknown. Therefore,

$$\frac{8}{x} = \frac{5}{4}; \ 5x = 32; \text{ and } x = 6\frac{2}{5}$$

The photo's depth must be cropped *to* $6\frac{2}{5}$ inches from 10 inches deep. The $3\frac{3}{5}$ inches to be cropped can be taken from the top, bottom, or partially from each, depending on the content. If the content will not permit this much cropping, the layout or the photo must be changed.

There are some disadvantages to the system described here. Working with strange fractions can be too time consuming. There is a possibility that errors will occur and result in unusable, costly engravings.

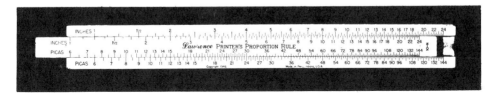

Figure 14-2. *A slide rule used to figure enlargement and reduction proportions of illustrations. The center portion slides to any position. If two dimensions are placed opposite each other, the fourth dimension will be found directly across from the third. (Note the solution to Example 1.)*

USE OF SLIDE RULE OR CIRCULAR SCALE

Most of the danger of human error can be eliminated by scaling with slide rules (Figure 14-2) and the circular scalers (Figure 14-3) that supply ready-made mathematical answers. These handy gadgets are often furnished free by printers and engravers, or can be purchased quite reasonably. Both work on the same principle; two of the dimensions are lined up across from each other on the scale; the missing dimension is then located directly across from the third known dimension.

Figure 14-3. *A circular scaler works the same way as a slide rule. The inner wheel is rotated until two dimensions are opposite each other. The unknown dimension is then located directly across from the third known dimension. As set here, the wheel shows that an 8 by 10 photo will reduce to 4 by 5. It also shows that when 10 reduces to 8, it is a reduction to 80 percent.*

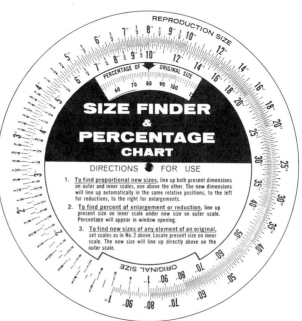

Another method, somewhat inaccurate but usable in most instances, employs a diagonal line to find any unknown dimension in picture scaling. No mathematics are involved; the work is done entirely by drawing and measuring lines on an overlay sheet, not on the photograph. Care must be taken so that the pencil does not press a line into the emulsion of the photo, for such lines show in the finished engraving or plate.

The diagonal method, illustrated in Figure 14-4, starts with the bisection of a rectangle by a line drawn diagonally from one corner to another. Any smaller rectangle formed by right-angle lines drawn from adjacent sides of the large rectangle to the diagonal line is proportionate to the large rectangle.

In Figure 14-5, the diagonal is used to solve Example 1 solved

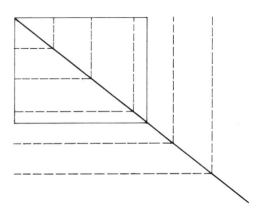

Figure 14-4. *Diagonal system of photograph scaling.*

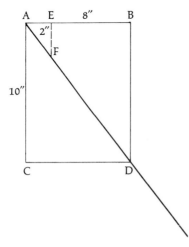

Figure 14-5. *Finding depth when width is known. The width (AE) of two inches is drawn across between A and B. The perpendicular (EF) from that point to the diagonal is measured to find the unknown depth of the reproduction.*

earlier by the arithmetical system (page 328). The larger rectangle represents the 8- by 10-inch photograph. The known engraving width of 2 inches is measured across the top. The perpendicular line dropped to the diagonal at that point (line E-F) is the depth the plate will be, 2.5 inches. The length of that line may be somewhat different, however, because this method is only as accurate as the drawing of the lines. If the perpendicular is not at exactly 90 degrees, the measurements will be slightly off; if the diagonal misses a corner, an inaccuracy also results. All inaccuracies in drawing lines affect the answer.

Figure 14-6 shows the use of the diagonal to find the width when the depth is known. The procedure is identical to that used in Figure 14-5, except that the perpendicular is drawn from the side (because the depth is known) to the diagonal.

Example 3 used earlier (page 328) in explaining the arithmetical system (finding the amount to crop) is worked out by the diagonal method in Figure 14-7. In this example both dimensions of the reproduction are known (it thus becomes the starting rectangle) and the diagonal bisects the rectangle representing the picture to be *cropped*. The amount to be cropped is found by measuring the distance between the intersection of the diagonal with the line B-D and the corner D.

Figure 14-6. *Finding width when depth is known. Measure known depth (2½") from A to G. The unknown width is then determined by measuring from point G to the diagonal (line GH).*

Figure 14-7. *Finding amount to crop. Lightly draw a rectangle with the dimensions of the reproduction. Then draw a diagonal for that rectangle. That diagonal will intersect the dimension of the original at the point where a crop mark could be placed. The distance from that point to the corner (D) is the amount to be cropped.*

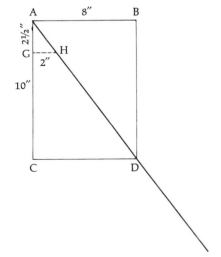

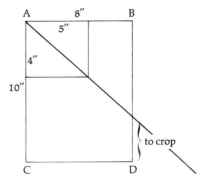

Finding the Percentage of Reductions or Enlargements

Platemakers usually translate the relationship of original photo to finished plate size into percentages because camera settings are determined by the percentage to which copy is enlarged or reduced.

It is often beneficial to do the same thing when editing photographs. One of the costs of platemaking is the camera work, and if several original photos can be shot (photographed) at the same time a same-focus reduction in price is given. Because plate dimensions can often vary without harming a layout, it may be wise to change them slightly so that several photos can be reduced to the same percentage of the original size.

For example, if five photographs are to be reduced respectively to 48, 49, 50, 50.5, and 51 percent of original size, they might all be shot at the 50 percent reduction in order to claim the same-focus price benefit. The percentage of reduction or enlargement is determined simply by dividing one dimension of the photo into the same dimension of the plate. In Example 1, a photo 8 inches wide was to be reduced to a plate 2 inches wide. By dividing 8 into 2, the reduction is found to be 0.25, or reduced to 25 percent.

Other Methods of Altering Photo Content

Cropping is not the only method by which the content of a photo can be changed. An artist can *airbrush* photographs to remove disturbing background or to emphasize certain portions of the subject (Figure 14-8). The platemaker can also do this and can manipulate his camera settings to *highlight* (make white) some sections of the picture subject that might otherwise be gray and dull.

Through the use of special plate finishes as described in Chapter 6 (silhouette, partial silhouette, vignette, geometrical shapes), the appearance and shape of photographs can be changed when they appear in print.

Although airbrushing and retouching require special skills, the journalist can get special plate finishes without an artist's assistance. Through the use of overlay sheets he can adequately communicate his desires to the platemaker who creates the special effect as he makes the plates. To order silhouettes, for example, an overlay sheet is fastened snugly to the photo and then the subject to be silhouetted

Figure 14-8. *An airbrush can be used to eliminate disturbing background in a photo.*

is lightly outlined with soft pencil. To avoid misunderstanding, "outline" or "silhouette" should be written in the area surrounding the line.

Vignettes can be indicated in similar fashion. The beginning and ending of the fade-out area can be drawn on an overlay. Mortises, notches, and geometric shapes (circles, ovals, irregulars) can also be shown on an overlay. The change in size brought on by enlargement or reduction in platemaking *must always be considered* when working with overlays.

An overlay sheet is also used to show desired highlight areas for highlight halftones and to locate line work on combination plates, both reverse and surprint. For letterpress printing, combination plates are expensive, but on many occasions are especially effective. If type matter or line illustrations must appear over a halftone (in white or in the color of the halftone) a combination plate is required. Along with the halftone copy, reproduction proofs of type matter or sharp black-on-white line drawings must be provided to the engraver so that he can make good combination plates. These techniques are also used in offset lithography, but they do not, of course, involve special *plates*. The special treatment needed in each case centers around the *negative* preparation in lithography.

For any method of printing, a size allowance must be made if illustrations are to run off the edge of the page. These *bleeds,* as they are called, must be given an extra eighth-inch for each edge that goes off an outside edge of the paper. This allowance is necessary so that the illustration will still bleed after the printed piece is trimmed; otherwise, folding, trimming, and binding operations cannot insure that a thin white streak will not appear on what were meant to be bleed edges.

Photomontages (composite pictures made by combining several photos into one) are usually made by pasting the photos together on mounting board. They can also be made by the photographer, in which case the negatives are used to print several subjects on one sheet of photo paper. The edges of the component photos can be sharp or blended into each other by an airbrush or by retouching. They require no special instructions for reproduction.

Specifying Screen and Metal for Halftones

The fineness of screen, which determines the quality of reproduction, must be specified for halftones that are to be duplicated by either letterpress or offset processes.

Generally speaking, the finer the screen the better the reproduction. In letterpress printing, however, this statement is true only insofar as the fineness of screen and the quality of paper are properly matched. Fine screens require smooth papers in letterpress; in offset lithography good reproduction of fine screens can be obtained on rough papers. The earlier chapters on illustrations and paper should be helpful as a guide to the proper matching of screen and paper. The screen desired may be indicated on the back of copy or with grease pencil on an unused portion of the surface in this fashion: 55-line, 65-line, 133-line, and so on. If any of the special screens discussed in Chapter 6 (mezzotint, circle, etc.) are desired, they must be specified.

Discussion to this point has been mainly limited to black-and-white photographic copy. Communication by graphic arts today requires the use of all kinds of illustrations, many of them in color. This does not infer that the journalist must be an artist or a color photographer; it simply means he must know the special effects at his disposal and be acquainted with the preparation and production requirements for all kinds of illustrations.

Line Drawings

Although they are the simplest and cheapest of illustrations, pen-and-ink drawings are highly versatile and effective. In letterpress printing, the required line etching is simple to make and is the least expensive kind of photoengraving. In offset, there usually is no special treatment and no extra charge required for line drawings. If the drawings are created in the same size as desired for reproduction, they can be pasted in position with type matter and processed with no special treatment or added cost. If they must be reduced or enlarged separately, a slight charge is usually involved.

For best reproduction, these drawings are done on white bristol board with black ink; the primary production demand is for sharp, clear, black lines on a contrasting background. Although a pen is most commonly used, brushes can produce good line illustrations also, as described in Chapter 6. The quality of reproduction is often enhanced when original drawings are reduced for reproduction; any drawing that can be reduced to 50 percent of its original size will lose many minor flaws that might have been present in the original art.

Line drawings and other artwork must be crop-marked, just as photos are, as they are being processed for publication. Although crop-marking is usually not needed to change the shape or content of a line illustration because the illustration usually was drawn to specifications, crop marks are needed to set the dimensions to be followed. As with photos, four marks are needed: two to set the horizontal dimension and two for the vertical.

Any drawing that contains only pure darks and pure whites is reproducible as a line drawing. This includes those that will appear to have middle tones because of Benday shading or drawn dots or lines; it is important to recognize the wide variety of artwork included in the line-drawing category. Cartoons, bar graphs, charts, diagrams, and maps are usually prepared for line reproduction.

Color in Illustrations

The preparation of copy for color reproduction is explained in Chapter 7. As mentioned there, both line and halftone copy can be reproduced in color. Full-color photographs or film transparencies, oil paintings, water colors, and other original full-color continuous-tone materials are reproduced by the halftone process through color separation. It is wise to determine the preferences of individual engravers or lithographers before submitting copy for separation negatives and plates. For color in line illustrations, separate drawings keyed for exact positioning must be provided for each color. Enlargements and reductions are possible for color reproductions just as they are for black and white.

Reading Proofs of Illustrations

Although the errors in illustrations differ from the misspellings, wrong fonts, transposed lines, and the like, that creep into type matter, they nevertheless demand careful attention. Engravers and lithographers provide proofs of their work with illustrations, just as printers do with type, and these proofs should be checked in time for necessary corrections to be made before deadlines.

It is difficult to discern some illustration errors; others are easy to spot. With a little care and practice, anyone can detect the common failings. Some of these errors result from poor work by the engraver or lithographer, but many are the result of improper preparation. Wherever the fault lies, it is essential to detect and correct all flaws before the final printing.

Here are some common failings:

1. Wrong dimensions. This error often can be traced to the person who marked the original copy, but occasionally a production person will err in figuring the percentage of reduction, or a camera operator may shoot the copy incorrectly. But whether an editor placed a crop mark incorrectly or an operator set his camera improperly, the negatives or plates must be remade to fit their space. The only debate is about who pays the extra cost.

2. Imperfections on the edges. Photo reproductions with jagged edges need not be tolerated. Engravers can smooth plate edges, and lithographers can recut mask openings to eliminate such blemishes.

3. Content not as desired because plate dimensions do not follow the crop marks. Sometimes an illustration will be reproduced in the desired size, but included in the reproduction may be material that was to be cropped out. If the original was correctly marked, the illustration is redone at no charge.

4. Scratches. Engravers and lithographers try to handle negatives and plates with care, but unsightly scratches sometimes do appear. Circle them on the proof so that the cause of the flaw can be located and corrected.

5. Spots. These should also be circled on the proof. Although spots often are only the result of a bad proof, it is possible that they are actually in the reproduction. If they are merely proof flaws, a new proof will prove the fact; otherwise the error must be corrected in the negative or plate.

6. Proof too gray or too contrasty. A good halftone requires accuracy in the determining and making of several camera exposures. Bad camera work or etching can cause a halftone to be a poor reproduction of the original. Mark the proof "too gray" or "too contrasty," and the engraver will deliver a better plate if the evaluation was reasonable.

7. Some faint handwriting on surface. Poor editing can be the cause of this problem. Any handwriting done on the back of a photo may show in a reproduction. If this shows up on a proof, the reproduction must be redone at the cost of publisher or supplier, whichever caused the flaw.

8. Paper clip marks on edge. This is also usually the fault of the editorial staff, not of the engraver or printer. Paper clips should not be used on photos; they often scratch or dent the emulsion. Such scratches or dents will appear in any reproduction.

9. Hairline cracks. These usually result from improper handling of

the photo. Photos should not be rolled or folded; emulsion cracks will result.
10. Dark line on part of an edge. Improper cropping can cause this failing. Lines should not be drawn to indicate a dimension of a photo; only marginal crop marks are needed. Any line drawn to show cropping will appear in a reproduction if it is slightly off angle.

Some imperfections in illustration reproductions can be seen only with a magnifying glass; others may only show up when the plate is put on a press. But most shortcomings that can cause serious difficulties can be detected by careful inspection of proofs. Time so spent is certainly worthwhile.

CHAPTER 15

Machine
Composition
and Presses

It is important for the graphic designer to
know something about type composition and presses. Because
foundry type is set by hand, it is time- and money-consuming.
Therefore, most composition for periodicals, books, and commercial
jobs is done by machine today, and the saving in time and money is
substantial. The typographer should understand the capacities and
limitations of the various machines in order to make the most economical use of them.

The pressroom is the heart of the publishing or printing plant.
Here the end product is mass-produced. The planning of the appearance of printed material reaches its culmination when type and auxiliary materials are reproduced in ink on paper. The press is the vital
link between the planning and the actual printed piece — periodical,
book, folder, leaflet, booklet, record jacket, bread wrapper.

Many kinds of presses exist, varying widely in speed, size, and
principle of operation. The typographer needs at least a rudimentary
knowledge of presses and their capacities and limitations. Only in
this way can he (1) select a printer with the right press for his specific
job or (2) tailor the job to the press equipment available in order to
achieve the desired results.

Type Composition

There are two basic methods of type composition (typesetting): hot
type and cold type. It is significant that the development of these
methods paralleled the development of what has come to be called

the "information explosion." For more than four hundred years after Gutenberg, all composition was done by hand. Machine hot-type composition is relatively recent. The first of these machines were introduced late in the nineteenth century. Today's models are capable of computer-controlled automation and can be operated at a rate several times faster than hand setting.

In this century the extent of man's knowledge has doubled every few decades and the need to communicate this information has kept pace. The most modern means of composing type — photo-electronic — is capable of assembling as many as 10,000 characters per second. Highly skilled hand compositors could do little better than one character per second. It has been forecast that photo-electronic composition will reach a rate of up to 60,000 cps.

HOT TYPE

Hot-type composition is the setting of type characters cast in metal. Such type may be precast and assembled by hand (see Chapter 3). More commonly, such composition is done by machines, which manufacture type as they are operated, either as a line of words on one type body (called a *slug*), or as single letters. Like hand-set or foundry type, the faces of the letters cast on these machines stand in relief. The reader should remember that printing by pressing paper against the inked faces can directly follow hot-type composition.

Four kinds of hot-type composition machines are in wide use: the Linotype and Intertype (together called *linecasting machines*); the Monotype, and the Ludlow.

THE LINECASTERS

These machines are fundamentally similar. Both cast a one-line piece of type. With the Linotype (Figure 15-1), the operator sits at the keyboard, labeled 1. As he punches the keys, much as a typewriter is operated, brass molds, called *mats* or *matrices* (plural of matrix), are released from storage in the *magazine,* 2. They drop through the *delivery channels,* 3, and are carried to the *assembly elevator,* 4. At this point *spacebands* are dropped between the words.

The line of mats and bands is moved to the *casting mechanism,* 5. Here molten metal is flushed against the line, thus casting a slug. Completed slugs are trimmed to proper thickness and type height before dropping into the *galley,* a metal tray, 6.

After casting, the mats and spacebands are raised by the *first elevator,* 7, to a point where they are transferred to the *distributing elevator,* 8. Here, the mats and spacebands are separated; the latter are re-

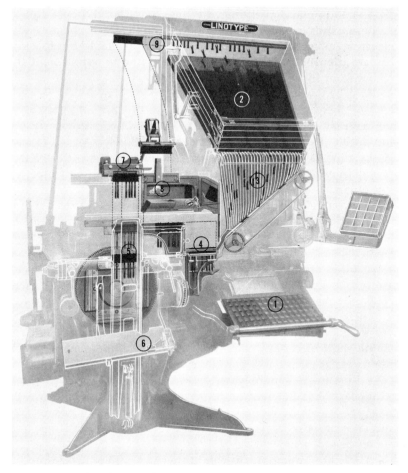

Figure 15-1. *The Linotype. (Courtesy Mergenthaler Linotype Company)*

turned to storage, ready for reuse, while the former are moved to the *distributor bar,* 9. The mats then move along the bar to their proper compartments in the magazine.

The mat (Figure 15-2) has been called the heart of the linecaster. These brass molds are of varying thicknesses, depending on the width of the letters they are to mold. Mats are generally two-letter, particularly in the smaller type sizes. The mat in Figure 15-2 carries an uppercase I, one in a roman version, the other in italic. Roman and boldface are another frequent combination on two-letter mats. This makes it possible for the machine to set roman with italic or with boldface from one magazine.

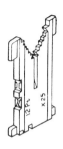

Figure 15-2. *The mat or matrix. (Courtesy Mergenthaler Linotype Company)*

Spacebands make justifying the lines possible. When a line is cast, these bands expand, filling the line completely on the measure. Noncasting mats of varying widths are also available for spacing. These are distributed manually within the line to supplement the spacebands or to letterspace where needed.

Advantages and Limitations

The typographer should understand what the linecaster can deliver economically. Here are some major considerations:

1. Leading can be easily achieved, for the operator can cast a face on a slug thicker than normal for the face. Thus, a 10-point type can be set on an 11- or 12-point body.

2. The range of faces stocked by compositors varies widely. Basically, a separate magazine is required for each font, but remember, two different fonts — e.g. roman and italic — may be cast from some mats, as shown in Figure 15-2.

Magazines are interchangeable, and some later-model machines carry four or eight magazines that can quickly be brought into use. Special thought should be given to using a font found in a *split magazine,* which is half the size of a regular magazine and thus contains fewer mats. Lengthy copy set from a split magazine may run the machine short of certain mats, thus forcing the operator to sit idle while he waits for them to run the cycle of the machine.

The linecasters generally set faces as large as 36-point; a few machines can handle sizes up to 60-point. Most printers, however, prefer to restrict their available faces to sizes up to 24- or possibly 30-point, and compose larger sizes by hand or on the Ludlow machine, to be discussed later.

3. There are limitations to combining two different faces in one line other than the two found on the duplexed mats (Figure 15-2), since the operator can usually compose from only one magazine at a time. It may be possible to mix faces by setting another slug from a different magazine and then using the needed portions of two slugs. Obviously, this means time and expense. Many compositors and printers have special machines, known as *mixer machines,* which are capable of setting a few different faces in one line.

4. Linecasters generally are restricted to 30-pica slugs. This does not mean one could not order, for example, 14-point Century set 36 picas wide. But it would entail extra cost, since the compositor would use *butted slugs.* This means that for each 36-pica line two slugs would be set and then combined to make one line. There are some linecasters that cast slugs as long as 42 picas.

5. Care must be given to corrections and alterations made in linecaster composition. To correct a single error or make a minor

change requires resetting the entire line and sometimes several lines above and below in order to rejustify the composition. This means that in correcting one error the operator faces the risk of making another. In reading corrected proofs, one should read the corrected line and several others above and below.

When checking proofs from composed type, it is wise to make alterations so that a minimum of lines must be reset. Printers charge for resetting lines in which changes from the original copy are made. These are called *author's alterations* or *AA's.*

6. Composition other than straight matter is more expensive, because of the time factor. It is difficult to set *tabular matter,* particularly when some of the columns are very narrow and perhaps require vertical rules as separators. This is because slugs have to be sawed into proper widths to be placed between the rules.

Sometimes, when it is essential to reproduce such tabular matter and only linecasters are available for composition, type can be composed without rules. Then a repro proof is pulled and lines are ruled on the proof with pen and ink, after which a line engraving is made.

Unless machines with automatic centering are available, centering type on the measure should be avoided whenever possible, for this demands special attention from the operator. Irregular line lengths and changing line lengths may also add to expense.

When an illustration or perhaps a headline cuts into text matter and type lines run around it, the composed text matter is called a *runaround.* To make a run-around the operator must set the copy to the required length on a slug of column width. Then the slug has to be sawed to the required width in order to make room for the illustration or head. Setting the copy short on the original slug requires slow hand spacing.

7. Spacing between words set on linecasters is often typographically imperfect. Spacebands vary in widths, thin to jumbo. This means that the operator uses narrow bands for small-size faces and wider bands with larger sizes. Most printers do not stock bands in a full range because of expense. They are likely to use perhaps only one or two for a fairly comprehensive number of type sizes.

THE LUDLOW TYPOGRAPH

Commonly called a Ludlow, this machine casts type on a single slug from mats assembled and distributed by hand. It is not strictly a machine but a semi-automatic means of type composition. Mats are assembled from storage cabinets and placed in a *stick,* which is actually a frame in which the line of mats is secured. Spacing and justifying are manual processes. The stick is inserted into the Ludlow machine and the line is cast from molten metal.

The Ludlow is widely used for casting display lines in sizes as large as 144-point. It is not a straight matter machine but is nonetheless often used for setting type as small as 4-point, particularly in job shops when only a few lines are needed, for example, on calling cards or letter heads. And, although it is akin to hand composition, it makes possible the use of fresh metal for each job printed.

THE MONOTYPE

In reality, the Monotype is two machines, a keyboard and a caster. These are shown in Figure 15-3. The keyboard operator perforates a paper tape, which is then fed into the caster. Holes in the tape represent the characters of the type font and the spacing required. The keyboard unit signals the operator when a line is ready for justifying and hyphenation. He codes the needed information into the tape.

As the tape is fed to the caster it activates levers to move a matrix case (Figure 15-4) backward, forward, and side to side. When the proper character matrix is over the mold, molten metal is injected into the mat to form the character. Casting is done at a rate of 150 per minute; as each character is cast, it is pushed into position until a full line is formed. Then another is started.

Figure 15-3. *The Monotype keyboard and caster. (Courtesy Lanston Monotype Company)*

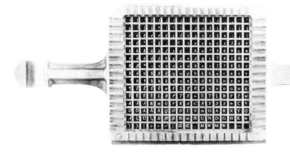

Figure 15-4. *The Monotype matrix case and one matrix, actual size. (Courtesy Lanston Monotype Company)*

The following advantages and limitations are worthy of attention:

1. The system is well-adapted to intricate composition such as tabular matter. A special tabbing scale on the keyboard makes such composition as well as runarounds and irregular line lengths relatively simple.
2. The system allows adjustments in set widths without effect on point size. A 10-point type might be composed in 10½-set or in 9½-set. This 5 percent flexibility allows for expansion or contraction of copy to fit within a certain area.
3. The Monotype offers greater precision in spacing between words so that composition is more eye-pleasing.
4. Although cost of composition on an hourly basis exceeds that of linecasters, it can prove less costly for complicated materials or quality book work.
5. Corrections made in the type are usually simpler than in the case of linecaster composition since the casting is not done by lines but individually, character by character.

AUTOMATED LINECASTERS

Linecasting machines can be equipped to compose automatically without an operator. Such machines are tape-controlled through an operating unit attached to the linecasters; the unit is fed perforated tape, such as that prepared on the Teletypesetter (*TTS*) (Figure 15-5).

Figure 15-5. *Close-up of tape operating control equipment designed for automatic operation of Monarch® and other linecasting machines. The tape is perforated with the necessary codes to release the matrices automatically in accordance with composition requirements. Spring-loaded plungers, or electronic sensing devices, read the holes in the tape and activate the keyboard of the typesetting machine. The whole process is quite similar to the operation of a player piano. (Courtesy Harris Intertype Corporation)*

The tape may be prepared locally on perforators or may be received via wire services.

There are two methods of controlling *h&j* (hyphenation and justifying). In one, the operator is signaled by his typewriter-like keyboard when a line ending is to be made. He makes the decision and codes into the tape the necessary h&j information. Such a perforator is aware of the number of units in a measure and also the number for the various characters in a font. As the latter are coded in, their increasing total units are subtracted from the measure count until a point is reached near the h&j range. Such keyboards are termed *counting keyboards.*

The process is speeded up by more modern *noncounting keyboards.* These perforators produce *idiot tape,* devoid of h&j codes. This *raw tape* (idiot tape) is fed to a computer, which does the counting and makes logical h&j decisions. It can do the latter much faster than a human operator. The computer then drives a tape punch to turn out a second tape, ready for use.

Some of the perforators are capable of producing *hard copy* (typewritten on paper) or displaying copy on a video screen. Some are capable of reading a perforated tape, displaying the copy to a point where a change is required. The operator types the changes and a revised tape is punched. Tape-operated machines are capable of more than double production and more intricate composition.

MAKEUP AND LOCKUP

The final composing-room functions following hot-metal composition are makeup and lockup.

Makeup merges type with illustrative materials and other printing elements. It is done by the stoneman at a large steel table called a *stone* (the top was originally stone). He follows instructions from the designer indicated in a dummy or on a layout, placing materials in proper position. Figure 15-6 shows a dummy being made.

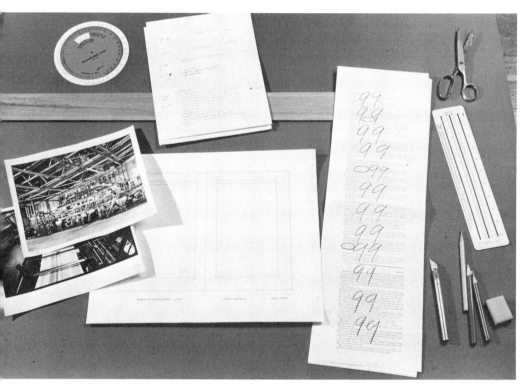

Figure 15-6. *Steps in the dummying of two pages of a book. (a) Materials used. From lower left, clockwise: photographs, T-square, scaling wheel, manuscript of caption copy, galleys, line gauge and pica ruler, blank dummy page.*

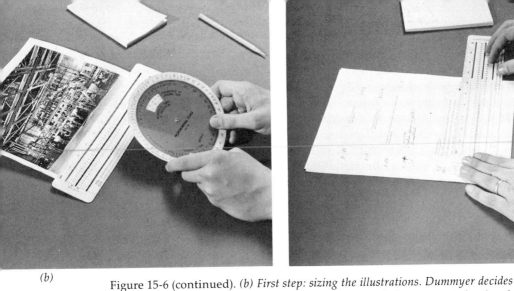
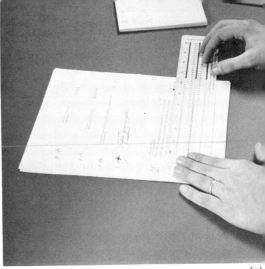

(b)

(c)

Figure 15-6 (continued). *(b) First step: sizing the illustrations. Dummyer decides where on the page the photographs, in conjunction with the text, are to be placed. He also assesses the content of each photo and decides whether or not to crop. He then reduces (or enlarges) the photos with all these factors in mind, with the aid of the scaling wheel (see page 329). Figures on pad above show original dimensions followed by reduced size. (c) Determining caption width and depth. As with the illustrations, dummyer decides on best dimensions and position for caption copy. Here, with line gauge, he measures original copy and determines printed size. (d) Stripping the galley. Dummyer cuts up galleys, which have already been set according to type page width, in preparation for pasting on appropriate dummy page. (e) Pasting the galleys into position. Dummyer, having waxed back of galley (a kind of gluing), now places it in the position on the dummy page where he judges it should go. Though he is skilled primarily in the art of graphics, he must also remember such makeup necessities as alignment of facing pages, prevention of widows, and so forth. (f) The finished dummy pages. Note outline of sized photos at upper left (they will be bleeds) and box for caption. The line figures at lower left and middle right are tear sheets to guide the compositor. Galley sections have been pasted in place also. Dummy will now go to compositor, who will follow exact positioning of art, captions, and text in page makeup. (Photos courtesy John King)*

(d)

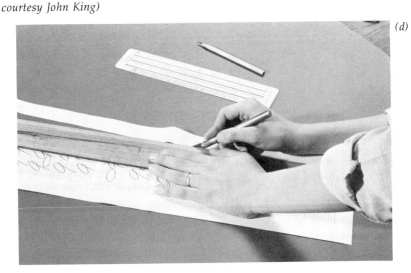

(e)

(f)

As soon as makeup of pages is complete, *page proofs* are pulled. These indicate how the finished job will look. After page proofs are O.K.'d and final corrections complete, the pages are locked up.

The lockup is done in a heavy, metal *chase,* which is actually a rectangular frame. The metal components do not necessarily fill the chase; the blank areas are filled with *furniture* (metal or wood). To secure the form, wedge-shaped *quoins* (pronounced "coins") are placed at the top and right of the chase. As they are expanded (tightened with a key), they exert pressure against the furniture and toward the form and the chase (see Figure 15-7).

Letterpress printing may, of course, be done directly from the locked-up form. However, much hot-metal composition is intended only for the preparation of copy to be reproduced by other printing

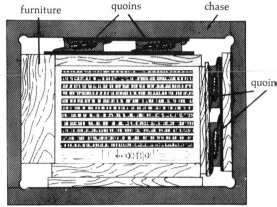

furniture   quoins   chase

quoin

Figure 15-7. *Lock-up of individual metal type pages in steel printing chase, left. Locked-up form, right.*

processes. Locked-up forms may be used for pulling repros, which are then photographed; they may be used for printing on clear glassine, which may be contact-printed on film for making reproduction negatives; or they may be transformed by other means. Together, such ways of using relief composition are called *image conversion.*

Another use of the locked-up form is common. It may be duplicated—made into electros or stereotypes. When this is done, type-high slugs (*bearers*) are locked up inside the chase to protect the form when pressure is applied. *Foundry proofs,* which are drawn from inked duplicates, carry heavy black borders formed by the bearers, which are removed from the duplicates before printing.

If the form is being readied for letterpress and consists entirely of plates—that is, engravings, electros, and/or stereotypes—lockup may be done by using a *patent base,* a metal base of honeycomb or diagonal groove design, as shown in Figure 15-8. The patent base is placed in a chase and plates are secured to it with special hooks. Plates can be moved individually in order to achieve close register.

Figure 15-8. *Patent base with plates locked on bed of press.*

COLD TYPE

Cold-type composition is characterized by direct imaging of type faces onto paper. There are several methods: (1) direct impression, (2) transfer lettering, (3) paste-down type, (4) photocomposition, and (5) electronic composition.

DIRECT IMPRESSION

This method of putting the type face on paper generally involves the use of a special typewriter. The technique is also referred to as *strike-on* composition. The most widely used of such machines are the Varityper, the Justowriter, and the IBM Selectric. All are capable of justified composition, produce composition that looks like type, and have proportional spacing (the sets of the letters vary, as in normal book fonts).

The Varityper requires two typings to achieve justifying. Faces can be mixed, and a wide range of type styles is available.

The Justowriter consists of two units: recorder and reproducer. The former produces a perforated tape and *hard copy* — that is, it also types on paper. The reproducer accepts the tape and automatically types justified copy in a type face. The reproducer has only one face in one size.

The IBM Selectric Composer requires two typings for justified copy. Different type faces are available; however, mixing is not feasible. An alternative use of the Selectric is possible. Typing can be done on a recorder, which places the message on coded magnetic tape and produces hard copy. The tape is processed in a console which has been given type format instructions — line width, leading, and so on. The tape drives a modified Selectric Composer. If errors are found in the first typing, corrections are recorded on a second tape. Together with the original tape it is fed into the console, which merges them to drive the composer. The system is known as the MT/SC (Magnetic Tape Selectric Composer).

PASTEDOWN AND TRANSFER

Transfer lettering and pastedown type are used for composing display type. Pastedown type is printed on transparent, adhesive-backed sheets. Letters are cut from the sheet and affixed to artwork. Letters are available in black or white. Borders, screen patterns, and a wide variety of symbols are also available. Transfer letters are not printed on but are affixed to the back of a transparent sheet. The letters can be positioned over the artwork and burnished; they transfer from the sheet to the artwork. They, too, are available in black and white.

Photocomposing machines operate on a common principle. They print type faces and other symbols onto paper (sometimes film) by flashing a light through film negatives of the desired symbols. One such system is shown in Figure 15-9.

High-quality negatives of various symbols are contained in the type disc in the example. The disc spins at a high rate of speed. The Xenon lamp flashes a brief fraction of a second, just long enough to "stop" the desired character. The beam of light strikes the mirror in the escapement system and is reflected toward the paper or film. En route it passes through the required lens for enlarging or reducing the image.

Note that the escapement system moves horizontally (right or left). This makes possible the composition of lines of type, left to right. The phototypesetting paper is capable of vertical movement, making possible composition in depth.

The symbol negatives are not carried on discs in all systems. In some they are affixed to drums; others use flat grids to which the negatives are attached. The film fonts are readily interchangeable

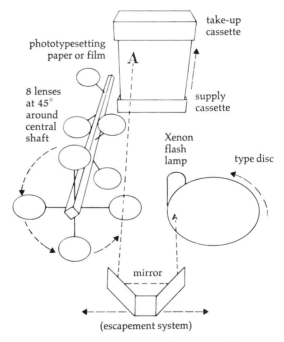

Figure 15-9. *Optical system of AM 748 phototype-setter. (Courtesy Varityper Division, Addressograph-Multigraph Corporation)*

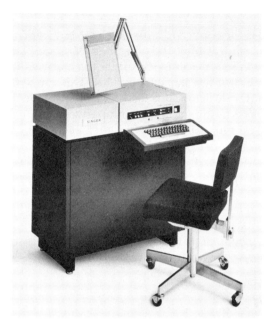

Figure 15-10. *Direct key-board-operated phototype-setter. (Courtesy Graphic Systems Division, The Singer Company)*

and the number of fonts a machine can hold multiplied by the number of sizes it can generate represents the number of different fonts it can mix on a single job. For example, one large-capacity machine can load a maximum of 18 fonts capable of being set in 23 different point sizes. Thus automatically it can mix 414 fonts.

Pi characters are also available in negative form. Such characters are not usually contained in a type font but are often needed in composition. They include math symbols, fractions, inferior and superior numerals, accent marks, and so on. Such symbols are available on linecaster mats but must be inserted by hand, since they are not carried in the magazines. In phototypesetting a nearly unlimited assortment is available for on-line production, and they can be imaged without a significant slowdown in production.

Photocomposing machines may be divided into two types: (1) automated and (2) hand-operated. The automated machines are more complex and are capable of production at higher speeds. They are utilized in composing block or straight matter, intricate tabular matter, and complicated formats such as advertisements.

Hand-operated machines compose at low production speeds, dependent on the operator's efficiency. Some of these typesetters operate directly under keyboard control. Shown in Figure 15-10 is such a machine, used for composing four different display faces in ten sizes from 12- to 96-point. The type fonts are interchangeable. Direct from the keyboard machines are also used for the composition of text sizes, $5\frac{1}{2}$- through 12-point, and are capable of composition to

24-point. The operator types the copy, and a display board in front of him informs him when an end-of-line decision must be made. He can make the decision for hyphen placement or order the machine to justify automatically, following a few basic logic rules. This range is less accurate than the operator decision. It is also possible to achieve hyphenless composition by ordering variations in interword and intraword spacing. Exposure onto paper is made after each line is completed.

The input to other hand-operated machines involves manual selection of characters and exposure of these elements one-at-a-time onto paper or film. Generally, such machines are used for setting display type in sizes as large as 150-point. These machines usually compose on single line strips; some are capable of composing several lines deep. A few of the machines can apply special optical treatments to the exposed type, as shown in Figure 15-11.

AUTOMATED COMPOSITION

Tremendous increases in composition speeds have been attained in the past few years through the introduction of automated equipment. The fastest of the automated phototypesetters are capable of

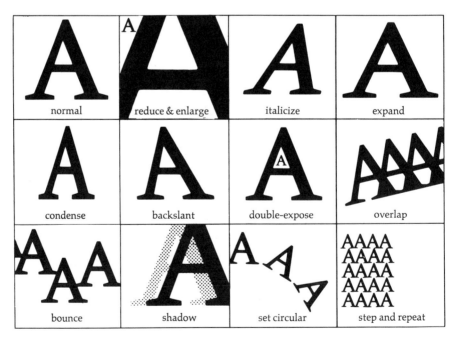

Figure 15-11. *Optical treatments of photocomposed display type. (Photo Typositor® type reproduced by permission of Visual Graphics Corporation)*

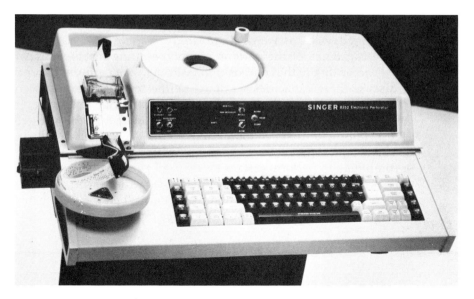

Figure 15-12. *Tape perforator. (Courtesy Graphic Systems Division, The Singer Company)*

production speeds as high as 190 lines per minute (11-pica lines of 9-point type, averaging 30 characters and spaces).

The manually operated linecasters, on the average, are able to produce some 200 similar lines per hour. Additional time is required for correcting galley proofs. Hyphenation and line spacing are, of course, time-consuming. On the average the operator is generating only three to four lpm (lines per minute).

We spoke previously of automated linecasters, operated by TTS attachments. Such machines can produce as many as 850 to 900 lines per hour — 14 to 15 lpm. Let's briefly recap how such a system works. First, the copy is written on a typewriter. It is then "retyped" by a punch operator whose machine turns out a raw tape. Such a machine is shown in Figure 15-12. The tape is then fed to a computer for h&j. The computer turns out a second tape to drive the linecaster. After type is set, it is proofed. If there are errors, it's back to the linecaster to set corrected lines. These are substituted for lines containing errors. Two typings, two tapes, and at least two sessions at the linecaster — plus a great deal of leg work, carrying paper tape and lines of type back and forth. Keep all this in mind. In the section on "Integrated Composition Systems" we will show how modern technology has simplified or eliminated many of these steps.

Logic and the computer are integral to the most modern typesetting devices, especially in the areas of phototypesetting and electronic composition. Most of these machines are driven by paper tape (in some cases by magnetic tape), although coded information is sometimes fed directly to them via wire connections from other text-processing devices, as we shall see later.

The capacities of the various phototypesetting machines range widely according to the composition tasks they can perform. In order to discuss these capacities we must define three terms. *Hardware* refers to the electronic components in a machine or computer. *Software* refers to the programs that direct the mathematical and logical functioning of the electronic components. As a result of calculations and logical decisions, these components activate the composers or computers to perform certain tasks. *Hard-wired logic* refers to certain "wired in" calculating and decision capacities incorporated in some of the limited-function phototypesetters when they are manufactured. Such machines cannot be further programmed.

(a) This line has been optically set flush left.
Notice the overhang of the 'T' in the line
above. Also note that type in this brochure
has been optically justified—all punctuation has been hung outside the margin.

(b)   This is an example of a line—set minus 1½ units.
This is an example of a line—set minus 1 unit.
This is an example of a line—set minus ½ unit.
This is an example of a line—set normal.
This is an example of a line—set plus ½ unit.
This is an example of a line—set plus 1 unit.

(c)

Tom says, "New York is a great state." This is a non-kerned line.
Tom says, "New York is a great state." This line shows how operator control over individual letters allows poorly spaced letter combinations to be improved.

(d) LESS THAN SOLID
LINE SPACING
IS POSSIBLE ON
ALPHASETTE

(e) **ALPHATYPE**
ALPHATYPE
ALPHATYPE
ALPHATYPE
ALPHATYPE
ALPHATYPE

Figure 15-13. *Examples of mini computer phototypesetter composition. (a) Hanging punctuation and optical line-up; (b) automatic letterspacing; (c) kerning; (d) negative line feed; (e) variable letterspacing. (Courtesy Alphatype Corporation)*

(a) **WINKER**

b.h.11, VictorySong-TillysFilly
Jean Guy Lareau, St. Mathias, Quebec

2:10 BR   1972 i1 1 1 0   1,023
2:09 Lon   1971 25 3 2 3   1,655

2:02¹—!—28,139

JEAN-GUY LAREAU, Blue, White

Trainer—J. Lareau

7- 6 BR ft clm2500	m :31⁴ 1:05 1:37² 2:09²	3	4	5	2⁰	2¹	2²¹	2:09⁴	8.20 J Lare	HighDarneau Winker ChiefMaynard	7
6-28 BR ft clm2000	m :30² 1:04¹ 1:37⁴ 2:10	5	2⁰	2	3	2¹	1¹¹	2:10	5.30 J Lare	Winker BoyTrust JHenryM	8
6-18 Sher ft pref-2	m :31² 1:04² 1:37 2:09	7	7	7	6⁰	5	5⁸	2:10³	11.30 M Chag	FarriorJugChief SylvieBunter AdiosCaretaker	
6-14 Sher ft qua	m :31² 1:04² 1:37 2:11	5	1	1	1	1	1³¹	2:11	NB M Chag	Winker ExpressCVolomite SilverSonnett	
4-24 BB! ft clm1500	m :31³ 1:05 1:37² 2:10	2	6	6	6	3²	4!	2:10	8.00 R Norm	ConsulRichelieu TommysPride JeffKirk	
4-18 BB! sy clm2500	m :32 1:05¹ 1:37³ 2:11	7	8	8	9	9⁹	5⁴¹	2:11	67.95 R Norm	DarnGoodScout MarshaMir LouAdio	
4- 5 BB! ft clm2500	m :32¹ 1:04² 1:35² 2:08	6	9	9	9	9¹⁸	8¹⁴	2:11¹	52.00 R Norm	FairwellLight HappyMir AnnieTopfield	

(b) It is one of the difficulties, but also delights, of teaching a course in Jacobian England, that most students arrive for the first class with strong preconceptions concerning the society they are about to study. The Jacobians, they almost universally agree, were inhib-

(c)   WASHINGTON (AP)—President Nixon asked Congress Wednesday to give the Coast Guard added authority to protect against

WASHINGTON (AP)—President Nixon asked Congress Wednesday to give the Coast Guard added authority to protect against oil spills and said he will seek $35

Figure 15-14. Examples of mini computer phototypesetter composition. (a) Tabular matter, columns justified; quad left, center, and right; (b) initial cap insertion; (c) standard setting from wire service has been stripped and line measure changed. (Specimens produced on a Mergenthaler V-I-P phototypesetter, manufactured by Mergenthaler Linotype, an ELTRA Company)

Most of the latter are capable of simplified hyphenation logic, justifying, mixing, tabbing, quadding, leadering (inserting leaders), letterspacing, variable line lengths, and variable leading. The keyboard machines are of this type. In addition, there are phototypesetters, without keyboard, that are hard-wired but require the input of tape.

The programmable photocomposers are the "big boys" in speed and flexibility. They contain minicomputers. Software is available for extending their capabilities well beyond those of the limited-function machines. The greater the computer core memory, the more flexible the typographic formats can be. Some machines can store formats numbering into the hundreds.

The greater memory capacity allows for more sophisticated means of h&j. The machines can story more fonts and thus can mix more faces and more readily switch from one format to another.

Some phototypesetters can *strip wire service codes*. This means that line-end codes on wire service paper tape can be ignored under proper program control and the text can be converted to another line length. Another important feature is the capacity of some of these machines to *reverse lead* (pronounced "led"). This refers to the capacity of the machine to move the film or paper in the opposite direction on computer command. Thus, additional columns of type can be *imaged* (exposed) alongside a first column, which has already been exposed. Some models can back the paper up as much as the depth of a newspaper page. Reverse leading also makes possible exposing images above the base line of the type. The ability to mix more faces and to compose multicolumns allows these machines to do *area composition;* this results in fewer pieces of paper to paste up when makeup of pages is done after all photocomposition is completed.

Under control of computer programming, phototypesetters are generally capable of greater horizontal and vertical spacing flexibility. Eight examples are shown in Figures 15-13 and 15-14.

(a) **SUMMER ARRIVES ON DOT** WITH SOFT SWEATER **DRESSING.** *Easy designs for travel or town by Matti of Lynne in airy, carefree Celanese Arnel triacetate with nylon sweater ribbing. Tank Topped Cooler in white dots on yellow, with yellow ribbing; or navy dots on white with navy*

(b) The following assumptions can be made: $\epsilon'_f \approx \epsilon_f$, and $\sigma'_f \approx \sigma_f$. (summaries of various methods of estimating ϵ_f and σ_f see [34].) Changes

$$\sum_{all \ i} 2N_f = \left(\frac{\sigma_f}{\sigma_a}\right)^{1+5n/n} = \left(\frac{108}{73}\right)^{14.1} = 260 \text{ reversals}$$

(c)

	4 WRC NBC
6 :00 :15 :30 :45	
7 :00 :15 :30 :45	7:45 Faith, Life News, Weather
8 :00 :15 :30 :45	Agriculture USA '' '' On Campus '' ''
9 :00 :15 :30 :45	Speaking Freely Ann Rand- Author, is Guest
10 :00 :15 :30 :45	Mass For Shut-Ins International Zone
11 :00 :15 :30 :45	Overview '' '' Issues '' ''
12 :00 :15 :30 :45	Dimension Washington Deena Clark's Moment With

Figure 15-15. *Examples of CRT composition. (a) Electronically generated condensed and sloped (italic); (b) variable base line composition for setting superior and inferior characters (phototypesetters are also capable of this treatment and CRT's can perform the various formattings of phototypesetters); (c) CRT mixing, alignment of different sizes and generation of horizontal and vertical rules. (Specimens produced on a Linotron 505 CRT phototypesetter, manufactured by Mergenthaler Linotype, an ELTRA Company)*

Because these typesetters generate type on a video screen, they are often termed CRT (cathode ray tube) machines. The generated images are focused by a lens onto paper or film; thus they are also referred to as CRT phototypesetters.

If phototypesetters are high-speed, machines in this group could be termed "super high-speed." They are capable of composing up to 3,000 newspaper lines per minute. In one newspaper application such a typesetter turns out full-size pages of classified reader ads, complete with rules, in approximately 70 seconds.

The flexibility of the CRT extends beyond that of the photo-typesetters. In addition to the capacity to do large areas they are capable of the same formatting techniques as other programmable photocomposers. In addition, because characters are generated on a video screen, they can be electronically manipulated to appear as roman, italic, backslanted, condensed, expanded, or bold—even in combinations of such treatments. Some CRT's can generate line art along with type. Experimentally, continuous tone art has been scanned and then converted to dot form in digital computers, later to be output as halftones.

Descriptive patterns for the generation of symbols are either stored in computer memory in digital form or matrix grids are scanned by a CRT (not the printout tube) which translates the character descriptions into digital coding. The descriptive coding, in either case, is utilized by the machine to direct the action of the printout CRT beam. This electronic beam "paints" the shapes of symbols on the screen in a series of parallel, vertical lines—as many as 1,440 per inch. The greater the number the greater the definition of characters, but the slower the composition rate. Type sizes run from 4- to 80-point in different models. In Figure 15-15 are shown some examples of CRT composition.

INTEGRATED PHOTOCOMPOSITION SYSTEMS

Consider the machines you have been introduced to so far. They include electric typewriters, tape perforators, VDT's, OCR's (see page 308), hard-wire logic and minicomputer phototypesetters, and CRT typesetters. In addition, you will be introduced to video layout machines and the computer.

Various configurations of these pieces of equipment can be developed in order to meet the needs of commercial printers and publishers. These configurations are called *text processing systems* and they range from the simplest to the most complex patterns, involving the use of every device listed above.

In using the term "system" we are speaking within the context of present-day systems engineering. This might be defined as the arrangement of a variety of machines and equipment to form a unity capable of performing a complex function; it also involves the interactions between people and the equipment involved.

We will discuss the various levels of sophistication in the text processing systems that have evolved. As we do so, the reader should keep in mind the methods of getting words into print involved in the hot-metal system — from the original typing through editing, design, composition, proofreading, and makeup. Each of these functions and the personnel involved have been greatly affected.

Let us look at the ways in which these machines can be utilized:

1. KEYBOARD-DRIVEN PHOTOTYPESETTER. This is the simplest use of photocomposition equipment. Output speed is limited by the operator's efficiency. Author's copy must be edited in the traditional manner. Thus two keyboardings — the author's and the operator's — are required. Errors are detectable on the photo paper output from the machine. The machine does offer the advantages of hard-wired logic.

2. PERFORATOR TO PHOTOTYPESETTER.[1] Greater programming flexibility is offered in this system if the typesetter has a front-end minicomputer rather than hard-wired logic. Again, double keyboarding is necessary, and editing is done in the traditional manner. The machines are *stand-alone;* that is, perforated tape is hand-carried from the first to the second machine.[2] Errors are first detectable on the typesetter photo paper output.

3. VDT-PERFORATOR TO PHOTOTYPESETTER. Here is an opportunity to eliminate double keyboarding. The author can write his original manuscript, seeing what he produces on a CRT (video screen) instead of paper. Once he is satisfied, he can *dump* his message — that is, perforate a tape. This can go to the typesetter or to another VDT operated by an editor. If the editor's VDT has a tape reader, he can see the results on his screen, effect changes, and produce a merged tape. This incorporates the writer's and the editor's efforts.

A variation is possible here. The editor's VDT could stand between the two machines in number 2 above.

It should be noted here that a system for the first time brings the editing function within its operation. Now the need for galley proofs, revised proofs, and page proofs is less necessary. Proofs in the hot-

---

[1] Throughout this section the reader should interpret "phototypesetter" to include the CRT typesetters.

[2] Input must be supplied to a stand-alone piece of equipment. In contrast, the input for a self-contained machine is generated on a keyboard that is integral to the machine.

metal systems are needed to reduce the number of errors human beings tend to make; machine logic is less likely to err. If tapes reach the phototypesetter "clean," the output will be "clean."

4. OCR TO VDT TO PHOTOTYPESETTER. This gives still more editing flexibility and can eliminate double keyboarding. The writer could prepare his copy on the proper typewriter and insert his corrections. The tape produced could go to an editing VDT for further processing.

THE COMPUTERIZED PHOTOTYPESETTING SYSTEM

Up to this point in our discussion of phototypesetting and CRT's we have only mentioned the small computers integral to these machines. Many large text-processing systems make use of large, separate computers to control the operations of the various machines. The latter may stand alone and communicate with each other via hand-carried tape, as we have seen. Or they may function as subsystems and become *interfaced* (hooked up directly) with the computer. The devices that are interfaced are termed *on-line*.

Before we examine computerized systems, let us briefly consider what a computer is and what it can do. Our discussion must of necessity be brief; however, the computer is becoming so much a part of life for those in graphic communication that they should become more knowledgeable about it. We recommend reading Crowley (1967), a paperback book that is written for the layman.

Basically, the computer is a fast decision-making machine. It is capable of 1,000,000 or more operations in one second. Contrary to what many people may think, it is not strictly a "math machine," although it can perform mathematical operations. It is also a logic machine. For example, it can decide where hyphenation should be made; it can alphabetize; it can evaluate alternatives and select "the best" in terms of what it "knows." It can even check its own accuracy.

All information fed in, processed, and output is in a binary code. For example, the commonly used TTS tape is 6-level. A 6-level tape can code 63 different commands from the keyboard ($2^6 = 64$). A hole in the tape represents 1, no hole represents 0. Lower case a, b, and c are represented as 011000, 010011, and 001110, respectively. Keys on the perforator keyboard bear operator-recognizable language. Circuits and devices in the computer are compatible with the binary code. Current either passes through wires or it doesn't. Relays are either open or closed. Transistors conduct or do not. Magnetic devices are charged or not charged. A magnetic charge or no charge may be deposited in patterns on magnetic tape, discs, or drums. Output is in

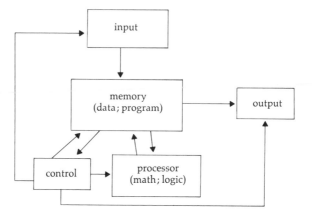

Figure 15-16. *Functional units of a computer.*

the same binary code, and a device is required to encode the information into human-recognizable language.

Figure 15-16 represents the major functional units of a computer. They are: input, memory, control, processor, and output. The input unit accepts instructions (program) and information to be processed. The memory has two major purposes—storage of the program and information to be processed. The control unit directs the execution of program commands in the required sequence. For example, information may be called from memory and sent to the processor for manipulation. The processor contains arithmetic and logic circuits. Processed information can be output or stored in memory.

The computer can be the central control unit of a *direct input system* in which no perforated tape is used. The most extensive use of this configuration, in which all equipment may be on-line, is found in the newspaper field. Let's examine such a system.

The four devices at the top in Figure 15-17 serve as system input, direct to the computer via hard wire. There is an additional input— the *video layout system* (VLS).

The electric typewriters are special units designed to output binary code signals. These, together with VDT's and OCR's, may be used in editorial as well as advertising (classified and display) departments.

The VLS has its own computer control, represented by the taller units behind the video screen terminals. Copy for display ads can be input from the terminal keyboards or from VDT's and OCR's. The VLS generates area composition up to 45 picas wide and a full newspaper page deep—it is capable of scrolling to that depth, although the screen is not that deep.

The operator can format the copy from his keyboard (see Figure 15-18), correct or change it in any manner. He can position display and text type as per layout. He can test the copyfitting and can control measures, type size, leading, and so on. The widths of the characters displayed on the screen vary according to font, so that, prior to dumping, he is able to get a full-width picture of how type in an ad will look from top to bottom—an ad as wide as 45 picas. The computer is needed to store copy before and after markup and makeup, to calculate copy fit, to calculate positioning, and to display type elements as the operator would like to see them. The ad data are moved to the main computer when called for by its control from storage in the VLS memory.

Note the VDT to the left of the central control computer. This serves for editing and proofreading the information called from central control unit memory. Operators at such VDT's can activate the monitor printers to produce hard copy for a record of what has been processed. These machines print out in either all caps or caps and lowercase at such high speeds that their effect on system throughput time is negligible.

We have described this system as being on-line. As such it is tapeless. However, a similar configuration could be effected in which

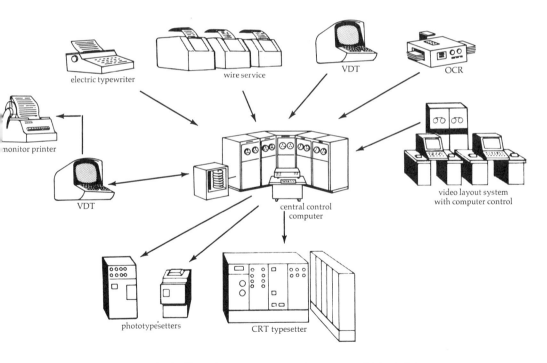

Figure 15-17. *Computerized, direct-input text processing system. (Adapted from literature supplied by American Newspaper Publishers Association Research Institute)*

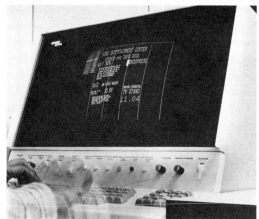

Figure 15-18. *The Harris 2200 Layout Markup Terminal, a VLS. (Courtesy Harris Composition Systems)*

tapes (paper and/or magnetic) would be used, with perforators instead of the on-line typewriters. In fact, some on-line systems are set up with machines equipped with tape read-and-punch facilities for emergency use in the event of system foul-up.

Several legitimate questions may arise in the reader's mind at this point:

1. What advantages does the on-line system have over the tape system? It allows greater speed. No tape punching and reading (by machines) is required. The feeding of tape through a punch or a reader is mechanical and consequently slower. On-line means lower operating costs — tape is expensive and personnel are needed for transporting and storing it. H&j, utilizing the larger memory of separate computers, can reach a high level of sophistication; more memory space can be given to the rules of logic and to dictionaries of *exception words*. VDTs on-line can display copy in line-for-line form, revealing awkward hyphenation.

2. Might the system "jam" with everybody working at once? Not likely. The central control monitors all operations and paces input, processing, and output. Machines control machines. Men and women can concentrate on ideas and words — writing, editing, and designing. This continuous operation is called *real time*.

3. How is it possible to keep track of all the copy that is being handled? One of the major advantages of the computerized system is that copy is entered into computer memory at a known address and is coded by source. At any time the user of a particular kind of copy can ask for a file. It can be displayed on a VDT and/or printed on a *high-speed printer* (monitor printer). Enough information is given to identify the copy and its space requirements. Consider this advantage in the case of myriads of small, classified ads. All ads from the previous day can be stored. New ads can be entered the next day and control, under proper programming, can delete "kills," sort out "skip ads" (they run again later), merge in the new ads, and output the current run. A central control computer can be programmed to place ads under the proper classification and even list them in a desired order there — for example, automobiles by make, model, and year.

4. Is there a relationship between computer size and the volume of work it can handle? To answer this we should first distinguish between *core memory,* or primary memory, and secondary memory. The former contains the program and the information being processed. The latter stores information prior to or following processing. Core size is usually stated as so many *K bytes*. One often hears "K" referred to as representing 1,000. Actually, it is 1,024, the closest binary equivalent number ($2^{10} = 1,024$). A byte is a series of bits, usually eight — capable of representing 256 symbols ($2^8 = 256$). A core memory of 12K bytes thus represents a capacity of 98,304 bits.

Information can be placed in or retrieved from core in a few microseconds (millionths), sometimes nanoseconds (billionths). Storage in or retrieval from secondary memory takes several milliseconds (thousandths).

Very large computers have a core as high as 196K and secondary memory representing many millions of characters. Since core represents program and amount processed, there is a relationship between computer size and system size.

In very large operations work areas are established, each with the number of input devices needed to prepare the required amount of copy, a computer of proper core capacity, the necessary amount of secondary memory, and a typesetter that matches the amount of text to be processed. Such work areas might, for example, be (1) news, (2) display advertising, and (3) classified advertising; or (1) news and display and (2) classified, depending on the volumes of work required.

PASTEUP

The ultimate output of these systems is print on photo paper, generated by phototypesetters and CRT's. The various pieces of paper are then pasted up to make page forms. These are photographed to make page negatives. To the extent that area composition is possible, the volume of pasteup work is reduced.

The existence of the VLS suggests that it will one day be possible to lay out full newspaper pages on a video screen, including halftones.

The page negative is used for making offset plates or engraved full-page plates (plastic or metal) for use on newspaper letterpress presses. Many newspapers today, although still utilizing letterpress, set type by the cold-type methods. In some cases the engraved page plates are used directly; in others, mats are formed from the engravings.

THE NEW VS. THE OLD

It is not difficult to develop a list of the advantages of cold-type composition over hot-metal methods. Figure 15-19 forms the basis for generating such a list. We might mention another advantage. The various cold-type machines have a sleek, modern style. They look like office machines as does the computer. The hot-metal machines, in contrast, have a manufacturing look. In the traditional composing room the atmosphere is generally that of a factory. Set in modern surroundings, complete with contemporary decor, soundproof ceilings,

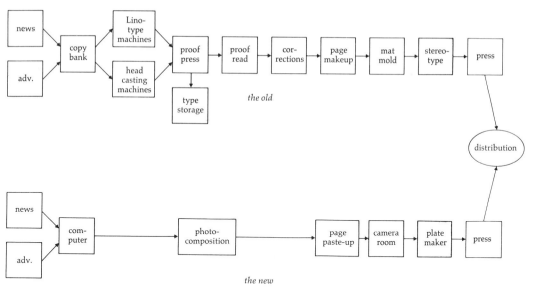

Figure 15-19. *The old versus the new: preparing for printing. (Courtesy American Newspaper Publishers Association Research Institute)*

and carpeting on the floor, the cold-type equipment presents an entirely different picture.

Presses

The planning of how printed materials should look reaches fruition when type and auxiliary elements are reproduced in ink on paper. Many kinds of printing presses exist, and they vary widely in principle of operation, speed, and size. It is probably true that there is a near-perfect press for every job.

For efficient mass communication by printing, it is therefore essential that the user of printing (1) select a printer with the right press for his specific job, or (2) tailor the job to the press equipment available to achieve his desired results.

KINDS OF PRESSES

Presses are usually described according to their principle of operation, whether they print on sheets or rolls of paper, whether they

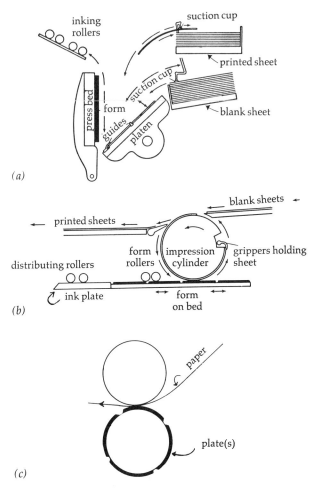

inking rollers

suction cup

printed sheet

press bed

suction cup

form

guides

platen

blank sheet

(a)

blank sheets

printed sheets

form rollers

impression cylinder

grippers holding sheet

distributing rollers

ink plate

form on bed

(b)

paper

plate(s)

(c)

Figure 15-20. *The three principles of press operation: (a) the platen press; (b) the cylinder press; (c) the rotary press. The printing surface (form) in a and b must be raised. The surface (plate or plates) in c can be raised, flat, or intaglio. (a, b: Reprinted from* Production in Advertising and the Graphic Arts *by David Hymes, by permission of the publishers, Holt, Rinehart and Winston, Inc.)*

print on both sides of the paper in one operation, and whether they print more than one color in each operation.

We will discuss presses here, separately, as three basic kinds: (1) platen, (2) flat-bed cylinder, and (3) rotary. These are shown in schematic diagram in Figure 15-20. Note that, in the first two, printing is done from type; thus they are limited to letterpress printing.

The rotary press, on the other hand, involves curved plates made from type. They may have a raised surface for letterpress printing, a flat surface for offset printing, or an indented surface for gravure.

Presses that print on sheets of paper are called *sheet-fed;* those that print on rolls are called *web-fed.* A press that prints on both sides of the paper in one operation is called a *perfecting press.* Thus the term used to describe the fast and efficient presses used by most newspapers is *web-perfecting rotary press.*

THE PLATEN PRESS

The simplest printing press is the platen press in which the form of type is placed in a vertical position. Paper is positioned against the platen, which closes in clamshell fashion to press it against the inked form. When the platen swings open to receive another sheet of paper, the form is reinked. Platen presses are often nicknamed *clamshells.* Platen presses are limited in size and are consequently used primarily for printing letterheads, cards, forms, and other small jobs.

THE FLAT-BED CYLINDER PRESS

Like platen presses, flat-bed cylinder presses print from raised surface materials. They can be one-color or two-color, web-fed or sheet-fed.

Much of the finest letterpress printing of past years has been done on these presses. Many magazines, books, and smaller newspapers have been printed on these machines. As pointed out in Chapter 12, however, much of the production that used to come off these presses is now going to photo-offset lithography because of some inherently slow characteristics of flat-bed cylinder production.

Cylinder presses are quite slow because they require two revolutions of the cylinder for one impression. As shown in Figure 15-20, the type form is locked in position on the press's flat bed. Blank sheets are then fed into the press and held to the impression cylinder by the grippers. This cylinder rotates twice for each impression that is drawn. In the first revolution the impression is made; in the second the cylinder rises to allow the paper to be removed.

These presses range widely in size from 9 by 12 inches to 50 by 73½ inches (these are dimensions of the paper sizes they accommodate). A production speed of 3,500 to 4,000 impressions per hour is typical.

Production rates are improved with the addition of a second cylinder to make a two-color press (Figure 15-21) or a perfecting press (Figure 15-22). On the press shown in Figure 15-22, one side of the

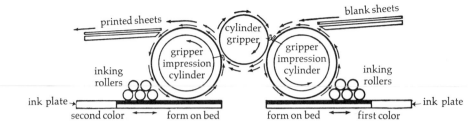

Figure 15-21. *A two-color cylinder press. (Credit same as preceding figure)*

web is printed by the impression of a four-page form on the lower bed; the web is perfected on the upper bed. Its capacity is approximately 3,500 papers an hour, delivered either as 8 full-size pages or 16 tabloid pages; consequently, it is used primarily for large weekly or small daily papers.

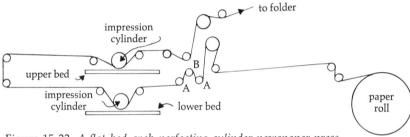

Figure 15-22. *A flat-bed, web-perfecting cylinder newspaper press.*

THE ROTARY PRESS

Rotary presses do not print direct from flat forms as in the case of flat-bed presses. Not only is the impression cylinder curved but so is the cylinder that carries the printing elements. In other words, printing in this operation is done from a curved surface.

This principle offers the opportunity for much greater speed, since each revolution of the impression cylinder puts ink on paper. Rotary presses, because they are constructed in units, are also highly adaptable to the use of color and to increasing volume; each additional unit increases capacity or permits the printing of another color. Many rotary presses are multi-unit.

Rotary presses can be sheet-fed or web-fed, single color or multicolor; they can be letterpress, offset, or gravure. Most large daily newspapers are printed on large, multi-unit rotary presses. Most large catalogs and Sunday newspaper pictorial supplements are printed on gravure rotary presses. Many magazines and an increasing number of daily newspapers are printed on web-fed rotary offset presses.

Letterpress Rotaries

The basic principle of a letterpress rotary press unit is shown in Figure 15-23. The unit consists of two kinds of cylinders, one that contains the printing plate and another that serves to press the paper against the plate. Figure 15-24 shows a unit of a web-perfecting newspaper press; each unit in this case consists of four cylinders, two of which carry page plates and two of which make the impression.

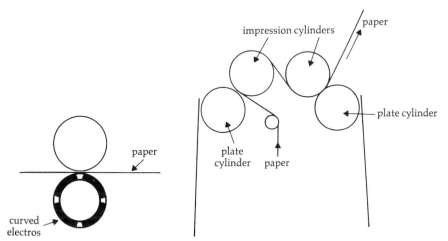

Figure 15-23. A sheet-fed rotary press—basic principle.

Figure 15-24. A newspaper web-perfecting rotary press unit.

The use of the rotary principle in letterpress necessitates an additional prepress production step: type and plates that have been put together in page form must be duplicated in relief on a curved plate to attach to the plate cylinder. This duplication is accomplished either by stereotyping or electrotyping. Newspapers traditionally have used stereotype plates (plates made by casting hot lead against a fiber mat) and magazines have used electrotypes (made by electrolytically depositing copper to form a printing surface) for rotary printing. Electros produce better quality plates but are more time-consuming and costly. The introduction of thin, shallow-etched plastic or metal plates that can be made photographically from page paste-ups has been a boon to newspapers with large rotary presses.

A multi-unit letterpress newspaper press, equipped with a folder, can produce as many as 70,000 newspapers containing up to 144 pages in an hour, completely folded and ready for delivery trucks. Provision can be made for color (even process color) but letterpress newspapers are not known for excellence in color reproduction. The accent instead is on speed—so much so that large presses even con-

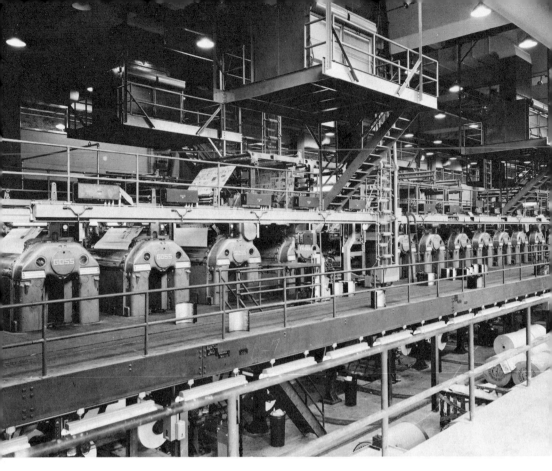

Figure 15-25. *A newspaper pressroom. (Courtesy MGD Graphic Systems Division, Rockwell International)*

tain devices called *flying pasters,* a splicing mechanism that automatically attaches the nearly exhausted roll of newsprint to a fresh roll. Thus it is not necessary to stop the presses every few minutes to splice a new roll of paper to the web manually. Figure 15-25 shows a large newspaper press.

Some large-circulation magazines, such as *Sports Illustrated,* also use rotary letterpresses. The magazine press shown in Figure 15-26 is capable of printing a 32-page magazine form, six colors on each side, at the rate of 2,000 feet of web per minute. Electronic monitors adjust alignment and register to guarantee quality work.

Offset Rotaries

The fact that offset lithography is a planographic printing process using thin, pliable plates made photographically from page pasteups has made it especially adaptable for rotary printing.

Offset plates, which are no thicker than cardboard, can be easily wrapped around a cylinder and clamped. Also, the rubber blanket,

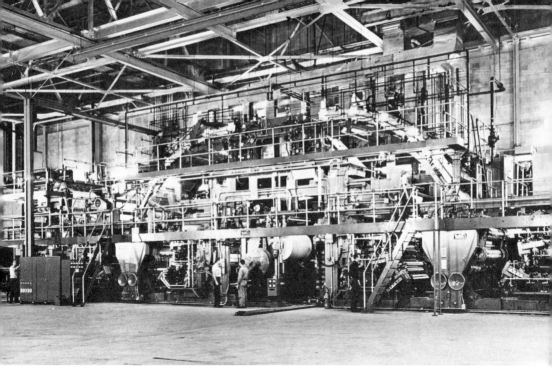

Figure 15-26. *This magazine press, designed to run at 2,000 feet per minute, is capable of printing a 32-page form, six colors on each side. Even while the press is running at full speed electronic monitors adjust the alignment and register, and a new roll of paper can be added. Top view of the same press, right. More electronic devices assure precise registration of colors and compensate for minute changes in temperature and humidity. At right, cut and folded page-units are delivered. (Courtesy Life; © 1963, Time, Inc.; photos: above: J. W. Clement Company; right: Sherwin Greenburg Studios)*

which actually does the printing, is thin and pliable and can be easily clamped around a cylinder.

Rotary offset presses can be sheet-fed (Figure 15-27) or web-fed (Figure 15-28). Web-fed presses are constructed on the unit principle, with the capacity in pages and/or additional color being determined by the number of units. The press shown in Figure 15-28 is printing one color on each side of four webs. One web can be fed straight through all four units to print four colors on each side.

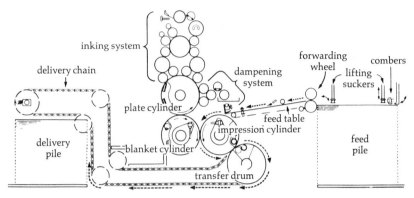

Figure 15-27. *A single-color, sheet-fed offset press. (Courtesy Lithographic Technical Foundation)*

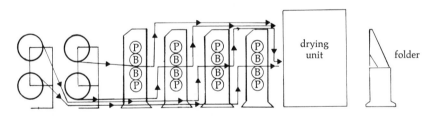

Figure 15-28. *A four-unit web-fed offset press.*

Most offset newspaper presses print a maximum of 16 to 32 full-size pages (double if tabloid) at speeds as great as 30,000 an hour. (However, some new offset presses can deliver up to 144 full-size pages at speeds up to 70,000.) A newspaper web offset unit is shown in Figure 15-29. Note that offset rotaries rely on one blanket cylinder to serve as the impression cylinder for another blanket cylinder.

The increased use of offset in the newspaper and magazine fields has greatly increased the use of the presses described here.

Rotogravure Rotaries

Rotogravure presses are either sheet-fed or web-fed, perfecting. Figure 15-30 illustrates a web-fed press and shows four units, each

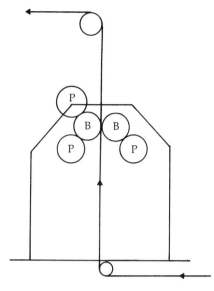

Figure 15-29. *A newspaper web-fed offset press unit.*

being used for a separate color. The web would next be turned over and fed through additional units for perfecting. The large cylinders, shown emerging from the rectangular bases, are the plate cylinders. Directly above each is an impression cylinder which presses the paper against the printing area so that the ink can be lifted from the depressed areas to the paper.

These presses are capable of producing excellent work in color or in black and white in huge runs; hence their popularity for newspaper supplements and illustrated catalogs.

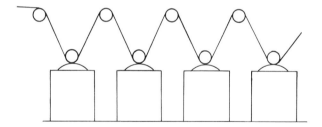

Figure 15-30. *A rotogravure press of four units.*

PRESSES THAT AREN'T PRESSES

A discussion of presses would not be complete without mention of *ink transfer devices* that serve the function of printing presses but cannot be accurately described in that fashion because they do not *press* ink to paper.

Xerox and other electrostatic machines are examples of such devices. They put ink on paper without an "impression." But it is most significant to note that the emphasis on research in production techniques has now shifted from type composition methods to presses. The end goal is a press system operated by a computer without plates or type in the traditional sense. The VDT's, OCR's, CRT's, and computerized systems mentioned earlier in this chapter are considered the ultimate breakthrough in prepress production steps. There will be modifications, improvements, and added uses devised for these systems, but no basic change seems to be needed, at least at this point.

Discussing the matter of press research, William Rinehart, director of the American Newspaper Publishers Association Research Institute, has said, "We have the jet engine in the composing room now, but we still have the steam locomotive in the pressroom."[3]

Rinehart and others point to the tons of metal and the hundreds of thousands — even millions — of dollars that are involved in large newspaper presses as being inconsistent with the new composing technology. Experiments with plateless printing (see ink-jet printing in Chapter 12) were well underway as this text was written. Predictions for success were optimistic but vague about specific methods or a timetable.

In the meantime, publishers and the occasional users of printing have a wide variety of efficient printing processes with amazing technological capability at their disposal. The technology for producing effective graphic communication is available; it is up to the user of that technology to produce content that is of equal quality.

[3] In remarks made at the ANPA technical seminar, Chicago, April 19, 1974.

CHAPTER 16 # Paper: Selection, Folding, Binding, Finishing

By now it should be obvious that successful graphic communication is possible only when the desires of the user of any printing process are closely coordinated with the mechanics of the process. Obvious, too, is the fact that although the user may wish to think only in terms of the esthetic values, or utilitarian properties, or both, of printed material, these qualities cannot be separated from mechanics and cost.

The interrelationship of mechanics and desired effects come into still sharper focus with a study of paper selection and imposition — the preliminary steps in printing; and folding, binding, and finishing — the final production stages.

A discussion of these also serves to stress the need for comprehensive advance planning that takes into account all phases of printing production. For, as will be shown, paper selection is affected by folding, binding is affected by paper, and so on. None of the steps in production can be separated from the others.

Paper Selection

There are several important factors to consider when selecting paper. Some are the immediate concern of the user; others are mainly of interest to the printer.

Paper shares full responsibility with type and illustrations in giving personality to any printed piece. It, too, contributes to the "voice" of the printed material. It can say quality or cheapness and speak loudly or softly. From the user's standpoint, this may be the most vital role of paper. But, although color, weight, and smoothness must be judged according to their esthetic contributions, these and other paper characteristics must be analyzed in other ways, too.

Practical properties, such as the ability to withstand age, are very important. Printed matter supposed to last for years may disintegrate long before its intended life span has expired if proper paper was not chosen. Or, faulty paper selection can cause printed pieces to fall apart at the folds before the material has completed its usefulness.

Cost, of course, is always a determinant. Paper is priced by the pound, with the rate according to the kind and amount of processing needed to give it the desired qualities. Thus weight, or thickness, becomes significant, increasingly so if the finished product is to be mailed. A small difference in weight per piece can multiply postage costs by thousands of dollars if great numbers are to be mailed.

Thus the user of printing is likely to be most concerned about these characteristics of paper: (1) the esthetic or psychological effect of its appearance and "feel," (2) its permanence, (3) its durability, and (4) its cost and weight.

The printer must, of course, share his customers' concern. But, because he is charged with the mechanics of production, he sees these characteristics from a slightly different angle, regarding many other technical properties with special meaning to him.

He must be aware of the opacity of paper, for example, because he knows that appearance can be ruined if the inked impression on one side shows through to the other. He tries to ensure that a printed piece is planned to fit a standard-size sheet of paper that matches his press capacity. By so doing, he can minimize the unnecessary costs that increase through wastage from trimming.

A letterpress printer knows that only with a smooth-finish paper can he reproduce fine-screen engravings to a customer's satisfaction. The offset lithographer or gravure printer requires other special papers for good reproduction.

Chemical and physical properties such as acidity, porosity, and surface-bonding strength must be checked. Papers with high acid content are fine for some work, but are not permanent enough for many uses. Ink spreads after contact with paper according to the porosity of the paper; surface-bonding strength determines a paper's resistance to "picking," the undesirable release of small bits of paper surface during a press run. If picking is excessive, press time can be lengthened because of the need for frequent cleanups.

Printers must always be conscious of the grain of paper. As paper is manufactured, the watery pulp is carried over fine wire cloth and the pulp fibers tend to lie in the same direction. In this way, the fibers give paper a grain, much like that in wood. Grain direction is important because it affects (1) the ease with which paper will run through a press, and (2) the folding and binding. In a magazine or booklet, for example, the grain should run parallel to the binding so that the sheets will lie flat when open. The bindery must always be consulted to be sure the grain is in the right direction for folding and binding.

The printer, then, in addition to the end-use properties of paper that may be apparent to his customer must also consider: (1) opacity, (2) sheet size, (3) special properties for particular printing processes, (4) capability of reproducing illustrations, (5) chemical and physical properties that affect presswork, folding, and binding, and (6) grain direction.

It is therefore essential that the user of printing work closely with the printer in selecting paper for any job. A basic knowledge of kinds, weights, sizes, and finishes is important to the user so he can adapt his requirements to those of the printer.

Basic Kinds of Paper

Paper can be classified in many ways; for example, *wood* papers and *rag* papers. Most paper is made of wood pulp, but some is made of rags or a combination of both.

The cheapest paper is made by grinding bark-free logs into a pulp that is formed into sheets without benefit of any chemical action to remove impurities. This *groundwood* paper is commonly used for newspapers and disintegrates quickly because of its imperfections.

Wood-pulp papers of more permanence are treated to be rid of substances that cause fast deterioration. Called *sulphate, soda,* and *sulphite* papers, they are used for all kinds of printing.

A 100 percent rag content paper is virtually imperishable, but is so expensive that its use is limited.

To order paper, one must know its four basic classifications named by appearance and proposed use: *bond, book, cover,* and *cardboard.*

Aside from its use for bonds and stock certificates, bond paper is standard for office use. Because its primary application is for letterheads and typewriter paper, it has a semihard finish ideal for typing or handwriting.

As the name implies, book paper is used for books, but it also is the vehicle for virtually every mass-printed medium of communication. It comes in textures ranging from rough to a smooth gloss.

Heavy and durable, cover paper has been formulated to withstand the extra wear on booklet and magazine covers. It is available in many colors and finishes. Publications are often "self-cover" — the cover is printed on the same stock and at the same time as the inside pages, but when special bulk or durability is desired, cover stock is specified.

Posters, stand-up advertising displays, and direct-mail promotion pieces are frequently printed on a stiff, heavy paper composed of several plies, or layers. Cardboard stock may also be referred to as *Bristol board* or by a number of suppliers as *postcard.*

In addition to the basic classes, there are special papers for special uses. *Offset* papers have properties designed to compensate for the moisture and other problems unique in offset printing. *Gravure* or *roto* paper is especially made to absorb the large amount of ink applied in rotogravure printing. There are other kinds of paper, but most are variations of those already described. Much of the variety comes from giving standard papers different finishes or surfaces.

Paper Surfaces

Paper sheets are formed during manufacture when pulp is passed between rollers. This is called *calendering,* and the amount of calendering depends upon the desired degree of surface smoothness.

Paper with a minimum of calendering is called *antique* or *eggshell* and is widely used for books and brochures. It has substantial bulk and is rough in texture. Although it is not suitable for reproducing letterpress halftone illustrations, its nonglare surface makes it desirable for lengthy reading matter. The bulk of antique papers is often reduced by additional calendering gentle enough not to eliminate the rough texture.

Fairly extensive calendering produces a smoother surface for paper called *machine finish.* Many magazines use it because of its good printing surface; *English finish* is very similar (slightly more calendering) and provides only slightly better letterpress halftone reproduction.

Supercalendered paper has been processed until its surface is slick enough to take all but the finest-screened letterpress halftone engravings. It also is popular for magazines.

Paper manufacturers, when confronted with the problem of finding a suitable surface for fine-screened halftones, developed *coated* papers. Originally these were brush-coated with a clay substance, and some still are, but most coating is now applied by machine as the paper is being made. Coated papers are expensive but essential for the finest quality of photographic reproduction.

Paper Weight and Sheet Sizes

Paper is priced by the pound but is sold in lots of a given number of sheets as well as pounds. Standard lots are a *ream* (500 sheets), a *case* (about 500 pounds), and a *skid* (about 3000 pounds). A *quire* is one twentieth of a ream and a *carton* is one quarter of a case.

It would be impossible, of course, to identify paper's weight by that of a single sheet. Instead, this vital element of paper, usually called *substance,* is expressed as the number of pounds in a ream of sheets of a basic size. Hence, paper would be labeled "100-pound" if 500 sheets of the basic size weighed 100 pounds.

Unfortunately, the *basic* size is not the same for all kinds of paper. Generally, the basic size is the most suitable and efficient for most common uses of any particular paper. The basic size for bond paper, for example, is 17 by 22 inches because it will fit most presses and will cut into four 8½ by 11-inch sheets.

Basic sheet sizes in inches are:

> *bond:* 17 by 22
> *book:* 25 by 38
> *cover:* 20 by 26
> *card (bristol):* 22½ by 28½

These must be kept in mind when ordering paper. Obviously, 500 sheets 25 by 38 inches will weigh a lot more than 500 sheets 17 by 22 inches of the same paper. The user of 20-pound bond who orders a 30-pound book paper expecting to get a sheet of more thickness will be shocked to find that it is, in fact, much thinner. (Equivalent paper weights are given in the table on page 251.)

In addition to the basic size, paper is available in many sizes said to be *standard* because they match press sizes or will cut or fold into standard-size booklets that, in turn, fit standard-size mailing envelopes. (Common sheet sizes are related to piece sizes in the table on page 250.)

Of course, the printer can use practically any size sheet of paper and cut it to fit a particular job. But when he does, waste results and, more importantly, a loss of efficiency occurs in each of the printing, folding, binding, and finishing steps that follow.

Imposition, Binding, and Folding

IMPOSITION AND SIGNATURES

As he produces booklets, magazines, books, or other such publications, a printer ordinarily prints several pages on a single sheet of paper. All of the type pages that are to print on one side of the sheet must be positioned so that, when printed, the sheet can be folded and bound with the pages in proper sequence. This arranging or arrangement of type pages is called *imposition*.

Each printed and folded sheet is called a *signature* and it makes up one or more sections of the publication. Any section of a publication in which pages have been printed on one sheet is a signature, but some impositions print more than one signature on one sheet.

The simplest of signatures can be two pages (one leaf printed on both sides), but ordinarily they range from four to 64 pages, in multiples of four. For booklets, books, or magazines, the most common signatures are eight, 16, 32, or 64 pages.

There are numerous kinds of impositions, especially for the great variety of intricately folded pamphlets and folders that are produced. In any case, the imposition a printer will use is dictated by the folding and binding that are to follow. It can likewise be said that much of the planning of the printed piece is dictated by the imposition the printer will use.

The problems of the editor of a 16-page publication, whether a newspaper, a magazine, or a public relations booklet, provide a good example. Whatever the publication, both its deadlines and any use of a color in addition to black are directly affected by imposition.

If, as is typical, the printer plans to print half the pages on one side of a sheet and half on the other, the editor must know which pages go on which side of the sheet. He can then set separate deadlines for each unit of eight pages that must go on the press at the same time. Only when all eight pages are complete right down to the last plate and the last line of type is the form ready.

If he plans to use a color in addition to black on only eight pages, or fewer, the editor, knowing the imposition, can assign color only to those pages that fall on one side of the sheet. By so doing he gets the color with only one additional press run; if one or more pages of color were to be assigned to each side of the sheet, two additional press runs would be required.

Imposition, therefore, is of great importance because press delays, missed publication dates, and unnecessary color costs can be avoided by a planner who knows what method the printer will use.

Kinds of Imposition

For most purposes there are two basic kinds of imposition. One of these is shown in Figure 16-1: half the pages in a signature are printed on one side of the sheet and the other half back up the sheet. This method is called *sheetwise* and is preferred by most printers for most jobs.

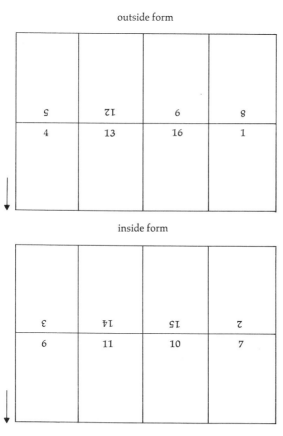

Figure 16-1. *A sheetwise imposition for a 16-page signature showing both sides of the sheet, eight pages printed on each side.*

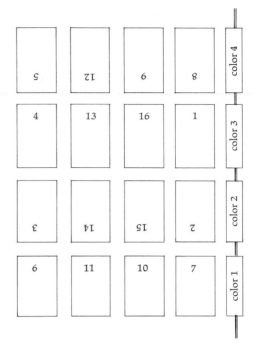

Figure 16-2. *A work-and-turn imposition for a 16-page signature; the complete signature is printed on both sides of one sheet, and the sheet is then cut to make two signatures. This diagram also shows how fountains and rollers might be split to put four different colors on a signature in one press run.*

In the other kind, all pages of a signature are printed on one side of a sheet for half the press run, and the sheet is then turned over for the same pages to be printed on the opposite side during the final half run. The sheet is then cut apart to form two signatures. Depending upon how the sheet is turned before it is backed up, this imposition has three variations—*work-and-turn,* which is most common, *work-and-tumble,* and *work-and-twist.*

In work-and-turn, the sheet is turned so that the left edge becomes the right edge, but the front (gripper) edge remains the same. In work-and-tumble, the sheet is tumbled so that the back edge becomes the gripper edge when the sheet is being printed on the second side. In work-and-twist all edges are reversed. Because work-and-turn employs the same gripper edge for printing both sides, it is used much more than the other two. Figure 16-2 shows a sheet that has been printed with this imposition.

The same figure shows a rather specialized printing technique which is of great importance to imposition. This is *split-fountain* or *split-color,* a technique that applies several colors to a sheet during one press run (Figure 16-3). Once a sheet has been printed in black, several colors can be added with one impression if they are planned to fall in "channels."

Although procedure varies, the ink fountain is usually split into several compartments (four, in Figure 16-2), which carry different colors. From these, the inking rollers, correspondingly split, carry the colors to their particular pages. As many colors can be printed simultaneously as there are sections of the roller. To plan color according to the channels covered by each roller section the designer must know the location of each page in a form.

This technique is used quite extensively by magazines to satisfy the color requirements of advertisers at minimum cost. Roller splitting for a one-time-only job may be too costly, but for magazines that can use cut rollers repeatedly it can offer substantial cost advantages.

WRAPS AND TIP-INS

Although good planning dictates a consideration of imposition and signatures, it is not always possible to produce a publication that will adhere to large signatures.

An advertiser, for example, will frequently insist that his magazine ad be on a special paper or other material. The ad must then be specially handled and inserted into the publication. In bookwork it is not unusual for the publisher to want a special glossy paper for reproducing the few illustrations to be used and to order the rest of the book printed on a cheaper stock.

Figure 16-3. *Split fountain: different color inks separated from each other in the ink fountains (wells at bottom) and transferred to rollers above. (Printing Corporation of America)*

In these and other cases where standard signatures cannot be used, the printer will most likely take care of the problem with a *wrap* or a *tip-in*. The former is a four-page insert placed around a signature before it is bound. Because they can be stitched into the binding with their signatures, wraps are as durably bound as the rest of the magazine or book. They are a problem to the editor, however, because he must plan their location carefully if he is to get the desired continuity of subject matter.

It is possible, but more time-consuming, to place four pages within a signature rather than around it. In that case the pages are simply called an *insert,* if they are in the center of the signature, or an *inside wrap* if they are put somewhere between the center and the outside.

A tip-in is a pasted-in two- or four-page section. Most tip-ins are of two pages — a single sheet. They are given a coating of paste in a narrow strip along the inner edge that is used to "tip" the sheet into position. Tip-ins are not so durable as wraps or inserts because they are not stitched during binding, but they are frequently used.

Although these inserting methods are common, their use is restricted to situations demanding such treatment. Only when substantial costs are avoided or imperative special effects are obtained should the use of units other than standard signatures be considered.

FOLDING, BINDING, AND TRIMMING

When the printed sheets come off the press, the work of the printer, as such, is completed. He may or may not process the work further; basically, the remaining work belongs to the bindery, or finishing specialists.

In most cases, bindery operations begin with folding, an often underrated step in publication production. Sheets sometimes must be cut before folding, but this step is avoided whenever possible. Even with the best cutting, the knife "draws" the paper as it goes through a stack, and a variation in page sizes results. Unbound circulars using bleeds, however, must be cut before folding.

Kinds of Folds

The most common fold, because it is used for books, booklets, and magazines, is the *right-angle* fold. Thus, a single sheet folded once becomes a four-page signature; folded again at a right angle it becomes an eight-page signature, and so on. An eight-page signature folded in this manner must be trimmed before the pages are free to be turned so that pages 2, 3, 6, and 7 can be read.

Figure 16-4. *Common folds for printed matter. A: single-fold four-page folder; B: eight-page accordion; C: eight-page folder with two parallel folds; D: six-page accordion; E: eight-page booklet or folder with two right-angle folds, also called French fold if printed one side and not trimmed; F: six-page standard fold; G: eight-page right-angle fold with first fold short; H: eight-page accordion; I: eight-page parallel, three-fold over and over; J: eight-page parallel map; K: eight-page reverse map; L: 10-page accordion; M: 12-page letter fold; N: 12-page broadside, first fold short; O: 16-page broadside; P: 16-page parallel booklet.*

A *French fold* is an eight-page unit made with right-angle folds and not trimmed. French-fold leaflets are often used in advertising and promotion work.

Parallel folds may be either *accordion,* where each succeeding fold is parallel but turned in the opposite direction, or *over-and-over,* where each fold is in the same direction. Like the French fold, these require no trimming. See Figure 16-4 for common folds.

Methods of Binding

Binding may be either a minor or a major contributor to the cost of any printing job. With simple leaflets it can be skipped entirely; for an elaborate sales presentation book it may be the major cost element. This influence on cost makes binding an important part of production planning. Binding also has a direct bearing on planning in signature units. This point can be more clearly seen with a comparison of two common binding methods.

SADDLE-WIRE BINDING. The most-used kind of binding, because it is inexpensive and adequate for many magazines and booklets, is *saddle-wire binding*. Signatures to be bound by this method are inserted one into the other, and wire staples are driven into the fold through to the center of the publication. As they are bound, the signatures resemble a saddle, hence the name.

Saddle-wire binding has some special advantages. Because there is no backbone, only a fold, pages will lie flat. Inside margins can be small, because the binding does not infringe upon the page. Separate covers can be used but are not necessary. Saddle-wire binding is limited, however, in the number of pages it can accommodate. Generally speaking, it is usable only for publications up to about one-quarter inch in thickness.

SIDE-WIRE BINDING. Thicker magazines or booklets (up to about one-half inch in thickness) may be *side-wire* bound. In this sort of binding, signatures are stacked on top of each other and staples are driven through from top to bottom. Because these staples are inserted about one-eighth inch from the backbone, they prevent side-wire publications from lying flat when open. A separate cover is usually wrapped around and glued to the backbone of side-wire publications. Figure 16-5 illustrates these two binding systems.

Once again, the effect of the mechanical operation on editorial planning should be emphasized. In this case, the pages that fall into each signature can vary according to the kind of binding. Except for the center signature, half the pages in each signature of a saddle-wire booklet come from the front of the booklet and the other half from the back. Thus, in a 32-page booklet of two signatures, the outside or

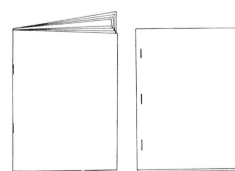

Figure 16-5. *Saddle-wire binding, left; side-wire binding, right.*

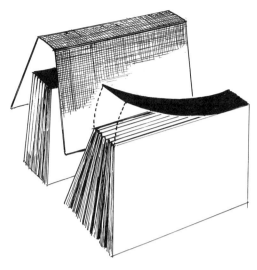

Figure 16-6. *Perfect binding: lining cloth is glued to backbone, then stiff paper cover is glued on.*

Figure 16-7. *Smyth sewing: a six-signature book, showing one row of Smyth-sewn stitches; thread holds signatures together at backbone.*

wrap signature contains pages 1 through 8 and 25 through 32. The center signature contains pages 9 through 24. On the other hand, all signatures in side-wire booklets have pages with consecutive numbering. The editor, therefore, must know which binding system is to be used as he completes the signatures to meet press deadlines.

The planner of a side-wire bound booklet or magazine must also allow a larger inside margin to compensate for the eighth-inch or more taken up by the binding.

PERFECT BINDING. The development of durable and pliable plastic glues has increased the use of the so-called *perfect* binding. This is a much cheaper method than traditional book binding, yet it can be used for volumes as large as municipal telephone books.

No sewing or stitching is needed in perfect binding. Instead, the backbone area is roughened by grinding, the pliable adhesive is applied to it, and lining cloth is then glued to the backbone. Paper covers are usually used with perfect binding (Figure 16-6).

TRADITIONAL BOOK BINDING. Several steps are involved in traditional book binding. Regular hard-cover books are said to be *sewn and case bound.*

After the signatures have been gathered, end papers are tipped (pasted) to the first and last signatures. Signatures are then sewn together (Smyth sewing), and the book is "smashed," or compressed before the three sides are trimmed. In Smyth sewing, signatures are saddle-sewn and sewn to each other at the same time (Figure 16-7).

Books are often *rounded* and *backed* after trimming. They are said to be backed when the backbone has been widened enough to compensate for the thickness of the covers to be added. When rounded, the backbone is made to form a slight arc. It is then reinforced with mesh and paper, which are glued to it, and the *case* (cover) is attached by gluing the end sheets to it.

LOOSE-LEAF AND MECHANICAL BINDINGS. Scores of loose-leaf and mechanical binding systems are being used today, ranging all the way from student notebooks to elaborate catalogues and price books.

The chief advantages of these bindings are that pages open flat, may be of different paper stock and even different sizes, and there is no need to be concerned about signatures.

All the mechanical binding systems use more or less the same principle. Sheets are punched with holes along the binding edge and are then bound together by plastic or metal rings or coils that are slipped through the holes.

SOME SPECIAL FINISHING OPERATIONS

Some of the so-called finishing operations may be carried out by the printer, but many of them are the responsibility of a binder or a firm specializing in the particular technique. In many cases, finishing techniques are used to increase the utility of the printed piece, but they are often also employed simply to enhance visual appeal.

The following list is by no means all-inclusive, but it does present the more commonly used techniques.

Die Cutting

Some printed pieces are much more effective if they are cut to special shapes. Any special shape—a company's product, a question mark, the outline of a state—can be made by die cutting. Several sheets of paper or cardboard can be cut at one time when *high dies*, very similar to rugged cookie cutters, are used. Some *steel-rule* cutting is done, however, on standard printing presses with only one or two sheets being cut at a time. For steel-rule cutting, the desired shape is cut into three-quarter-inch plywood with a jigsaw, and steel rules are cut and bent to fit the shape. The rules, when put into the cutout, are sharp enough and high enough to make the desired cut with each press impression.

Easeling

Finishers have stock sizes of easels, which are applied to display cards and other printed pieces so that they can stand on counters,

Figure 16-8. *Steps from imposition to sewing of signatures.*

(a) Stripper lining up negatives on a goldenrod flat according to folding and binding imposition (offset process, see page 270). Light table enables him to follow ruled-up master form underneath.

(a)

(b) Exposed plate ready for developing and fixing.

(c)

(b)

(c) Putting finished plate on press.

(d)

(e)

(f)

(g)

Figure 16-8 (continued). (*d*) *Taking printed sheet out of delivery end of press.* (*e*) *Banding skid of printed sheets for delivery to bindery.* (*f*) *Cutting printed sheets according to specifications.* (*g*) *Skids of printed sheets ready to be placed on Dexter quad folding machines in background. Skid in left foreground holds stacks of sheets cut and prefolded in half, each half containing a 64-page signature (32 pages on each side of sheet). Folded signatures are at right.* (*h*) *Signatures being Smyth sewn before binding. Spools of thread are at upper left; stack of signatures is in front of each operator. (Photos a–e: courtesy New York Lithographing Corporation; f–h: courtesy Montauk Book Manufacturing Company, Inc.)*

(*h*)

desks, and table tops. Either single- or double-wing easels are used, depending upon the weight of the board or the width of the base.

Embossing

Initials, seals, medallions, and other designs can be raised in relief on paper or other material by running the material in a press between a relief die (below) and an engraved die (above). Embossing may be either blind (no color applied) or printed. Inks or paints are applied before embossing. The major expense is in the making of the dies, but careful make-ready is also required.

Gumming

Labels and other stickers may be gummed by hand or by machine either before or after printing. Machines can apply gum in strips of any number and in any direction. Many printing problems are avoided if gumming follows presswork.

Indexing

Indexing is a die-cutting process for providing the tabs needed on such items as index cards, address books, telephone pads, and so on.

Numbering

Most letterpress printers can easily and cheaply provide numbering because numbering machines can be locked in a chase with or without other plates and type matter. These machines can number consecutively or repeat.

Other printing processes require the use of special press attachments.

Pebbling

Any texture can be added to paper following printing by running the paper through rollers embossed with the desired design. Paper manufacturers offer a *pebble* stock, a paper with a textured surface, as well as other uneven finishes, but as a finishing term pebbling means the addition of *any* texture after printing. Linen and other clothlike surfaces are included.

Applying texture to paper as a finishing process instead of during paper manufacture eliminates the problems connected with running rough stock on letterpress machines.

Perforating

Either the printer or the finisher can do perforating. If it is done by the printer, ink is carried to the paper at the perforating line because the sharp rule used is slightly more than type-high. A perforating wheel is attached to the cylinder if the technique is to be done on a cylinder press.

The kind of perforating found on postage stamps is the work of a finisher who uses a rotary machine that punches rows of tiny holes. The purpose of perforating, of course, is simply to make tearing easy.

Punching

Standard male and female dies are used to punch holes for the various styles of loose-leaf or mechanical binding.

Scoring

Scoring, like perforating, is done to make tearing easier or to aid in folding. A sharp steel rule is used to cut the outer fibers of the paper slightly; if heavy stock or cardboard is being used, the rule may have to cut partially through the board.

Scoring should not be confused with *creasing,* a similar operation in which a dull, rather than sharp, rule is used. Creasing is also an aid to folding, but its other purpose is to make tearing more difficult, not easier. The blunt rule merely compresses the fibers, making the stock more durable at the fold.

To avoid confusion, it is wise to tell the finisher *why* the technique is being requested.

SECTION 6

HISTORICAL BACKGROUND

CHAPTER 17
Evolution of Graphic Communication

CHAPTER 17 Evolution of Graphic Communication

Information transferral by means of visual imagery has been a part of human life since the very dawn of history. In fact, the basic definition of history sets the division between prehistoric and historic at the point where the ability to record knowledge in visual form became a part of human civilization.

The evolution of graphic communication from cave drawings to cathode ray tubes and computers consequently parallels closely the evolution of man from primitive existence to a highly complex industrialized and technological society.

The story of man's striving to solve his communication problems closely follows his striving for a better life. As his efforts advanced toward a society that would grant him his spiritual and physical needs, so did his means of communication. It was no coincidence, for example, that the primitive method of written communication was revolutionized in the fifteenth century by Johann Gutenberg and others — this was the period of the Renaissance in Europe. It was also no coincidence that a flood of significant developments in printing occurred about four centuries later — Western civilization was in the midst of a great industrial revolution. And today's flurry of changes, after more than half a century of virtual inactivity, are reflecting the vast social and technological changes in our concepts of space, speed, and time. Space exploration, with its reliance on computer and video technology, was the seedbed for the unprecedented growth in the computer-related printing technology of today.

Our current fast, efficient methods of graphic communication have resulted from our ability to solve several perplexing problems. The first of these was the need for a set of symbols that singly and in groups could visually represent both real objects and mental concepts. A workable alphabet made this possible. Then we needed suitable materials on which these symbols could be viewed and retained for long periods of time, even permanently. Video tubes and a wide variety of papers have given us almost limitless flexibility for the display and storage of information. Long ago, the invention of ink made it possible to put symbols on paper; centuries later, movable type, type-composition machines, and printing presses made it possible to reproduce visual messages in great quantity. A need for illustrations to supplement the symbols was satisfied with the invention of photography and photoengraving techniques. And finally, the need for a machine that could substitute for the mental functions of human beings themselves — a device with the capability of making logical decisions and of storing information in its memory — was met with the introduction of computers. The combination of computer capability and photographic techniques forms the base of the current technological revolution in graphic communication.

At the Beginning: Prehistoric Efforts

Too involved in a desperate struggle for survival to have much concern for communication, prehistoric man felt little need for any efficient means of recording or transmitting information in visual form.

There is evidence that he knotted cords and notched sticks to send a few messages of importance and to register the feats of tribal leaders. Eventually, he also scrawled crude drawings (pictographs) on stones, weapons, utensils, and the walls of caves, but these drawings were limited to physical objects.

Contributions of Early Civilizations

As he advanced to a more civilized state in some areas of the world, notably Egypt and China, man became concerned with the supernatural as well as with the world around him.

The Egyptians, for example, made substantial contributions to our alphabet with their *hieroglyphics* (sacred writings). Generally considered the forerunner of our modern alphabet, they served to provide symbols for thoughts as well as for physical objects. The Egyptians also discovered a writing surface called *papyrus,* from which our name for paper has come. Papyrus was a grasslike plant whose pith could be pressed into sheets, and its use can be traced back as far as 3500 B.C. (McMurtrie, 1943).

But it was the Chinese who gave us paper as we know it today; its invention was reported to the emperor in A.D. 105 (Carter, 1955). How many years the Chinese may have used paper before that date is not known. This early paper was made from hemp, cotton rags, and the bark of trees. Although crude according to today's standards, it represented one of the most important steps in the evolution of printing.

The Chinese were also the first to manufacture a substance similar to ink (about A.D. 220), and they later invented a true ink. They first used tree sap or cochineal insects to get a dyelike substance to serve the purpose. Then, during the fourth or fifth century, they used lamp black and water-soluble gums to produce what is now known as "India" ink because it was introduced to the Western world via India.

Phoenicia, a small country that lost its identity when it became a part of Syria in 64 B.C., is credited with being the source of our modern alphabet. The Phoenicians simplified the cumbersome hieroglyphics into an alphabet and gave phonetic values to their symbols (Figure 17-1). Later modifications by the Greeks, Romans, and Anglo-Saxons gave us our present twenty-six-letter alphabet.

Thus, from the early civilizations of the East and Middle East came solutions to three basic communications problems—the need for a workable set of symbols, an adequate writing surface, and a printing substance. With sufficient time and labor, knowledge at last could be recorded somewhat efficiently, though slowly.

It had taken centuries for man to reach this point, and it was centuries later that any significant further advances were made. That it took so long to produce printing is remarkable. Certainly the Romans achieved a high degree of civilization as they built their empire. In government, philosophy, road building and other forms of engineering, as well as in many of the elements of culture characteristic of an advanced civilization, the Romans excelled. Certainly, as their influence spread to all parts of the Western world, there would have been a great opportunity for some form of printing to be introduced. The failure of the Roman Empire to evolve any, however, was probably caused by the lack of a sufficiently strong need for new methods. With an ample supply of slave scribes, the Romans could produce enough books without feeling a need for the further efficiency of printing.

		Egyptian		Phoenician	Greek			Latin			Hebrew
1	eagle	𓅃 𝒵	𐤀	A	A 𝙖 α	A	A	𝙖 ɑ a	א
2	crane	𓄿	𐤁	ﬖ B	B β	β	B	B b	ב
3	throne	𓊨 Z	𐤂	ﬖ Γ	Γ ℾΥ	⟨	C	{C ℭ𝔠𝔰𝔤	ג
4	hand	⟅	△	△ △ 𝔰 δ	D	D	∂∂d	ד
5	maeander	⌘ m	⅃	⅃ E	Є ε	F	E	ε e	ה
6	cerastes		⅄	⅄ ΥF	ϝ	F	F	ℱⅎ	ו
7	duck	𝒵	𝚰	𝚰 Ⅰ	Z Ζℂ	𝚰	Z	z	ז
8	sieve	O 𝒪	𐙀	𐙀 H	H h η	𐙀	H	h h	ח
9	tongs	⊜	⊕	⊕ ⊙	O θ ϑ	⊗			ט
10	parallels	⑄ 𝑦	⅃	⅃	Ⅰ ⅈ ι	Ⅰ	Ⅰ	i j	ﬠ
11	bowl	⌐ ⅄	⅄	⅄ K	K κ ϰ	K	K	k	כ
12	lioness	⌇ ⅃	⅃	∨ ∧ λ λ	L	L	⎱⎰	ל
13	owl	𝒷	Ⅿ	Ⅿ M	M μμ	𝘙	M	𝔪 m	מ
14	water	⌇ ⅂	⅂	N N ν ν	𝘙	N	n n	נ
15	chair-back	⎯	‡	‡ ☰ ϡ Ⴀ	⊞	+	X x	ס
16	. . . .		O	O O O o	O			ﬠ
17	shutter	⬛ 𝒷	⅃	⅃ Γ	ㄲ π ϖ	P	P	P	פ
18	snake	⌐ 𝒻	⌐	⌐ M	⅃	⌐			﬩
19	angle	Δ 𝒶	φ	φ ϙ	Q	Q	q q	ק
20	mouth	⌐ 𝒶	⅄	⅄ P	ℙ ℘P	𝘗	R	℘ℾ	ר
21	inundated garden	⌇⌇ ⅄	w	⅄ ⅃	⟨ C ⊂σ	𝒮	S	𝒮ℐ𝒮	ש
22	lasso	⎰ 𝒷	✝	✝ T	T Τ 𝒯	T	T	⅃ t	ת
		I	II	III	IV	V	VI	VII	VIII	IX	X	XI

Figure 17-1. *The Egyptian and Phoenician contributions to the evolution of the Greek, Latin, and Hebrew alphabets. (Reprinted from* The Story of the Alphabet *by Edward Clodd, by permission of the publisher, Appleton-Century-Crofts, Inc.)*

With the fall of the Roman Empire during the fifth century, the Western world underwent such vast changes that little thought was given to books. The Church became the dominant influence in the life of the Middle Ages, and for centuries man's attention was diverted from the mechanical innovations that would provide a way to a greater production of worldly goods. It was approximately one thousand years after the Roman Empire deteriorated that the Renaissance brought modern printing to the world.

The Renaissance and Printing from Movable Type

In the fourteenth and fifteenth centuries, Italian scholars started a radical shift in attention from the religious to the humanistic. Out of a spirit of rebellion against the church-dominated society of the Middle Ages, they turned to a study of the classical culture of ancient Greece and Rome. The movement, based on the past, was considered a rebirth of culture and society and had a profound influence on art, architecture, education, and the philosophy of life itself.

The breakthrough that gave us modern printing was the invention of typography—printing from movable types—by Johann Gutenberg of Mainz, Germany (Figure 17-2). He did not actually invent printing, for the Chinese and others had printed from wood blocks many years previously, but in about the year 1448, he perfected a method for casting and using movable pieces of type. Although some authorities say that a Laurens Coster of Haarlem, Holland, did similar printing two years before Gutenberg, there is no doubt that the latter so developed the idea as to be principally responsible for the far-reaching effect of printing on our civilization. After painstaking

Figure 17-2. *Johann Gutenberg (1400–1468), founder of modern printing, and the Gutenberg press, based on the contemporary wine press. The lever-operated screw lowered the platen to press the paper against the type. (Reprinted from* A New History of Stereotyping *by George A. Kubler, by permission of the Certified Dry Mat Corporation)*

labors, Gutenberg found what were, for his day, satisfactory solutions to each major problem of printing: (1) a system of movable type in which the letters could be arranged in any order and reused as needed, (2) a method of making these pieces of type in quantity both easily and accurately, (3) a method of holding the type in place for printing, (4) a system of making the type impressions on paper, and (5) an ink that would provide a readable impression from type to paper.

Gutenberg first cut pieces of type separately from pieces of wood and held them together in lines by running wire through a hole drilled at the base of each piece. Then he invented a frame into which the type could be wedged and held in place. The wooden wine presses of his day gave him the idea for making impressions on paper. Type was placed on a flat bed of wood, and, by means of a lever-operated screw, a wooden platen was lowered to press the paper against the type (Figure 17-2).

When he found that ink softened his wood types and that the press wore down the letters quickly, he cut types from lead. When lead proved too soft, he tried harder metals, but these cut through the paper. At last he found a satisfactory combination of lead, tin, and antimony—still the basic components of today's types. With a satisfactory alloy in use, he turned his attention to a means of making pieces in quantity. His brass type molds were the answer, and with their use modern printing was born. Then, since earlier inks had run and blotted when used with type, he emerged with a satisfactory solution to this problem, thus providing his final significant contribution to all five basic aspects of modern printing. Those who followed had only to devote their talents to devising type designs, faster presses, speedier means of type composition, and other printing methods to meet the needs and tastes of contemporary life.

Gutenberg, like so many other inventors, was an impractical person who profited little from his ingenuity. Financial backing for his work came through a partnership with John Fust, a goldsmith who was to share the profits and was given a mortgage on Gutenberg's equipment as security on his investment. Fust, after Gutenberg had devoted about five years to his famous 42-line Bible, brought suit against him and received virtually all the inventor owned. Together with Peter Schoeffer, an excellent printer who had worked with Gutenberg, Fust completed the 1,300-page Bible in 1456, six years after its inception.

Meanwhile, Gutenberg obtained financial help from another source and set up a competing shop. There he did some notable work, but he died in 1468 still heavily in debt.

Printing spread to other countries soon after its introduction in Mainz, and artisans of different nationalities brought about worthy improvements in type as they created designs reflective of their backgrounds. Yet, aside from type design and a few minor changes, the printing art once again stagnated for centuries. For example, the first printing press in the United States, established as an adjunct to Harvard College by Stephen and Matthew Daye in 1638, was patterned closely after the nearly two-hundred-year-old Gutenberg press. Neither presses, type composition, nor the manufacture of paper was to change until the Industrial Revolution.

Effects of the Industrial Revolution

In the first phase of the Industrial Revolution beginning around 1760, advances in technology brought great changes in the way of life for the people of England, Europe, and eventually the rest of the world. Industry moved from the home workshop to the factory; machines did the work of countless men at far less cost and in much less time. New markets opened up for the increased goods, money found its way into more pockets, the desire for goods grew and in turn fostered the production of still more goods.

As prosperity spread, so did public education; literacy increased, and more and more people had the time, ability, and interest to want more and more to read.

The second phase of the Industrial Revolution in the 1800s brought the inventions of the telegraph, the steamship, and the locomotive to provide opportunities for speed of communication and transportation; but numerous factors kept the production of printed matter from taking advantage of the accelerated pace. Hand composition, the lever press, and the hand manufacture of paper were all too slow to meet the mounting demands for more printed communication. When the effects of the Industrial Revolution finally spread to printing, innovations helped each of these areas to catch up with amazing rapidity.

THE COMING OF STEAM POWER AND THE CYLINDER PRESS

The magic of steam was first put to use in printing in Boston by Daniel Treadwell in 1822 and by Isaac Adams in 1830. Both men applied power to the familiar Gutenberg bed-and-platen presses. Treadwell's press (Figure 17-3) met with little success, but Adams's was used extensively for book work for several years.

This application of steam power to an inherently slow method was not enough for newspapers, whose circulations were mounting rapidly. Too much time was wasted in lifting the platen away from

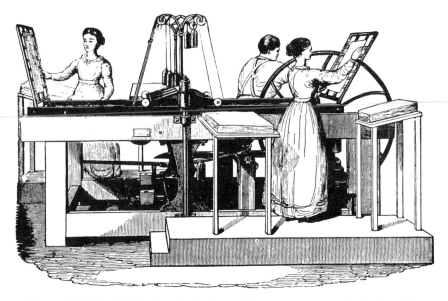

Figure 17-3. *Daniel Treadwell's bed-and-platen power press, the first application of steam power to a printing press. (Reprinted from* A Short History of the Printing Press *by Robert Hoe)*

the type or in moving the type away from the platen under the old system, and a basic change was called for.

It was answered by the substitution of a cylinder for the platen. The first steam-powered cylinder press came from Friedrich Koenig, a German who received financial backing for his work in England. Koenig's press, with a cylinder to pick up the paper and carry it over a moving type bed, was patented in 1810 and was first used for newspaper work by the London *Times* on November 28, 1814. By using two cylinders, Koenig made his presses *perfecting;* that is, they printed on both sides of the sheet. Two of his steam-driven two-cylinder presses were used by the *Times* to produce 1,100 copies an hour, a quite remarkable achievement for that day.

THE TYPE-REVOLVING PRESS

The first press based on the principle now used for the highest-speed newspaper production was built by R. Hoe & Company and put into operation at the Philadelphia *Public Ledger* in 1846. Called the Hoe Type Revolving Machine, the new press was designed to rotate the type, instead of to hold it stationary. Type was locked into place on a large cylinder by means of wedge-shaped rules between columns. In miraculous fashion, the cylinder could revolve at rather high speeds without letting the type fly in all directions.

Hoe's first type-revolving press used four impression cylinders around the central type cylinder and was capable of turning out 2,000 sheets per hour for each impression cylinder, or a total of 8,000 per hour. One man was required to feed each impression cylinder and corresponding type bed, and the press printed one side of a sheet. To increase output, Hoe eventually grouped as many as ten impression cylinders around the type cylinder (Figure 17-4).

The Hoe Type Revolving Machine was important because of its rotary principle. It cleared the way for *stereotyping,* a process that led to the modern rotary newspaper presses, which put printed impressions on paper about as fast as an electric-powered cylinder can rotate and paper can be fed to it.

STEREOTYPING AND PRESENT-DAY WEB-PERFECTING ROTARY PRESSES

A disadvantage of the Hoe type-revolving press was the need to lock countless type pieces onto the main cylinder. This cut speed and restricted type display to one-column widths because of the wedge-shaped column rules. Although long lines of display type in advertising and headlines that can spread across columns are commonly accepted as necessities today, it was the demand for still greater speed —not large headlines—that encouraged the experimentation resulting in the use of stereotype plates in newspaper printing.

Figure 17-4. *The Hoe Type Revolving Machine. The original press used four impression cylinders; for increased production, this later model used ten cylinders. (Reprinted from* A Short History of the Printing Press *by Robert Hoe)*

Briefly, *stereotyping* is a method of making, with type metal, "perfect facsimiles of the faces of pages composed of movable type" (Kubler, 1941). Modern stereotyping methods were known and used as early as 1690 in Germany and other parts of Europe. Credit for the invention of stereotyping is generally given, however, to Claude Gennoux, a French printer who obtained a patent for it on July 24, 1829.

Gennoux used the "papier mâché" or "wet mat" process for making duplicate plates. By pressing the wet mat made of several layers of paper against the type area, Gennoux made a mold that, when dried, was used to cast the plate from molten metal. Today's dry mats came into use in this country after 1890.

In 1849, Jacob Warms of Paris obtained a patent for making curved stereotype plates by placing a wet mat in a curved mold. The idea was introduced in this country by Charles Craske, a New York engraver who made the first curved stereotype plate for a rotary press of the New York *Herald* in 1854. His first attempt was not entirely successful, but in 1861 he started stereotyping the regular editions of four New York newspapers,and the process has been used regularly since that time.

Stereotyping made it possible to put full newspaper pages, in the form of single curved pieces of metal, on press cylinders that could then revolve at tremendous speeds, making impressions on paper as they went. To be fully efficient, rotary presses using stereotype plates had to be improved to (1) make it possible to print both sides of the paper at once and (2) make it possible to feed paper from a continuous roll instead of from sheets. The first rotary press to incorporate these two features was devised by William Bullock of Philadelphia in 1865. His press was said to be web-perfecting because paper was fed from a roll (web) and printed on both sides of the sheet (perfecting). As is the case with most inventions, it contained some unreliable mechanical features.

A greatly improved web-fed rotary press was introduced by R. Hoe & Company in 1871 and was widely accepted after being put to use at *Lloyd's Weekly Newspaper* in London and the New York *Tribune*.

The Hoe company pioneered other notable improvements in rotary presses, including the manufacture of presses that used several units to multiply production capacity. Its Double Supplement Rotary Press installed at the New York *Herald* in 1882 consisted of two units and could print 24,000 12-page papers an hour. The Hoe Quadruple Newspaper Press installed at the New York *World* five years later produced 16-page papers at the same rate.

Improvements in Composition Methods

As presses were developed to meet the mounting pressures for increased production of newspapers and other printed material, attempts were also made to eliminate the three shortcomings of hand composition of type: (1) the matter of time and effort needed to get the pieces of type from their storage places and set them into lines; (2) the tedious problem of spacing between either words or letters or both to fill out lines flush on the right; and (3) the distribution of the type back to its storage places.

Most of the early machines succeeded in speeding up only one or two parts of the typesetting operation. The mechanization of the setting phase seemed to cause the least difficulty: machines that would eject type pieces from their storage places when an operator pressed a key on a keyboard were quickly devised. A solution to the distribution problem was presented by the Unitype, manufactured in 1870 by the Wood Nathan Company. As a substantial improvement over other machines, this was used in many newspapers plants for years. Although justification still had to be done manually, the Unitype was said to be able to do the work of four hand compositors (Olson, 1930). Its operation was keyed to two cylinders, one above the other. The top cylinder automatically distributed the type into proper positions in the lower cylinder, from which the pieces could respond to keyboard action.

MERGENTHALER AND THE LINOTYPE

On July 3, 1886, in the New York *Tribune* building, a man named Ottmar Mergenthaler set the first line of type on a machine that was to be christened the Linotype (Figure 17-5); this machine was destined to make automatic composition practical in every respect. Mergenthaler, its chief inventor, was a German-born watchmaker who had been working in Baltimore as a skilled constructor of patent models. His work in perfecting a typecasting machine had been financed by a group of publishers including Whitelaw Reid of the *Tribune,* in whose building the Linotype was introduced.

Mergenthaler's machine was based on a new principle that involved the casting of lines of type by injecting molten metal into brass molds during the setting process. It met all the requirements for a typesetting machine: casting was performed by hitting a keyboard; both the distribution of the molds and the justification of lines with expandable spacebands were automatic. In addition, using molds instead of pieces of type was an added bonus: every line

Figure 17-5. *Ottmar Mergenthaler (1854–1899), inventor of the Linotype, and the original Linotype. (Courtesy Mergenthaler Linotype Corporation)*

that came from the machine was newly cast, the type itself was saved from constant wear.

Although several of the first Linotypes were installed in the shops of newspapers, it was not until 1890 that improvements made the machine function efficiently. For example, when it was first introduced, the Linotype used blasts of air to move type molds; the later models let the force of gravity pull the molds into position.

Several completely automatic composing machines were introduced with enthusiastic praise by their backers in the 1890s, but most of them failed to meet production tests. The manufacture of a device called the Paige machine, for example, was supported by Mark Twain to the extent of $190,000. According to Twain, it could do everything but drink, swear, and go on strike (Mott, 1962). But when tested in the Chicago *Times-Herald* office in 1894, it did not perform properly.

OTHER EARLY TYPE-CASTING MACHINES

The Intertype machine, chief competitor of the Linotype today, was produced by Herman Ridder, publisher of the New York *Staats-Zeitung,* and was first put into operation at the New York *Journal of Commerce* in 1913. It is a linecasting machine similar to the Linotype.

The Monotype, invented by Tolbert Lanston in 1887 and employed for production in 1898, gets its name from the fact that it casts single letters instead of line slugs. It also differs from Linotype and Intertype because it consists of two machines: one is a device like a typewriter that makes a perforated tape; the other does the casting as the tape is fed to it, much like a player piano.

Still another machine, the Ludlow Typograph, was introduced by Washington I. Ludlow in 1909 and later developed by William A. Reade. Designed mainly to produce the large sizes of type that had previously been set most economically by hand, the Ludlow system is widely used today. Although it is not an automatic system (molds are handset and then cast into lines), it offers some important improvements over hand composition. Each line is fresh new type in one piece and is, consequently, easier to handle.

FOURNIER AND THE POINT SYSTEM

Early type designers and founders made no attempt to base type sizes on any uniform set of measurements. For printers the result was at times utterly confusing. Type from one founder could not be mixed with that from another; the fact that spacing materials were different made each incoming order of type a new puzzle to be solved.

A French printer, Pierre Simon Fournier, is mainly responsible for bringing order to type measurement. In his *Manual Typographique* of 1764, he tells of his efforts (Jahn, 1931):

> To clear this chaos and to give . . . typography an order which never before reigned there, is the subject which has gained my attention. Through the invention of *typographic points,* I think that I have been fortunate enough to succeed with an exactness and precision . . . The typographic point is nothing more than the separation of the bodies of types by equal and definite degrees, which I call points . . . I have divided the standard scale into two inches; the inch into twelve lines, and the line into six typographic points; making altogether 144 points in two inches . . . The invention of these points is the first service that I rendered to typography in 1737.

The introduction of the point system by Fournier was indeed a service and a major step forward. But more than a century passed before the point system came into use in the United States in 1878. In that year the foundry of Harder, Luse & Company of Chicago, a leading type manufacturerer, was destroyed by fire. When it rebuilt, the company decided to introduce the point system for all the type it made. Finally, in 1887, The United States Type Founders' Association adopted a system using points equal to 0.01384 inch, a modification of Fournier's plan. It is standard in this country today.

Machine Papermaking

Until it was mechanized during the Industrial Revolution, the manufacture of paper was a slow, tedious hand process. The first papermaking machine was invented by Nicolas Robert at Essonnes, France, in 1798. Henry and Sealy Fourdrinier bought his patent and, with the aid of an engineer, introduced the first practical paper machine in 1803; this marked the real beginning of large-volume mechanical papermaking.

Reproduction of Photographs

Early American letterpress printers and publishers had to content themselves with woodcuts for illustrations until the 1870s, when zincographs (line illustrations etched by acid on zinc) came into use in this country. Introduced in Paris in 1859, these were an improvement over woodcuts, but did not provide a means for reproducing on a plate all the tones of a photograph.

Authorities differ about the discoverer of the halftone photoengraving process which eventually overcame this obstacle. Undoubtedly many men from several countries were instrumental in perfecting the process. William Talbot, an Englishman, is said to have made the first halftone in 1852 by using a cloth screen and sensitized coatings to put a continuous tone image on a relief printing plate. Frederick Ives of Philadelphia, with successive inventions in 1878 and 1886, is generally given credit for the modern halftone process of photoengraving. In experimentation at Cornell University, Ives produced a crossline screen on glass similar to the screens used today. At about the same time, Stephen H. Horgan made a halftone plate that was the first to appear in an American newspaper; this was "Shantytown," used by the New York *Daily Graphic* on March 4, 1880.

But the work of these men would not have been possible, of course, had it not been for the basic idea of photography itself. This had made its debut when Joseph Niepce produced the first photographs around 1827 in Europe.

Discovery of Offset Printing

Two accidental discoveries set the stage for what might be called the "age of competition" in graphic communication. Both incidents, though many years apart, brought about a new printing process, called *photo-offset lithography*—commonly called "offset" or "photo offset"—now a strong competitor for the traditional letterpress system of Johann Gutenberg.

In 1796, a little-known but imaginative Bavarian actor and playwright named Aloys Senefelder discovered that he could print from the flat surface of a stone. Senefelder, because he could not afford to have expensive engravings made for printing his plays, was trying to learn the art himself by practicing writing backwards. For his practice he substituted a flat stone for engraver's copper because the stone could be more easily scraped and used again.

One day as he was polishing a stone slab, his mother came into his workshop and asked him to write a list of linens to be washed before the laundress, who was outside waiting, took the clothes with her. With neither paper nor ink at hand, Senefelder used a greasy substance he had been working with to scrawl the laundry list on the stone. Later he noticed that when the stone was coated with water, the greasy inscription repelled the water.

This basic principle—that greasy surfaces accept only ink and reject water, and vice versa—is still the basis for lithographic printing. It is however, about the only aspect of commercial lithography that has not changed.

Even in primitive form the new process revealed some special advantages. Any number of images, for example, could be applied to the stone, thus providing for the printing of several copies at once. And, generally speaking, the process provided a faster, more economical method for producing illustrations than did designing on copper plates, the competing method of the day.

In 1825 when Goya did his famous "Bullfighter" lithographs, he established lithography as an artist's medium. Commercial work in color by the new process soon followed, and lithography began to develop into a printing process known for giving color in various tones economically.

Among the early users of lithography in this country was Nathaniel Currier, who learned the technique as an apprentice to William and John Pendleton of Boston. Currier set up his own shop in New York in 1835 and hired an artist, J. M. Ives. Ives later became a partner in the firm, and under the name Currier & Ives it produced lithographic prints that are still popular.

The first lithography presses were of the hand-operated, flat-bed variety. R. Hoe & Company introduced a power press in 1869, but real progress was delayed for twenty years until thin sheets of zinc replaced stones as the printing surface, and a direct rotary lithography press became possible. Actually, the switch to zinc plates wrapped around a cylinder made the term lithography (taken from *lithos,* "stone" and *graphos,* "drawing") a misnomer.

The process picked up its most common name, *offset* printing, as the result of the second accidental discovery. Ira Rubel, a New Jersey lithographer, was feeding paper into his press when he noticed that occasionally a surprisingly precise image would show up on the back of a sheet. This occurred when a sheet first failed to feed; the image was then transferred onto the impression cylinder and would appear with amazing clarity on the back of the next sheet.

Rubel incorporated the transfer, or offset, idea into a press he introduced in 1905. A special cylinder covered with a rubber blanket was used to receive the image from the plate and in turn to "offset" the image onto paper. The Harris brothers of Niles, Ohio, who were manufacturers of a rotary letterpress machine, also introduced a press with the plate-to-rubber-blanket principle in 1906.

The first commercial use of an offset press was in the plant of the Republic Bank Note Company of Pittsburgh in 1906. This press and others to follow showed that offset lithography was an excellent means for producing quality illustrations on even the roughest papers. The resilient rubber blanket, because it squeezed the image into, rather than just on, the paper, made quality work possible on any surface.

About the same time the offset principle was added to presses, photography was adopted as a means of making lithographic plates. The ability to put the image on the press plate photographically was a giant step forward, but offset was slow to gain wide acceptance. Since World War II, however, it has been turning the printing world upside down.

The Era of the Computer and Video Tube

Offset's emergence as a behemoth of the printing industry was one of the significant developments that marked the 1950s and 1960s as a period of competition and change for graphic communication.

At the root of offset's great growth were the significant changes in type composition that were making even the automated casting of lines of type in lead outmoded. The widespread use of the computer and the video tube in the production of mass media communications in the 1970s marked that decade as a revolutionary new era in printed communication.

The new era created a new alphabet and a new language with abbreviations such as VDT, CRT, and OCR and words such as *interface, on line, cursor,* and *computer* leading the way to a new understanding of the new technology. The emphasis was entirely on the word new, because there was no resemblance between the computerized media operations and those still using Gutenberg and Mergenthaler technology.

Today, newspapers such as the Davenport (Iowa) *Times-Democrat* function without typewriters (the *Times-Democrat* keeps one for staff memos) and without traditional metal type. Reporters type their stories at video display terminals which place the stories in a computer's memory. An editor then calls the story from the computer and onto his video screen for correction and headlining. The corrected story is returned to the computer and then goes to the photocomposing machine. The paper type proof of the story and headline are then pasted into page position for photographing and reproduction on an offset press.

Others, such as the Richmond (Virginia) newspapers, rely on optical character recognition scanners to get the words of the reporter into type. In such cases, the reporter still types his story on paper which is edited and then fed into a machine that scans the editor's instructions and the story before feeding it into a photocomposing machine. Or, the story may go directly from the reporter to the scanner and then be brought out on video display terminal for editing. Instead of ending up on an offset press, the page plate may be etched by laser beam and printed by letterpress.

These and other technical systems have been described on earlier pages. Their variations are countless; in fact, most complete systems are tailored directly to the unique needs of the individual publication. And they are only a part of the current picture. You need only pick up occasional copies of weekly news magazines to read of new marvels in the printing processes: type being set by cathode ray tube devices; trade marks being electrostatically printed on the shells of eggs without crushing them; new newspaper plants being built near their suburban readers because the output of the news and ad departments can be transmitted to the plants electronically; and other equally remarkable achievements.

These rapid changes have been called an information explosion and a communications revolution. Regardless of the name given to them, they obviously exemplify the need that now exists for a greater breadth and depth of knowledge about the techniques of producing printed materials. Anyone who plans a career with any medium of communication must be prepared to use any system skillfully. His finished product must also meet higher standards than ever before and must be produced more quickly.

To be successful today, any printed material — newspaper, magazine, brochure, poster, newsletter — must be prepared with a talent, finesse, and speed never before demanded with such urgency. This demand stems, as did events during the Renaissance and the Industrial Revolution, from the necessities of a society in the midst of great flux.

Television's booming voice and powerful image changed the living habits of Americans, as well as the role other communications media must play in society. Communication satellites soaring in outer space bring the promise and the challenge of a global flow of information with consequences difficult to imagine for the world in general and communications in particular. Indeed, the marriage of electronics and printing seems to be the primary answer to current and future informational needs. The ever-growing population is making ever-widening demands for quicker distribution of information.

New industries and vastly altered old ones are requiring a continuing system of education via the media of communications. In engineering and other professions graduates are discovering before the ink is dry on their diplomas that significant new knowledge already outdates what they have just learned.

These developments mean that designers of printed literature must learn new methods and use old ones with dexterity in order to get the printed word into the minds of their readers faster and easier.

We hope that the preceding chapters have provided a foundation of knowledge for the preparation of fast, efficient graphic communications.

Glossary

abstraction Isolating specific features from a sum total of stimuli for purposes of interpretation (decision-making). Examples: the human information processing system allows us to interpret lines (low order abstraction) to be forming angles (higher order abstraction); or "chickens (low order abstraction), which are fowl (higher order), may also be assets (highest order) to a farmer."

agate Name for 5½ point type; agate line is unit of ad-space measurement, 1/14-inch deep, one column wide.

ampersand The symbol &, meaning "and."

area composition Output of a photocomposing or cathode ray tube composing machine that is greater than a single column in width.

art Photographs, drawings, and hand-lettering. Also paste-up of materials for camera copy, as in offset and rotogravure.

astonisher Name sometimes used for headlines that include a short line above and/or below the main lines. Also printers' slang for exclamation point.

author's alterations Abbreviated "AA's," refers to changes in proofs not due to printer's error. The publisher or author pays the charges.

backbone Portion of book binding between front and back covers; the *spine*.

back lead The ability of a photocomposing or cathode ray tube machine to roll exposed photopaper back to a starting point for added exposures.

back slant The opposite of italic type stance; available through some cathode ray tube or photocomposing machines.

banner Newspaper headline crossing full width of page. Also called streamer or ribbon.

bar graph A graph using varying lengths of bars to show relative quantities.

base alignment Alignment, by means of photocomposing or cathode ray composition, of type faces with varying x-heights on a common optical base line.

basis weight   The weight of a ream of paper at standard size (book 25 by 38; cover 20 by 26; index 25½ by 30½), also called "substance."

Benday process   A method of applying shading and tinting (lines or dots) to line artwork.

binary digit   The amount of information needed to resolve uncertainty between two alternatives. The number of alternatives determines the binary digits needed.

binding   In broad sense, any further treatment of stock after printing; includes cutting, folding, trimming, gathering, stitching, gluing, and casing.

bit   Contraction for binary digit.

bleed   An illustration filling one or more margins and running off the edge of the page.

blind keyboard machine   A tape-perforating machine which does not display hard copy.

blueprint (or **blue** or **blueline**)   A fast proof on paper from an offset flat or negative; all printing is blue.

body type   Type for main message; generally under 12-point size. Also called text type. Opposite of display type.

boldface (bf)   A variation of a type face which is heavier and darker than the fullface or lightface versions.

bond paper   A paper stock suitable for business purposes, such as letterheads and forms.

book   Trade slang for magazine.

book paper   A paper stock for periodical printing as well as books and direct literature (promotion and so on).

box   Printed matter enclosed in rules.

break-of-the-book   Allocation of space in a magazine.

brownline or Vandyke   Same as blueprint except printing is brown.

build-up   An excess of ink sufficient to cause smudging or filling-in of letters.

bulk   Thickness of paper, without reference to its weight.

bullet   Large dot used as an attention-getter and sometimes as a divider.

butted slugs   Two or more linecaster slugs placed together to form a single line of type. Slugs must be butted when the printed line is to be longer than the machine can set.

byte   A series of bits capable of identifying a number of tape symbols; usually a series of 8 bits, which would identify 256 (2^8) symbols.

calendering   A rolling operation during paper making that produces smoothness of surface. Super-calendered paper is rolled between polished steel cylinders to create an especially smooth surface.

caps and small caps   Capitals (upper case) and small capitals. Small capitals are the same height as lower-case letters in any type face but have upper-case formation.

caption   Text accompanying illustrations. Also used to describe the overlines or "heads" above newspaper illustrations.

carding   A command in type composition by photocomposing machines and CRT machines whereby spacing is provided between lines to enlarge the type area to a desired depth.

case Storage drawer for foundry type. Also the stiff cover of a book and the mold in electrotyping.

case-bound A book with a hard cover.

cathode ray tube (CRT) A television screen; in graphics, a typesetting machine using the screen or a keyboarded terminal used by reporters and editors for putting copy into a computer for typesetting.

channel The medium through which a message is transmitted in the communication process.

chase Metal frame to contain type and plates for printing or for molding duplicates.

chunking A recording by grouping bits of information into new items. Example, the word "house" is composed of isolated bits representing the letters *h,o,u,s,e;* together these bits now represent a single, recognizable unity. The process expands the capacity of human memory.

clean tape Tape containing only the necessary codes for operating linecasting, photocomposing, or electronic type generating equipment with all errors and extraneous codes having been removed by an editor or a computer.

coated paper Paper to which a surface coating has been applied for a smooth finish.

cold type Type composed by other than traditional methods (hot type or foundry)—namely, photocomposition, paste-down, or "typewriter methods." Such type is printlike in varying degrees.

collage A combination of several distinct pictures into a composite picture.

collotype *See* **photogelatin.**

colophon Symbol or trademark identifying a printer or publisher.

color print Color photograph viewed by reflected light as compared with a transparency, which is viewed by transmitted light.

color separation Process of preparing separate primary color prints (plates) which, when printed in register, produce a full-color illustration.

combination Line and halftone combined into a single illustration. Also a run of several different jobs at one time on one press.

composing stick A device in which foundry type is assembled and justified into lines.

comprehensive A hand-drawn layout or dummy, carefully prepared and finished to approximate the piece in print.

concept An event or object isolated as unique because of characteristics it has in common with similar events or objects.

contact print A print on photo paper from negative or positive in contact, as opposed to enlargement or reduction.

context Peripheral information from the environment surrounding an object or event from which information is being received.

copy Text or art to be printed or reproduced.

copyediting Correcting, improving, and marking copy to be printed.

copyfitting Determining (1) space required for copy, (2) amount of copy to be written for allotted space, (3) size of type to accommodate an amount of copy in an allotted space.

copyreading Reading copy for errors and marking copy for printer.

copy schedule An inventory sheet kept by copy desk chief of a newspaper; contains sufficient information about each item for a dummy to be made.

core memory The computer memory that holds program and type-element information that is being processed.

core size The capacity of the core memory of a computer. Stated in numbers of K of words; e.g., 8K, 8-bit word would be $8 \times 1,024 \times 8$ or 65,536 bits. The larger the K, the larger the computer core memory.

coquille board A textured board used to produce shading in drawings.

counting keyboard machine A tape-perforating machine that signals the operator when hyphenation and justification directions must be punched into the tape.

cover stock Special paper suitable for covers of booklets.

crop To mark artwork or photographs indicating which portions are to be reproduced.

CRT Cathode ray tube (q.v.).

cursive type Any type face resembling handwriting, but with disconnected letters. A form of italic in some recent book faces.

cut A photoengraving (line or halftone) for letterpress printing.

cutlines Text accompanying illustrations. *See also* **caption.**

cut-off rule A rule that prints a line used horizontally across columns in newspapers to separate items and guide the reader.

cylinder press A press on which paper is held to a cylinder that revolves, rolling the paper across a flat, inked letterpress form to receive impressions.

dead matter Printing materials (type and illustrations) no longer needed (foul matter).

decoding Extraction of meaning from symbols or cues used in communicating meanings.

deep etch Special offset technique for long runs in which plates are made from film positives instead of negatives.

dial-in To indicate to a hard-wired logic photocomposing or cathode ray tube machine the format specifications by setting the controls.

die-cut A printed piece cut into special shape by dies made by shaping steel blades into the desired form.

dingbat Typographic decorative device such as a bullet or star.

direct image master Short-run offset plate, usually of paper or plastic, and made without photographic negatives or positives.

display type Type larger than body.

doctor blade The blade on a gravure press that wipes excess ink from the plate before the impression.

double-burn In offset, the exposure of light in succession through two separate flats onto the same plate; in many cases one flat contains halftones and the other contains line copy.

doubleprint A surprint, for example, a black line appearing on a tone area.

dropout A halftone without dots in unwanted areas; produced by a number of photomechanical means.

dummy Proofs of text, illustrations, captions (or measured holes for each element), and display pasted into position on sheets in specific page arrangement for compositor's guidance in making up pages. In newspapers and magazines the elements may be sketched in place.

dump To release copy from a video display terminal's screen to the perforator.

duotone A two-color reproduction of a halftone from separate plates. When two plates are made from a single black-and-white photo (one high-key carries color, the other normally carries black) it may be called a duograph.

ear Small amounts of type, illustration, or both on either side of a newspaper name plate. Also refers to the hook on letters *r* and *g*.

electronic composition Composition of type by generation on a TV type picture tube.

electrostatic printing A technique of affixing a printed image in powder form on paper by means of electrostatic charges.

electrotype A metal plate cast from a wax mold of the original type page.

Elrod machine for making rules, leads, slugs, and borders.

em The (nonprinting) square of a type body of any size. Also incorrectly used as a synonym for pica in expressing linear measurement.

embossing Pressing a relief pattern of type, art, or both into paper or cover materials.

emotion A reflection of an evaluation of an object or event; such an evaluation is "wired in" or cognized—i.e., the result of decision-making.

en Piece of spacing material half as wide as it is high (half the width of an em).

encoding Selection of symbols or cues used in communicating meanings.

end papers Paper glued to the inside covers of a book; often left blank but may contain printing.

engraving A printing plate etched by acid from photographic or other copy; a copper plate into which letters are hand-etched in reverse for printing invitations, calling cards, and so forth. Also a synonym for a cut or photoengraving.

ephemera Printed material of a transitory nature, generally materials other than books.

exception dictionary A computer memory store of hyphenation codes for words not amenable to the logic algorithm for breaking.

face The printing surface of type or plate. Also the name for a specified type.

fake process color Full-color reproduction from a black-and-white photo, effected by the engraver's manipulation of four separate negatives so that they represent the respective primaries and black. *See* **process color.**

feedback A response from the receiver to the sender of a communication, which interprets his reaction; a return of information concerning a past event or object to a control, allowing the latter to adjust its output.

file management A computer program that organizes input within memory so that it may be retrieved for further use.

filling in   Excess ink builds up to a point where letters, notably those with bowls (*g, e, a*), plug or close up.

first revise   A proof of type with corrections made after first proofreading.

flag   Name plate of a newspaper.

flat   A vehicle for holding film positives or negatives in position for exposing onto plates. Offset flats are usually goldenrod paper; photoengraving and gravure flats are usually glass.

flatbed press   A direct-from-type (or engraving) press using either platen or cylinder to print from a flat, as opposed to curved, type form.

flat color   Simplest form of spot color; each color stands alone, solid or screened—colors do not overlay each other to form additional colors.

flat piece   A printed sheet delivered to customer unfolded.

flexography   A relief printing method using liquid fast-dry ink on rubber plates.

flop   To reverse art laterally—image, when printed, is opposite from original.

folio   A page number.

folo head   Headline over a small story related to and placed directly following the main story.

font   All the letters and characters in one size of a type face.

form   Type and engravings locked in a chase, ready for printing or duplicating.

format   The shape, size, and style of a publication; also the typographic requirements for composition, such as line length, type face, size, and so on.

foundry type   Hand-set type.

fullface   The standard or normal weight and width of a type face.

furniture   Metal or wooden material used to fill in large nonprint areas of a letterpress form.

galley   A metal tray for storing type. Also, the usual term for a galley proof.

galley proof   Proof from type in a galley; after correction, stored type is made into pages.

gang   To run several jobs on one press at a time. Also, to make several engravings—all at same enlargement or reduction—at one time.

gauge   *See* **line gauge.**

general-purpose computer   A computer capable of preparing composition tape as well as performing other functions.

goldenrod   Opaque golden-orange paper that serves as the vehicle for an offset flat.

Gothic type   Those faces with, generally, monotonal (noncontrast) strokes and no serifs; also called sans-serif, contemporary, or block letter.

Greek golden mean   An elegant and universal ratio manifested in natural growth and development and applicable to graphic design.

grid   A division of design space into orderly and regular rectangular areas that serve to contain printed elements thereby establishing a structural relationship among them.

gripper edge   The edge of a sheet held by the gripper on the impression cylinder press or sheet-fed rotary; it represents an unprintable $3/8$ to $1/2$ inch.

gutter   The inside margin of a page at the binding.

halftone   A printing plate made from a photograph, wash drawing, and so forth. Gradation of tone is reproduced by a pattern of dots produced by interposition of a screen during exposure.

h&j   Hyphenation and justification; codes for hyphenation and justification incorporated into perforated tape produced by a computer which has been fed idiot tape or produced from a counting-keyboard perforator; such codes may also be on-line (q.v.).

hanging punctuation   Placement of all punctuation marks falling at the ends of justified lines to the right of these lines.

hard copy   A printed, usually typewritten, record produced (1) simultaneously when the message is perforated onto tape, or (2) as print-out from a computer that has prepared composition tape. Used for editing purposes.

hardware   The actual computer and its other "hard-to-the-touch" components.

hard-wired logic   Wired-in capacity of an automated phototypesetter or CRT to perform certain mathematical and logical functions. Such machines are not programmable and can perform only their wired-in functions.

hed sked   A headline schedule, the newspaper inventory sheet showing all headlines the newspaper normally uses.

highlight   The lightest portion of a photo or other art or reproduction of same. To highlight a halftone is to remove mechanically or photographically the dots in certain areas. Such a halftone is called a highlight or drop-out halftone.

hot metal   *See* **hot type.**

hot-metal pasteup   Methods of ad makeup for letterpress newspapers in which stripped type slugs and plates are affixed to a plastic base; base plus slugs, plates, and stereo casts are type-high. The plastic base is marked off in grids to delineate columns and facilitate location of elements. The pasteup is placed in the page forms for mat rolling.

hot type   Type composed by machine from molten metal; sometimes includes foundry type.

IBC   Inside back cover.

idiot tape   Perforated tape without h&j codes (also called raw tape).

IFC   Inside front cover.

image (verb)   To expose a type element photographically.

image conversion   Any of several techniques for adapting hot-metal composition to film negative images for making offset or roto plates.

imposition   The location of pages in a form or on a sheet so that when the printed sheet of signature is folded, the pages will fall in proper order.

impression   The pressure of type or plate against paper in printing. Also, "impressions per hour" refers to number of sheets being delivered.

initial A large letter used to start a copy area.

insert A separately printed piece placed in a publication at the time of binding.

intaglio Process of printing from depressed areas carrying ink.

interface To hook various text-processing devices directly via hard wire in lieu of using perforated tape for intermachine communication.

Intertype A keyboard-operated, circulating mat linecaster.

IPS Information processing system; a biological or man-made system capable of accepting information, interpreting (processing) it, and reacting after making a decision.

italic type that slants right; counterpart to roman posture, which is upright.

jet printing Plateless printing system using fast-moving, computer-driven ink jets to put an image on paper.

jim dash A short dash (about three ems long) used between headline decks in some newspapers.

jump To carry over a portion of a story from one page to another. Also the continued portion of the story.

justify To space or quad out a line of type to make it full to the right margin.

key plate The printer (plate) in color printing which is laid first and to which others must register.

kicker A short line of type above and/or below the main part of a headline; used mainly for feature story headlines.

layout Often used as synonym for dummy. A pattern, roughly or carefully drawn, to show placement of elements on a printed piece.

leadering Inserting leaders.

leaders A row of dots used to guide vision across open areas of tabular material.

leads (pronounced "leds") Thin metallic strips used to provide extra space between type lines.

legibility That degree of visibility which makes printed matter read easily and rapidly.

letterfold The basic fold given to business letters and to most direct literature.

letterpress The traditional system of printing from raised (relief) areas.

ligature Two or more letters joined together as a single unit, such as *ffl*, *fi*, *ff*, *ffi*, *æ*, *œ*.

line In advertising, an agate line; in illustrations, it refers to artwork and plates composed only of extreme tones as opposed to halftone illustrations.

linecaster A machine, such as Linotype, which casts type in line units.

line conversion A relatively new technique of converting photographs to line illustrations for special effect.

linecut An engraving, usually on zinc, containing no gradation of tone unless applied by Benday or similar means.

line gauge   Printer's ruler marked off in picas and other printing units of measure.

line spacing   Extra space between lines in photocomposition; similar to hot-metal leading.

Linotype   A keyboard-operated circulating mat linecasting machine.

lithographic conversion   Lithographic printing of plates originally made for letterpress. Plates can be chalked and photographed directly or proofs can be pulled and photographed.

lithography   A system of printing from a flat surface using the principle that grease and water do not mix. *See also* **offset.**

lockup   The securing of type, engraving, and furniture in a form prior to plating.

logotype   Several letters, words, or a slogan cast in one piece of type such as an advertiser's signature or a newspaper name plate.

long term memory (LTM)   Human "permanent" memory of vast storage capacity and very long duration, perhaps a lifetime.

lowercase   Small letter, as distinguished from a capital.

LTM   Long term memory (q.v.).

Ludlow Typograph   A typecasting machine usually used for display type; molds are hand set in lines and then the line is cast as a single slug.

makeready   Preparation of page forms or plates that involves padding and other means of adjusting the contact between printing surfaces and paper to produce uniform impression during printing.

makeup   Arrangement according to design of type, illustrations, and other elements into pages.

mark up   To put composition instructions on copy or layout. As a noun, refers to ad layouts so marked. Also, to give command codes to a photocomposition machine or computer indicating typographic formats.

mask   A sheet of opaque paper used to prevent light from striking the plate while making offset or engraving plates; areas are cut from the mask so that the desired image will be exposed on the plate. Masks may also be made photographically on film.

matrix   A mold of a typecasting machine from which a type character or other element is cast. Also the sheet of papier-mâché or composition material used as a mold in stereotyping.

measure   Page, line, or column width expressed in picas.

mechanical   A pasteup with all elements in proper position, marked, and ready to be photographed and made into a plate.

mechanical binding   Type of binding using plastic, metal spirals, or rings instead of traditional sewing or stapling.

mezzotint   An illustration that has been given a textured impression through the use of a special halftone screen.

miniature   A small layout prepared as a preliminary to executing a full-scale layout.

moiré   A pronounced screen pattern that results from the clash of dot patterns when two or more screens are used; corrected in full-color and duotone work by changing screen angles.

monitor printer   A high-speed impact printer that produces hard copy of computer-stored information.

Monotype   A typecasting machine; casts single letters rather than lines and uses both a tape-punching unit and a casting unit to do this.

montage   A combination of several distinct pictures into a composite picture; usually called a collage unless the edges of the component pictures are made to blend into each other.

mortise   A cutout area in an engraving, which permits the insertion of type or other matter; if the cutout is from outside edges, it is usually called a notch.

name plate   The name of a newspaper, usually at the top of page one.

negative   In photography, engraving, and photographic printing processes, the film containing a reversed (in tone) image of the copy photographed.

noise   External or internal interference that impedes proper interpretation of meanings being communicated.

nonpareil   A size of type, 6-point.

notch   A portion cut out from one or more edges of an illustration.

OBC   Outside back cover.

OCR   Optical character recognition (q.v.).

OFC   Outside front cover.

offset   A lithographic printing method in which the inked image transfers from plate to rubber blanket to paper. Often called indirect or photo-offset lithography.

on-line   Electronic text processing machines that are directly connected via hard wire.

optical alignment   The projection of certain letters beyond the left margin to give a more esthetic appearance, for example, the stem of a capital *T* aligned with the left stem of an *N* in the succeeding line, with the *T* cross stroke left of the margin.

optical character recognition (OCR)   Scanning of typewritten or printed characters, followed by conversion of the message to magnetic or perforated tape.

overhang cover   A cover that, after trimming, projects beyond the dimensions of inside pages.

overlay   Transparent or translucent sheets of paper or acetate used over art and photos to show location or shape of special treatments. Camera copy that combines on the same plate with the art or photo underneath, or overprints it in another color, may also be placed on an overlay.

overset   Type that is set but not used.

page proof   Proof of type matter in page form together with illustrations or with holes left for them.

parameters   Specifications for photocomposition or CRT composition; the details of formatting.

pasteup   To paste visual elements (proofs from hot-metal or cold-type composition) to a layout board in exact positions; the pasteup is then photographed before making printing plates.

patent base   A frame locked up in a letterpress form and to which duplicate plates less than type-high may be attached by hooks.

perfect binding   A method of binding books with paper in lieu of case and flexible glue instead of stitching.

perfecting press   A press capable of printing on both sides of a sheet or web at the same time.

photocomposing   Automatic, repeated exposure of a flat on a single offset or wrap-around plate. Each printing impression from the plate, when it is run, results in several copies of the same image. Also, synonym for photocomposition.

photocomposition   Type composed by exposing negatives of the characters on film or paper.

photoengravings   Original letterpress plates used to reproduce line and halftone illustrations.

photogelatin process   A screenless printing process using gelatin plates, especially suitable for reproducing tone illustrations; also called collotype.

photostat   A photocopy, either positive or negative (reversed in tone), same size, enlarged, or reduced.

pi   Type that is mixed up and hence unusable.

pica   Standard unit of linear measurement (12 points); approximately $\frac{1}{6}$ of an inch.

pi characters   Characters not found in the normal font of type.

pictograph   A graph using pictures of objects to show relative amounts of data.

pie chart   An illustration showing a circle divided into segments to show relative quantities of statistical data.

platen press   A flat-surfaced relief press. Paper is supported on one surface, type on the other. The two are brought together for impression.

point   Printer's unit of measuring size of type and of rules, border, spacing material; there are 12 points to a pica and approximately 72 points to an inch. As unit of measurement for thickness of cardboard, equals $\frac{1}{1000}$ of an inch.

posterization   A special technique for reproducing halftone illustrations in which the two absolute tones (white and black) are combined with only one middle tone.

press proof   One of the first copies off the press; it offers a final opportunity to make changes in the job.

process color   The reproduction of continuous-tone color originals by separating out each color and recording it on film; then plates are made from these films to carry the respective colors to paper.

progressive proofs   Proofs of process color plates; each color is shown separately, then in combination with each other. For four-color process a set of "progs" would show seven printings.

proof   A trial printing of type, negatives, or plates, to be checked for possible errors.

quad   In hand composition, a less-than-type-high spacing material used within lines; an em quad is the square of the type size. In photocomposition, in-line spacing created by moving the escapement system without exposure of type elements. In automated composition, quad left is the same as flush left and quad right the same as flush right. Quad middle is the same as flush left and right.

quire   Usually 25 (sometimes 24) sheets of paper of the same size and quality.

quoin   A wedge-shaped device used in locking up letterpress forms.

ragged right   Type composed without having the right edge made to be flush to the edge.

rated speed   The capacity of a photocomposition or CRT typesetting device expressed in lines per minute, usually based on 8-point, 11 picas (approximately 30 characters and spaces per line).

raw tape   *See* **idiot tape.**

ream   Usually 500 (sometimes 480) sheets of paper of the same size and quality.

redundance   Excess of information needed to make a decision.

register   Placement of forms, plates, or negatives so that they will print in precise relation to or over other forms, plates, or negatives, as in color printing.

rehearsal   Repetition of information to be learned (transferred from STM to LTM).

reproduction proof   A proof on special paper of exceptional cleanness and sharpness to be used as camera copy for offset, rotogravure, or relief plates (usually called "repro").

retrieval   The recall of information from LTM to STM.

reverse   Reproducing the whites in an original as black and the blacks as white.

reverse lead   *See* **back lead.**

roman   A type characterized by serifs; also refers to vertical type commonly used for typesetting as distinguished from italic.

rotary press   A press that prints as paper passes between a cylindrical impression surface and a curved printing surface.

rotogravure   Printing and printing presses using the rotary and gravure principles; intaglio process.

rough   A preliminary layout not in finished form.

routing   Cutting away of excess metal from nonprinting areas of engravings or duplicates.

rule   A strip of metal that is type-high and produces a line on paper. Rules vary in thickness and length.

run   The number of copies to come off the press.

running heads   Titles or heads repeated at the top of book and publication pages usually followed by or preceded by folio.

saddle-stitch   To fasten a booklet together by stitching or stapling through the middle fold of the sheets.

sans serif   Type having no serifs. *See* **Gothic type.**

scale   To find any unknown dimension when enlarging or reducing original art for reproduction to size.

Scan-A-Graver   A machine that electronically reproduces plates as halftones on plastic for newspaper use.

score To crease paper or cover stock to facilitate folding without breaking.

screen Cross-ruled glass or film used in cameras to break continuous-tone copy into halftone dots. The number of lines per linear inch on the screen governs the fineness of engraving. Also a tint block or flat tone.

script Types that simulate handwriting in which letters appear to join.

scroll On video display terminals, to roll the text material up across the face of the video tube for reading; permits seeing previous input that has gone off the screen. (Similar to rolling paper up or down in an ordinary typewriter.)

self-cover A cover that is part of one of the signatures of a booklet and of the same paper.

series The range in sizes of a type face.

serif The finishing cross stroke at the end of a main stroke in a type letter.

sheet-fed Referring to presses that accept sheets, not rolls (webs).

sheetwise An imposition calling for printing half the pages in a signature on one side of the sheet, the other half on the other side.

short term memory (STM) Human memory of short duration and limited capacity; information quickly forgotten unless moved to LTM.

side-stitch To fasten sheets together sideways through the fold.

signature A number of pages printed on one sheet of paper; when folded and trimmed, the pages fall in numerical order. A book signature may contain 8, 16, 32, or 64 pages.

silhouette Reproduction of art or photo with background removed.

silk-screen process A process of printing by which ink or paint is "squeegeed" through a stencil-bearing silk screen to the paper beneath.

slug A line of type from a linecasting machine. Also, between-line spacing material of metal 6 points or greater in thickness. Also, the word or two to identify a story.

small caps *See* **caps and small caps.**

soft copy Copy seen on a video display device.

software The programs that direct the operation of a computer as it performs mathematical and logical functions.

split-fountain printing In printing, the ink receptacle (fountain) can be separated into compartments corresponding to segments of the ink roller, which has also been split. By putting different colors in each fountain segment, more than one color can be printed from a form during one press run.

split mag Half-size linecaster magazine, likely to run short of molds during composition.

split page A magazine page that is part advertising and part editorial.

split-roller *See* **split-fountain printing.**

spot color Any color printing other than process printing.

square indention A newspaper headline pattern in which all lines are uniformly indented from the left; a modification of the flush-left headline.

square-serif Types basically Gothic in nature but having monotonal serifs.

stand-alone   Electronic text processing machine that is not on-line.

stereotype   A letterpress duplicate metal plate (flat or curved) made from a mold similar to cardboard.

STM   Short term memory (q.v.).

stock   Paper or cardboard.

straight matter   Text copy composed in normal paragraph form, as contrasted with tabular matter.

strike on   Cold-type composition produced on machine that resembles a typewriter.

strip   The computer function of removing h&j codes from wire-service tape and inserting new h&j codes in a second tape.

stripped slug   A type slug that is shaved underneath; it can then be mounted at any angle on base material that brings it type-high.

stripping   Affixing film negatives or positives to a flat. Also, cutting linecast slugs to less than type height. *See* **stripped slug** and also **hot-metal pasteup.**

substance   A term for the basis weight of paper.

surprint   A combination plate made by exposing line and halftone negatives in succession on the same plate.

syntax   The relationship of verbal (sometimes visual) elements arranged so that they impart imformation clearly.

tabbing   Composing copy in even columns within a specified line measure.

teletypesetter   An attachment that automatically operates a mat-circulating linecasting machine from perforated tape.

Text   A type face with an "Old English" look. Also any body type (written with lower case *t*). Also the body of a book excluding front and back matter.

text-processing system   Combination of various electronic composition gear that puts author's original copy into type on photo paper or film.

thermography   A printing process that produces a raised impression simulating an intaglio engraving. An image is put on paper in the usual way; it is powdered while wet, then heated so that powder and ink fuse to a raised image.

thumbnail   A miniature layout. Also a half-column photoengraving.

tint block   A photoengraving used to print tints of any percentage of color. Also refers to the panel printed from a block.

tip-in   A single sheet or partial signature glued into a book or magazine. It is often of smooth stock used for halftone printing while remainder of publication may be printed on a cheaper stock of paper.

tombstone   The typographical effect that results from side-by-side placement of two or more headlines too similar in size and face to stand as separate units.

transparency   A color photograph that may be viewed by transmitted light.

type-high   In letterpress printing, .918 inches, the desired height for all elements in a form.

typo   A typographical error.

upper case Capital letter.

VDT Video display terminal (q.v.).

vellum Originally a calfskin or lambskin prepared as a writing surface; now used to label a paper stock with a good writing surface.

Velox A screened photographic print similar to a photostat positive, but usually sharper in definition.

video display terminal (VDT) A cathode ray tube keyboard-operated device for viewing material as it is keyboarded into or drawn from computer storage.

video layout system (VLS) A video-screen, keyboard-control unit-system for area composition of advertisements up to $1/2$ newspaper page width and full page depth.

vignette The treatment given a photograph or halftone so that edges fade away into the background without breaking sharply.

visual STM Human memory of very short duration in which information is held long enough to ascertain whether it is useful.

watermark A faint design or lettering pressed into paper during its manufacture that can be seen when the sheet is held up to light.

web-fed Paper fed into a press from a roll

white print A photocopy (contact print or enlargement) from a negative (halftone or line).

widow A short line at the end of a paragraph; always to be avoided at the top of newspaper or magazine columns or book pages, but its presence elsewhere may or may not be disliked.

word wrap The capability of a VDT to end each line with a full word. Adding a word to any line will push as many words forward as necessary to make room, perhaps involving several lines. The change of characters is instantaneous.

work-and-tumble A system resembling work-and-turn (below) except that the sheet is turned so that a new edge is grabbed by the grippers.

work-and-turn A system of printing both sides of a printing piece on one side of a sheet, then turning the sheet so that its gripper edge remains constant and the sheet is printed on the reverse side.

work-up A fault in relief printing that causes a spot to be printed because spacing materials or blank portions of type slugs have risen high enough to gather ink.

wrap An insert into a magazine or book. Unlike a tip-in, it is wrapped around a signature.

wraparound press A relief press (sheet- or web-fed) that utilizes a shallow-etch curved plate made from a flat similar to that used in offset.

wrong font (wf) A letter or character that is of different size or face from the type that was specified.

xerography A dry system of printing based on electrostatic principles.

zinc A photoengraving, line or halftone, made of zinc.

Bibliography

Adler, Mortimer J. *The Difference of Men and the Difference It Makes.* New York: Holt, Rinehart and Winston, 1967.

American Photoengravers Association.*The Fundamentals of Photoengraving.* 1966.

American Photoengravers Association. *Line, Halftone & Color—An Introduction to Modern Photoengraving.* 1959.

Arnold, Edmund C. *Ink on Paper.* 2nd ed. New York: Harper & Row, 1972.

Arnold, Edmund C. *Modern Newspaper Design.* New York: Harper & Row, 1969.

Bain, Eric K. *The Theory and Practice of Typographic Design.* New York: Hastings House, 1970.

Baker, Stephen. *Advertising Layout and Art Direction.* New York: McGraw-Hill Book Co., 1959.

Baker, Stephen. *Visual Persuasion.* New York: McGraw-Hill Book Co., 1961.

Bauer, Raymond A., and Greyser, Stephen A. *Advertising in America: The Consumer View.* Boston: Harvard Graduate School of Business Administration, 1968.

Biggs, J. B. *Information and Human Learning.* Glenview, Ill.: Scott, Foresman and Co. 1971.

Biggs, John R. *Basic Typography.* New York: Watson-Guptill Publications, 1968.

Birren, Faber. *Color: A Survey in Words and Pictures.* New Hyde Park, N.Y.: University Books, 1963.

Bockus, H. William, Jr. *Advertising Graphics.* 2nd ed. New York: Macmillan Co., 1974.

Bowman, William J. *Graphic Communication.* New York: John Wiley & Sons, 1968.

Bragdon, Claude. *The Beautiful Necessity.* New York: Alfred A Knopf, 1922.

Branden, Nathaniel. *The Psychology of Self-Esteem.* New York: Bantam Books, 1969.

Brown, J. "Information Theory." In *New Horizons in Psychology,* edited by Brian M. Foss. Baltimore: Penguin Books, 1966.

Burt, Sir Cyril. *A Psychological Study of Typography*. London: Cambridge University Press, 1959.

Butler, Kenneth. *Practical Handbook on Effective Illustration in Publication Layout*. Mendota, Ill.: Butler Typo-Design Research Center, 1952.

Butler, Kenneth; *Practical Handbook on Headline Design in Publication Layout*. Mendota, Ill.: Butler Typo-Design Research Center, 1954.

Butler, Kenneth; Likeness, George C.; and Kordek, Stanley A. *Ken Butler's Layout Scrapbook, 101 More Usable Publication Layouts*. Mendota, Ill.: Butler Typo-Design Research Center, 1958.

Butler, Kenneth; Likeness, George C.; and Kordek, Stanley A. *101 Usable Publication Layouts*. Mendota, Ill.: Butler Typo-Design Research Center, 1954.

Butler, Kenneth; Likeness, George C.; and Kordek, Stanley A. *Practical Handbook on Double-Spreads in Publication Layout*. Mendota, Ill.: Butler Typo-Design Research Center, 1956.

Cardamone, Tom. *Advertising Agency and Studio Skills: A Guide to the Preparation of Art and Mechanicals for Reproduction*. New York: Watson-Guptill Publications, 1970.

Carter, Thomas F., and Goodrich, L. C. *Invention of Printing in China and Its Spread Westward*. 2nd ed. New York: Ronald Press Co., 1955.

Cherry, Colin. *On Human Communication*. 2nd ed. Cambridge, Mass., and London, England: M. I. T. Press, 1957.

Cheskin, Louis. *Color for Profit*. New York: Liveright Publishing Corp., 1951.

Chomsky, Noam. "Language and the Mind." *Psychology Today* 1 (1968), no. 9.

Clodd, Edward. *The Story of the Alphabet*. New York: Appleton-Century-Crofts, 1918.

Corcoran, D. W. J. "Acoustic Factors in Proofreading." *Nature* 214 (1967): 851–852.

Crowley, Thomas H. *Understanding Computers*. New York: McGraw-Hill Book Co., 1967.

Croy, Peter. *Graphic Design and Reproduction Techniques*. New York: Hastings House, 1968.

Dair, Carl. *Design with Type*. Rev. ed. Toronto: University of Toronto Press, 1967.

deSausmarez, Maurice. *Basic Design: The Dynamics of Visual Form*. New York: Reinhold Publishing Corp., 1964.

Dixon, N. F. "The Beginnings of Perception." In *New Horizons in Psychology*, edited by Brian M. Foss. Baltimore: Penguin Books, 1966.

Dondis, Donis A. *A Primer of Visual Literacy*. Cambridge, Mass.: M. I. T. Press, 1973.

Eighth Graphic Arts Production Yearbook. New York: Colton Press, 1948.

Faw, T. T., and Nunnally, J. C. "The Effects on Eye Movement of Complexity, Novelty, and Affective Tone." *Perception and Psychophysics* 2 (1967): 263–67.

Felten, Charles J. *Layout 4*. St. Petersburg, Fla.: Charles J. Felten, 1970.

Fletcher, Alan; Forbes, Colin; and Gill, Bob. *Graphic Design: Visual Comparisons*. New York: Reinhold Publishing Corp. 1964.

Frank, Lawrence K. "Tactile Communication." The Journal Press: *Genet. Psychol. Monographs* 56 (1957): 209–15.

Garner, Wendell R. *Understanding Structure in Psychological Concepts.* New York: John Wiley & Sons, 1962.

George, Ross F. *Speedball Textbook for Pen & Brush Lettering.* 18th ed. Camden, N.J.: Hunt Pen Company, 1960.

Gill, Bob, and Lewis, John. *Illustration: Aspects and Directions.* New York: Reinhold Publishing Corp., 1964.

Golden, Cipe Pineles; Weihs, Kurt; and Strunsky, Robert. *The Visual Craft of William Golden.* New York: George Braziller, 1962.

Gombrich, E. H. "The Visual Image." In *Communication, A Scientific American Book.* San Francisco: W. H. Freeman and Co., 1972.

Gregory, D. L. *The Intelligent Eye.* New York: McGraw-Hill Book Co., 1970.

Gregory, D. L. *Eye and Brain.* 2nd ed. London: World University Library, 1972.

Gross, Edmund J. *101 Ways to Save Money on All Your Printing.* North Hollywood: Halls of Ivy Press, 1971.

Haber, R. N. "How We Remember What We See." *Scientific American* 222(5) (1970): 104–12.

Hambidge, Jay. *The Elements of Dynamic Symmetry.* New York: Brentano, 1926.

Hanson, Glenn. *How to Take the Fits out of Copyfitting.* Fort Collins, Colo.: Mul-T-Rul Co., 1967.

Heron, W. "The Pathology of Boredom." In *Frontiers in Psychological Research,* edited by S. Coopersmith. San Francisco: W. H. Freeman and Co., 1966.

Hill, Donald C. *Techniques of Magazine Layout and Design.* 2nd ed. Huntsville, Ala.: Graphic Arts and Journalism Publishing Co., 1972.

Hoe, Robert. *A Short History of the Printing Press.* New York: Gillis Press, 1902.

How to Prepare Artwork for Letterpress, for Lithography. Neenah, Wis.: Kimberly-Clark Corp., n.d.

Hubel, P. H., and Wiesel, T. N. "Receptive Fields, Binocular Interaction, and Functional Architecture in the Cat's Visual Cortex." *Journal of Physiology* 160 (1962): 106–54.

Hubel, P. H., and Wiesel, T. N. "The Visual Cortex of the Brain." *Scientific American* 209 (1963): 54–56.

Hubel, P. H., and Wiesel, T. N. "Receptive Fields and Functional Architecture in Two Nonstriate Visual Areas (18 and 19) of the Cat." *Journal of Neurophysiology* 28 (1965): 229–89.

Hubel, P. H., and Wiesel, T. N. "Receptive Fields and Functional Architecture of Monkey Striate Cortex. *Journal of Physiology* 195 (1968) 215–43.

Hunter, David. *Papermaking.* New York: Alfred A. Knopf, 1947.

Hymes, David. *Production in Advertising and the Graphic Arts.* New York: Holt, Rinehart and Winston, 1958.

Jackson, Hartley E. *Printing: A Practical Introduction to the Graphic Arts.* New York: McGraw-Hill Book Co. 1957.

Jahn, Hugo. *Hand Composition.* New York: John Wiley & Sons, 1931.

Karch, R. Randolph. *Printing and Allied Trades*. 5th ed. New York: Pitman Publishing Corp., 1962.

Kepes, Gyorgy. *Language of Vision*. Chicago: Paul Theobald and Co., 1944.

Kubler, George A. *A New History of Stereotyping*. New York: J. J. Little & Ives Co., 1941.

Kuffler, S. W. "Discharge Patterns and Functional Organization of Mammalian Retina." *Journal of Neurophysiology* 16 (1953): 37–68.

Lewis, John. *Typography: Basic Principles*. New York: Reinhold Publishing Corp., 1964

Linderman, E.W. *Invitation to Vision: Ideas and Imaginations for Art*. Dubuque, Iowa: Wm. C. Brown Co., 1967.

Lindsay, Peter H., and Norman Donald A. *Human Information Processing*. New York: Academic Press, 1972.

Mackworth, N. H., and Morandi, A. J. "The Gaze Selects Informative Details within Pictures." *Perception and Psychophysics* 2 (1967): 547–51.

Mathews, Frank. *A Survey of the Graphic Arts*. Champaign, Ill.: Stipes Publishing Co., 1969.

Maurello, S. Ralph. *How to Do Pasteups and Mechanicals*. New York: Tudor Publishing Co., 1960.

McMurtrie, Douglas C., *The Book: The Story of Printing & Bookmaking*. New York: Oxford University Press, 1943.

Melcher, Daniel, and Larrick, Nancy. *Printing and Promotion Handbook*. 3rd ed. New York: McGraw-Hill Book Co., 1966.

Meyer, Hans. *150 Techniques in Art*. New York: Reinhold Publishing Corp., 1963.

Miller, G. A., and Isard, S. "Free Recall of Self-Embedded Sentences." *Information and Control* 7 (1964): 292–303.

Mott, Frank Luther. *American Journalism*. New York: Macmillan Co., 1962.

Murgio, Matthew P. *Communications Graphics*. New York: Van Nostrand Reinhold Co., 1969.

Nelson, Roy Paul. *The Design of Advertising*. 2nd ed. Dubuque, Iowa: Wm. C. Brown Co., 1973.

Nelson, Roy Paul. *Publication Design*. Dubuque, Iowa: Wm. C. Brown Co., 1972.

Newell, Allen, and Simon, Herbert A. *Human Problem Solving*. Englewood Cliffs, N.J.: Prentice-Hall, 1972.

Ninth Graphic Arts Production Yearbook. New York: Colton Press, 1950.

Norman, Donald A. *Memory and Attention*. New York: John Wiley & Sons, 1969.

Olson, Kenneth E. *Typography and Mechanics of the Newspaper*. New York: Appleton-Century-Crofts, 1930.

Oparin, A. I. *The Origin of Life*. New York: Dover Books, 1962.

Partridge, C. S. *Stereotyping. The Papier-Mâché Process*. Chicago: Mize & Stearns Press, 1892.

Paterson, D. G., and Tinker, M. A. *How to Make Type Readable*. New York: Harper & Row, 1940.

Pinney, Roy. *Advertising Photography*. New York: Hastings House, 1962.

Pocket Pal. New York: International Paper Co.

Postman, L. J.; Bruner, J. S.; and Postman, L. "Familiarity of Letter Sequences and Tachistoscopic Identification." *J. Genet. Psych.* 50 (1964): 129–39.

Printer 1 & C. Washington, D.C.: U. S. Government Printing Office, 1954.

Pye, David. *The Nature of Design.* New York: Reinhold Publishing Corp. 1964.

Roberts, Raymond. *Typographic Design.* London: Ernest Benn, 1966.

Robinson, David O; Abbamonte, Michael; and Evans, Selby H. "Why Serifs Are Important: The Perception of Small Print." *Visible Language* 4 (1971): 353–359.

Romano, Frank J. "Markup for Photocomposition." *Inland Printer/American Lithographer* 171 (1973), no. 6.

Ruesch, Jurgen, and Kees, Weldon. *Nonverbal Communication.* Berkeley: University of California Press, 1966.

Schachter, S., and Singer, J. E. "Cognitive, Social, and Psychological Determinants of Emotional State." *Psychol. Rev.* 69 (1962): 379–99.

Scharf, Aaron. *Creative Photography.* New York: Reinhold Publishing Corp., 1965.

Schlemmer, Richard M. *Handbook of Advertising Art Production.* Englewood Cliffs, N.J.: Prentice-Hall, 1966.

Schuneman, R. Smith, ed. *Photographic Communication.* New York: Hastings House, 1972.

Scott, Robert Gillam. *Design Fundamentals.* New York: McGraw-Hill Book Co., 1951

Shannon, Claude E., and Weaver, Warren. *The Mathematical Theory of Communication.* Urbana: University of Illinois Press, 1963.

Sperling, G. "On the Information Available in Brief Visual Presentations." *Psychol. Monographs* 74, no. 11 (1960).

Stent, Gunther S. "Cellular Communications." In *Communication, A Scientific American Book.* San Francisco: W. H. Freeman and Co., 1972.

Stevenson, George A. *Graphic Arts Encyclopedia.* New York: McGraw-Hill Book Co., 1969.

Stone, Bernard, and Eckstein, Arthur. *Preparing Art for Printing.* New York: Van Nostrand Reinhold Co., 1965.

Story of Lithography, The. New York: Lithographers National Association.

Sutton, Albert A. *Design and Makeup of the Newspaper.* Englewood Cliffs N.J.: Prentice-Hall, 1948.

Swann, Cal. *Techniques of Typography.* New York: Watson-Guptill Publications, 1969.

Tinker, M. A. *Legibility of Print.* Ames: Iowa State University Press, 1963.

Tinker, M. A. "Recent Studies of Eye Movements in Reading." *Psychol. Bul.* 54 (1958): 215–31.

Travers, Robert M. W. *Man's Information System.* Scranton, Pa.: Chandler Publishing Co., Intext, 1970.

Tschichold, Jan. *Asymmetric Typography.* New York: Reinhold Publishing Corp., 1967.

Westley, Bruce. *News Editing.* 2nd ed. Boston: Houghton Mifflin Co., 1972.

Wiener, Norbert. *Cybernetics: Control and Communication in the Animal and the Machine.* New York: John Wiley & Sons, 1948.

Yule, John A. C. *Principles of Color Reproduction.* New York: John Wiley & Sons, 1967.

Zachrisson, Bror. *Studies in Legibility of Printed Text.* Stockholm: Almqvist & Wiskell, 1965.

Characters Per Pica: Selected Type Faces

Character-per-pica counts for a number of selected type faces are presented in the following table as a tool for practice in copyfitting. Copyfitting can be accurate only when the characteristics of the individual type design are taken into account, since types of the same size but of different faces use differing amounts of space according to the design of the face.

There has been no attempt to make this list complete; only a few of the more common body and display faces are included. Information about other type faces can be obtained from compositors and type manufacturers. It should also be noted that the space required by many type faces varies slightly according to the manufacturer (e.g., the Baskervilles of two makers may differ from each other) or according to the method of composition (e.g., Linotype Palatino differs from Linofilm Palatino). Specific information about such variations can be obtained from compositors and type manufacturers when needed.

Face	Point sizes							
	8	9	10	11	12	14	18	24
Baskerville	3.22	2.96	2.64	2.46	2.3	2.01		
Benedictine	3.0		2.5		2.1	1.9		
Bernhard Gothic Medium	3.75		2.96		2.64	2.29	1.75	1.33
Bernhard Gothic Medium Italic	3.61		2.94		2.61	2.17	1.74	1.31
Bernhard Modern Roman	3.59		2.99		2.54	2.15	1.74	1.31
Bodoni with Italic	3.13		2.6		2.36	2.11	1.64	1.28
Bookman	3.11	2.88	2.6	2.37	2.21	1.84		

Face	Point sizes							
	8	9	10	11	12	14	18	24
Caledonia	3.12	2.87	2.63	2.44	2.26	2.00		
Caslon 540	3.39		2.91	2.56	2.21	1.86	1.49	1.06
Caslon 540 Italic	3.39		3.16	2.76	2.38	1.99	1.59	1.16
Century Schoolbook	2.97		2.43		2.12	1.75	1.4	1.1
Century Schoolbook Italic	2.99		2.46		2.17	1.81	1.44	1.13
Cheltenham	3.56	3.2	2.99	2.72	2.53	2.15		1.42
Clarendon	2.6	2.4	2.3		2.0			
Cloister	3.56		3.11	2.97	2.75	2.45	1.93	1.46
Cooper Black	2.6		2.03		1.75	1.42	1.09	.83
Dominante	2.6	2.5	2.3		2.0			
Egmont Light	3.4		2.7		2.3	2.2		
Electra	3.2	2.88	2.68	2.5	2.4			
Franklin Gothic	2.66		2.1		1.89	1.63	1.26	.98
Futura Medium	3.6		2.87		2.42	2.11	1.61	
Futura Medium Oblique	3.6		2.87		2.43	2.11	1.61	
Garamond with Italic	3.37	3.18	2.95	2.7	2.59	2.3	1.77	1.38
Goudy Old Style with Italic	3.36		2.74		2.42	2.01		
Helvetica	3.03	2.68	2.45		2.10	1.97	1.53	1.17
Kaufmann Script			3.12		2.84	2.54	1.94	1.5
Melior	3.08	2.75	2.48		2.14			
Optima	3.28	2.95	2.67		2.29	1.97	1.53	1.17
Palatino	3.08	2.75	2.48		2.14	1.87	1.44	1.11
Park Avenue					2.83	2.54	2.07	1.64
Scotch Roman	3.18		2.85	2.7	2.26	1.87	1.45	1.12
Stymie Bold	2.92		2.29		2.02	1.67	1.31	1.03
Stymie Bold Italic	2.86		2.22		1.98	1.63	1.29	1.01
Times Roman Bold	3.14	2.90	2.73	2.53	2.31	2.07		
Times Roman Italic	3.14	2.90	2.73	2.53	2.31	2.07		
Ultra Bodoni	2.18		1.97		1.56	1.46	1.12	.82
Ultra Bodoni Italic	2.18		1.98		1.57	1.43	1.13	.84
Vogue	3.51		2.63		2.44	2.12	1.67	1.28
Wedding Text	3.71		3.01		2.7	2.47		
Weiss Roman	3.76		3.16	2.93	2.58	2.27	1.7	1.37
Weiss Italic	4.54		3.51	3.38	2.92	2.66	2.09	1.69

Some Commonly Used Type Faces

The type faces shown on this page and the following seven pages represent designs commonly used for body and/or display in all forms of printed matter. They are set in a moderate size to show their suitability for different purposes. By analyzing the distinctive characteristics of various letters, students can quickly learn to recognize many of these common designs.

Alternate Gothic

ABCDEFGHIJKLMNOPQRS
TUVWXYZ&
$1234567890
abcdefghijklmnopqrstuv
wxyz

Baskerville

ABCDEFGHIJKLMNOPQR
STUVWXYZ&
abcdefghijklmnopqrstuvwxyz
$1234567890

P. T. Barnum

ABCDEFGHIJKLMN
OPQRSTUVWXYZ&
$ 1 2 3 4 5 6 7 8 9 0
abcdefghijklmnopq
rstuvwxyz

Baskerville Italic

ABCDEFGHIJKLMNOPQR
STUVWXYZ&
abcdefghijklmnopqrstuvwxyz
$1234567890

Benedictine

A B C D E F G H I J K L M N
O P Q R S T U V W X Y Z &
$ 1 2 3 4 5 6 7 8 9 0
a b c d e f g h i j k l m n o p q
r s t u v w x y z

Benedictine Italic

A B C D E F G H I J K L M N
O P Q R S T U V W X Y Z &
$ 1 2 3 4 5 6 7 8 9 0
a b c d e f g h i j k l m n o p q
r s t u v w x y z

Bernhard Gothic Medium

A B C D E F G H I J K L M N
O P Q R S T U V W X Y Z &
$ 1 2 3 4 5 6 7 8 9 0
a b c d e f g h i j k l m n o p q
r s t u v w x y z

Bernhard Gothic Medium Italic

A B C D E F G H I J K L M N
O P Q R S T U V W X Y Z &
$ 1 2 3 4 5 6 7 8 9 0
a b c d e f g h i j k l m n o p q
r s t u v w x y z

Bernhard Modern Bold

A B C D E F G H I J K L M N
O P Q R S T U V W X Y Z &
$ 1 2 3 4 5 6 7 8 9 0 ¢
a b c d e f g h i j k l m n o p q
r s t u v w x y z

Bernhard Modern Roman Italic

A B C D E F G H I J K L M N
O P Q R S T U V W X Y Z &
$ 1 2 3 4 5 6 7 8 9 0
a b c d e f g h i j k l m n o p q
r s t u v w x y z

Bodoni

A B C D E F G H I J K L M N
O P Q R S T U V W X Y Z &
$ 1 2 3 4 5 6 7 8 9 0
a b c d e f g h i j k l m n o p q
r s t u v w x y z

Bodoni Italic

A B C D E F G H I J K L M N
O P Q R S T U V W X Y Z &
$ 1 2 3 4 5 6 7 8 9 0
a b c d e f g h i j k l m n o p q
r s t u v w x y z

Bookman

ABCDEFGHIJKLMNOPQ
RSTUVWXYZ&
abcdefghijklmnopqrstuv
wxyz
$1234567890

Bookman Italic

ABCDEFGHIJKLMNOPQ
RSTUVWXYZ&
abcdefghijklmnopqrstuv
wxyz
$1234567890

Caledonia

ABCDEFGHIJKLMNOPQRS
TUVWXYZ&
abcdefghijklmnopqrstuvwxyz
$1234567890

Caledonia Italic

*ABCDEFGHIJKLMNOPQRS
TUVWXYZ&
abcdefghijklmnopqrstuvwxyz
$1234567890*

Caslon

ABCDEFGHIJKLMN
OPQRSTUVWXYZ&
$ 1 2 3 4 5 6 7 8 9 0
a b c d e f g h i j k l m n o p q
r s t u v w x y z

Caslon Italic

*ABCDEFGHIJKLMN
OPQRSTUVWXYZ&
$ 1 2 3 4 5 6 7 8 9 0
a b c d e f g h i j k l m n o p q
r s t u v w x y z*

Century Schoolbook

ABCDEFGHIJKLMN
OPQRSTUVWXYZ&
$ 1 2 3 4 5 6 7 8 9 0
a b c d e f g h i j k l m n o p q
r s t u v w x y z

Century Schoolbook Italic

*ABCDEFGHIJKLMN
OPQRSTUVWXYZ&
$ 1 2 3 4 5 6 7 8 9 0
a b c d e f g h i j k l m n o p q
r s t u v w x y z*

Cheltenham Medium

ABCDEFGHIJKLMNOPQRS
TUVWXYZ&
abcdefghijklmnopqrstuvwxyz
$1234567890

Cheltenham Medium Italic

*ABCDEFGHIJKLMNOPQRS
TUVWXYZ&
abcdefghijklmnopqrstuvwxyz
$1234567890*

Clarendon

A B C D E F G H I J K L
M N O P Q R S T U V W X
Y Z
$1234567890
a b c d e f g h i j k l m n o p
q r s t u v w x y z

Clarendon Semi-Bold

**A B C D E F G H I J K L
M N O P Q R S T U V W X
Y Z
$1234567890
a b c d e f g h i j k l m n o p
q r s t u v w x y z**

Cloister

ABCDEFGHIJKLMNOPQRS
TUVWXYZ&

abcdefghijklmnopqrstuvwxyz

$1234567890

Cloister Italic

*ABCDEFGHIJKLMNOPQRS
TUVWXYZ&*

abcdefghijklmnopqrstuvwxyz

$1234567890

Cooper Black

**ABCDEFGHIJKLMN
OPQRSTUVWXYZ&
$1234567890
abcdefghijklmnopq
rstuvwxyz**

Craw Modern

**ABCDEFGHIJKL
MNOPQRSTUV
WXYZ&
abcdefghijklmn
opqrstuvwxyz**

Dom Casual

**ABCDEFGHIJKLMN
OPQRSTUVWXYZ&
$1234567890
abcdefghijklmnopq
rstuvwxyz**

Dominante

ABCDEFGHIJKLMN
OPQRSTUVWXYZ&
$1234567890
abcdefghijklmnop
qrstuvwxyz

Dominante Bold

**ABCDEFGHIJKLMN
OPQRSTUVWXYZ&
$1234567890
abcdefghijklmnop
qrstuvwxyz**

Egmont Light

ABCDEFGHIJKLMN
OPQRSTUVWXYZ
$1234567890
abcdefghijklmnopqrst
uvwxyz

Egmont Light Italic

*ABCDEFGHIJKLMN
OPQRSTUVWXYZ
$1234567890
abcdefghijklmnopqrst
uvwxyz*

Electra

ABCDEFGHIJKLMN
OPQRSTUVWXYZ&
$1234567890
abcdefghijklmnopq
rstuvwxyz

Electra Italic

ABCDEFGHIJKLMN
OPQRSTUVWXYZ&
$1234567890
abcdefghijklmnopq
rstuvwxyz

Futura Medium Italic

ABCDEFGHIJKLMNOPQRSTU
VWXYZ&
abcdefghijklmnopqrstuvwxyz
$1234567890

Electra Cursive

ABCDEFGHIJKLMN
OPQRSTUVWXYZ&
$1234567890
abcdefghijklmnopq
rstuvwxyz

Garamond

ABCDEFGHIJKLMN
OPQRSTUVWXYZ&
$ 1 2 3 4 5 6 7 8 9 0
abcdefghijklmnopq
rstuvwxyz

Franklin Gothic

ABCDEFGHIJKLMN
OPQRSTUVWXYZ&
$1234567890
abcdefghijklmnopq
rstuvwxyz

Garamond Italic

ABCDEFGHIJKLMN
OPQRSTUVWXYZ&
$ 1 2 3 4 5 6 7 8 9 0
abcdefghijklmnopq
rstuvwxyz

Franklin Gothic Italic

ABCDEFGHIJKLMN
OPQRSTUVWXYZ&
$1234567890.,-:;!?'
abcdefghijklmnopq
rstuvwxyz

Goudy

ABCDEFGHIJKLMN
OPQRSTUVWXYZ&
$1234567890
abcdefghijklmnopq
rstuvwxyz

Futura Medium

ABCDEFGHIJKLMNOPQRSTU
VWXYZ&
abcdefghijklmnopqrstuvwxyz
$1234567890

Goudy Italic

ABCDEFGHIJKLMN
OPQRSTUVWXYZ&
$ 1 2 3 4 5 6 7 8 9 0
abcdefghijklmnopq
rstuvwxyz

Helvetica

ABCDEFGHIJKLMN
OPQRSTUVWXYZ&
$1234567890
abcdefghijklmnop
qrstuvwxyz

Helvetica Italic

ABCDEFGHIJKLMN
OPQRSTUVWXYZ&
$1234567890
abcdefghijklmnop
qrstuvwxyz

HUXLEY VERTICAL

ABCDEFGHIJK
LMNOPQRSTU
VWXYZ
$1234567890

Kaufmann Script

ABCDEFGHIJKLMN
OPQRSTUVWXYZ&
$1234567890¢
abcdefghijklmnopqrs
tuvwxyz

Kennerly

ABCDEFGHIJKLMNOPQRS
TUVWXYZ&
abcdefghijklmnopqrstuvwxyz
$1234567890

Lightline Gothic

ABCDEFGHIJKLMNOPQRS
TUVWXYZ&
abcdefghijklmnopqrstuvwxyz
$1234567890

Melior

ABCDEFGHIJKLMN
OPQRSTUVWXYZ&
$1234567890
abcdefghijklmnopq
rstuvwxyz

Melior Italic

ABCDEFGHIJKLMN
OPQRSTUVWXYZ&
$1234567890
abcdefghijklmnopq
rstuvwxyz

News Gothic

ABCDEFGHIJKLMN
OPQRSTUVWXYZ&
$1234567890
abcdefghijklmnopq
rstuvwxyz

News Gothic Condensed

ABCDEFGHIJKLMN
OPQRSTUVWXYZ&
$1234567890
abcdefghijklmnopq
rstuvwxyz

Optima

ABCDEFGHIJKLMNO
PQRSTUVWXYZ
$1234567890
abcdefghijklmnopqr
stuvwxyz

Optima Italic

ABCDEFGHIJKLMNO
PQRSTUVWXYZ&
$1234567890
abcdefghijklmnopqr
stuvwxyz

Palatino

ABCDEFGHIJKLMN
OPQRSTUVWXYZ
$1234567890
abcdefghijklmnopqr
stuvwxyz

Palatino Italic

ABCDEFGHIJKLMN
OPQRSTUVWXYZ
$1234567890
abcdefghijklmnopqr
stuvwxyz

Park Avenue

ABCDEFFG
HIJKLMNO
PQRSTUVW
XYZ&
abcdefghijklmno
pqrstuvwxyz
$1234567890

Scotch Roman

ABCDEFGHIJKLMNOP
QRSTUVWXYZ&
abcdefghijklmnopqrstuvw
xyz

$1234567890

Scotch Roman Italic

ABCDEFGHIJKLMNOP
QRSTUVWXYZ&
abcdefghijklmnopqrstuvwxyz

$1234567890

Stymie Bold

ABCDEFGHIJKLMN
OPQRSTUVWXYZ&
$1234567890
abcdefghijklmnopq
rstuvwxyz

Stymie Bold Italic

ABCDEFGHIJKLMN
OPQRSTUVWXYZ&
$1234567890
abcdefghijklmnopq
rstuvwxyz

Times Roman

ABCDEFGHIJKLMNOP
QRSTUVWXYZ&
abcdefghijklmnopqrstuvw
xyz
$1234567890

Times Roman Italic

ABCDEFGHIJKLMNOPQ
RSTUVWXYZ&
abcdefghijklmnopqrstuvwxyz
$1234567890

Vogue Bold Italic

ABCDEFGHIJKLMNOPQRSTU
VWXYZ
abcdefghijklmnopqrstuvwxyz
1234567890

Ultra Bodoni

ABCDEFGHIJK
LMNOPQRSTUV
WXYZ&
$1234567890
abcdefghijklmnop
qrstuvwxyz

Wedding Text

ABCDEFGHIJ
JKLMNOPQR
STUVWXYZ&
$1234567890
abcdefghijklm
nopqrstuvwxyz

Ultra Bodoni Italic

ABCDEFGHIJK
LMNOPQRSTUV
WXYZ&
$1234567890
abcdefghijklmnop
qrstuvwxyz

Weiss Roman

ABCDEFGHIJKLMNOPQRST
UVWXYZ&
abcdefghijklmnopqrstuvwxyz
$1234567890

Venus Bold Extended

ABCDEFGHIJKLMNOP
QRSTUVWXYZ&
abcdefghijklmnoprstuv
wxyz
$1234567890

Weiss Italic

ABCDEFGHIJKLMNOPQRS
TUVWXYZ&
abcdefghijklmnopqrstuvwxyz
$1234567890

Vogue Bold

ABCDEFGHIJKLMNOPQRSTU
VWXYZ
abcdefghijklmnopqrstuvwxyz
1234567890

Windsor

ABCDEFGHIJKLMN
OPQRSTUVWXYZ&
$1234567890
abcdefghijklmnop
qrstuvwxyz

Index

A

AA's, *see* author's alterations
Abbamonte, Michael, 64
accordion fold, 246, 247, 387
acknowledgments page, 243
Adams, Isaac, 405
advertising, newspapers, 237–238
　copy markup, 305–306
　see also design; newspaper make-
　　up, inside pages
agate line, 53, 54
air brush, 332–333
all caps, effect on legibility, 65–66
alphabet, evolution of, 401–402
angle-cut fold, 247
antique paper, *see* paper, types
appendixes in books, 243
appropriateness of type, 70–72
area composition, 358
Arnold, Edmund C., 212
art director, 179
Art Nouveau, *see* modern art
ascender, 39, 40
astonisher, 209
asymmetrical balance, 86–88, 161–
　162
attention and attraction, 156

author's alterations, 343
average word, definition, 67

B

balance, in design and layout, 82–88,
　161–162
　magazine layout, 184
　newspaper makeup, 227–228
banner, 208
bar graphs, 100–101, 336
bar line, 206, 207
basic paper sizes, 248–249
basis weight, 250, 381
Baskerville, John, 46
Bauer, Raymond A., 5
Bauhaus Institute, 47, 79
beard, *see* type parts
Benday process, 111
Bennett, James Gordon, 205
bibliography in books, 243
Biggs, J. B., 16, 27, 30
Biggs, John R., 65
bimetal plates, 271
binding, types, 387–390
binocular rivalry test, 63
bit of information, *see* information
　theory

black letter type, 42
blanket-to-blanket printing, 374
bleeds, 81, 184, 249, 250, 334
block letter type, 47
Bodoni, Giambattista, 46
body type, defined, 40, 61
   effect on legibility, 16
   in newspapers, 214–218
boldface, 50
   paragraphs, 220–221
bond paper, 250
   see also paper, types
book, binding of, 389–390
   design, 80–81, 243
   format, 243
booklet, copy preparation, 305–306
   defined, 242–243
   design of, 243–245, 248–249, 252–
      255
   envelopes for, 250
   format, 242–245
book paper, 250, 251
   see also paper, types of
border, 54, 55–56
bowl, *see* type parts
boxed heads, 220–221
boxes, 220–221
brace makeup, 231
braces, 55
brackets, 55
Bragdon, Claude, 163
Branden, Nathaniel, 23
break for color, 134
break-of-the-book, 179–180
bridging the gutter, 192–193, 255
broadside, 246
brochures, *see* booklet
Brown, J., 21
Bruner, J. S., 21
brush and ink drawings, 109
Bullock, William, 408
Burt, Sir Cyril, 61, 63, 64, 66, 67, 68, 69
butted slugs, 342

C

calendering, 380
camera lucida, 314
caps, 43, 66

caps and lower case, 43
   legibility, 65–66
captions, 189
carbon tissue, 282
card stock, *see* paper, types of
cartoons, 100–101, 336
case bound, 389
Caslon, William, 44
cathode ray tube, composition, 358–
      359, 415
   halftone reproduction in, 359
   see also video display terminal
Caxton, William, 43
center-body letters, 40, 52, 58, 73, 154
channel, capacity, 11, 12
   of communication, 9–10
character-count copyfitting, 319–321
chase, 349, 350
Cherry, Colin, 19
Chinese and printing, 400–401
Chomsky, Noam, 75
Christian Science Monitor, 233
chroma, 128
circus make-up, 227
c.l.c., *see* caps and lower case
close register, *see* color, register
coated stock, 250
cold-type composition, 36, 351–366
   letterpress, 266–268
   offset, 278
color, analogous, 131
   background for type, 69, 139
   balance, 132
   build-up, 139
   chroma, 128
   complementary, 130
   contrast, 130–132
   correction, 138
   cost in printing, 135–136
   dimensions, 127–128
   fidelity, 136–138
   functions, 130
   hue, 125
   intermediate, 127
   key-line, 134
   illustrations, 120–124, 336
   in light, 126–127
   monochromatic, 131

color—*continued*
  nature of, 126
  overlay, 134
  over use, 140
  paper, 69, 251–252
  practical pointers, 138–140
  preference, 133
  primary, 125, 127
  printing, 133–134
  process, 133, 252
  proportion, 132
  psychology, 128–129
  register, 134
  rhythm, 132
  schemes, 130
  second color, 130
  secondary, 127
  separation, 122–123, 136–137
  shade, 128
  split complementary, 130–131
  tint, 127
  tone, 126
  type printed in, 69, 139
  unity, 132
  value, 127
column separators, 217–218
  rules, 217–218
  white space, 217
column width, newspapers, 216
combination plates, *see* combination
  reproductions
combination reproductions, 118–
  120, 334
common space, 58
communication process, 7–11
  channel, 9
  concepts, 22–24
  decoding, 9
  definition, 14
  encoding, 9
  feedback, 10
  message, 9
  model, 7, 11
  noise, 10
  percepts, 16–22
  receiver, 10
  see also meaning; information proc-
    essing system

composition, *see* type composition
compositor, 262
comprehensive layout, 154
computer, 361–366, 414
  as central control, 362
  core memory, 365
  K bytes, 365
  OCR use with, 311–312
  VDT use with, 310–313
concepts, formation of, 22–24
  decision-making in, 23
  feature analysis in, 23, 24
condensed type, 50
constructionism, *see* modern art
consumer magazine, 176–178
contemporary newspaper makeup,
  234–237
contemporary type group, 47
contents page, in books, 243
  magazine, 200–201
context, 20
continuous tone, 103
  see also halftone reproduction
contrast, in design and layout, 84,
  88–89, 156–161
  magazine, 195
  newspaper, 225–226
copy correction, 298–302
  symbols, 297, 300
copyfitting, character count, 319–322
  character count scale, 320
  display type, 322–323
  em system, 315–318
  short-cuts, 322
  square-inch, 319
  unit-count, 322–323
copy preparation, verbal, 296–324
  copyfitting, 315–324
  copyreading symbols, 297
  markup, 305–306
  newspaper procedure, 303–305
  printer's instructions, 302
  proofreading, 256
  proofreading symbols, 300
copy preparation, visual, 325–338
  airbrushing, 332
  bleeds, 334
  color, 336

copy preparation, visual — *continued*
  cropping photos, 325–327
  highlighting, 332
  line drawings, 335
  outlining, 334
  photomontage, 334
  proofs, 336–338
  retouching, 332
  scaling, 327–331
  silhouetting, 332
  vignetting, 334
copyreading symbols, 297
copyright page, 243
copy schedule, 223, 305, 365
coquille board, 110
Coster, Laurens, 403
counters, *see* type parts
cover, magazine, 198–199
  treatment in booklets, 245, 253
cover paper, 251
  see also paper types
Craske, Charles, 208, 408
creasing, 395
creativity, defined, 74
cropping photos, 325–327
  for content, 327
  marks, 326
  to fit space, 327
CRT, *see* cathode ray tube and video
  display terminal
cues, meaning, 9
Currier and Ives, 413
cursive type group, 48, 76
cursor, 312
cut-in, *see* run-around
cut-off rules, 217
cuts, *see* halftone reproductions; line
  reproductions
cylinder press, 369–370, 405–406
  flat-bed web-perfecting, 369–370
  two-color, 369–370

D
Dadaism, *see* modern art
dashes, 54, 217–218
Daye, Matthew and Stephen, 405
decision-making, 14, 18, 19, 20, 23,
  27, 28–29, 31

human capacity, 169
  in emotions and motivation, 30–31
decoding, 9, 11
decorative devices, in newspaper
  makeup, 220–222
decorative type group, 48
deep etch plates, 271
descender, 39, 40
design, balance in, 161–162, 184–186,
  227–228
  contrast, 156–161, 195, 225–226
  evaluating, 74
  eye movement, 167–169
  gridding, 148–150
  harmony, 164–166, 195, 227–230
  meaning in, 143
  movement, 146, 166, 191, 231
  proportion, 162–163
  rhythm, 163–164, 193
  unity, 73, 166, 230
  valuing, 74
  vocabulary in, 145–150
die cutting, 390
Dijit system, 294
dingbats, 189–200
direct image master, 271
direct input system, 362
direct literature, defined, 241
  by mail, 241
  types of, 241–248
display type, copyfitting of, 322–324
  defined, 40, 61
divisions of a book, *see* book format
Dixon, N. F., 17
doctor blade, 283
Dondis, Donis A., 75
double burn, offset plates, 271
double cylinder perfecting press, *see*
  cylinder press
drawings, 98
drop-out halftone, *see* highlight halftone
dry brush drawings, 110
dummy, defined, 151
  magazine, 307
  newspaper, 222–223, 304
dummying, 347–349
dumping, 360

duotone, 120
duplicate plates, electrotypes, 371
  how made, 263–266
  plastic, 266, 371
  stereotypes, 263–266, 371
  uses of, 266

E

ears, 218–219
  see also type parts
easeling, 390
eggshell, *see* paper, types of
electronic composition, 358–359
electrostatic printing, 292–294, 376
  production steps, 293–294
  Xerox, 292–293
electrotype, 350, 371
em, 53–54
embossing, 394
emotions in information processing,
  30–31
emphasis, *see* typographic emphasis
em system copyfitting, 315–318
encoding, 9, 11, 26
English finish, *see* paper surfaces
engraver, proofs, 336–337
  work of, 262–263
engravings, *see* halftone reproductions; line reproductions
envelopes, 250
ephemera, 79–80
  design of, 81–82
exception words, 365
extended type, 50
Evans, Selby H., 64
eye camera, 63, 129
eye movement, 21–22, 167–169

F

family, type, 49–51
  variations within, 50–51
feature analysis, 18, 19, 23, 24
feature heads, 210
feedback, 7, 8, 11
feet, *see* type parts
fill-in, 256
finish dash, *see* dashes
finishing operations, 386–395

fixation, in reading, 62–66
  in viewing illustrations, 21–22
flag, *see* nameplate
flat-bed web-fed perfecting press,
  see cylinder press
flat, in offset, 270
flat-color, 133
flat piece, 245
flat tones, 133
Flesch, Rudolph, 63
flush left headlines, 208
flying paster, 372
focal point, newspaper, 223
focus makeup, 231
folder, defined, 246
  design of, 252–255, 245–247
  effect on information processing,
    246–247
  factors regarding use of, 248
  printing press, 371, 374
  types of, 246–247
folding, types of, 246–247, 386–387
folios, 243, 253
folo heads, 210
font, type, 51
form, importance of, 4
  printing, 36
format, magazine, 181
42-line Bible, 42
foundry type, 37
Fourdrinier, Henry and Sealy, 412
Fournier, Pierre, 411
Frank, Lawrence, 71
Franklin, Benjamin, 217
French fold, 387
front matter, 243
furniture, 349
Fust, John, 404

G

Gannett, laser plate system, 266
Garamond, Claude, 44
Garner, Wendell R., 144
Gennoux, Claude, 408
glossary, in books, 243
golden mean, 162–163
goldenrod, use in offset, 270
Gombrich, E. H., 61

Gothic type group, 46–48, 64–66, 80
graphic art, 5
graphic communication, extent of, 5
graphic elements in design, 60, 61,
    143
  interaction of, 156
graphic reproduction process, prin-
    ciples of, *see* printing process
graphics, effects of mechanics on, 6
  importance of, 4
Gregory, D. L., 16
gravure, advantages and disad-
    vantages, 281–286
  negatives for, 282
  photogravure, 282
  production steps, 282–285
  rotogravure, 282, 284–285
  screen for, 282
  uses, capabilities of, 286
grid, 148–150, 189–191
gripper edge, 249
grippers, 249, 369
groove, *see* type parts
gumming, 394
Gunning, Robert, 63
Gutenberg, Johann, 6, 35, 72, 259,
    399, 403–404
gutter, 183

H

Haber, R. N., 28, 70, 72, 166
hairline register, *see* color
hair space, 59
half-title page, 243
halftone reproductions, dots, 104, 106
  fill-in of, 256
  finishing, 120–124
  inventors of, 412
  letterpress, 262
  moiré, 120–121
  offset, 270
  plugging of, 256
  screens, 106, 116–118, 334–335
  shapes, 112
  use on CRT composing machines,
    359
Hambidge, Jay, 163
hand composition, 35, 57, 340

h&j, *see* hyphenation and justifi-
    cation
hanging indention, 206, 207
hanging punctuation, 92
haploscope, 63
hard copy, 347, 363
  monitor printer, 365
hardware, 356
hard-wired, 356
harmony, in design and layout,
    164–165
  magazines, 195
  newspapers, 229–230
  typographic, 71–72, 229
Harris, Ben, 217
Harris brothers, 414
headlines, capitalization and punc-
    tuation of, 212–213
  counting, 322, 324
  importance of, 89
  newspaper, 205–212
  photographic treatment, 90
  reversed, 91
  self-descriptive, 90
  shapes, 83, 90–92
  special considerations, 89–92
headline schedule, 212
Hearst, William R. 205
hed sked, *see* headline schedule
Heron, W., 16
hieroglyphics, 400–401
highlight halftone, 114, 332
Hoe, R. & Company, 406–408, 413
hook, *see* type parts
Horgan, Stephen H., 412
horizontal spacing, 57, 358
hot-metal composition, 36
Hubel, D. H., 16, 17, 64
hot type, 36, 38, 262, 340
house organs, 279
hue, 123
Hvistendahl, J. K., 65, 67
hyphenation and justification, 346,
    354, 355, 357

I

idiot tape, *see* raw tape
illustrations, functions of, 98–102

illustrations — *continued*
  types of, 98–103, 108–112
images, importance of, 97
imposition, definition of, 382
  effect on magazine layout, 180,
    388–389
  types, 383–385
imprinting, 248
indexing, 394
Industrial Revolution, 47, 405
information processing system, 15
  capacity, 26
  codes in, 27
  emotion in, 30, 31
  memory subsystems, 24–30
  model of, 29
  motivation in, 30, 31
information retrieval, 27, 28
information theory, 12–14
  amount of information, 11, 12,
    14, 169–172
  bit of information, 12, 13
initial letter, 55, 95, 188, 189, 220–221
  rising, 95
  set-in, 95
ink, build-up, 139
  discovery of, 401
  effect on legibility, 69
insert, 386
intaglio, *see* gravure
interfaced, 361
intertype machine, invention of, 410
  use, 262
introduction page, in books, 243
inverted pyramid, 206, 207
IPS, *see* information processing sys-
    tem
irregular right, *see* ragged right
Isard, S., 144
italic type, 50
Ives, Frederic, 412
Ives, J. M., 413

J

Jenson, Nicolas, 43
jet printing, 294, 376
jump heads, 210
jumps, 223

justifying, 57

K

kern, *see* type parts
keyboard, counting, 346
  noncounting, 346
key line, 134
kicker, 209
Koenig, Friedrich, 406
Kuffler, S. W., 16, 17

L

Lanston, Tolbert, 411
laser plates, 266, 415
layouts, headlines in, 172–173
  illustrations in, 173–175
  symmetrical design in, 83, 85–88
  see also magazine; design
layout tools, 154
leaded, 40
leadering, 357
leaders, 54
leading, defined, 54
  effect on legibility, 66, 71, 73
  linecasting composition, 342
leads, 54, 57
legibility, applying rules for, 69–
    70, 72–73
  defined, 62
  display type, 76
  tests, 62–63
letterfolds, effect on design, 246–247,
    387
letterpress printing, laser plates, 266
  makeready, 263
  paper requirements, 263
  plates for, 262
  presses, 369–372
  principles of, 261
  production steps, 261
  rotary, 263
  stereotyping, 263–266
letterspacing, 58, 59
ligatures, 37
light, effect on legibility, 68
Lindsay, Peter H., 16, 19, 60
linecasters, 340–347, 355
line conversions, 111

line, in design vocabulary, 145–150
  see also agate line
line gauge, 38
line graphs, 100–101
line illustrations, 102, 335
line length, effect on legibility, 66–67, 72
line reproductions, 335–336
  Benday process, 111
  description, 102
  functions, 170–172
  how made, 103
  negatives in offset, 268, 278
  plates for letterpress, 262
  plugging of, 256
line spacing, 54
Linotype, advantages of, 342, 343
  invention of, 409
  operation, 340–342
lithography, discovery of, 413
  see also offset lithography
lockup, 36, 347
logotype, 57
long-term memory, 27–30
loose-leaf binding, 390
loose register, see color, register
Los Angeles Times, 228, 230
Louisville Courier-Journal, 233
LTM, see long-term memory
Ludlow Typograph, invention of, 411
  operation, 343–344
  use, 262, 344
Ludlow, Washington I., 411

M
McElroy, John, 63
McGraw-Hill, 280
machine composition, 340
machine finish, see paper, surfaces
Mackworth, N. H., 21
magazine, ad placement, 180
  alignment, 189
  backward readers, 180
  balance, 184–186
  captions, 189
  contents page, 199
  contrast, 195
  copy marking, 306

cover, 198–199
dummy, 307
format, 181
functions, 181
gridding, 189–191
grouping, 188, 189
gutter, 183
harmony, 195
initial letters, 188, 189
linkage, 192
margins, 183
optical center, 183
pocket size, 181
rhythm, 193
signatures, 180
simplicity, 184
split pages, 200
subtitles, 189
table of contents, 199
titles, 189
visual syntax, 181, 186
white space, 183
Magnafax Telecopier, 293
Magnetic Tape Selectric Composer, 351
makeready, 263
makeup, 347, 363
  see also newspaper; magazine; tabloid
Manutius, Aldus, 50
maps, 100–101
margins, book, 80–81
  booklets, 253
  effect on legibility, 68, 73
  gutter, 183
  magazine, 183
  names of, 68
markup, 303–305, 306, 313, 363
masthead, magazine, 200
matrix, 340, 343
matrix case, 345
meaning, as result of decision-making, 14, 18–19, 23, 31
  in concept formation, 24
  in design, 143–145
  in perception, 16–22
  signification, 144
  storage in LTM, 24, 28

meaning—*continued*
  structural, 144–145
measure, *see* line length
measurement of type, 38–40
mechanical binding, 390
memory, effect on proofreading, 256
  systems, 24–32
  tests, 129
message, 9
mezzotint, 116
miniature layout, 151–153
Mergenthaler, Ottmar, 409
Miller, G. A., 26, 144
mimeographing, 294
minicomputer, 357
modern art, 77–78
modern Roman type, 45
moiré, 120–121
Mondrian, Piet, 78, 148, 192
Monotype, invention of, 411
  operation, 344
  use, 262, 345
monotypographic harmony, 229
montage, 334
mood types, 49
Morandi, A. J., 21
mortise, 114
motivation in information processing, 30–31
movable type, invention, 403
MT/SC, *see* Magnetic Tape Selectric Composer
movement, in design and layout,
  166, 231

N

nameplate, 218–219
National Observer, 236–237
Nelson, Roy Paul, 67, 238
newsmagazine, 176–177
newspaper flat-bed perfecting press,
  see cylinder press
newspaper makeup, body type, 214–
  218
  brace, 231
  circus, 227
  column separators, 217–218; rules,
    217–218; white space, 217

column widths, 216; spread leads,
  216; varying for effect, 216
dashes, 217–218
decorative devices, 220–222; boldface paragraphs, 220–221; boxes,
  220–221; dingbats, 220–221;
  initial letters, 220–221; simulated boxes, 220–221; special
  paragraph beginnings, 220;
  subheads, 220; thumbnails, 220–
  221
design elements, 223–231; balance, 227–228; contrast, 225–
  226; harmony, 227–230; motion,
  231; unity, 230
dummy preparation, 222–223,
  303, 304
ears, 218–219
factors causing change, 203
focal points, 223
headlines, 205–213; capitalization, punctuation, 212–213;
  functions, 205, 206; modern
  trends (flush, kicker), 208–209;
  schedule, 212; special (boxed,
  feature, folo, jump, standing),
  210–211; traditional (bar line,
  hanging indention, inverted
  pyramid, step line), 206–209
inside pages, 237–238; double
  pyramid, 237–238; pyramid to
  right, 237–238; well, 237
nameplate, 218–219
Scripps-Howard, 204–205
tabloid, 238–240
New Typography, 76–82
nicks, *see* type parts
Niepce, Joseph, 412
noise, 10
nonpareil, 38, 53
Norman, Donald A. 16, 19, 26, 60
notch, 114
Novelty type group, 48, 49
numbering, 394

O

oblique type, 50
Ochs, Adloph S., 205

OCR, *see* optical character recognition
off-center fold, 247
offset lithography, advantages, 273–278
  discovery of, 414
  first presses, 414
  growth in use, 279–281
  parts of press, 272
  plate preparation, 270–271
  presses, 372–374
  press operation, 271–273
  principle of, 267
  steps involved in, 268–277
  uses, 279–281
offset paper, 251
  see also, paper, types of
Old Style Roman type group, 45
on-line, 361, 363
  advantages of, 365
Oparin, A. I., 3
optical alignment, 356
optical center, effect on magazine design, 183
  in design, 85, 161
optical character recognition, 308–310, 359–362, 414
  copy marking for, 309
  use with VDT, 310
optical letter alignment, 92
ornaments, 55
outline halftone, 113, 344
over-and-over fold, 387
overlay, 134–135
overset, 315

P

page dummy, 151, 304
pamphlets, *see* booklets
Pannartz, Arnold, 43, 44
paper, carton of, 381
  case of, 381
  chemical properties, 378
  color, 251–252
  cost, 378
  discovery of, 401
  effect on design, 250–252
  effect on legibility, 69

effect on mailing costs, 252, 378
  effect on process color, 252
  first machine making, 412
  grain, 379
  letterpress requirements, 263
  properties of, 378
  ream of, 381
  selection, 250–252, 377–379
  sheet sizes, 248–249, 369, 381
  skid of, 381
  substance, 381
  surfaces, 380–381
  types of, 250, 379–380
  weights and sizes, 248–251, 252, 381–382
papyrus, 401
parallel fold, 246, 387
paragraph beginnings, 220
parentheses, 55
pasteup, for letterpress, 262, 302, 366
  for lithography, 302, 313–314
  type, 351, 366
patent base, 350
Paterson, D. G., 63, 65, 68
pebbling, 394
perception, 16–22
  as a cognitive process, 19
  context as an aid to, 20
  decision-making in, 18, 19
  eye and brain in, 17–18
  feature analysis in, 18, 19
  redundancy as an aid to, 20–22
perfect binding, 389
perfecting press, 406
perforating, 394–395
perforators, 346, 365
photocomposition, 36, 352–366
  automated, 354–366
  computerized, 361–366
  hand operated, 353–354
  integrated systems, 359–366
  keyboard-driven, 360
photoengravings, 35–36, 412
  see also halftone reproductions; line reproductions
photogelatin printing, 290–292
  production steps, 290–291
  uses and limitations, 291–292

photographs, air brushing, 332–333
  bleed, 334
  cropping, 325–327
  editing, 325–326
  functions of, 98
  highlighting, 332
  in offset, 278
  montage, 334
  outline, 334
  retouching, 170, 332
  scaling, 327–331
  silhouette, 332
  vignette, 334
photogravure, see gravure
photo-offset lithography, see offset
  lithography
pica, 38, 39, 53
pica rule, see line gauge
pi characters, 353
pictographs, 100–101
pie charts, 100
pin mark, see type parts
platen press, 369
plates, bimetal, 271
  deep etch, 271
  for letterpress, 262
  for offset, 270–271
  trimetal, 271
plugging, 256
pocket magazine, 181
point, in design vocabulary, 145
  in paper measurement, 57
  in type measurement, 52–57
point system, adoption in U.S., 411
  explanation of, 38, 52–57
  invention of, 411
posterization, 117–118
poster type, 37
Postman, L., 21
Postman, L. J., 21
preface page, 243
preliminaries, 243
presses, history of, 404–408
  types of, 367–375
  units, 317, 374–375
press sheets, checking of, 255–256
printed pieces, sizes of, 250
printer's instructions, 302

printing process, principles of, 259–295
  selection of, 295
  types of, 36, 259
  see also gravure; jet; letterpress;
    offset; photogelatin; silk-screen;
    electrostatic
process color, 120–124
  etching, finishing, proofing, 124
  halftone negatives, 124
  reproductions, 120–124
  scanner, 123
  separation negatives, 122–123,
    136–137
  transparencies, 122
progressive margins, 68, 183, 243
proofreading, galleys, 300–302
  press proofs, 255–256, 302
  study of, 256
  symbols, 256, 300
proofs, engraver's, 336–338
  foundry, 350
  galley, 302
  of illustrations, 336–338
  page, 301, 349
  press, 255–256, 302
  reproduction, 350
  revise, 301
proportion in design and layout,
  162–163
proportioning photographs, see
  scaling
psychogalvonometer, 129
public relations magazine, 178
Pulitzer, Joseph, 208
punch operator, 355

Q

quadding, 357
quads, 57, 58
quoins, 349

R

ragged right, 59, 68, 72
raw tape, 346, 355
Raymond, Henry J., 205
readability tests, 63
Reade, William A., 411

reader interest, effect on legibility, 71
reader size type, 40
real time, 365
receiver, 10
recognition, 18, 19
  of shapes, 21–22
redundancy, 20–22
reference section, 243
register, color, 134
  marks, 134–135
Reid, Whitelaw, 409
relief printing, *see* letterpress
Renaissance and printing, 403–405
reproduction proof, 350
reticular activating system (RAS), 60
retouching, 332
reverse combination, 120
reverse leading, 357
reverse line reproductions, 108–109
rhythm in design and layout, 163–164, 193
Ridder, Herman, 410
right-angle fold, 386
Rinehart, William, 376
rivers of white, 59
Robert, Nicholas, 412
Robinson, David O., 64
Roman Empire and printing, 401–402
roman type, 50
Roman type group, 43–46, 64–66, 73
rotary presses, 371–375
  letterpress, 371–372
  offset, 372–374
  rotogravure, 374–375
rotogravure, 36
  presses, 374–375
  see also gravure
rough layout, 153–154
Rubel, Ira, 414
rules, 54, 217–218
runaround, 343
running heads, 243

S

saddle, in letterpress, 266
saddle-wire binding, 388
Sans-serif type group, 47

scaling illustrations, 327–332
  arithmetical system, 328–329
  diagonal line system, 330–331
  percentage in, 332
  slide rules, circular scales, 329
scanner, *see* optical character recognition
Schachter, S., 31
schematic diagrams, 100–101
Schoeffer, Peter, 404
scholarly magazine, 176–177
scoring, 54, 395
Scott, Robert G., 74, 75
screens for halftone, color, 121–124
  gravure, 282
  lines per inch, 104
  offset, 278
  silk-screen printing, 287–289
  use, 104
screen process, *see* silk-screen printing
Scripps, E. W., 205
Scripps-Howard papers, makeup, 204, 205
Script type group, 48, 76
scrolling, 312, 362
self-cover, 242
self-mailer, 248
Senefelder, Alois, 413
sentence embedding, 144
series, *see* type series
serifs, 45
  see also type parts
set em, 53
set of letters, 52, 67
set solid, 40
set width, 345
shading sheets, 111
Shannon, Claude, 7
shapes, basic, 150
  halftone, 112
  in design vocabulary, 150
  of lines of type, 83
  recognition of, 19–22, 65
sheet-fed presses, 369, 370, 374, 375
sheetwise, 383
short fold, 247
short-term memory, 25–26, 29, 32
  capacity, 26, 29–30·

short-term memory—*continued*
  encoding in, 26
  visual, 24–25
shoulder, *see* type parts
side-wire binding, 388
signatures, 180, 382–385
silhouette, 113, 332
silk-screen printing, 286–290
  production steps, 287–289
  stencil preparation, 287–289
  uses and capabilities, 290
Singer, J. E., 31
skyline, 226
slug, 340
slugging system, 305
Smyth sewing, 389
software, 356
source, communication, 8
spaceband, 340, 342, 343
spaces, 57, 58
spacing, materials, 57, 58
  of type, 54, 57, 58, 84, 91
special characters, 56, 57
specimen book, 40
Sperling, G., 25
spirit duplicating, 294–295
split color, 384
square-inch table, 319
split-fountain, 384, 385
split pages, magazine, 200
spot color, 133
spread leads, 216
square finish halftone, 105
square-inch copyfitting, 319
square indention, 209
Square-serif type, 48
stand-alone machines, 360
standard fold, *see* letter fold
standard sizes of printed pieces, 248–250
standing heads, 210–211
Standing, L. G., 28
Stent, Gunther S., 16
step line, 206, 207
stereotype, curved, 208, 371
  definition, 408
  illustrations of, 264–265
  invention of, 208, 407–408
stick, 343

STM, *see* short-term memory
stone, 347
strike-on composition, 262, 351
stripping, 270
  of wire service codes, 357
subheads, 220
substance, 381
subtitles, 189
surprint, 119
Sweynheym, Conrad, 43, 44
symbols, 9
  in concept formation, 22
symmetrical design, 76, 82–85, 86
syntax 4, 144

T
table of contents, magazine, 199
tabloid makeup, 238–240
tabular matter, 343
tachistoscope, 63, 129
Talbot, William, 412
type punch operator, 347
Teletypesetter, 345–347
textbook, use of offset, 280
text processing system, 359–366
text section, 243
text-size type, 40
Text type group, 42–43
texture in design vocabulary, 150
texture board drawings, 110
thick and thin strokes, *see* type parts
thumbnail, layouts, 151
  photographs, 220–221
tight register, *see* color, register
time comprehension tests, 63
Tinker, M. A., 20, 63, 65, 68, 69
tint blocks, 107, 133
tip-in, 385–386
title page, 243
tombstone, 225
tone in design vocabulary, 150
traditional composition, 36
transfer type, 351
Transitional Roman type, 45, 46
transparencies, 122
Travers, Robert M. W., 13, 27, 169, 170
Treadwell, Daniel, 405
trimming, 386

trimetal plates, 271
TTS, *see* Teletypesetter
Twain, Mark, 410
two-revolution press, *see* cylinder press, one-color
type body, 38, 40
type case, 262
type classification, 41–52
type composition, cold type, 36
    hand, 37, 57, 409
    hot metal, 36, 38
    legibility in reverse, 69, 72
    photocomposition, 36
type comprehensive, 154, 339–367
type face, 38
    effect on legibility, 64
    identifying, 52
    psychological implications, 70, 71
type groups, 42–49
type high, 41, 263, 340
type in color, 69
type materials, 37–38
type page, 183
type parts, 40, 52
type races, *see* type groups
type series, 52
type size, determining, 39
    effect on legibility, 66
Typograph, *see* Ludlow
typographic emphasis, 83–85
typographical patterns of headlines, 83, 84–89

U
unit-count copyfitting, 322–324
unity, in design and layout, 166, 230
    in design with type, 72–73
Unitype, 409
upper case letters, *see* caps

V
Varityper, 351
VDT, *see* video display terminal
Veloxes, 114
verbal elements in design, 60, 143
vertical spacing, 57, 358
video display terminal, 310–313, 359–365, 414

command codes, 313
cursor, 312
editor's use, 312
markup, 312
on-line, 310
reporter's use, 311
scrolling, 312
Videojet, 294
vignette, 113, 334
visual elements, *see* graphic elements
visualization, 151
video layout system, 362–364
visual short-term memory, 24–25, 29
visual syntax, 75, 145–150, 181, 193, 246
VLS, *see* video layout system
vocabulary, 4
    in design 145–150, 181, 186, 189

W
Warms, Jacob, 408
Weaver, Warren, 7
web-fed presses, 369–370
wf, *see* wrong font
Wiener, Norbert, 7
Wiesel, T. N., 17, 64
windows in offset flats, 270
wood type, 40
work-and-tumble, 384
work-and-turn, 384
work-and-twist, 384
wrap-around fold, 246
wraps as inserts, 385, 386
wrong font, 51

X
xerography, production steps, 292–293
    uses, 292–293
Xerox, offset plate preparation, 271, 376
    Magnafax telecopier, 293
x height, *see* center-body letters

Z
Zachrisson, Bror, 63, 64, 65, 68